Classic Steelhead Flies

Classic Steelhead Flies

HEADWATER BOOKS

STACKPOLE BOOKS

Published by

STACKPOLE BOOKS
5067 Ritter Road
Mechanicsburg, PA 17055
www.stackpolebooks.com

Printed in China

10 9 8 7 6 5 4 3 2 1

First edition

Photos by the author except where noted

Library of Congress Cataloging-in-Publication Data

Shewey, John.
Classic steelhead flies / by John Shewey.
pages cm
Includes bibliographical references and index.
ISBN 978-0-8117-1332-0
1. Flies, Artificial. 2. Steelhead fishing. I. Title.
SH451.S526 2015
688.7'9124—dc23

2014033011

CONTENTS

Foreword *By Trey Combs*	vii
Acknowledgments	ix
Introduction	xi
Notes on Methodology	xiii
CHAPTER I: The Golden Age of the Steelhead Fly	1
CHAPTER II: John S. Benn Paves the Way	9
CHAPTER III: Embracing the Classics	15
CHAPTER IV: The Classic Patterns	23
CHAPTER V: Style Conversions of Classic Patterns	189
CHAPTER VI: Notes on Tying	199
Fly Recipe Appendix	243
Bibliography	259
Notes	261
Index	267

FOREWORD

John Shewey stands tall among international fly-fishers. The editor-in-chief of three regional fly-fishing magazines, he has authored numerous books, including *Steelhead Flies* (2006), a classic and a feast for the eyes that displays his brilliant fly-tying skills.

John called me in 2013 and described a new book he was writing on the history of steelhead flies. He asked me about an obscure fly fisherman, John S. Benn, known to both of us. I had come upon this angler 40 years ago in an issue of *Forest & Stream* newspaper dating to the 1890s. Benn had put his name on one of the earliest flies known in our sport, but I knew little else. John explained that he was searching Northern California census figures for the period in an effort to determine exactly where the man lived when he was fishing for steelhead. Once he was located, perhaps more information would follow.

I was extremely impressed by the depth of John's research and excited that his book would shed new light on old histories, and put into context the evolving types of steelhead flies that have appeared during the past 30 years. I could not have chosen a more perfect person to write such a book.

John and I share a common passion for steelhead flies. They speak to us. They have stories to tell and offer tantalizing mysteries. We see the flies first as a creative art form, a reflection of ourselves, revealing what fly fishers find and have found attractive and full of angling promise. We are both traditionalists, too, and tie steelhead flies that are historical testimonials to flies born on Great Britain's legendary salmon rivers. We've both studied flies as simple as a bare hook impaling a strip of black rabbit, to patterns so complex that a single fly could sell for hundreds of dollars. Somewhere, on some river, steelhead will strike them all.

For this book, *Classic Steelhead Flies*, John selected over 120 steelhead patterns from thousands with names and originators who had championed their use. These flies, so painstakingly chosen, seamlessly tie together the history of steelhead fly fishing. John organized this book so text appears next to a large image of each fly, photographed on a background carefully selected to complement the fly's origins or form. John tied most of the flies that appear herein, adhering as closely as possible to the original dressings.

John Shewey has added to our angling literature an eloquent and visually lavish chronology of steelhead fly-fishing history.

—Trey Combs, author of *The Steelhead Trout* (1971),
Steelhead Fly Fishing and Flies (1976), and
Steelhead Fly Fishing (1991)

Wielding a two-handed rod on a Columbia River tributary.

ACKNOWLEDGMENTS

This book rests firmly on the foundations built by a handful of authors who took it upon themselves to research and record the origins of thousands of fly patterns. Their work enables further research and chronicling, and I remain thoroughly indebted to, among others, Joseph D. Bates, Jr., Harold Hinsdill Smedley, Ray Bergman, Arthur Lingren, and especially Trey Combs, without whose tireless research in the 1970s a book like this would be impossible. So much of what Trey recorded would have otherwise been lost to the ravages of time. Additionally, Jack Berryman's "Pioneers & Legends" columns from *Northwest Fly Fishing* magazine proved invaluable in conducting research for this project, and it was with great interest and enthusiasm that I edited many of his installments of that column. Finally, I offer sincere thanks to the fly tiers, most of them no longer with us, who most shaped my own intrigue and fascination with steelhead flies: Ed Haas, Cal Bird, Walt Johnson, and David McNeese.

Summer-run steelhead have inspired generations of fly designers from Northern California to Alaska. This fish took a featherwing Parmachene Belle, a pattern first fished for steelhead around 1890.

INTRODUCTION

The first snow of autumn dusts the ridges above a beautiful Northwest steelhead river.

Just out of high school in the early 1980s, I took a summer job at a new fly-fishing shop in Salem, Oregon. By then I had already developed a small commercial tying business. I had spent the past couple years supplying flies to small tackle stores in the area, and while trout flies were their primary interest, I also supplied them with a few basic steelhead patterns: Skunks, Purple Perils, and Polar Shrimps mostly. But one Saturday afternoon that summer, the fly shop's manager, a fellow named Matt Kayser, unpackaged a few small boxes of steelhead flies tied by Ed Haas, the Northern California master tier. Haas's steelhead flies were perfect, each fly identical to the others of its pattern, as if it had come from an automated factory line.

Matt gave me about two dozen of the flies and gently suggested that I upgrade my own steelhead patterns to be more like the gorgeous Ed Haas flies. Matt was not a fly tier himself at the time, but he recognized superbly tied flies when he saw them. Frankly, my own standard hair-wing steelhead flies were pitiful compared to the artistry of Ed Haas. But serendipity intervened, and I now had a boxful of his flies to study. I went home that night and cut apart one of Haas's Polar Shrimps; in doing so I discovered his reverse-wing technique for making indestructible hair wings and gained a new appreciation for precision tying. I tied steelhead flies deep into the night, then continued apace the next day. Monday morning I opened the shop early and placed a dozen Skunks and a dozen Polar Shrimps, all tied on size 4 hooks, on the counter near the register in small cardboard Danville thread boxes. When Matt arrived, he noticed the flies immediately. While my ruse to trick him into mistaking my flies for Haas flies failed, he was quick to compliment the colossal improvement, for I had come close to replicating Haas's work. A steelhead fly tier was born that weekend.

I devoured the available literature on steelhead flies and fly tying, what little of it there was at the time. One monumental tome became my pattern bible: *Steelhead Fly Fishing and Flies* by Trey Combs, which had been released a few years earlier by Frank Amato Publications. I was mesmerized by the color plates of steelhead flies, many of them tied by now-legendary Washington angler Harry Lemire, whom I met and befriended a few years later. Combs's book, and the flies therein, provided a wellspring of practice projects, and I would often pick patterns from the book at random and tie them until I felt they approximated an Ed Haas version.

Just two years later, I went to work for David McNeese at his fly shop, which had opened in downtown Salem in 1977. McNeese had built his business in part by supplying rare and unusual materials to tiers of Atlantic salmon flies, as well as traditional Catskill-style trout patterns, but at the same time he was quietly revolutionizing the classic steelhead fly. Influenced by the works of Preston Jennings and the traditions of dressing Atlantic salmon flies, McNeese retooled traditional steelhead flies. Although other affectations defined the McNeese style, the bodies and tails were unique: dyed seal dubbing for bodies instead of yarn or chenille and dyed golden pheasant crest feathers for tails rather than hackle fibers. By the late 1980s, the McNeese style of steelhead fly was well established, but at the time, these flies hadn't reached a national audience, despite magazine articles penned by myself, Deke Meyer, and McNeese himself. But in 1991, Trey Comb's next big project, *Steelhead Flies*, featured color plates of McNeese's flies, many of them his intriguing and artistic renderings of classic old patterns. That book and later the rise of the internet propelled the McNeese style into the forefront. Classic patterns bore a new face, and tiers all over the Northwest and beyond began exploring these new, more stylistic versions of old dressings.

As one of the early adherents to this more elegant form of steelhead flies who is still enamored with them today, I approach the topic of classic steelhead flies wistfully. As styles changed, many of the older classics I first knew—such as those perfect hair wings dressed by Ed Haas—retreated into obscurity. This book stems from my desire to slow the inevitable, to breathe life into the steelhead flies of old, flies with vivid histories and stories to tell. As I delved into the flies and their pedigrees, I embarked on a voyage of discovery whose bounds I had not anticipated. I tied patterns I had never before tied; I learned about their originators; I gained new insights on the rivers that spawned the flies; and I redoubled my longstanding reverence for the steelhead, which has inspired such superlative efforts by fly tiers and anglers for 150 years.

Through the process of assembling this book, a steelhead tier was reborn. My sincerest wish is that my own enthusiasm might inspire other fly dressers to embrace the classics—to tie them, to study them, to fish with them, and to keep their legacy alive.

John Shewey
August 2014

NOTES ON METHODOLOGY

A historian should always strive to confirm or disprove information by digging for the most reliable sources. It is hardly enough to rely on the writings of previous authors as fact; independent verification is always desirable. That fly fishing is not seen as a place for sound historical research is no excuse for shoddy workmanship, and angling authors should challenge themselves to become better historians. The alternative is to compound mistakes: one author presents inaccurate material, and the next author on that subject uses the first as a primary and only source, and so on down the line—fictions are created where none were intended.

I've seen this happen in ways that are almost humorous. In my own research on Spey flies from nineteenth-century Scotland, I discovered that the lovely Glen Grant pattern was created by Major James Grant, who at the time was the proprietor of the famous Glen Grant distillery near Rothes. Uncovering these facts was easy with historical research, yet other writers—on the strength of assumptions rather than research—have matter-of-factly stated that the fly's inventor was a fellow named Glen (a "glen" is a narrow ravine, and in this case refers to the glen behind the distillery, where Major Grant's beautiful gardens thrive to this day). They also claim that Grant was a member of the Grant family of Castle Grant (he was not of that Grant line, and Castle Grant—seat of the Countess of Seafield in those days—is 25 miles upriver from Rothes).

Naturally, historical inquiry can only extend to the bounds of one's resources, but within those bounds, a writer must exhaust all avenues before continuing. Conscientious research allows future historians to continue the quest for ever-more refined and accurate details. To that end, throughout this work I have included citations and endnotes, not only to cite my sources and thus provide a springboard for future inquiry, but also, in some cases, to provide interesting additional details on the flies and their creators; I hope readers will take the time to read these notes. So too, a record of sources allows for easier correction: eliminating errors is always difficult, but disseminating historical details in a book like this opens further avenues of inquiry for curious, knowledgeable readers.

Swinging a fly through a narrow run on Oregon's John Day River.

CHAPTER I

The Golden Age of the Steelhead Fly

Although the pioneers of the sport were wont to use standard patterns of trout and salmon flies, experience soon taught that the best results were obtained with special patterns, which, like the salmon flies of Britain, varied not only with the locality of the river and season, but also with the condition of the water.

—William Bayard Sturgis, *Fly-Tying,* 1940.

The earliest flies designed specifically for steelhead were variations on popular trout flies of the day, such as the Coachman, Royal Coachman, and Parmachene Belle. By the 1920s, feather wings were beginning to be replaced by more durable hair wings, especially those made from bucktail.

Discovery

When John Sutter and James W. Marshall accidentally discovered gold flakes in the tailrace of their lumber mill site on the South Fork of the American River in 1848, they were wise enough to know they should keep their find a secret. But when Sutter's Mill employees paid for goods at the local store owned by Samuel Brannan, the cagey Brannan immediately realized the opportunity for profit—not from the gold itself, but from selling mining implements to fortune seekers in San Francisco. Brannan launched the Gold Rush, and it made him stupendously wealthy; Sutter enjoyed no such fortune. In 1849, with the news of the discovery of gold on the American River having spread across the continent, the land was overrun and everything the widely traveled and industrious Sutter had worked for was ruined. All told, some 300,000 fortune seekers flocked to California, swelling the population that until then had been dominated by Native Americans, as well as Mestizo and Mexican colonials.

The population boom was unprecedented in North America. The new arrivals found remote mountains and valleys never before seen by nonindigenous people, Native American seasonal encampments and villages, and highly developed agrarian Mexican/Mestizo settlements. They also found rivers teeming with anadromous fish and streams swarming with trout. The massive influx of people from the East likely introduced fly angling to California. On July 10, 1860, the *Daily Alta California* reported,

> Amateur anglers . . . have been scouring the streams for trout . . . We are informed by the proprietor of a sportsman's emporium [in San Francisco] that the demand for fishing tackle has been greater this season than ever before . . . Fly fishing is seldom practiced among our California anglers, albeit the sport is infinitely preferable to the old-fashioned way of baiting constantly with worms and grasshoppers.

With so many bait fishers, snaggers, netters, and trappers, fly anglers were the exception in California, but so explosive was the population growth after 1849 that just about any material want could be accommodated by innovative and opportunistic entrepreneurs. By June 9, 1851, Warren & Company, Sacramento, was advertising "various kinds of fly hooks [flies] ready for use" in the *Sacramento Daily Union*.

Even before the occasional fly angler was exploring the waters of the American River drainage, pre–Gold Rush fishermen

With the discovery of gold on the American River, people swarmed to California both over land and by sea. San Francisco's population exploded almost overnight and the harbor became so crowded that vessels often had to wait days to unload passengers and goods.
PHOTOGRAPHER UNKNOWN

had long benefitted from the river's natural bounty, and on November 29, 1850, a resident who had preceded the forty-niners reported in the *Sacramento Transcript*, "In addition to the mountain game, our rivers afford a large supply of the finny tribe. The salmon and salmon trout appear to be the general favorites. The latter is taken in large quantities twenty miles, and probably higher up the American river."

The term "salmon trout" was used to describe two species of fish. On the east side of the Sierra Nevada crest, the huge native trout of Lake Tahoe and the Truckee River earned the title salmon trout—we know them now as Lahontan cutthroat trout. An adventurous fur trapper who wrote a story for the August 18, 1855, *Sacramento Daily Union*, titled "Notes of a Prospecting Tour in the Sierra Nevadas," reported, "July 24—Started at sunrise, and arrived at Lake Bigler [Lake Tahoe] at 10 o'clock, distant from Carson Valley eight miles. We camped here, and went fishing. Had good luck, catching enough salmon trout [Lahontan cutthroat] and smelt to last five of us three or four days. For supper we had fried fish, boiled fish, and fish chowder. Retired to bed with light hearts and heavy stomachs."

On the west side, the name salmon trout was applied to the peculiar and mysterious salmonlike trout—or was it a troutlike salmon?—that seasonally migrated into the streams in California's Central Valley and all along the California Coast: steelhead. In the Central Valley, steelhead ranged throughout the San Joaquin and Sacramento Rivers; they spawned in every tributary with suitable, accessible habitat. In those waters and on the coastal streams, virtually all steelhead were winter steelhead—they ascended the rivers in autumn and winter to spawn immediately upon reaching their natal waters. Even if California's pioneering fly anglers had intentionally targeted these fish, they would have found the prospects daunting due to cold, swollen flows of winter. However, unlike winter steelhead on coastal rivers, for the Central Valley winter steelhead "peak immigration seems to have occurred historically from late September to late October," according to "Salmon, Steelhead, and Trout in California," a report by Peter B. Moyle, Joshua A. Israel, and Sabra E. Purdy, which offers a thorough treatment of current and historical steelhead populations and life histories in California, including details about Central Valley steelhead. So mid-nineteenth-century anglers may have found conditions more conducive to fly angling for these fish. Certainly anglers eagerly pursued winter steelhead with every other method of harvest. For example, the February 3, 1858, *Daily Alta California* reported, "Since the rise of water in the mountain streams, the salmon trout have commenced ascending, numbers of which have been taken by the Californians. We have seen some splendid specimens offered for sale in the streets." Perhaps some of those specimens were taken on fly-fishing tackle, but records of such feats remain elusive.

But the American River system, the heart of the gold country, also hosted robust runs of summer steelhead—fish that arrived between late spring and midsummer and overwintered in the rivers before spawning the following late winter or early spring; other streams in the San Joaquin River watershed and the Sacramento River watershed may also have hosted summer runs. Moyle and his coauthors note that while only winter-run steelhead occupy Central Valley streams today, "There is indication from fish counts before the era of large rim dams that summer-run steelhead . . . once existed in the system. . . . In the American River, summer steelhead apparently migrated upstream in May–June and were fairly abundant."

If fly fishers of the 1850s sought battle with those summer-run steelhead instead of winter steelhead, they would have found much easier treading. Moreover they would have formed the vanguard of our sport.

While I can supply no direct evidence that Gold Rush-era anglers purposely fly fished for the summer-run steelhead in the American River system, it seems likely they would have done so, even if there were only a few fly casters. So I think the American River system is probably the true birthplace of dedicated steelhead fly angling. That possibility has seldom been considered simply because the summer-run steelhead disappeared from the American River drainage many decades ago when dams blocked off their spawning grounds.

Also by the 1850s, anglers were fishing the coastal streams of the San Francisco Peninsula and nearby. Such waters as Paper Mill Creek (now known as Lagunitas Creek) became popular destinations as early as the 1860s. And May was ". . . the month above all other, in California, during which the angler for trout achieves his greatest triumphs," reported the *Daily Alta California* (May 10, 1862), which also noted, "For the last week, every stream, within a radius of twenty miles around this city [San Francisco], has been visited by disciples of the ancient 'Izaak.'" Based on the timing of some of the best fishing on the coastal streams (late spring) and the reports of prodigious catches of trout, it seems likely that salmon and steelhead smolt were the primary catch, but with so many anglers afoot, adult salmon and steelhead were also part of the catch and were targeted at times when they invaded the rivers on their spawning runs.

As San Francisco grew—from just 850 people in 1848 on the eve of the Gold Rush to 150,000 people by 1870—the number of fly fishers increased, and the prosperity of the city's upper and middle classes engendered a class of sporting enthusiasts able to pursue the bountiful game and fish of nineteenth-century California. Fly-fishing opportunities were legion, and significantly, the traditions, techniques, and tackle were of British and Northeast origins, including the fly patterns. Because so many new Californians had arrived from the East, the most popular flies were the standard East Coast and British patterns of the day. In 1863, Elam & Howes, Clay Street, stocked artificial flies (and rods, reels, silk lines, silkworm gut, and trout hooks) from the famous New York City tackle firm, Conroy's, advertising their wares in the *Daily Alta California*; and by 1870, according to listings in *Langley's San Francisco Directory*, the city had five fishing tackle dealers; a decade later, it had at least 10.

Far to the north, in Oregon, one proprietor was already importing fishing tackle from San Francisco in the 1860s. The *Daily Mountaineer*, a pioneering newspaper in The Dalles, announced on April 15, 1866, "Our friend Juker, ever alive to the wants of the public, has just received a large and fine assortment of fishing tackle, consisting of fly hooks [flies] of all shades and colors, poles, reels, Limerick hooks, baskets, &c.,

direct from San Francisco. . . . Now is the time for the followers of Izaak Walton to prepare for amusement."[1]

By then, trout anglers were venturing farther and farther afield throughout California and Oregon, but another two decades would pass before the Eel River in distant Northern California was attracting increasing numbers of anglers from San Francisco, drawn by rumors of excellent sport fishing. By the late 1880s, commercial salmon fisheries at the mouth of the Eel had been operating for more than thirty years, yet a new name for one of the common fish in the Eel, the salmon-trout, was just coming into vogue: steelhead. This term seemingly originated from the Columbia River far to the north. In July, 1877, the United States Fish Commissioner, Professor Livingston Stone, visited the Clackamas River area (near Portland) to determine if the river was a suitable location for a salmon hatchery, and the local *Oregon City Enterprise* (July 19, 1877) then reported, "The projectors of this scheme have objected to this location, alleging that only 'steel-heads' ascend the Clackamas." Likewise, *The Daily Astorian* (May 15, 1879) suggested "steel heads" were "entirely different fish from the Columbia river salmon proper," and to settle the matter legally, in 1882, the state circuit court determined that steelhead were not salmon in the eyes of the law.

And on the Eel River, there was something special about these steelhead: substantial numbers of them ran up the river in the summer and fall. The Eel, like the American, had summer steelhead, and they would soon form not only a popular fishery for local and traveling fly fishers, but also the foundations of steelhead fly fishing itself. By 1890, San Franciscan John S. Benn (see Chapter II) had already garnered considerable fame as a professional fly tier, but in that year, or perhaps a bit earlier, he joined a party of friends in journeying to the Eel, and he alone among them was strictly a fly angler.

On October 25, 1891, *The Morning Call* (San Francisco) ran a story titled, "An Angler's Outing on Eel River—The Steel-Heads," reporting:

> Since the return of a party of well known anglers from the wilds of Humboldt County questions such as, What are "steel-head" trout? and What is the definition of the word "species," as applied to trout and salmon? have been asked and remain unanswered . . . it has been said by noted anglers, who have taken these fish by means of rod and line from several rivers between here and Alaska, that they are of the same formation and resemble in every particular the gamy white-trout of Europe. The so-called "chub" salmon is gamy and is a different fish in formation and appearance to the steel-head, specimens of which have not, as yet, been submitted to the Fish and Game Commissioners for classification.
>
> . . . .a majority of the gentlemen remained at Fortuna, a small town situated near the river and about thirty miles from Eureka. . . . [John] Gallagher and [E.R.] Swain took a flying trip, as an experiment, to Scotia from Fortuna on the day prior to their return home, and had most excellent sport . . . On the strength of the information received [that fishing had improved since the first party returned to San Francisco] the following gentlemen have made preparations for a trip north this week: A. Wilson, N. B. Turner, W. Stone, Dr. von Hoffman and John Ben [sic].

The following year, an April 24 *San Francisco Call* article noted that some years prior, John Benn ". . . was first to discover that both salmon and trout, during certain months of the summer season, would readily rise to an artificial fly."

Steelhead fly fishing was born, and in its first two decades it would be dominated by the then-popular trout flies and minor modifications of them, along with a few popular Atlantic salmon flies. Hence, such famous feathered lures as the Coachman, Royal Coachman, Parmachene Belle, Professor, and Gray Hackle served faithfully for the first generation of steelhead fly anglers.[2] Naturally fly dressers eagerly sought to improve upon these standard patterns and also put their own stamp on their newfound pursuit. John S. Benn (1840–1907) was among the first to alter standard dressings to arrive at California originals, such as his Benn's Coachman and Benn's Black Prince; moreover, he devised many patterns that were entirely new, not so reliant on the patterns from back east for their design. These included his Benn's Martha, named for his daughter, as well as his most famous steelhead fly, the Railbird.

In keeping with the times, all of these early steelhead flies were featherwing patterns. But in time, steelheaders would largely switch to more durable hair for the wings in their flies. The earliest hair-wing flies were called bucktails, and while their genesis is murky, they would soon come to define the steelhead tier's craft.

Rise of the Bucktails

By the 1920s, hair-wing steelhead flies were beginning to replace the older featherwing patterns on steelhead rivers from California to northwest Washington. William Scripture is often credited with inventing bucktail flies in New York in the first decade of the twentieth century when he began substituting long deer tail hair for feathers in the wings of his streamers. Author Emerson Hough and his friend William Wood designed their bucktail flies shortly thereafter. All three men were preceded in the development of hair-wing flies by Carter H. Harrison, who in 1903 created his Trude fly as a joke one evening while staying at A. S. Trude's Algenia Ranch on the Snake River in eastern Idaho (Trude was a banker from Chicago; Harrison was longtime mayor of that city). But the lineage of the hair-wing fly goes back even further, at least to the 1880s when Theodore Gordon created his Bumblepuppy for pike. A few years later, John P. Hance of Indiana coined the phrase for this group of flies when he invented a bass pattern that he dubbed the Fort Wayne Bucktail.

Harold Smedley recorded in his 1943 book *Fly Patterns and Their Origins* that Emerson Hough "traveled and fished the length and breadth of North America and wrote interestingly of it." He fished the Rogue River for steelhead, apparently in the fall of 1915, and chronicled his experiences for *The Saturday*

When autumn color tinges the leaves, steelhead anglers enjoy their most prosperous season. As the earliest steelhead fly casters discovered on California's Eel River, summer steelhead runs peak in September and October on many Northwest rivers. Here an angler swings a fly on the Snake River upstream from Asotin, Washington.

Evening Post in 1916, noting, "The steelhead will follow the fancy of fresh-water trout in its own selection of flies. In habits somewhat like the freshrun [Atlantic] salmon, it still rather favors the freshwater trout; and it is not customary to angle for it with the gaudy flies that alone serve in salmon angling. In summer evenings the local anglers favor gray hackles, brown hackles, or some modest fly of that description."[3] Hough does not say whether he tried his bucktail flies on those Rogue River steelhead, so whether his personal appearance on the river had any bearing on the spread of the bucktail flies is impossible to ascertain.

Regardless, bucktail flies quickly gained a following, and by 1912, one Portland, Oregon, tackle dealer—the influential Backus & Morris, part owned by casting champion Walter Backus—was offering them for sale and promoting them in advertisements in the city newspaper. In the June 20, 1912, issue of *The Sunday Oregonian*, Backus reported on a recent trout-fishing expedition to one of the forks of the Willamette River near Eugene, and noted, "That popular fly, the yellow bucktail proved to be the best killer . . . they all fell for that queer-looking fly with the deer hair wing."

Although we can't pin down the moment at which a bucktail fly was first used for steelhead, Backus or his angling companions may well have inaugurated the trend in the early twentieth century on their forays to Oregon's Rogue River, which by then—even before novelist Zane Grey introduced the river and its steelhead to a widespread audience through his writings—had become a popular destination for anglers from all over the nation.

So too, the first bucktails may have come from California. No less an authority than George McLeod—inventor of the iconic Skykomish Sunrise and Purple Peril—relates that his original fly-tying instructor, E. B. George, brought bucktails to Washington from California. E. B. George was active in the Seattle-area fly-fishing community and a member of the Steelhead Trout Club that formed in 1928. Though hailing from California, he had come to Washington from Portland, and may have lived in Salem even earlier. Despite the lengthy journey in those days, George annually traveled to the Rogue for fall steelhead fishing in the 1930s.[4]

Whatever their exact point of origin, bucktails were rapidly embraced by steelhead anglers, and much of their popularity is due C. Jim Pray (1885–1952), the legendary fly tier and tackle dealer from Eureka, California, and the well-traveled writer and Klamath River addict, Peter J. Schwab.

Schwab hailed from Chicago (though he was born in Pennsylvania) where he was associated with well-known angler and casting champion Fred Peet, best known for his Cains River streamer patterns designed for Atlantic salmon and adapted to steelhead patterns—particularly the Demon series—by Pray in the 1930s. But prior to his invention of the attractive Cains River series of streamers in 1923, Peet, with his friend Charles Antoine, developed their Squirrel Tail Trout Flies in 1917; another Chicagoan, Call J. McCarthy, had developed his Prismac Hair Flies, with their bodies, hackles, and wings all made from bucktail. Even in 1912, before McCarthy, Peet, Antoine, and others developed their own hair-wing flies, the South Bend Bait Company in Indiana was selling its South Bend Bucktails. (The lineage of the bucktails, though still incomplete and controversial in its details, was outlined briefly by Larry St. John in *Practical Fly Fishing*, published in 1920; he identified originators of the early flies and notes the year they were invented.)

So Schwab was already well versed in hair-wing flies by the time he fell in love with the Klamath River and its steelhead in the mid-1920s. He traveled the Northwest in search of steelhead and steelhead fly fishers, and though he found few of either at first, he did meet Portland's Harry Van Luven, a Rogue River regular who relied almost exclusively on his Red Fly, which Schwab would later rename the Van Luven, or Van Luven Bucktail. Schwab began designing his own bucktail flies for steelhead soon after, and in the 1930s, Pray not only designed new bucktail flies, but marketed, popularized, and sold them. By then, bucktail flies were popular on the Rogue, and they would soon dominate the steelhead angler's arsenal from the Eel River to the North Umpqua River.

Washington steelhead fly anglers were likewise quick to adopt bucktail flies. Emil Faulk, around 1923, used bucktail for the wing on his Faulk. The superb fly tier and angler Al Knudson based his Al's Special on either Dan Conway's Yellow Hammer or Conway Special, but he used bucktail for the wing; so too, George McLeod added wings of bucktail to the Yellow

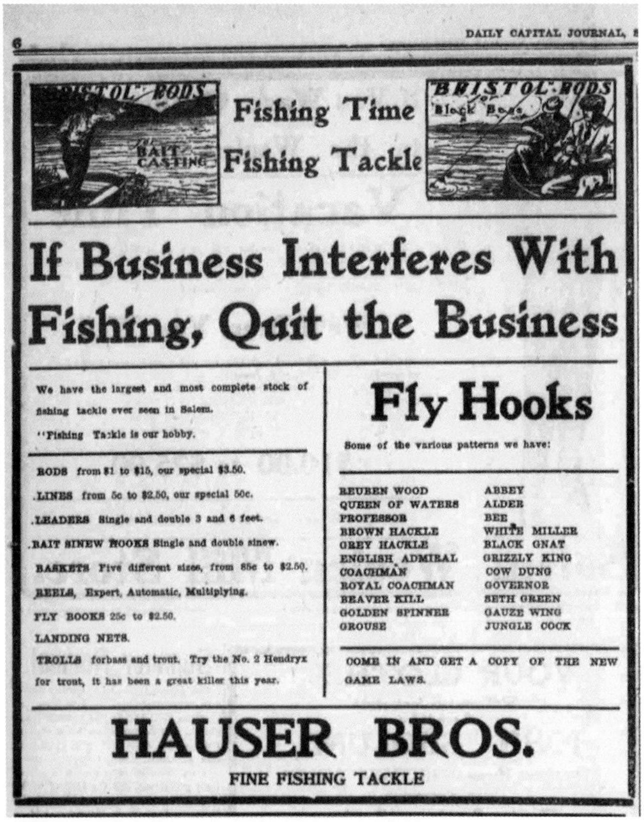

By the dawn of the twentieth century, fly fishing was a well-established tradition throughout the Pacific Northwest, as demonstrated by this 1905 newspaper ad from Hauser Bros., in Salem, Oregon. The popular flies of the day were standard patterns originated in the American Northeast and in Great Britain.

Hammer, and by the time the young McLeod, son of famous angler Ken McLeod, designed his Skykomish Sunrise in 1938, bucktail flies were pervasive from the Eel River in California to the Skagit River in northwest Washington. The floodgates of steelhead fly design were fully open.

Moreover, while this class of flies carried the name bucktail owing to the type of hair most commonly used for the wings, steelhead tiers quickly seized upon the other types of hair available to them, each with its own characteristics. Harold Smedley notes in his discourse on Schwab's bucktail flies in *Fly Patterns and Their Origins*, "The principal hairs used are those of gray squirrel tails, black bear and skunk tail, Eastern white tail deer in natural and dyed yellow, orange, and red, and polar bear in the same colors." Steelhead fly tiers throughout the Northwest employed these hairs and others.

It was the golden era of steelhead flies. From the 1920s through the 1970s—a span of more than half a century—new patterns were legion, a fact well represented by Trey Combs in *Steelhead Fly Fishing and Flies*, which features over 200 patterns in the color plates alone, with many others described in the text. By the time that book was released, steelhead tiers had already branched out from the popular bucktails. Combs dutifully recorded their efforts: Syd Glasso and Dick Wentworth and their gorgeous Spey-type steelhead flies; the elegant original patterns by Harry Lemire and Walt Johnson; the intricate designs of Ralph Wahl and Wes Drain. Notably all these men were Washingtonians. Not coincidentally, the evolution in steelhead fly design had shifted north from its birthplace in California, for the demise of steelhead populations was well underway. Commercial harvest and widespread habitat destruction caused the range of robust and healthy steelhead runs to retreat ever northward, shrinking along the way, a trend that continues today.

ROGUE RIVER
AND ITS
GAME FISH

JOE WHARTON
THE AUTHOR IN FISHING GEAR

(The text in this booklet is adapted from an article published in FOREST & STREAM, in June, 1928, America's most popular outdoor magazine.)

In the founding days of steelhead fly fishing, fly and tackle shops were the vanguards of the sport, delivering the latest fly patterns and fishing acumen to their customers. One of the most significant of the pioneering tackle stores north of California was Joe Wharton's Sporting Goods, opened in Grants Pass—on the Rogue River—in September, 1907. Wharton would become an institution on the Rogue, and in the 1920s the local newspaper re-worked an article he wrote for *Forest & Stream* into an 11-page booklet titled *Rogue River and Its Game Fish*.

End of an Era

While the widespread runs of summer steelhead upon which steelhead fly fishing was founded declined in both range and numbers, the sport itself continued to gain new adherents. Inevitably there were fewer steelhead for more anglers and there were many more fly tiers to tinker with designs, to contemplate the reasons a steelhead takes a fly, and to attempt to create better and more effective patterns. Anglers have always tried to create better patterns, but prior to the 1980s, fly tying was less pervasive among fly anglers, and fly anglers were less numerous. But as the sport grew, so did the craft of fly tying, and the industry itself was quick to introduce new materials to the point that a fly-tying materials catalog of today bears little resemblance to a materials catalog from the 1970s or before.

Through the 1970s and well into the 1980s, fly shops stocked hairs from many different mammals and dubbings made from many different furs. Routinely available were squirrel tails, bucktails, elk hair, deer hair, moose hair, fitch tail, skunk hair, black bear hair, and others; while most of these are still easily procured, the furs used for dubbing are far more difficult to source now: seal, beaver, muskrat, nutria, opossum, Australian opossum, mink, otter, and rabbit. In their place, however, came the synthetics, and synthetic dubbing now dominates the fly tier's craft. Likewise came the age of the popular plastic materials such as Flashabou and Krystal Flash—these products launched a revolution in fly tying, and such materials are common now.

With the sudden insurgence of so many different artificial fly-tying materials, steelhead tiers began designing not only new patterns, but entirely new classes of flies. Articulated flies, tube flies, and any number of plastic- and lead-adorned patterns soon began competing for bin space and media press, and the number of classic hair-wing patterns seen not only in fly shop bins and mail order catalogs, but also on the rivers being wielded by anglers, shrunk noticeably. The decline of the classic steelhead flies divested the sport of some of its romance in the same way that the decline of the classic full-dress Atlantic salmon fly or the Maine featherwing streamers denuded those fisheries of a some of their charm and allure.

In his highly informative *A Steelheader's Way* (2009), Lani Waller observes, "By the more romantic among us, flies are often revered to the point of worship. . . . Some of us elevate our flies into the realm of the supernatural as magic amulets, secret concoctions, invisible allies, and fetishes." My own three-decade affinity for my trusty Spawning Purple probably bears witness to Waller's assessment. So too, however, are those among us for whom steelhead represent the pinnacle of our sport, and who insist that the way we fish for them must honor their stature in our eyes. For anglers like me, the new breed of steelhead flies—regaled in plastic and metal—only dilute fly fishing of some of its charm, some of its enrichment and heritage. So while I hardly cling to particular flies as magic amulets, I do venerate the classic steelhead patterns, for embodied in each of them is the history of our sport—the hopes and passions and innovations of the anglers who shaped steelhead fly fishing, who forged traditions and codified an ethos.

For these reasons I shun weighted steelhead flies; I don't dress flies with plastic parts; I prefer good old-fashioned hooks over shanks, tubes, and articulations; I have no interest in turning steelheading into trouting by dead-drifting flies; and I refuse to fish for summer-run steelhead in their spawning season of spring. These are voluntary guidelines that frame my personal philosophy on steelhead fly fishing because for me and many other steelhead anglers, the method makes the sport. Without the classic flies fished in the traditional method, steelhead angling would lose much of its appeal in the same way that wingshooting loses its appeal without the partnership of a well-trained dog.

As the esteemed author Roderick Haig-Brown said in *Fisherman's Spring* (1951), "In sport, method is everything. The more skill the method calls for, the higher its yield of emotional stir and satisfaction, the higher its place must be in a sportsman's scale of values." In other words, to again quote Haig-Brown, an angler is under "at least a moral obligation to understand what makes his sport and why."

Thanks to the pioneers of our sport, we know how to fish effectively for steelhead, and as tackle has improved, our success has increased even as steelhead continue to decline in numbers in the rivers on which the sport was founded. But effectiveness is not the true measure of a fly angler, for if the total catch was paramount, we would choose methods even more deadly than fly angling. Instead we opt for the grace and beauty of the long rod, and in doing so, we willingly and knowingly concede potential effectiveness—the fly angler, over the course of seasons, can hardly hope to beach more steelhead than the angler skilled in the use of jigs and spoons and bait and other such attractants. Yet we value the method more than the body count, even if, often, the artistic side of fly fishing for steelhead seems to erode in the face of tactics and flies aimed to make fly fishing emulate gear fishing.

But one thing that cannot be tempered is the steelhead itself. Any angler attracted to the allure of the king of American gamefishes should have the chance to meet the steelhead on its most sporting terms: a fresh-run fish willing to leave the comfort of its keep in the river and chase down a fly swinging near the surface. It is then, at that moment of contact between fish and fly and fisher, that the neophyte understands the addiction of the veteran; it is then that the words of Rogue River great Joe Wharton in his 1928 book *Rogue River and Its Game Fish* ring so unforgettably true: "When one of these fellows takes the fly it sends a galvanic thrill through the angler that no other strike does."

The sport of steelhead fly fishing—with that galvanic thrill of the take being its pinnacle—would be incomplete without the classic patterns and their individual histories. Still, I am continually amazed and impressed at the artistry displayed by many contemporary fly dressers in creating the new breed of steelhead flies. These tiers and their increasingly labyrinthine articulated patterns and other ornate, skillfully designed styles are redefining the genre. But of course they do so on the shoulders of the anglers who fabricated the sport itself. If the new breed of steelhead flies overwhelms the classics, it will mean the end of an era, but the historical record, with luck, will be secure.[5]

CHAPTER II

John S. Benn Paves the Way

In 1846, during the Mexican–American War, Captain John Berrien Montgomery of the USS *Portsmouth* captured the Mexican settlement of Yerba Buena, raising the American flag at the Mexican customs house, which was renamed Portsmouth Square in honor of the ship. The following year, the settlement was renamed San Francisco. Today, Portsmouth Square is a city park located in the city's Chinatown district. PHOTOGRAPHER UNKNOWN

The trout is crafty and cunning, but the [steelhead] is the fighter of the world. He comes for a fight and only for a fight, and having come, he does his best to make it an interesting one. Incidentally, the [steelhead] is also one of the most prolific sources of inspiration for breaking the ninth commandment.

—"Descriptive of many Grants Pass Scenes," *Rogue River Courier,* October 16, 1908.

The taxonomy of the steelhead—was it a salmon or a trout?—was nowhere near settled when famous fly tier John S. Benn first ventured north from his home in San Francisco to pursue rumors of fabulous fishing on the Eel River in Northern California in the late 1880s. By then, anglers in California, and likely in Oregon and Washington, had taken plenty of steelhead on flies, but usually in the pursuit of trout, not comprehending what these troutlike salmon or salmonlike trout really were. Hence West Coast fishermen soon began calling these silvery denizens of wild rivers salmon-trout, and heated debates ensued, continuing past the turn of the century—were they trout or were they salmon?

The fish remained enigmatic, as did the juvenile salmon encountered so frequently in the coastal rivers by pioneering anglers who had no doubt begun casting flies on California waters as early as 1849. And just as scientists of the day were figuring out how to classify all these Pacific Coast salmonids, Benn began a targeted pursuit of the salmon-trout—the steelhead—with flies. At first, he and the anglers who joined him on the Eel during the early 1890s used the trout flies that had earned their trust, but Benn tied them a bit larger; the names are familiar, for among these early flies cast for steelhead were such stalwarts as the Coachman, Royal Coachman, Red Ibis, and Professor—flies hailing from the British Isles and the American Northeast.

The old Irishman Benn, originally a millwright, honed his fly tying and fly angling on the Blackwater and Shannon Rivers—famous for their runs of Atlantic salmon—in his native land. But America beckoned, as it did to so many Irishmen, and Benn's family came to America not long after the feverish California Gold Rush and reached the Golden State in the 1860s.

Once in California, Benn engaged in the business he knew, and according to the 1875 *San Francisco Directory*, he partnered with Mary Bergin to form American Mills at West Fourth Street, San Francisco. However, stricken by rheumatism "to such an extent that twice he was rendered totally blind and became crippled for seven years," Benn, after recovering, sought a more sedentary occupation. Having long been an ardent angler and fly tier, he decided to make flies his business ("The Fly-Maker: The Story of a Craftsman of Sport," *San Francisco Call*, June 9, 1907). Indeed, by 1882, five years after launching his fly-tying enterprise, the 1882 *San Francisco Directory* listed Benn as an "artificial flymaker" at his residence, 603 Brannan Street. Over the ensuing 25 years, Benn would move to various San Francisco residences, but always he remained a fly tier by trade. He even taught his daughter Martha the craft, and she joined him in the business.

Not only was Benn among the early fly anglers who explored the streams of the Central California coastal region,[6] but he also opened the door to luring the grand gamefish of the Pacific Coast to the fly, being "the first of the fraternity of stream whippers to discover that the steelheads of Eel River will rise to a fly when the feathered lure is properly presented to the game fishes" (*San Francisco Call*, November 27, 1897).

Annually by the early 1890s, Benn and a number of his angling comrades formed parties that resided for several weeks on the banks of the Eel in the fall. The journey was arduous: they had to travel by steamship to Humboldt Bay, or endure the even more troublesome and lengthy overland route. Benn impressed the locals not only with his ability to catch copious numbers of steelhead on his flies, but also with his feat in landing massive chinook salmon—notoriously lockjawed where flies are concerned even to this day—on fly tackle. Upon their return to San Francisco, Benn and his cohorts found a waiting audience of anglers eager to hear of their exploits in the faraway Humboldt country, and the November 6, 1892, *San Francisco Call* noted that Benn and his friends, after their 1892 trip to the Eel:

> . . . tell wonderful things concerning the finish battles they engaged in with the great fighting fisher known as king salmon. Benn, who fished altogether with flies of his own manufacture, astonished the natives, who did not surmise that the king of fresh-water fishes [chinook salmon] could be captured by means of fly-casting. Benn used a royal coachman, and with this well-known

John S. Benn was a prolific and esteemed professional fly tier from San Francisco; in addition to being credited as the first fly angler to target steelhead on the Eel River, he created many original fly patterns, including such steelhead patterns as the Benn's Coachman, Benn's Martha, Soule, and Carson Coachman. Born in Ireland, where he learned to tie flies and fish for Atlantic salmon, Benn was an early member of the San Francisco Fly Casting Club. His daughter, Martha, tied flies professionally as well and continued to do so long after her father's death in 1907. Washington-based artist and fly dresser Sean Dahlquist rendered this likeness of Benn. SEAN DAHLQUIST

> fly he had grand luck, hooking and landing several small and large salmon daily. The largest fish he landed weighed 30 1/2 pounds. It took him exactly two hours and ten minutes to kill this fish with a 15-foot bamboo rod which did excellent service, however, although rather light in construction for this kind of sport.

By that time, Benn, industrious and innovative, was the most celebrated fly tier in the West, and his fame spread even more through the 1890s as his flies, and those tied by his daughter Martha, earned accolades and awards at the California State Fair, the Universal International Exposition in Paris, the Saint Louis World Fair, and the Lewis and Clark Exposition in Portland. In 1904, upon examining Benn's flies at the California State Fair, a reporter for the *Amador Ledger* (July 29) decided the display was "unquestionably the finest at the exposition from any state or country."

Meanwhile—decades ahead of British Columbia's Roderick Haig-Brown or the North Umpqua's Vic O'Byrne—Benn was wielding long, two-handed rods for salmon and steelhead on the Pacific Coast, no doubt taking his cue from his upbringing on the Irish salmon rivers. So too, Benn—one of the early members of the San Francisco Fly Casting Club that formed in 1894—won the two-handed salmon-rod casting event at the club's inaugural casting tournament held on May 4, 1894, at Stow Lake in Golden Gate Park. The *Sportsman's Journal* (May 19, 1894) reported:

> The double handed salmon casting event had three entrants. John S. Benn, the veteran fly tyer and salmon fisher, was the first to wield the 18 foot, 6 joint bamboo rod, which some called a mast. After several attempts the heavy Japanese twist line began to cut the air and 70, 80, 90 feet were soon passed. Then resting for apparently a second Mr. Benn gathered himself, drew line from the reel and right in the teeth of the wind shot his salmon fly straight through the air and scored 105 feet, his fly dropping almost along the buoys. Great shouts of applause rent the air and Mr. Benn rested on his laurels, as he was tired. As in the other events there was no telling what he would have scored had there been no wind.

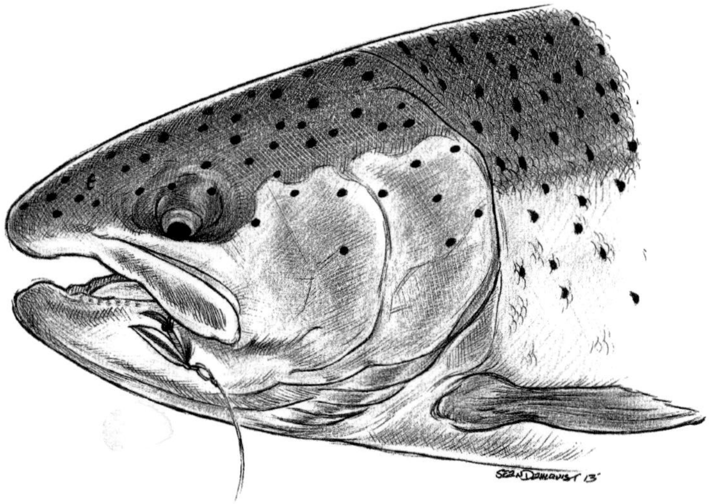

In the late 1880s when John S. Benn pioneered the dedicated pursuit of steelhead with fly tackle, these enigmatic fish were poorly understood and their taxonomy was disputed. They behaved like trout, and they looked like trout, but they went to sea like salmon, which they also resembled. Hence, the term salmon-trout was in widespread use, and the name steelhead or "steel-heads" would soon come into vogue. SEAN DAHLQUIST

Benn beat his nearest competitor by 14 feet in the face of stout trade winds blowing in off the Pacific. The Midwinter Fair fly-casting tournament had been modeled after the casting tournaments that had been held back East for a decade or so, and it was the first casting competition in the West. Rules required that each competitor actually cast a fly (the hooks were clipped at the bend to prevent hooking any of the prodigious numbers of rainbow trout stocked in Stow Lake by the California Fish and Game Commission) and Benn even designed a "Benn's tournament fly," dressed on size 5 hooks.

Some years prior, Benn had invented a new, improved fly wallet; he applied for a patent for the product, providing a highly detailed description and drawings, and the wallet was in production by around 1890, when the *Mining and Scientific Press* (January–June, 1891) reported, "Many of our local anglers pronounce this book of Mr. Benn's the most convenient on the market." He continued to sell his fly wallets into the early 1900s, and *Sunset* magazine (Vol. 8, 1901/1902), in a story about the fly-casting championships of 1902, notes that among the prizes were "Benn's fly books and flies."

By then, Benn's flies were famous and eagerly sought by anglers throughout the region. There's no way of knowing how many different Benn patterns he and his daughter turned out, but among the many popular Benn trout flies were Benn's McCloud and Benn's Orange-Gray and Brown. His version of the Royal Coachman became especially popular, and his flies were recommended wherever stories about California fishing appeared, including in such magazines as *Forest and Stream* and *Western Field*, and books, such as *Shasta: The Keystone of California Scenery* (1889), wherein E. McDonald Johnstone recommended Benn patterns alongside the most popular flies of the day, the Professor, Royal Coachman, and Black Gnat. One angler carried Benn flies all the way to the trout streams of Germany and reported back to the *San Francisco Call* (February 29, 1896), ". . . We caught a few small fish from one of the small streams that empty into the Rhine on John Benn's famous coachman . . ."

All through California—the centerpiece of nineteenth-century fly fishing in the West—anglers exalted Benn's flies and venerated their maker. Members of the San Francisco Fly Casting Club (which included essentially all the well-known fly-angling devotees of the city in the club's infancy), "apparently scorn to go in quest of trout with any lure other than the flies made by John Benn or some equally famous artificer," said the *San Francisco Call* (April 9, 1906). And a disparaging word about the popular Benn could bring quick retort, as on

June 18, 1893, when the *Call* took umbrage at what might seem a minor indignity and jumped to Benn's defense:

> Ramon G. Wilson has contributed an article to the book, *Favorite Flies*, in which he says of our local expert fly-tier, John Benn: "Benn is most ingenious and prolific in his devices for new flies, but few of them, however, are in general use." Mr. Wilson certainly must have been mind-wandering to some distant land when he wrote the above, as Benn's flies are in great demand on this coast, and unlike the imported truck, which is only answerable for fingerling fishing, the homemade fly can be always relied upon no matter how large or vigorous a fighter the fish may be. As for artistic finish Benn's flies are far superior to the English lure.

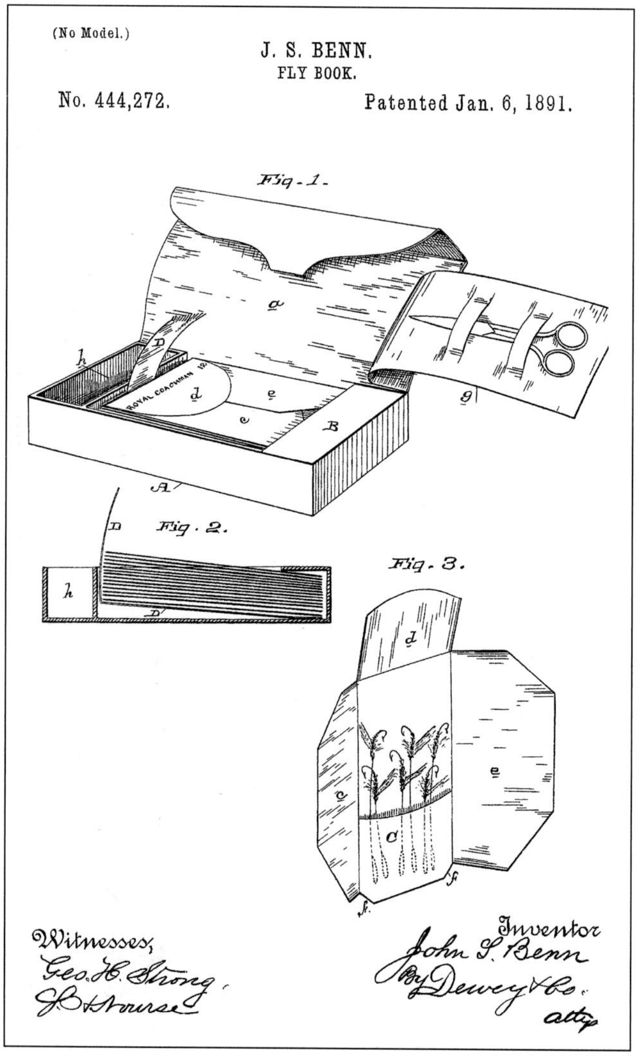

In 1890, Benn applied for a patent for a new fly book, which was an improvement over the fly books available at the time. The patent was granted in 1891. In the specification for his patent, Benn explained, "I have so constructed my improved fly-book that the flies are readily accessible, while at the same time a large number can be carried in a small space. Each variety can be kept in its separate receptacle, and by indexing and numbering only the envelope desired need be opened and examined."

North to the Eel

Benn's trout flies enjoyed widespread popularity, and so not surprisingly he and others began fishing some of them for steelhead. The *San Francisco Call* reported on the successful angling excursions to the Eel River by the city's leading sport fishers, and soon the river found itself swelling with visitors; the tiny communities there began catering to the travelers, and as the popularity of steelhead fly angling grew, Benn—and eventually others—began designing flies specifically for these abundant fish that provided such superb sport.

So enamored with the Eel and its steelhead was Benn that in the mid-1890s, he decided to move permanently to the river's banks, leaving behind San Francisco and all his angling friends there; by then his daughter Martha had married, and Benn's dear old angling partner John Butler had, reported the *San Francisco Call* (November 27, 1897), "arranged to plant John for the balance of his days in a comfortable dwelling on the banks of the famous Eel River, in Humboldt County, where the old angler can enjoy happy moments at his favorite pastime during times when business is slack."

Like Benn, Butler was an original member of the San Francisco Fly Casting Club and both men were champion casters. The *Breeder and Sportsman* (October 7, 1905) noted, "Butler was a member of the fraternity of Eel River enthusiasts who lived in San Francisco and annually made the journey to the Eel; he is on record as having bested a 16-pound Eel steelhead in September, 1905."

By trade, Butler was purveyor of wines, ales, and spirits, and owner of Butler's English Ale House in the city; one can only imagine the angling conversations that occurred in Butler's, described by author Daniel O'Connell in his *The Inner Man: Good Things to Eat and Drink and Where to Get Them* (1891) as a "resort of many old countrymen who love to drink their half-and-half from the shining pewter." Butler imported spirits from around the globe, specializing in fine sherry and other inebriants; he had bourbon made to order ("Butler's Chicken Cask") and brought in sherry-cask-finished Scotch whiskey; "cold and delicious pig's head" was the "piece de resistance of Butler's lunch table, and in the trouting season, an appetizing fish, deliciously cooked, caught by Mr. Butler himself, who is a successful and enthusiastic angler."[7]

Butler must have harbored great respect and admiration for his friend and frequent fishing partner, yet despite his intent to provide Benn permanent accommodations on the Eel River, Benn never made the move. The *Breeder and Sportsman*, January 8, 1898, reported, "John Benn is still at the old stand, 402 Montgomery Street, attending to orders for his famous flies of yore. The announcement that John contemplated taking up his residence at Fortuna was premature. He will not leave the city for Eel River until next fall, if he goes at all." Two months later, the *San Francisco Call* (March 12), likewise noted, "Anglers will be pleased to learn that John Benn, the famous dresser of trout flies, has not left this city to reside in Humboldt County. Benn is industriously at work tying favorite flies at his old place on Montgomery Street, where he will be pleased to see at any time his old friends of the angle."

Printed in the *San Francisco Call* of October 23, 1897, these drawings carried the headline, "John Benn, the Well-Known Dresser of Trout Flies, Recently Returned From a Two Weeks' Outing on Eel River." A short caption explained, "The pictures show the old angler in the act of teaching the wife of a prominent physician at Fortuna how to cast a fly scientifically. After which Benn takes a nap in his fishing-boat and was shot by a camera artist while enjoying happy moments."

While previous sources have said that Benn moved to the Eel, I have found no corroborating evidence, and in fact the strongest evidence suggests that he intended to move to the Eel, but ultimately never did so. On my behalf, Joan Berman, special collections librarian at Humboldt State University Library in Arcata, undertook a search to determine whether any record existed of John Benn residing in Humboldt County, and she reported finding no evidence of Benn having lived there. Her searches included various issues of a city directory that included Fortuna, Rohnerville, Rio Dell, and Scotia; the major history collection; the Susie Baker Foundation Collection name index; the *Southern Humboldt Papers*; and the index of the *Humboldt Historian*, newsletter of the Humboldt County Historical Society.

Circumstantial evidence hints at the reason that Benn never made the planned move to his beloved Eel: the previous autumn—September, 1896—Benn's daughter Martha married Peter Calderwood, who seems to have been something of a degenerate. As reported in the *San Francisco Call* (March 2, 1899), she divorced him in mid-1898, but she may have separated from him much earlier, possibly by the winter of 1897. (Sadly, the couple's five-month-old daughter, Alice, died on May 4, 1898). When John Benn, with aid of a deliveryman, went to Calderwood's residence to move a piano, Calderwood threatened to kill both men. Benn may have been retrieving the piano for a daughter who had recently moved back home, and the threat from his son-in-law was so sincere that Benn swore out a court warrant for Calderwood's arrest, according to the *San Francisco Call* (March 3, 1897).

The situation escalated rapidly when two weeks later, Calderwood, with an accomplice named Charles Nevins, allegedly drugged Benn and attempted to have him admitted to the "Home for Inebriates." After being arrested, Calderwood and Nevins insisted they had Benn "conveyed to the institution for his own good, as he was a hopeless inebriate," but according to Benn, the men intended to rob him, and they succeeded in absconding with "a lot of trout flies" from Benn's shop. Ultimately Nevins and Calderwood appeared before a judge to answer to a charge of administering a drug with intent to commit a felony, and at the request of Benn's attorney, the case was dismissed (*San Francisco Call*, March 20 and March 23).

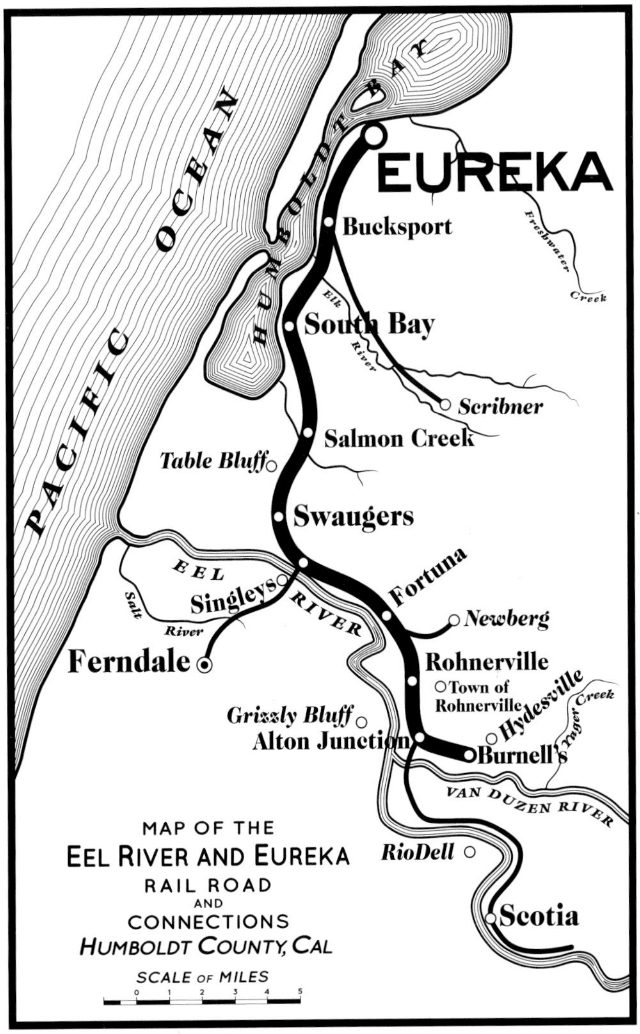

Started in 1882 by a group of Eureka businessmen, including William Carson (see Carson Coachman, page 53), the Eel River and Eureka Railroad was running passenger trains twice daily (three times a day on Sundays) by 1896. The train allowed travelers who arrived by ocean-going steamers to easily reach the Eel River from Humboldt Bay and Eureka. Reproduced from the vintage original map by Pete Chadwell of Dynamic Arts.

So it seems at exactly the time that Benn was hoping to enjoy the rest of his days on the banks of the Eel River, through the benefaction of John Butler, domestic strife forestalled his plans. But the famous old fly tier continued to make his living selling his wares to the burgeoning community of California anglers, and he continued as the preeminent artisan in the field until his death on December 9, 1907. By then he had founded an entirely new lineage of flies: patterns designed and dressed specifically for steelhead.

John S. Benn, along with his wife, Alice (1837–1912), and daughter, Martha (1878–1939), are interred at sprawling Cypress Lawn Memorial Park in Colma, California. R. WHITE.

"Honest" John Butler died suddenly only a few months prior to the passing of his old friend John Benn. He had been traveling in Rome with his niece a year after massive fires largely obliterated downtown San Francisco after the big earthquakes of 1906; his long-established saloon was lost in the tragic conflagration. "Butler had planned after the disaster to visit England, his birthplace, with his niece, Miss Bertha Butler, and then tour Europe, returning to San Francisco this summer," reported the *San Francisco Call* of April 17, 1907, which continued, ". . . Butler was a man of many peculiarities and strong traits. His integrity was never questioned and he built a fortune in his business. His real estate ventures in later life added to his riches."[8]

Sadly, Benn has almost vanished from the narrative of our sport. His flies and his sterling reputation as an angler and fly dresser virtually died with him, and outside the earliest works from author Trey Combs—*The Steelhead Trout* (1971) and *Steelhead Fly Fishing and Flies*—Benn's connection to steelhead and steelhead flies has hardly been mentioned, let alone chronicled, since his own lifetime. Subsequent generations of California steelhead anglers—Sam Wells and then C. Jim Pray, for example—would forge a lasting imprint on steelhead flies and fly fishing, helping to define the genre, but their accomplishments were built upon the foundation laid by John S. Benn.[9]

CHAPTER III

Embracing the Classics

Oregon's John Day River is the third-longest free-flowing river in the lower 48 states; it annually hosts a small and imperiled run of native summer-run steelhead that arrive in late autumn.

Some days they take the fly greedily and some days not all the art in the world nor all the flies can lure a rise.

—"Rogue River Angling," *Medford Mail Tribune,* October 26, 1911.

Steelhead can be perplexing—if you allow them to be. Many anglers do. But I find steelhead perfectly decipherable in that I have abandoned any notion that the particular fly I use to tempt them matters to the steelhead. I have also decided I know nothing of why steelhead take swung flies anyway. To suggest that a fly lacking a particular hue or shape or feather or fur or tinsel renders that fly less effective than all others is nonsensical; to insist that one pattern, dressed in one specific manner, is more deadly than all others defies logic.

Yet not all successful steelhead fly fishers abide by the same logic that guides my own passion. When flies and steelhead behavior are the topic, there is a continuum: at the one end are the strict rationalists, such as myself, and at the other are those who insist that a single attribute of a particular steelhead fly makes all the difference. In each of those two camps reside successful anglers. All along the continuum are anglers who hold their own less extreme notions of what renders a particular fly effective and find their efforts rewarded by steelhead, which have proven themselves amendable to so many different flies since the vanguard generation of steelhead fly casters first swung Coachmen and Professors and Gray Hackles through the then-uncharted waters of Northern California.

History, I submit, is on the side of the skeptic: if one style or shade or pattern of steelhead fly were more effective than all others, then by now we would all be using it, for we have had nearly 14 decades to compile evidence and form conclusions on that score. Essentially, however, the opposite has occurred in that we now have more varieties and styles of effective flies than ever before. On December 21, 1967, the revered outdoor writer Enos Bradner (1892–1984), in his long-running "The Inside on the Outdoors" column for the *Seattle Times*, wrote, "Steelhead patterns, as developed in the Pacific Northwest, are many and varied. In fact, there are almost as many patterns in use as there are steelhead anglers."

And nearly 50 years later, the development of new steelhead flies continues unabated, and all of them attract steelhead. In doing so they tell us much about the fish itself: a Pacific Coast steelhead is no mere trout, and it takes flies for reasons largely unrelated to the reasons trout take flies. Should you find rising trout during a hatch of Green Drakes, you can conclude that the fish are feeding on the mayflies; moreover, you can verify your suspicion through simple observation. You can reason that if you imitate the insects upon which the trout are feeding, and then skillfully fish your imitation, you will rise trout *because* your fly mimics what they are eating.

But steelhead are different. Their reasons for chasing feathered forgeries are entirely their own. Certainly there are situations when some steelhead eat food—salmon eggs or other

A Golden Demon—one of the most famous and iconic of all steelhead flies—adorns the jaw of an autumn buck. Such fleeting scenes inspire many modern steelhead anglers to continue using the old classic patterns.

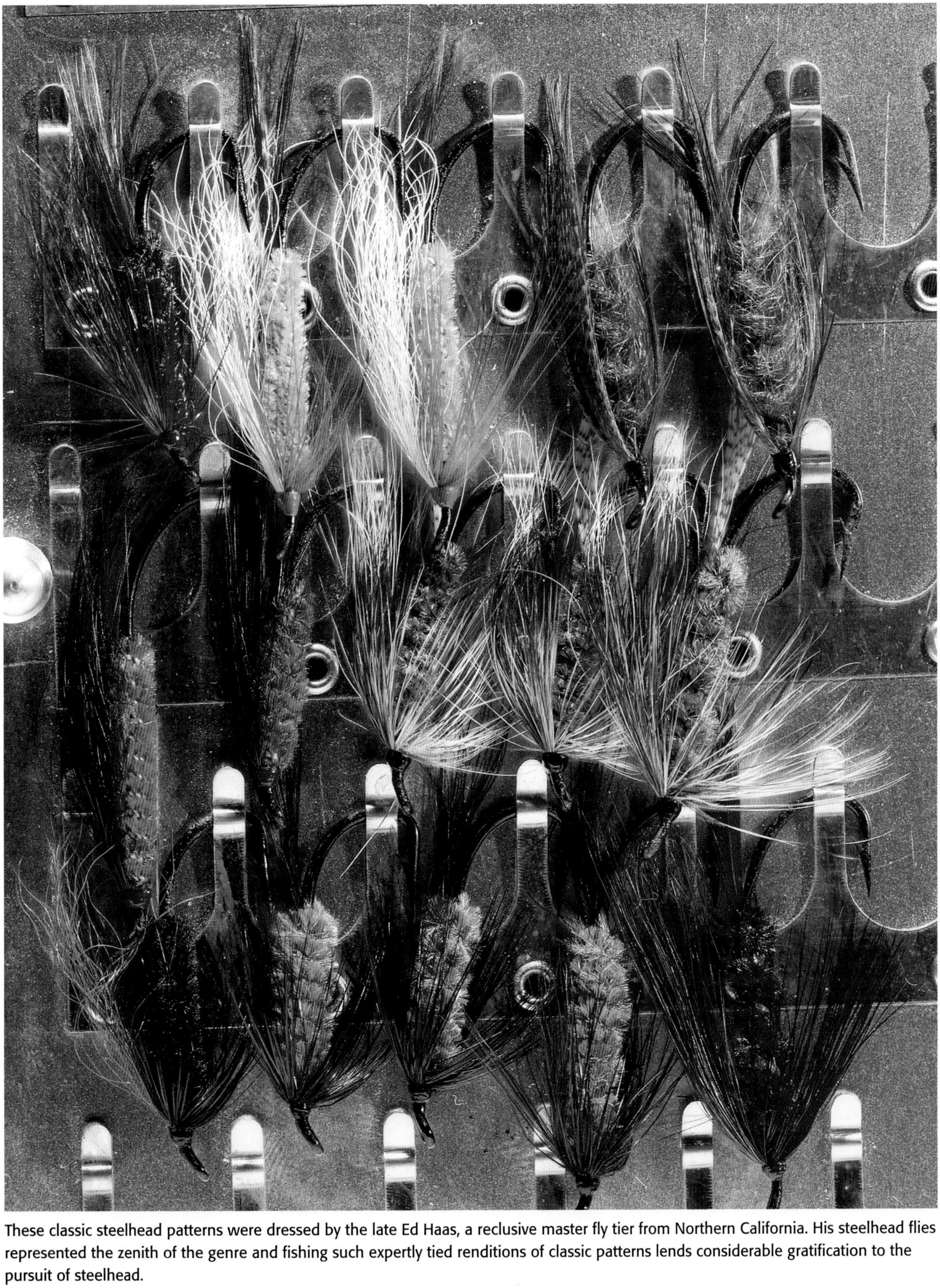

These classic steelhead patterns were dressed by the late Ed Haas, a reclusive master fly tier from Northern California. His steelhead flies represented the zenith of the genre and fishing such expertly tied renditions of classic patterns lends considerable gratification to the pursuit of steelhead.

Steelhead fly angling takes anglers to remarkable places, and the traditional and highly repetitive tactic of swinging flies allows ample time for contemplation and introspection.

spawn and insects—but these circumstances hold no interest to me, for the steelhead is at its sporting best as a fish that chases down swung flies for reasons we can't codify. It is their enigmatic nature coupled with the traditional method of catching them that makes steelhead so special. Frank Colby, tackle store owner and steelheader of yesteryear on Oregon's Rogue River, put it succinctly when he told author Syl MacDowell (*Western Trout*): "Nobody knows steelhead."

Theories abound as to why a steelhead will suddenly chase down a fly swinging across the flow. In decades past, I admit to having held to some of those theories, but upon the strength of many seasons chasing steelhead, I long ago abandoned any notion that I or anyone else will ever satisfactorily explain why these fish behave the way they do. Moreover, I embrace their abstruseness, for the mystery embedded in the pursuit makes it all the more thrilling.

So too, the steelhead's proclivity for flies of all descriptions fosters the artistry of the fly dresser's craft, for it's hardly accidental that some of the world's most beautiful flies belong to types of angling in which the fly choice matters little to the fish: salmon fishing in the British Isles in the nineteenth century, streamers dressed for Maine's landlocked salmon and brook trout a century ago, and of course steelhead on the Pacific Coast. Particularly germane was the Atlantic salmon debate of the 1800s, when fly tying reached its zenith with the gaudy and gorgeous full-dress salmon flies of the Victorian era. George M. Kelson, among the greatest of the British fly tiers and author of *The Salmon Fly* (1895), insisted that for want of a single fiber of some feather from an exotic bird, a fly could be rendered all but useless. His detractors immediately took issue, among them such intellectuals as Sir Herbert Maxwell.

Kelson advised his readers that the salmon in each river had preferred colors, and that salmon changed their tastes for particular patterns over time in direct response to anglers using those patterns; he wrote, for example, that "In the afternoon I usually dress flies with gold tinsel ribbing instead of silver, which answers best earlier in the day." But Maxwell, ahead of his time, scoffed at the cultlike adherence to river-specific flies and Kelsonesque dogma, noting in *Salmon and Sea Trout* (1898), "The popular theory encourages the extraordinary delusion that every river requires its peculiar combination of silk, wool, tinsel and feathers to take the salmon which frequent it."

The two camps diverged, with Kelson and Maxwell representing opposite ends of the continuum. But for every angler who has promoted Kelsonesque ideas—and I've heard and read many of them, such as "this fly is designed specifically for shallow glassy tailouts in the last hour of light between late June and late July" and "the band of orange floss in the tag of this fly is

Steelhead are decidedly unconcerned about the particulars of fly patterns, so anglers can choose flies that appeal to their own sense of art and function. Many hundreds of classic patterns have proven equally effective.

the trigger mechanism that causes steelhead to strike"—I would argue that these cases involve heavy doses of self-fulfilling prophecy and minimal doses of rational thinking.

Many steelhead anglers—upon spending enough seasons catching fish—become comfortable with the idea that the specific fly matters to them, but not to the steelhead. Michael Baughman, in his intelligent book *A River Seen Right* (1995), tells a story about this:

> I can trace my reluctance to place a lot of importance on fly pattern back to 1971, which was when I made my one-and-only contribution to fly tying by inventing the Right-Wing Special. Both the name of the fly and the pattern were offered to the well-to-do and mostly Republican Steamboat Inn guests in the spirit of good-natured fun.
>
> The fly was tied to imitate a tiny American flag, with a red tail, a body made of bands of red, white, and blue chenille, a wing formed of layers of red, white, and blue bucktail, and a red head.
>
> I gave out dozens of them over the summer and used them myself. I sincerely believe that, per hours fished, they caught as many steelhead as any other pattern. Stan Knouse finally tied a few dozen up and offered them for sale, and people actually bought them. I still keep a few in my fly box, and they still catch steelhead, but I don't know of anybody else who continues to use them. . . . Given the political climate these days, though, perhaps the time is right for the pattern to make a comeback.
>
> The real point is that if the Right-Wing Special can catch a steelhead, just about anything can.

Anglers who stubbornly disbelieve the idea that the nuances of their carefully crafted, sagaciously chosen flies are of no consequence to steelhead should consider the observations of Lee Spencer, a man who for many years has volunteered to guard the steelhead of a critical feeder stream to the North Umpqua River. The waters in his charge are closed to fishing, but historically prone to poaching; however, under Spencer's watch, such depredations are nonexistent. Spencer has spent numerous hours (11,000 in his first 15 years by his own count) just observing steelhead as they gather in an important pool where they are easily seen and studied in the clear water. He takes copious notes and keeps accurate records, and he often reports his observations and musings in his column titled "Notes from the Big Bend Pool" in the *Steamboat Whistle*, newsletter of the Steamboaters

On an October day on Oregon's Lower Deschutes River, three divergent patterns accounted for three steelhead. One of the fish took this "Duck Fly," created in jest by the author, but also fished to good effect. The episode demonstrated that anglers care far more about pattern particulars than do steelhead.

club. In the Fall 2013 issue, for his fifteenth season studying the pool, Spencer reported:

> I feel that I can say with absolute accuracy that by far the largest majority of the summer steelhead that return to the North Umpqua River have absolutely no interest in any fly they may see during the course of their stay in the fly water. This is perhaps particularly true for fish that can be seen from the edge of the highway. If you have seen a steelhead that means that four other anglers have seen it too and thrown their fly box at them.
>
> Also I am ignoring the flies that are swung into the face of a steelhead. When a steelhead takes a weighted fly, it is likely done for a different reason than a steelhead that shows an interest in a fly presented on the swing. During my time on the pool, I have always paid attention to what the steelhead in the pool showed an interest in and these things have made it into my seasonal natural history notes (all of which may be examined on The North Umpqua Foundation web page). So, over the last fourteen seasons I have documented a total of 2,538 approaches by steelhead to 1,200 items. Note that more approaches than this have undoubtedly occurred; these are simply the ones that I observed and managed to write down over my time here.
>
> These 2,538 steelhead actions are a small proportion of all of the generic rises seen every season, just as the 1,200 items are less than 0.0001% of the leaves, twigs, seeds, and other things that drift through the pool each season. In fact, these 1,200 items—only 22% of which are insects and crustaceans—make up far fewer than 0.001% of simply the insects that drift over the pool during the course of a season. I make this point because most *rises* are not for the purpose of approaching anything other than the surface and most *approaches* do not, in fact, make contact with the item approached.
>
> The term *approach* is the general term used herein to identify any behavior that appears to be for the purpose of getting close to an item, and includes rises to items, mouthings or nudgings, swimming close to and turning away, approaching and taking and expelling, or approaching, taking and keeping items. Thus the juxtaposition of a steelhead with an item is not documented as an approach unless it appears to be for the purpose of positively approaching that item. Now, my time with Sis and Maggie at the pool suggests unambiguously that by far most of the approaches I have documented represent curiosity on the part of the steelhead in question. . . . whatever that means in steelhead terms. Finally, let me observe that, for the most part, these approach behaviors do not seem angry, fearful, or aggressive.
>
> Do the steelhead in the pool approach items for the same reasons that the steelhead in the North Umpqua River fly zone approach flies? Who knows, probably even the steelhead don't, but I expect so. I have watched as my good friend Ed Kikumoto rose a steelhead to a waking stick and I have risen one to a pistachio shell.

An examination of the data recorded by Spencer reveals that when items approached by steelhead are categorized, leaves are their favorite (or perhaps just the most numerous). Yet no one I know ties and fishes leaf flies. Just as revealing, however, is that Spencer has observed steelhead approaching so many different items that he created a "miscellaneous" category in which to lump all the unique approaches, and that list includes:

> feathers, area of a trout rise, otters, kingfisher, alder cones, mergansers, beavers, unknown plant parts, dead sticks, pieces of wood, bats, Styrofoam, bark, bubbles, fungus on a steelhead tail, fir needles, immature fir cones (reddish), sugar pine needle bundles, lichened sticks, cedar branchlets, lichens, leaf stems, blue-green algae, squirrel, stick with plant down attached, lichened bark, six–eight inch cutthroats, broad-leaved maple seeds, steelhead skin flap, parr with an autumn caddis, minnow carcass, six-inch ring-necked snake, racers and garter snakes, scales from a fir cone, alder catkins, large pink mushroom, spiders dragged by their airborne webs, water strider, the shadow of a waking insect projected onto the stream bed by the late afternoon sun.

I suspect no angler in the steelhead world is more qualified to know whether the fly he chooses any given day is the "right" fly. Spencer knows they are all the right flies. Far from raining on the proverbial parade, I find such evidence to be emancipating: I know a steelhead will take any fly I care to swing for them, and that knowledge allows me to approach the fly-tying part of the equation purely from my own sense of art and my own steelhead angling ethos.

As I write this, I'm fresh from an October trip on the Lower Deschutes River. Fishing had been reputedly slow, but three fish nonetheless rewarded my efforts, and each came to a different fly. The first pounced on a Spawning Purple, the second devoured a Silver Demon (those two flies could hardly be less alike), and the third inhaled a fly I had tied up the night before as something of a joke: my cousin Al Shewey—a particularly adroit steelhead fisherman—is a graduate of Oregon State University, whereas my degree comes from the University of Oregon. The two schools are rivals in athletics, and the so-called Civil War football game earns bragging rights for a year. I decided a bit of good-natured fun was in order, and I dressed a fly in the colors of the Oregon Ducks—green and yellow, two colors that are completely out of fashion for steelhead flies these days. After pontificating fictitiously about how steelhead perceive and react to different colors, I presented the fly to Al with great fanfare, suggesting he use the green-and-yellow pattern, as it would—according to my research—be the best choice for the current light and water conditions. With mounting suspicion, Al listened to my vociferous discourse and finally, as I knew he would, spurned the green-and-yellow fly. With the stage thus set, the second half of my scheme—hatched purely for entertainment among steelheading comrades—was to take a fish on the new fly, and that evening a fine little native accommodated my efforts. As we beached the fish, I turned to Al and told him, "I might be a little hard to live with for a while."

The Duck Fly, the Spawning Purple, and the Silver Demon—three disparate patterns, all fished the same day, all successful. What can you learn from such events? Only that steelhead don't concern themselves with pattern specifics; it is enough that when a swinging fly—probably any swinging fly—and a willing steelhead happen to converge in time and space, the fish is likely to "approach," to use Lee Spencer's terminology, and the game is on.

My own conclusions on steelhead and steelhead flies are hardly unique. The battle between the rationalists and the disciples of Kelson has raged for generations on the steelhead coast. The *Rogue River Courier*, on October 26, 1915, reported, "The big fellows are taking the fly in great shape, and little preference is shown to the exact kind of fly. . . . B. F. Skillman put his trust in the 'Professor,' and brought in seven big fellows, all taken on that fly, to prove his judgment. But then Joe Wharton duplicated the catch and used the 'Royal Coachman,' 'Abbey,' 'English Admiral' and 'Silver Doctor' indiscriminately, thereby proving to his entire satisfaction that it is not the fly, but the man."

Wharton was right. There are two ends of a steelhead angling outfit, and the end doing the casting has far more influence over the results than the end bearing a steel hook adorned in fur, feather, and tinsel. It's where, when, and to a lesser degree how that fly is fished that determines the steelhead fly fisher's fate. In this fact we find an invitation: the steelhead by their nature invite us to dress and fish flies that capture our imagination, that embody our sense of artistry, that reflect the spirit of the chase, and that honor the traditions of our sport.

CHAPTER IV

The Classic Patterns

Classic steelhead flies engender ample room for artistic expression by individual fly tiers.

Flies are the expression of the times and character of the rivers and their people—what they do, how they fish their favorite streams. Each has a special flavor.

—Bob Arnold, Washington steelhead angler

Autumn color tinges the foliage along a remote Northwest steelhead stream; waters like this and the steelhead that return them each fall inspired the creation of hundreds of beautiful flies.

Some steelhead flies are easily defined as classics—the Purple Peril, Skykomish Sunrise, Umpqua Special, and Golden Demon, for example. These patterns are classics because they are iconic; they are inextricably wedded to the foundations of steelhead fly fishing; and they have been familiar and widely recognized for decades. Yet categorizing a steelhead fly pattern as a classic need not rely on the rigid standards set by those stalwart flies. So too among the classic steelhead flies are those patterns that meet various other criteria: they were regnant at one time, they were historically significant in the development and evolution of this genre of the fly tier's art, or they were devised and espoused by the legendary anglers of the steelhead coast. Other criteria may also apply in the inexact and admittedly biased nature of adjudging fly patterns for inclusion on a list of classics, and I hardly claim the list presented here is complete or uncontestable.

Most of the flies presented here I tied the way I interpret their dressings through the lens of my own idea of style and form and craftsmanship. The flies may not strictly adhere to the form in which their originators tied them. Still, I have made every effort to stick to the proper recipes. Some flies photographed for this work come from my collection of patterns dressed by tiers I admire, most of whom I have counted among my friends: the late Al Brunell, longtime resident of Gold Beach, Oregon, before he retired to Corvallis; Bob Roberts of Grants Pass, Oregon; the late Walt Johnson, of Stillaguamish River fame; and even Ed Haas, the acknowledged master of tying steelhead flies.

Chapter VI details tying techniques for steelhead flies, but a few notes on materials are in order here. Except in certain cases, the recipes (which are listed in the Appendix, starting on page 243) do not specify hook models or sizes because those choices are largely at the discretion of the individual tier: you might prefer a standard black-finish, straight-shank, upturned-eye salmon/steelhead hook for a particular pattern, whereas another tier might dress the same fly on a bronzed down-eye wet-fly hook. Historically, heavy-wire bronze hooks were the norm, but by the 1920s, black-finish salmon hooks were becoming increasingly common among steelhead fly anglers, the idea having been borrowed from (and the hooks obtained from) the British. By the 1980s, with the launch of David McNeese's Partridge Bartleet hooks and the similar Alec Jackson Spey hook, the range of specialty hooks available for steelhead flies increased dramatically. So style dictates hook choice, although function comes into play as well: wet flies that are somewhat buoyant by nature fish better on heavy-wire hooks, and of course steelhead dry flies perform best when tied on light-wire hooks. Most steelhead flies are adaptable to a wide range of hook sizes, with sizes 1/0 through 8 typical of the classics.

In most cases, fine-diameter threads—sizes 6/0 and finer—serve best for steelhead flies, with black thread being most commonly used. However, for flies with silk or tinsel bodies, and in general for creating tips and tags of fine oval tinsel or silk, use white, small-diameter multifilament, unwaxed thread that flattens easily, such as UTC 70 denier or size 6/0 Danville's Flymaster (be sure to get unwaxed). Once these components of the fly (tip and tag, and/or silk or tinsel body) are complete, switch to black thread (or other color as specified) to finish the remainder of the fly.

Like the hooks used for classic steelhead flies, many of the materials are interchangeable. The body of a Purple Peril, for example, can be made from chenille, wool yarn, dubbing, or other material that suits your fancy. Sometimes it's a matter of what works best for a particular size hook, but usually personal preference dictates your choice in body materials. The same holds true for wing materials, although ease of use also may play a part. For hackles, the recipes to follow generally do not specify saddle hackle or neck hackle because in most cases they are interchangeable. I have chosen to list only the hackle color where rooster saddle or neck hackles are appropriate. My own

A sniff of good Scotch helps the author ponder creative variations on classic steelhead patterns.

Steelhead are unconcerned with pattern specifics; that fact serves as an invitation to steelhead anglers to dress flies that appeal to their sense of artistry.

preference, except on small hooks (sizes 4 and smaller), is to use hackles from a large capon rooster, dyed the appropriate shade, because these feathers tend to have somewhat softer fibers than do saddle hackles. Saddle hackles often serve better on small hooks.

Steelhead flies allow you ample latitude for personal preference and stylistic interpretation. A pattern bearing an orange butt, red body, brown hackle, and orange-over-white wing is still a Brad's Brat, no matter what combination of materials you choose to arrive at the finished product.

Admiral (recipe on page 243)

All didn't end well in the career of U.S. Navy Rear Admiral Eustace Baron Rogers (1855–1929), for it seems the old sea dog ran afoul of his boss, Secretary of the Navy George von Lengerke Meyer, who served in that capacity throughout Grover Cleveland's presidency. Early in 1910, Rogers testified against Meyer's plan to reorganize the Navy department, and no wonder: as Paymaster General for the Navy, Rogers was so efficient that he managed to turn a $500,000 account into $12 million, and also stockpile substantial stores of supplies; he had an unprecedented ability to plan storage and pack supplies for seafaring fleets. The Naval pay and supply system had never been so efficient.

In early February of that year, Meyer targeted Rogers, along with Rear Admiral Washington L. Capps, and the *Los Angeles Herald* on February 8, 1910, opined, "We cannot believe he [Meyer] intends to vitiate his admirable record by disciplining Admirals Capp [sic] and Rogers for giving testimony unfavorable to his plan for the reorganization of the navy department."

Then in April, Rogers, given only a few days to prepare himself, was hauled before Congress at the behest of Meyer—seemingly as both punishment for his earlier testimony and also to facilitate his removal so that Meyers could begin his new plan for the Navy. Still, Rogers prevailed, but in something of a Pyrrhic victory, as he was granted full retirement—after thirty years in the Navy—with the rank of rear admiral.[10]

It seems that while Congress sided with Rogers, he was nonetheless cornered into retirement after decades of service, rather than willingly retiring "from active service in 1910 to pursue his favorite pastime of angling," as stated by Harold Smedley in *Fly Patterns and Their Origins* (1942), wherein he also says Rogers was a "veteran angler and skillful fly caster." Still, retirement no doubt gave Rogers, a San Francisco native and graduate of the University of California, opportunity to enjoy time on the water, and whether this fly was invented by him or by someone else and named to honor him remains obscure. Famous San Francisco fly tier John Benn often named flies for his friends, so it is certainly possible that the Admiral is a Benn original.

Al's Special (recipe on page 243)

In the 1930s, Ken McLeod was part of the second contingent of Seattle-area steelhead anglers who became so enamored of the summer runs on the North Fork of the Stillaguamish (sometimes called the Stilly) that they bought parcels of land on the river at the famous Elbow Hole. Then, beginning with Walt Johnson in 1943, the anglers started building cabins on the properties.

But both of these legendary anglers had been preceded in exploring these waters with a fly rod by their friend Al Knudson. Walt was a gentleman of the highest order, congenial, convivial, articulate, and intelligent. A superb fly fisherman himself, but ever humble, Walt once told me that the finest steelhead angler he ever knew—and all the Washington greats were his friends and peers—was Knudson (1901–1980), who bought a lot near Walt's and erected a picnic-style shelter rather than a cabin.

Knudson, considering the times, was a remarkably well-traveled steelhead angler, and among the first to take steelhead on flies—including dry flies—from the North Fork Stilly, having hooked his first there in 1926. In 1929, the Great Depression cost him his job, so Knudson moved to Grants Pass, Oregon, on the Rogue River, and tied flies—at first in a window display at the Del Rogue Hotel, where he lodged in a back room. For the next few years, he moved around the Rogue Valley a bit, and back to northwest Washington for a spell, and even lived in Northern California for a time. No doubt some of the many variations of the Rogue River Special came from his tying bench during his prolific years in southern Oregon. According to Jack Berryman's September/October 2007 "Pioneers and Legends" column in *Northwest Fly Fishing*, Knudson sold prodigious numbers of flies to his numerous wholesale accounts and helped popularize the Rogue as a destination for anglers in the 1930s.

During that decade, he arrived at his simple but elegant Al's Special, a fly which he based on the Conway Special devised by Seattle's Dan Conway—one of the few patterns Knudson relied on while fishing for winter steelhead on the Skagit, Skykomish, and Stilly during the 1940s.

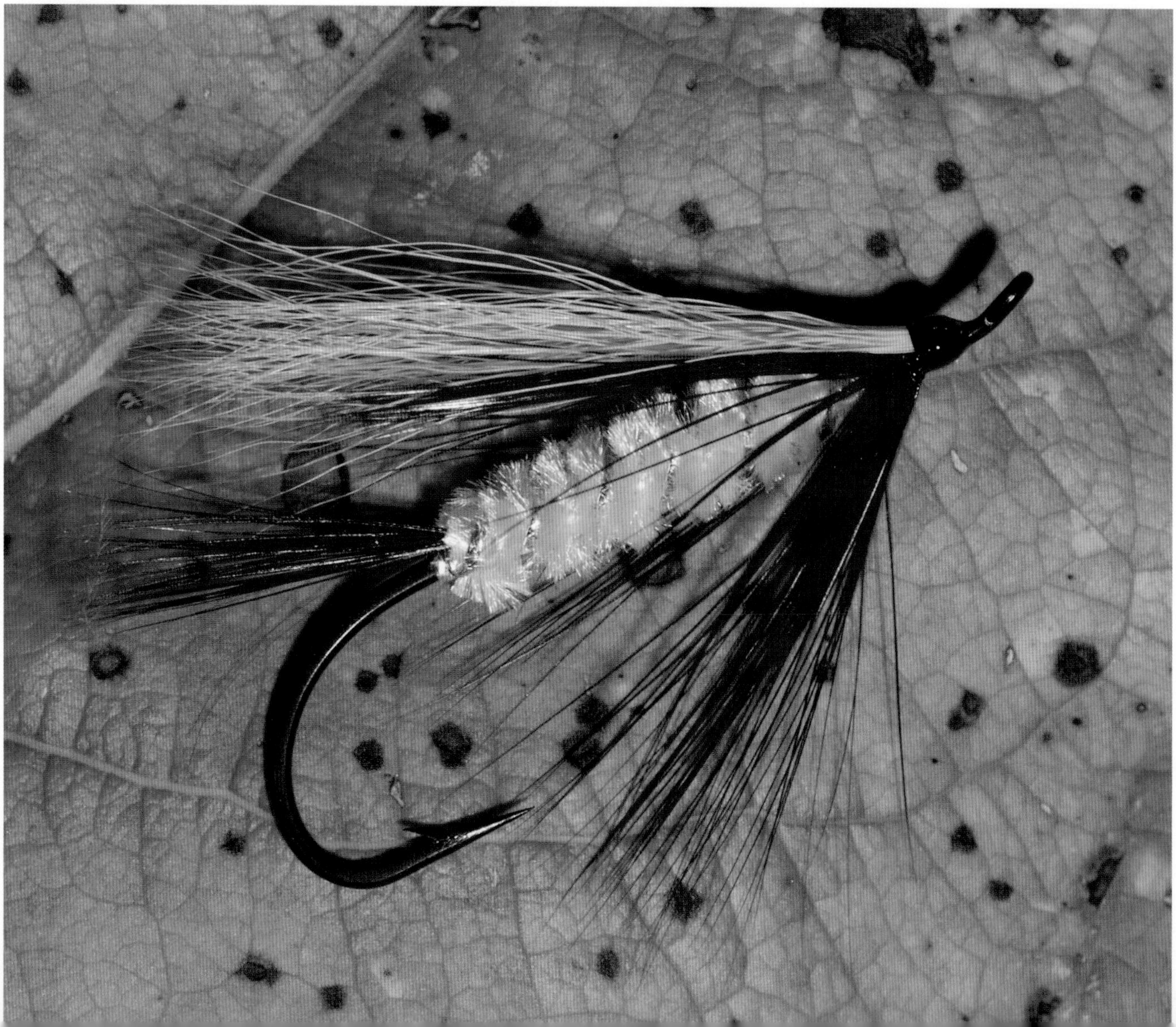

Alaska Mary Ann (recipe on page 243)

Joseph D. Bates, Jr., tells the story of this early bucktail fly in *Streamer Fly Tying & Fishing* (1950), and his story is often repeated, sometimes with introduced error. Frank Dufresne, longtime U.S. Fish and Wildlife Service employee in Alaska and eight-year veteran as head of the Alaska Game Commission, replicated a lure used by indigenous people near the Kobuk River. The lure was made from ivory, whalebone, a cooper's nail, polar bear, and a "very small red corner from the mouth of the guillemot bird." (The pigeon guillemot, *Cepphus columba*, is a small seabird about the size of a teal duck that breeds along the inshore and nearshore strip from Southern California to Alaska; the birds nest on cliffs, islands, and sea-stacks, and they spend winters at sea.)

Dufresne retired in 1950 after thirty years of continual federal public service, and wrote several books, including the memorable *No Room for Bears* (1965) and the intriguing *My Way Was North: An Alaskan Autobiography* (1966), which his friend Corey Ford described in the introduction as filled with riveting "descriptions of primitive Eskimos, of dog-sledding over the Bering ice, of sour-doughs he knew along the Yukon, of caribou and mountain goats and bears, of the old Alaska which will never be again."

Like many of the early patterns, the Alaska Mary Ann became a de facto steelhead fly; it was designed for trout and other species in the far North. I, too, first used the Alaska Mary Ann as a trout fly, but not at such a high latitude. On a trip to Fairbanks in the 1990s, my friend and local fly shop owner Howie Van Ness handed me a fistful of Alaska Mary Anns to take back home to Oregon; though long aware of the fly, I'd never given it any further consideration. But that October, on a small coastal river just above tidewater, I gave one of those flies a swim for sea-run cutthroat, and it proved irresistible to the moody fish that day, providing me with my most memorable outing for the increasingly beleaguered "harvest trout." The nickname harvest trout comes from the time of year (autumn) that anadromous cutthroat return to fresh water. Sadly these iconic Northwest fish have seen their range shrink markedly and their numbers dwindle in many rivers once teeming with them.

Those sea-run cutthroat have remained tight lipped about their lust for the Alaska Mary Ann, as have I about their location, and Dufresne's fly remains rarely used outside of Alaska. But on the steelhead streams of that grand state, the Alaska Mary Ann still has its adherents.

Bekeart's Special (recipe on page 243)

Philip Baldwin Bekeart (born 1861) was the son of a forty-niner—the name for members of the first wave of the California Gold Rush in 1849 after gold was discovered at Sutter's Mill. Jules François Bekeart (aka Frank Bekeart) reached California that year, after having fought in the Mexican–American War, but upon finding that gold mining was hard work, he started a highly successful gunsmith and gun sales business in a wood frame and canvas building; a fire took the wood building in 1852, but it was replaced by a brick building, which is said to be Coloma's oldest structure, still standing today. Bekeart had immigrated to New York City from England in 1835 and apprenticed as a gunsmith there. His California store, which he moved to San Francisco after the Civil War, prospered, and continued to do so after Frank sold the business to his youngest son Phil in 1890. Phil would garner lasting fame among handgun aficionados for his design of target weapons. He was a competitive shooter, a highly respected western representative for various well-known Eastern firearms manufacturers, and a dedicated fly angler.

Bekeart had worked for Allen's Gun Store prior to purchasing his father's business, and by the early twentieth century, he was a well-known angler and hunter. He, along with several of the city's other notable sportsmen, including Will and Henry Golcher of Golcher Bros. Sporting Goods, were members of the so-called Salmon Creek Club, which held private water on that stream. Bekeart and the Golcher brothers fished and hunted together, shot competitively against one another, and enjoyed considerable success in their respective sporting goods dealerships. The Golchers were members of the San Francisco Fly Casting Club, and Bekeart once hosted the national casting champion, from New York, for a few days of sampling California streams. All of these men, running in the same circle of anglers, would have known John S. Benn, the famous fly tier, and if Bekeart himself did not originate this fly, then perhaps Benn invented and named it.

English author A. Courtney Williams, in *Trout Flies* (1932), credits the fly to Bekeart, but with these early flies that were named for individual anglers, it is usually difficult to determine whether the names they carry mean they were named by that person or in honor of that person, and Benn was known to name flies after his friends (e.g. Carson Coachman and The Soule). Nonetheless, Bekeart was certainly a fly tier, as Portland's Bunnell sisters credited him as one of the tiers who helped tutor them in fly tying, according to a story about them in the *Sunday Oregonian* (July 27, 1947).[11]

Benn's Black Prince (recipe on page 243)

To tiers who know the long-popular Black Prince, this dressing described firsthand by a newspaper reporter in John S. Benn's San Francisco fly-tying studio in 1907 will come as something of a minor departure—and a pleasant surprise. Benn was prolific, skilled, and widely admired; he and his daughter Martha invented many original patterns and devised numerous variations on standard patterns. Most of their dressings are lost to us, but a few survive. This version of the Black Prince, with its gold tag, yellow tail, and black ostrich butt, hints at the English Black Prince of Atlantic salmon traditions, devised by the renowned Major John Popkin Traherne, but retains, in the remainder of the dressing, the character of what Mary Orvis Marbury called "the Black Prince of American origin."

A writer for the *San Francisco Call* visited John and Martha Benn in their fly-tying studio and wrote a profile of them for the June 9, 1907, edition. He described the fly as such: "The Black Prince is tipped with gold; the tag is black ostrich, the tail a bit of feather dyed yellow, the body black floss, wound diagonally with silver thread; coal black wings, hackle and head complete the Black Prince."

Like many Benn patterns, his version of the Black Prince faded into obscurity, but the better-known Black Prince of North Umpqua lore, designed by legendary lodge owner Clarence Gordon, remained in use into the 1980s on its home river. Though arcane, Benn's Black Prince is elegant when rendered by an expert tier; enchanting when swung across the emerald flows of a steelhead stream; and riveting when pinned in the jaw of the great seagoing rainbow.

Benn's Coachman (recipe on page 243)

While the earliest fly-caught steelhead no doubt came from nearer his Bay Area home, famed fly tier and angler John S. Benn was among a small cadre of adventurous anglers who traveled north to discover then-unparalleled sport offered by the Eel River. At that time, fly anglers remained a rare sight on the Eel; Eureka local E. F. Pettengill reported to Mary Orvis Marbury for her 1892 book *Favorite Flies and Their Histories*, "Fly-fishing is in its infancy here as yet, but it is getting more popular every season."

John Benn would help change all that and make the Eel the first hub of dedicated efforts at taking steelhead on flies. He, probably in the company of John Butler and John Gallagher and others, made the arduous journey as early as the late 1880s and soon thereafter the autumn angling adventure to the Eel became an annual extravaganza—in 1898, reported the *San Francisco Call* (July 28, 1899), more than 50 men from San Francisco alone made the trip to the Eel; the next year John Butler organized a party numbering perhaps 75, said the *San Francisco Call* (September 2, 1899). But it was Benn alone, among bait and spin fishers, who first cast a fly for steelhead on the Eel at least a decade earlier:

> Many of the anglers of the state have had their lessons from the old man and every one who has had the pleasure of fishing the Eel river may thank him for it, for it was he who opened fishing there, being the first man to use a fly in those waters.—*San Francisco Call*, June 9, 1907.

Reaching the Eel River, as Benn had done by 1890, was no simple undertaking by today's standards. Overland routes were lengthy, circuitous, and impractical. Although numerous railway lines penetrated much of Northern California by then, they had not yet been congealed to create a direct rail route from San Francisco to Humboldt Bay or the Eel River. Instead, the most direct route was by steamer from San Francisco Bay to either the Eel River itself or to Humboldt Bay just to the north; in 1893, San Franscisco-based travel writer Mable H. Closson reported that the journey took 20 hours. From either of those two points, branch rail lines—built in the mid-1880s for the thriving lumber trade of the area—took both freight and passengers along the Eel itself. Thanks to regularly scheduled travel on steamers such as *City of Chester* and later *Eureka*, *Humboldt*, and others, Benn and his fellow anglers would arrive in Fortuna and Fernbridge to find thriving, prosperous communities fed by the forest products industry, not to mention the commercial salmon fishing and canning business.[12]

Though on a smaller scale compared to faraway San Francisco, the towns of the lower Eel River offered first-rate accommodations and services, including the popular Star Hotel in Fortuna, which was the first town on the river to gain electric lighting when, in the early 1880s, a pair of prosperous local mill owners decided to build a generating plant for both their mill and the town itself. In the 1890s, Eel River locals increasingly catered to visiting anglers, offering excellent accommodations on the river. Benn continued his annual visits to the Eel into the early 1900s, usually residing for at least two weeks at Weymouth's or Greig's Resort, and no doubt being something of a celebrity. The *Ferndale Enterprise* (October 18, 1904), reported, "J.S. Benn of San Francisco has been rusticating at the Greig resort near Singleys for the last week or more. The gentleman is the maker of the famous Benn flies, well known to the anglers of this section."

The famous old fly dresser befriended many of the best-known local anglers, and named flies after some of them; his flies garnered great popularity on the river. Among his many original patterns, for both trout and steelhead, was his version of the ever-popular Coachman. Benn's Coachman remained a popular fly on the Eel for decades, its distinguishing feature being the addition of red to the otherwise white wings.

Benn's Martha

(recipe on page 243)

Martha Benn, John Benn's daughter, must have learned the art of fly tying early on from her father, for by the early 1890s, he was, according to the *San Francisco Call* (May 13, 1894), "proud of a daughter who has placed the old man in the shade so far as polished work in fly dressing is concerned."

A tumultuous marriage, a troublesome divorce, and the death of an infant daughter may all have contributed to Martha moving back home with her father and joining him in the production of flies for sale to anglers in their home city of San Francisco and throughout California—and may also have been a factor in the famous old fly dresser canceling his plans to retire to the banks of the Eel River. Born in 1878, Martha married Peter Calderwood at age 18, but less than three years later, she filed for divorce, citing "failure to provide." With the divorce soon granted, she suffered through the death of her 5-month-old daughter Alice—named after Benn's wife—and little could she have known she would earn a minor headline in the *San Francisco Call* when her first divorce was ruled invalid and a new decree had to be issued.

Her personal tribulations aside, Martha was an astute fly tier: a writer for the *Call* (May 13, 1894), upon seeing a selection of Martha's flies, said "They were the equal, if not the superior, of anything he has seen in years. . . . Small flies are her specialty and for durability and finish they are par excellence." After her father's death in 1907, Martha continued commercial fly tying, setting up her studio at 604 Haight Street in a beautiful corner-lot house about half a block from her mother's residence on Pierce. The *San Francisco Directory* for 1908 listed her profession as artificial flymaker. These neighborhoods remain relatively intact and the Haight Street house is still there today. Martha later married Lon C. Cloer, 18 years her senior, who died in 1936. Martha herself passed away at the age of 61 in 1939.

Benn's Martha was in later years typically referred to simply as Martha—a truncation of the sort that always endangers the genealogy of a fly. It enjoyed substantial popularity in Northern California. Benn's Martha seems to date to about 1900, perhaps a few years prior; it was called such in a story titled "When You Begin Trout Fishing" in the January 4, 1902, edition of the *Breeder and Sportsman*. The fly is beautifully designed, and deserves resurgence among today's anglers.

Black Beauty (recipe on page 243)

On October 8, 1962, well-traveled California-based steelheader Karl Mausser (1909–1999) caught a 42-inch, 33-pound steelhead on the Kispiox River in British Columbia; at the time, this monstrous buck was the largest steelhead ever taken on a fly.

Mausser, an electrical contractor by trade (in the San Mateo-Burlingame area), was a natural for confronting the challenges of big, brawling steelhead rivers: his athleticism served him well. As a teenager, he had been a local tennis star, and the *Modesto Bee and News-Herald* (November 5, 1927), reported that Mausser was the "San Mateo county singles champion, a six-footer with a hard service and smashing game." By the 1940s, perhaps earlier, he was traveling north to fish the Eel, but eventually, reports of massive fly-caught summer-run steelhead of British Columbia would draw him northward, where he would become completely enraptured by the Kispiox, Morice, and other now-famous rivers in the Skeena River system.

In 2008, long after steelhead recruitment in the Skeena system began a serious decline, one of Mausser's longtime fishing partners, respected fisheries biologist Dr. James Adams—who had once caught a *Field & Stream*-record steelhead from the Kispiox—filed a guest editorial with the *Smithers Interior News*; it subsequently was included in the BC Ministry of Environment's "Consultation Report Phase 1 (January–March 2008) Skeena Quality Waters Strategy." In the unedited letter, supplied by Adams to www.moldychum.com, he recalled, "I have seen the August steelhead runs in the Morice River go from a superlative fishery in the 1960s to a complete failure by the 1980s. I knew Karl Mausser of Burlingame since I was in grade school, and started to fish various rivers with him in 1951. I listened to Karl tell me with tears in his eyes about the devastation of his favorite August dry-fly fishery for steelhead on the Morice."

Adams posted a poignant warning in recalling conversations with his old friend, providing us with a stark reminder that the geographical range of wild steelhead is being pushed ever farther north. Once upon a time the Eel and Rogue, the Columbia watershed, the North Fork Stilly, and the Olympic Peninsula rivers hosted mind-boggling runs of fish. Those populations are now shadows of their former abundance. The Canadian runs are waning, and eventually the Alaskan runs may, too. After that, the native steelhead has no sanctuary left for retreat.

While those Canadian rivers beckoned, Mausser frequented waters closer to home, especially the Klamath, and it was for this river that he invented the Black Beauty.

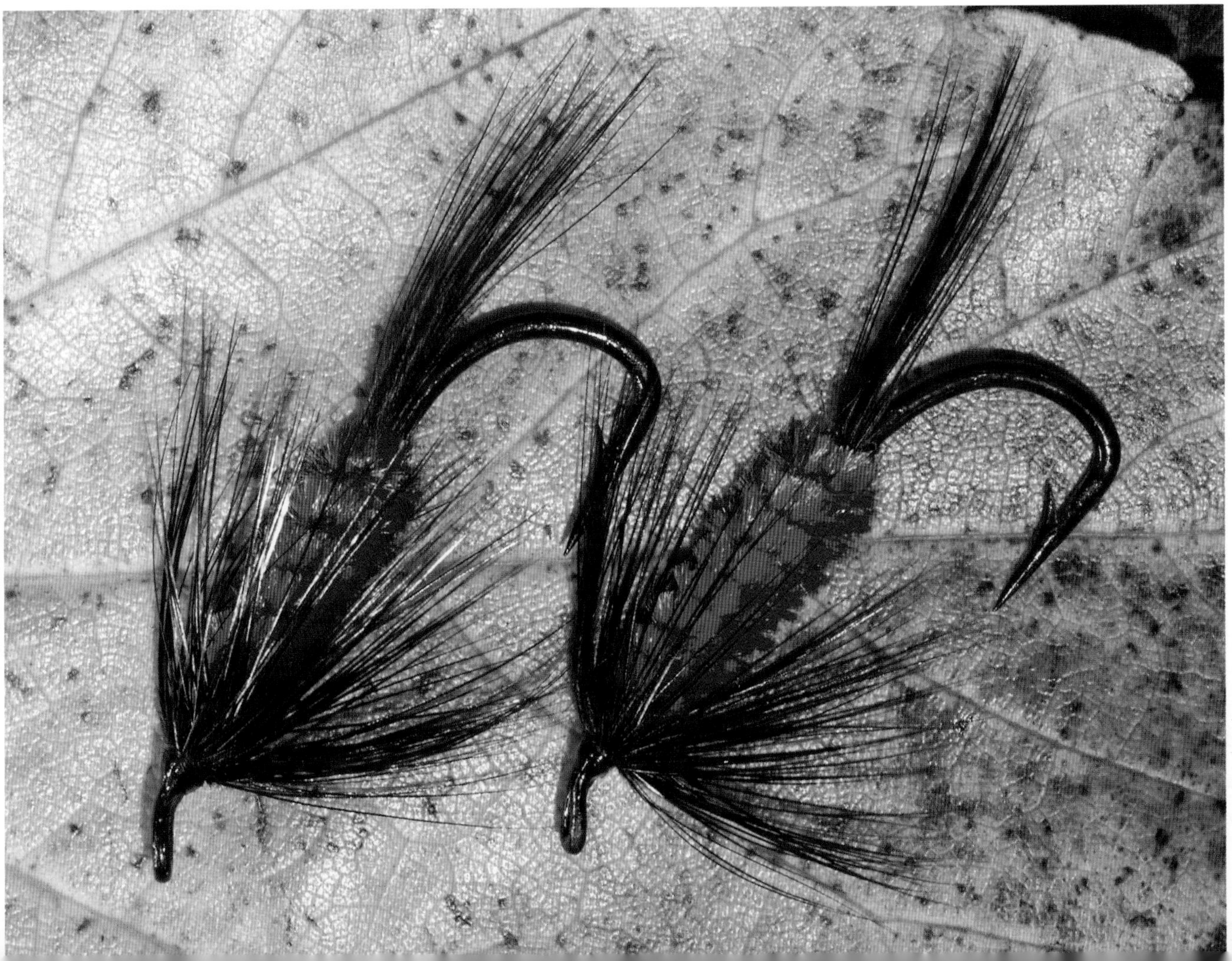

Black Demon (recipe on page 244)

The original Black Demon, devised by C. Jim Pray, the famous Eureka fly shop owner, is essentially just a Silver Demon with a black wing instead of the light-colored wing. Over the years, the name misled some tiers to dress the body with black silk rather than silver tinsel, and thereby a second version of the Black Demon arose to little fanfare (but apparently to the appreciation of the steelhead I've caught using this lovely variation). Pray himself told Joseph D. Bates, Jr., for Bates's 1950 book, *Streamer Fly Fishing*, "Originally I tied it with a silver body, no tail, orange throat, and a black bucktail wing. Since that time other tiers have incorporated a wood duck tail, and some have used gold for the body. . . ."

The Black Demon never generated as much enthusiasm as Pray's Silver Demon, but it proved a successful dark-wing alternative. The Black Demon had its adherents on the rivers of the Northern California and on Oregon's Rogue, and was, for a time in the 1940s during the infancy of fly fishing for winter steelhead, popular on Washington's Skagit River. In the 1990s, Walt Johnson told me the pattern was "a good producer on the Skagit [in the mid to late 1940s] especially in bright weather." Both renditions—the original silver-tinsel-body creation by Pray and the later gold- and then black-body variations—are fetching flies, worthy of a more devoted following.

In addition to standard bucktail styles, Pray tied some of his Silver Demons in the Cains River streamer style that had gained a following in New Brunswick in the 1920s. These colorful flies included tails of barred wood duck flank, probably explaining why such tails often appear on the Black Demon. Among the various methods of attaching the tail, I prefer to cut an extra-wide segment of wood duck flank and then fold it in half lengthwise before mounting it on the hook. I first saw this trick performed by Cal Bird. Not long after, I enjoyed studying steelhead flies by Oregon's little-known but exceptionally talented Jim Stovall; he mounted such folded wood duck-flank tails on his Demons with excellent results. Stovall served as a police detective and rarely dressed flies in public, but fortunate were we few at McNeese's Fly Shop in those days who persuaded him to edify us at the tying table. We sometimes enjoyed the opportunity to study wallets full of his flies and discuss with him his tricks and well-honed techniques.

Black Diamond (recipe on page 244)

Harry Lemire, the gifted tier and celebrated steelhead angler who gave us the Grease Liner, the skating fly that inspired so many anglers to fish dry flies for their favorite gamefish, had a knack for simple, elegant steelhead dressings. He combined materials in creative ways, and developed a number of patterns that gained popularity in Washington beginning in the 1960s. Among them was his Black Diamond, named for the town in which he lived, and on which he took a 13-pound winter fish on his home river, the Green, in 1970.

Black Diamond, still a small community, sits in the Green River Valley, 20 miles east of Federal Way. Incorporated in 1959, the community was established in the late 1880s after coal deposits were discovered. Coal would shape the town's history. "The area is cooler than Seattle and twice as wet," notes Lauren Landis for the Black Diamond Historical Society, "which means much of Black Diamond's history took place in the rain."

Green River Coal Company was founded on the claims of a group of four men in 1873, and they were soon bought out by a California speculator. Still, the coal fields remained largely undeveloped until the early 1880s, when California-based Black Diamond Coal Company finally began shipping Washington coal to San Francisco. By 1885 the Mount Diablo coal mines in California were tapped out, and the company sent its miners, most of them Welsh, north to the Green River area where they founded the small town of Black Diamond. Myriad difficulties plagued the mining efforts, from rugged terrain to clashes between management and labor, but by 1907, production reached a peak of 970,000 tons of coal, and by 1915, the mines employed 1,400 people.

The 1920s brought keen competition from alternate energy sources—primarily oil and electricity. Landis, on the Black Diamond Museum website, explains that the 1920s "witnessed some of the most tragic and violent labor disputes in the history of the State of Washington. In the late 1930s, the company disposed of Black Diamond and its residences, bringing to an end the company's total domination of the community's economic and social life. Miners were given the opportunity to buy their houses. If they did not choose to buy, the houses were sold to any interested party."

Black Gnat Bucktail (recipe on page 244)

The surest route to steelheading fame for any fly in the nineteenth century was to prove itself first as a trout fly on the waters of the American Northeast or in the British Isles, and then carry that reputation west in the California Gold Rush era and thereafter. It was the famous trout flies that anglers originally used to hook what were then called "salmon-trout" in California. These salmon-trout were odd: they looked like trout; but they came in from the sea like salmon. Their taxonomy would be disputed for decades. But they were accommodating; they proved far more obliging of the fly angler's efforts than those notoriously lock-jawed salmon so plentiful in the rivers from the Bay Area northward.

Fly fishers soon realized that their trout wet flies worked well for salmon-trout, and they began to fish them in sizes more attuned to these big, hard-fighting fish that were coming to be known as "steel-heads." A size 6 fly hook may seem dainty to modern steelhead anglers, but they were a departure from the more diminutive Black Gnats, Coachmen, Professors, and Hackle flies occupying the fly wallets of the trout fishers of the nineteenth century. Of the Black Gnat's origins in England, little is known except that the fly dates back to the eighteenth century; John Hawkins mentions it in his 1775 edition of Izaak Walton's venerated *The Compleat Angler*. Thereafter, the Black Gnat appears frequently in the English fly-fishing literature of the early nineteenth century.

The origins of the Black Gnat Bucktail as a steelhead fly are also murky, but no doubt it hails from California, the probable birthplace of the steelhead bucktails. Enos Bradner, in his 1950 classic *Northwest Angling*, acknowledged as much when he said the fly was "a southern pattern that is used in Puget Sound waters." Indeed, an early variation used on the North Fork Stillaguamish was Clyde Hoyt's Special, which in turn became the inspiration for George McLeod's all-dark fly, the McLeod Ugly.

Black Gordon (recipe on page 244)

The fly water of the North Umpqua River stretches for more than 30 miles, and around every bend of the winding highway that runs beside the swift, serpentine river, the traveler enjoys spectacular scenery. In places, deep pools reflect verdant forested slopes; around the next bend, the river fans out across a bedrock-studded tailout and then bounds over silvery cascades; in still other reaches, basalt walls and scree, tinged bright green with lichen and moss, squeeze the flow into swift, narrow chutes. In many places, the North Umpqua hides from the highway that traces its course, inviting those enamored of wild rivers to pull over in a wide spot and discover, on foot, what wonders might greet the eye.

Amid all the river's splendors, there are a few iconic vistas, one of them being the beautiful pool, some distance downstream from the famous Camp Water, known as Elevation or Rip Rap Point. Here, on the south bank opposite the road, a dramatic cliff towers over a gorgeous emerald tailout that at times in autumn offers promise to skated-fly enthusiasts. And here, too, a dam was once proposed, but the legendary guardian of the North Umpqua, Frank Moore, led the charge to stifle such insanity. After returning from duty in the European theater in World War II, Frank guided for Clarence Gordon, then owner of North Umpqua Lodge, and eventually took over the business. Gordon created the Black Gordon fly as a specialty for the North Umpqua, and I decided one summer many years ago that catching a North Umpqua steelhead on each of the river's classic fly patterns—such as the Umpqua, Cummings, Black Gordon, and a few lesser-known flies—would be a gratifying challenge.

In that pursuit, I one day found myself fishing near Rip Rap. Upstream, not far, are several good buckets, a couple of them easy to decipher, another requiring a discerning eye followed by a rather disquieting wade. In this latter spot—little more than a slick formed in just the right manner and fishable from a precarious submerged perch—a Black Gordon tempted a mighty steelhead that fine September evening. To recount the tale of just how that steelhead finally came to hand would only serve to call into question my sanity, but suffice it to say that the outcome involved equal doses, respectively, of elation, consternation, trepidation, terror, and finally euphoria.

Black Prince (Unknown Origin) (recipe on page 244)

Although now rarely found in fly wallets, the Black Prince enjoyed substantial popularity in the latter decades of the nineteenth century on the steelhead streams of California. But by the turn of the new century, the Black Prince—a purely American fly not to be confused with the Atlantic salmon fly of the same name devised by Major John Traherne—was waning in popularity. Mary Orvis Marbury, in *Favorite Flies and Their Histories* (1896), writes elegantly of the Black Prince:

> Perhaps no fly, since the ever-famous Fiery Brown, was more discussed and written of, for a few years, than the Black Prince. As with the Black Knight of romance, there was a mystery connected with this Black Prince; no one seemed to know, or perhaps be ready to declare, just whence he sprang, and to assert his true rights; and many were the doubts as to the correctness of his colors, whether the doublet should be of silver or gold. Even the tiny plume of red was declared out of place on this black knight, but finally the Prince with doublet of gold, scarlet plume, and sable mantle held his own, and was accepted as tried and true and admired of all, and has since fought and conquered in many a royal battle.

The Black Prince described by Marbury was, according to her, a lake fly, and the path to its conversion to a steelhead pattern is no less obscure than the pedigree of the original dressing, an Eastern invention to be sure—and one that at times was tied with a silver tinsel body, further confusing the issue of its true form. William C. Harris, in "The Trouts of America" from the book *Salmon and Trout* (1904), records the dressings as "Tail, scarlet ibis; body, silver tinsel; legs, black hackle; wings, black."

Likely the Black Prince followed the familiar path: first used as a trout fly in the West (it was recommended for such work by several writers of the period) but eventually charged with attracting steelhead on the rivers of Northern California. Today, a version of the Black Prince that sports a yellow butt, and the ubiquitous hair wing, is well known by steelheaders; it hails from the North Umpqua River (see the next entry).

Black Prince (Gordon's) (recipe on page 244)

A well-known pattern, popular in Oregon into the 1980s (when we tied many of them for customers at McNeese's Fly Shop in Salem), the Black Prince of twentieth-century steelhead fame comes from the North Umpqua. Beyond that, however, authors have failed to identify the fly's originator, but I confirmed my suspicions on the subject in the summer of 2013, on a visit to Frank Moore, the legend of the North Umpqua, and his wife of 70 years, Jeanne, at their lovely, secluded log home perched on a forested ridge high above the river.

Without hesitation, Frank told me the Black Prince was a Clarence Gordon fly, which made sense considering its similarity to the Black Gordon. "Have you seen my photos of Clarence?" Frank asked. I had not, so Frank, who had first guided for Gordon, and then purchased North Umpqua Lodge from him in the 1950s and operated it for many years, glided out of the room and up the stairs with a litheness belying his 90 years. He reappeared carrying several large frames and with his famous smile painted from ear to ear, exclaiming, "John, you won't believe this, but look at the fly Clarence is tying in this photo."

Sure enough, in an old black-and-white photo showing Gordon at his tying bench, he has a Black Prince under construction and several more finished and laying on the table. All of us—Frank, Jeanne, and my friend Doug Butler, a World War II historian who had wanted to meet Frank and learn a bit about his wartime service in Europe after landing at Utah Beach on D-Day—were thrilled at the serendipity.

Bobbie Dunn and Queen Bess (recipes on pages 244 and 254)

Peter J. Schwab (1887–1956) lived the kind of vagabond fly-fishing life many anglers dream about. The Pennsylvania-born angling aficionado began wandering westward in the early twentieth century and while living in Illinois, Schwab landed a masthead title as motor-camping editor for the Chicago-based *Outdoor Recreation* magazine. After this, explained historian Jack W. Berryman, in *Fly-fishing Pioneers & Legends of the Northwest* (2006), "He and his wife [Bess] pulled a large 'motor coach' around behind their car and spent months at a time visiting fishing destinations that were considered exotic in the 1920s—Montana, Wyoming, Idaho, Northern California, Oregon, Washington, and British Columbia." But one fish in particular, the steelhead, and one river, the Klamath, would end Schwab's wanderlust, for when in the late 1920s he first went scouting for steelhead fishing and steelhead fly fishermen, the seeds of addiction were planted. Until the early 1950s, Schwab, with Bess, continued to travel and fish widely around the West, but by then he was completely enamored with the Klamath and its steelhead, and spent all of his autumns there. Also by the 1950s he had compiled an impressive résumé as an outdoor writer. Always inventive, Schwab designed rods, lines, flies, and other angling implements, with his innovations frequently aimed at conquering tactical problems in steelhead fishing.

An early proponent of bucktail flies, Schwab developed a series of wire-body patterns that gained popularity in California. He experimented with weighted flies, using metal wire under the typical wool-yarn bodies, and discovered that even when the yarn got eaten away by sharp teeth, the steelhead continued to take the battle-worn flies. So he began tying wire bodies, and among his numerous dressings were the Queen Bess, named for his wife, and the Bobby Dunn, named for a fishing partner. He designed many others, and as Berryman explained, "He would shine the body, wipe it clean, and then cover it with a thin lacquer to prevent tarnish with age."

In addition to Berryman's account of Schwab, Trey Combs wrote extensively of him in *Steelhead Fly Fishing and Flies* (1976). The details provided by both authors are complementary in that they each offer unique details about this intriguing character.

Bosquito (recipe on page 245)

As a longtime professional fly tier, San Pedro, California, resident Roy Donnelly (1893–1975) was probably better known, in the 1930s and 40s, for his creative Variant dry flies than for his steelhead flies. His friend and fishing partner, Claude Kreider—author of *Steelhead* (1948)—called these delicate dry flies, tied with oversize hackles of two different shades, western variants of the Light and Dark Cahill. The Variant-type fly, little used these days, is simple in design, but also specialized. Hackles up to two times larger than standard are used, so, for example, a size 14 Variant would require a hackle matched to about a size 10 hook. The tail is extra long, and made from stiff dry-fly hackle barbules; tiers generally make the body from stripped peacock herl or stripped hackle stem, and standard or 1X short light-wire dry fly hooks are the norm. Properly tied Variants land delicately on the water's surface, and the true artist in fishing them makes the fly dance and skitter with gentle tugs of line.

No doubt the accomplished Donnelly was one such artist, given his high regard for Variants, but like Kreider, who lived nearby in Long Beach, Donnelly was also a dedicated steelhead angler who annually fished his favorite pools on the Klamath River in Northern California. The Bosquito is one of several Donnelly steelhead flies that gained a following on the rivers of Northern California, as well as on Oregon's Rogue River. The Donnelly Coachman is probably his best-known steelhead pattern.

Just before publisher Frank Amato released the seminal *Steelhead Fly Fishing and Flies*, by Trey Combs, in 1976, Donnelly passed away in Southern California. Not long before, Combs had written that the Tennessee-born Donnelly "is something of a West Coast steelheading institution, a professional fly tier since 1926, who has annually fished the Klamath at Weitchpec for as long as anyone can remember."

AMOUS
GROUSE
shop

Boss (recipe on page 245)

Modern steelhead fly fishers have no claim on the origins of weighted flies, as dominant as such patterns seem to be these days. In fact, pioneering steelhead enthusiasts began experimenting with various means of sinking their flies nearly as soon as the great rivers that sired the traditions of the sport began spawning their own river-specific patterns.

Among the mid-twentieth-century innovations in the arena of weighted steelhead flies were the Comet patterns, with their characteristic long tails made from dyed bucktail. They are uncomplicated and attractive flies, but their genesis is murky. Trey Combs determined that ". . . one Hap McNew, the son of Lon McNew [1878–1966] who operated McNew's Sporting Goods in Eureka, California, began tying bucktails with bead chain in 1940, appropriately calling them 'popeye flies.'"

Combs reports further that "This dressing practice was never particularly popular until comet flies made their appearance," and he notes that the Boss, dating to about 1949 and invented by Virgil Sullivan, was likely the first of the Comets to gain ascendancy on the Russian River, where they were best known. However, the first Comet flies may have hailed from the Klamath and perhaps the Eel as well; the style may have been first introduced, sans eyes, by Eureka's Ralph Cole. In Sean M. Gallagher's book, *Wild Steelhead* (2013), the learned California angler Jim Adams says, "There was a plumber in Eureka, Ralph Cole, who invented the Comet style of tying with a calf's tail, a gold body, a bead chain eye, and a hackle."

Comet patterns enjoyed resurgence in popularity in the late 1970s and 1980s, perhaps because of the publication of Combs's second book, *Steelhead Fly Fishing and Flies*, wherein he mentions these flies.

Hap McNew, inventor of the popeye flies, if not the actual Comet, inherited the tackle shop from his father and also owned a bar in Eureka. Notably he married divorcee Bessie Greenwood, a remarkable outdoorswoman whose mother had been Oregon's first female homesteader. Bessie (1917–2012) "was a very noted wet- and dry fly-fishing expert, tied her own flies, and for many celebrities (movie stars); she was the best skill pool player in the area. She out-gunshot the best, and was a very active hunter and fisherman," noted her obituary in the *Las Vegas Review-Journal* in August, 2012. Such details conjure the possibility that the Comet flies could have come from Bessie, though evidence to that effect has not been forthcoming.

Boxcar (recipe on page 245)

Back in the 1980s when McNeese's Fly Shop exerted a palpable influence on the way classic steelhead flies were dressed, David McNeese had a modest frame of about a dozen Wes Drain (1914–1993) steelhead flies. He proudly hung the frame near the door of the shop; we all admired those flies tied by one of the most gifted steelhead fly tiers to lay feather to steel in the twentieth century. Best known for his beautiful Drain's 20 pattern (named for a record 20-plus-pound steelhead he took on the fly), Drain was among the cadre of Seattle-area anglers who formed a little colony of steelhead enthusiasts near the famous Elbow Hole on the North Fork of the Stillaguamish beginning in the 1940s.

Among others in that group, such as Walt Johnson, Drain saw no reason not to fish dry flies for summer-run steelhead, and his Boxcar contributed to that particular genre. Indeed, the summer fish of the Stilly, in those decades when the run was still robust, tended to be excellent dry-fly takers. They were relatively small steelhead, with 3- to 6-pounders being typical, and at times they could behave quite troutlike. Walt told me of the numerous occasions on which he fished upstream with dry flies, dead-drifting them for the Stilly's summer-runs, with considerable success. It was a tactic Walt greatly enjoyed, and decades later he touted Drain's Boxcar as a reliable fly for such work, alongside some of his own beautifully designed patterns.

The Stilly, in those days, ranked among the truly great summer steelhead streams, a fact which may be difficult to reconcile with the degraded fishery this once mighty river sustains today. But legendary *Seattle Times* outdoor writer Enos Bradner was entirely accurate in the accolades he bestowed on the North Fork in a lengthy 1945 column called "Summer Steelhead":

> New Brunswick may have its Restigouche and England its Wye, both world-famous salmon rivers; New York may have its Beaverkill, the noted brown trout stream; but our own Washington has its Stillaguamish, a great summer-run steelhead river. Not only does the North Fork of the Stillaguamish afford some of the best steelhead fly fishing in the West, but it has the added distinction of being the only steelhead stream in the world open only to a fly.

So exceptional was the North Fork summer fishery, and so reliable was the dry-fly action—with the flies usually skated, though Walt and others embraced the idea of dead-drifting them—that the river fostered the development of numerous dries, such as the Boxcar. Little known today, moreover, is that one of the most iconic of classic steelhead flies, George McLeod's Purple Peril, was actually first dressed as a dry fly.

Brad's Brat (recipe on page 245)

Which pattern is the most iconic Washington steelhead fly? That question could stir debate for several pitchers worth of pints at a brewpub in Seattle: Purple Peril? Skykomish Sunrise? Orange Heron? You could defend those choices, but some anglers would make a case for the Brad's Brat, an enduring steelhead fly from the fertile imagination of Washington's most revered outdoor writer, Enos Bradner. Bradner, a Michigan native and graduate of the University of Michigan, visited Washington in 1929 and fished the renowned North Fork of the Stillaguamish River, where Al Knudson and a few others pioneered steelhead fly angling. Bradner fell in love with the place and soon moved to Seattle, where he opened Bradner's Bookshop and began fishing and hunting all over the region, as described by Jack W. Berryman in a thorough biography of Bradner in *Northwest Fly Fishing* magazine (Winter, 2003).

The famous one-armed fly tier, Dan Conway (see Conway Special page 59), taught Bradner to tie flies in the early 1930s, and he was soon a regular on the Stilly and its famous tributary, Deer Creek. He and others founded the Washington Fly Fishing Club in 1939, and through dogged determination eventually convinced the state game commission to restrict the North Fork Stilly to fly-fishing-only, a law that took effect in 1944. By then, the venerable Sasquatch of the Stilly—Walt Johnson—had grabbed up a small cabin lot on the Elbow Hole, and Bradner and others followed suit, with Bradner—just two doors up from Walt and adjacent to Frank Headrick—calling his cabin "Camp Bucktail," as Walt explained to me in 1995.

At about that same period, in 1943, Bradner accepted an offer to become the outdoor sports columnist for *The Seattle Times*, and for the next 26 years, three times per week, his column, "The Inside on the Outdoors," offered insights on a variety of subjects, with fly fishing—and fly fishing for steelhead in particular—his favorite topic. In 1950, his first book, *Northwest Angling*, was released to substantial acclaim. Book reviewer Robert B. Brown, in the *Michigan Alumnus Quarterly* (1950), warned, "Let devotees of Izaak Walton handle this book with care, for here is powerful medicine that may lead them to desert their favorite riffles on the Au Sable and the Thunder Bay and head for the far Northwest."

Bradner, essentially the dean of outdoor reporters in the Pacific Northwest, is memorialized by the Northwest Outdoor Writers Association (NOWA), which he helped form, with its Enos Bradner Award for "long time outstanding support of NOWA and upholding the high professional standards of outdoor journalism practiced by Enos Bradner."

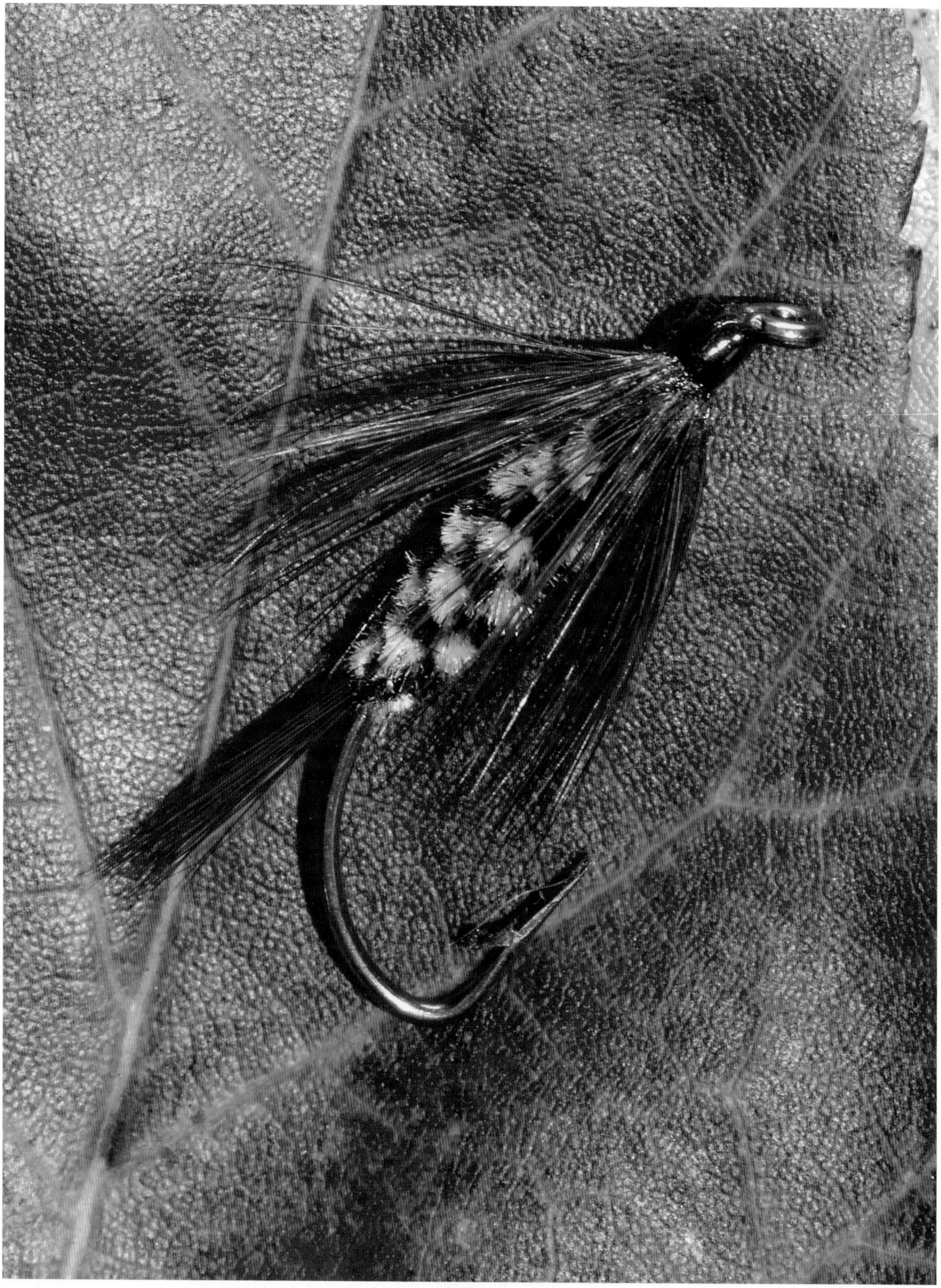

Brindle Bug (recipe on page 245)

Prolific designer of steelhead flies and near-lifelong resident of Eureka, California, Lloyd D. Silvius (1902–1973) devised the Brindle Bug around 1960 and—like many Silvius patterns—this simple but spritely little fly soon gained a substantial following on the Eel, Klamath, and Rogue Rivers. Among anglers who still swing flies on the Northern California steelhead rivers—particularly the Klamath and its tributary, the Trinity—the Brindle Bug remains a standard.

At the onset of World War II, the US Navy chose Eureka as a prime location to build floating dry docks—Humboldt Bay had no spanning bridge, so the huge floating dry docks could be hauled out to the Pacific without hindrance. No local company had the expertise or resources for such manufacture, so the Navy tasked Chicago Bridge & Iron Company (CBI) with the project and almost overnight Humboldt County became home to a production effort that employed some 3,000 people by 1944.

Though today nothing remains to hint at such a massive industrial effort on the shores of Humboldt Bay, the war proved a turning point for Silvius; prior to the war, he had been a baker, first for the Log Cabin Bakery, and then, in 1938, opening his own Silvius Bakery. But then came the war, and he and his wife Leona went to work for CBI. In 1946 after the war ended and the Navy shut down the CBI facility, Silvius opened the Lloyd Silvius Tackle Shop in Eureka, and thereafter his repute as a steelhead addict and expert spread throughout region.[13]

California Coachman (Yellow Royal Coachman) (recipe on page 245)

The popularity and influence of the Coachman and its progeny can hardly be overstated, and as Trey Combs wrote in *Steelhead Fly Fishing and Flies*, this fly of English origin, ". . . has sired more steelhead and trout flies than any other pattern, American or English."

The most famous of the Coachman's offspring—better known even than the original—is the Royal Coachman, iconic in American fly fishing for many decades. Both the Coachman and the Royal Coachman were popular steelhead flies in the late 1800s and well into the twentieth century, and both went through endless variations. One such offshoot of the Royal Coachman was John Fricke's California Coachman, also known as the Yellow Royal Coachman. Fricke, an ardent angler, was president of a school and office furniture supply firm founded in San Francisco, and also vested in mining interests. Born to German immigrants in 1868 (or 1866) in Illinois, he lived for a time in Oregon, where he married his wife, Birdie.

Fricke, according to the *San Francisco Call* (October 1, 1912), was among the early fly anglers to discover the massive trout of Oregon's then-remote Williamson River, traveling there in 1912 with pioneering California entrepreneur C. F. Weber, founder of school furniture supplier C. F. Weber & Company, which had offices in numerous cities and opened in Portland in 1894; Fricke was an owner of the company and president of the San Francisco-based firm.

Fricke's most frequent stomping grounds for trout were the Feather River and its tributaries, and upon his return from a trip there in 1912, the *San Francisco Call* ran a photo of him fishing the East Branch Feather. "During my visit," he told the newspaper, "I used artificial flies exclusively, and while fellows who were baiting with the helgamites [sic] they managed to dig out from under the rocks surpassed me in the matter of number of trout taken, I caught larger rainbows than they could lure with their bugs, and I had ten times as much fun. As everybody knows, a fish that rises to the fly is the gamest fighter in the stream."

By that time, Fricke was such a frequent visitor to the Feather, that, according to the *San Francisco Call*, he and one of his fishing buddies, Dr. E. H. Hadlock, bought a small miner's cabin on Mill Creek, a tributary of the Feather River, and set up their own fishing lodge. No doubt Frick intended the California Coachman as a trout fly, and by 1906, it had become one of the hot new patterns as far away as northwest Oregon, where Salem-based sporting goods store Hauser Brothers advertised it alongside the McGinty and March Brown in the July 13 issue of the *Daily Capital Journal*. Like so many of its fellow trout patterns, it soon found success in larger sizes as a steelhead fly.[14]

Carson Coachman (Carson Royal Coachman; Carson) (recipe on page 245)

If the city of Eureka, California, has a single iconic landmark, it is the bedazzling, flamboyant Carson Mansion, built in the 1880s by the famous timber baron William Carson (1825–1912). In 1947, a story in the *Humboldt Times* explained that this was a period in Victorian architecture "when houses were judged by the complexity of decorations that could be put upon them. Cupolas, towers and bay windows were in vogue." The Carson mansion bore such affectations in spades.

Carson had pioneered commercial timber harvest in the redwood forests of Northern California, having first emigrated from his native New Brunswick in search of gold; he found his fortune in redwoods instead. According to the Ingomar Club website, Carson "purchased a pack of horses and proceeded to the gold fields in Trinity County, along the Trinity River. However, the endeavor proved unsuccessful and by 1854 Mr. Carson was operating a mill in Humboldt County," from where, in 1855, he shipped his first load of redwood south to San Francisco, where previously only fir and spruce timber had been available. In 1863, Carson partnered with John Dolbeer, who would revolutionize logging with his steam-powered "logging donkey," and the company partnership lasted 87 years. Involved in many other local business ventures and worth $20 million at the time of his death, Carson "never failed to lend help to the less fortunate. All of his charities were not made public, but after his death, his will contained 116 beneficiaries, many company employees, as well as churches, hospitals and other community agencies."

His middle son, Charles Sumner Carson (1873–1933), one of five children Carson had with his wife Sarah, was a keen angler and sportsman. So too was the older brother, John Milton ("Milt") Carson (1865–1941), with whom well-known Eureka fly tackle dealer Sam Wells was once arrested under the specious grounds of taking more than a daily limit of salmon, in this case smolts as part of a limit of trout, according to the May 25, 1923, *Ferndale Express*. The Carsons, along with Wells, enjoyed high repute as anglers, enough that their expertise hardly escaped Eel River regular Clark C. Van Fleet, who, in his famous book *Steelhead to a Fly* (1954), recalled, "Eureka developed some of the best rod-wielders to be found on the West Coast, and the Eel was famous, not only for its monster fish, but for its expert fly fishermen as well . . ."

According to A. Courtney Williams, author of *Trout Flies, A Discussion and a Dictionary* (1932), the highly esteemed John S. Benn of San Francisco created and coined this pattern, in honor of one of the Carsons—or perhaps for the family in general.

Carter Fly and Carter's Dixie (recipes on page 245)

So dominant were the University of California Berkeley football teams of the early 1920s under coach Andy Smith that they earned the nickname the "Wonder Teams." From 1920 to 1925, Cal went unbeaten in 50 games, racking up 46 wins and 4 ties. The Golden Bears beat cross-bay rival Stanford 5 straight times from 1919 to 1923, cumulatively outscoring Stanford 131 to 17. Harley Carter (1900–1956), who played tackle for Stanford, never played for a team that beat Cal, but the cardinal-red of Stanford (which in the 1920s had no official mascot) must have run deep, for his son, Wayne, would follow in his footsteps as a tackle for Stanford 24 years later.

Football was but one of Harley Carter's athletic talents; he was also the West Coast intercollegiate boxing champion, according to a story in the *Berkeley Daily Gazette* (November 21, 1945), and, by the time the famous Eureka fly tier C. Jim Pray met him in the early 1930s, he was building a reputation as a dedicated steelhead angler—not to mention a fearless wader—on the rivers of Northern California, and on Oregon's Rogue River.

"The first time I saw him was on the great Big Bar Riffle below Orleans," recalled Pray in the late 1940s. "Harley had sneaked up for a day's fishing on his way North and had forgotten his waders. When I first saw him he was up to his arm pits in the cold water fly fishing with nothing on but a pair of pants, a shirt and an ordinary pair of shoes. He stayed there for several hours until he caught quite a few nice steelhead. I shivered in my waders watching him. Verily, he was quite a man!"

Pray created the Carter's Dixie (Carter's Dixie Bucktail) and the Carter Fly (Carter Fly Bucktail) in 1934 and 1938, respectively. The former fly he had devised before meeting Carter, but the fly had no name; after witnessing Carter's waderless fishing feat, Pray named the bucktail-style fly for the Berkeley resident. (Yes, Carter lived in Berkeley despite his strong ties to Stanford.) A few years later, at the behest of Carter, Pray created a dark-wing version of the Dixie, and called it the Carter Fly, as explained by Pray in his notes to Joseph D. Bates, Jr., for *Streamer Fly Fishing*.

Chappie (recipe on page 246)

In the midst of Prohibition, when the idea presumably did not spring from a late-night session with friends and a bottle of Scotch, I'm unsure how one decides to drive nonstop—meaning no stops for anything, including food, fuel, or bathroom—from Canada to Mexico. But that's exactly what outdoor adventurist and writer C. L. "Outdoor" Franklin did in the mid 1920s, completing the 1,606-mile feat in less than 55 hours in a brand-new 1925 Standard Six Buick. Not surprisingly, in October Franklin and his companion endured virtually nonstop rain all through Washington and Oregon, and in Oregon they had to abide by the state's 35-mile-per-hour speed limit, as stopping for any reason, including a police siren, would mean starting the journey from scratch. They rigged a big onboard extra gas tank with which they refueled the Buick on the fly. They reached Tijuana to great fanfare, concluded a story about the feat in the *Port Arthur News* on October 19, 1924.

The tri-country nonstop drive from Canada to Mexico was quite tame compared to Franklin's adventures driving the Baja Peninsula, as described by Erle Stanley Gardner in *Off the Beaten Track in Baja* (1967). Baja adventurers in the early decades of the twentieth century—necessarily self-sufficient—jury-rigged their vehicles with all manner of innovations to help them combat the rugged, unforgiving, remote, and oft-dangerous Mexican desert. As Gardner (who wrote the *Perry Mason* novels) warned, "It is to be borne in mind that when one takes one of these machines off the beaten path in Baja California, he is playing for keeps. If there are any 'bugs' in a machine you want to find out about them before you get down in Baja California."

The well-traveled Franklin, a Southern California resident who wrote a column for the *Los Angeles Times*, no doubt found the northward trip to the land of steelhead far more mundane, but addicting nonetheless, for he fell in love with the Klamath. "He fished it to the exclusion of almost all others for thirty years, and is responsible for naming many of the riffles between Hornbrook and Hamburg," explained Trey Combs in *Steelhead Fly Fishing and Flies*. Franklin's Chappie, which he used almost exclusively, has spawned several descendants, most of them varying in the color of the body, such as the Donnelly Chappie (yellow body) and the Flame Chappie (fluorescent flame-red body).

Cliff's Special (recipe on page 246)

Art Lingren, the British Columbia author and historian, says in his *Fly Patterns of British Columbia* that a description of the Cliff's Special as a standard pattern in 1946 probably indicates the fly, designed by Cliff Welch, dates to well before that time. It's a logical assumption; the showy, bright orange fly was touted alongside silver-bodied bucktails, the General Money, and the venerable Royal Coachman by W. F. Pochin in *Angling & Hunting in British Columbia*, Lingren's source.

By the mid-1940s, hair-wing patterns had superseded most of the featherwings. The Cliff's Special was no exception, and it too would fade into obscurity, but not before it had reigned for many years as "one of the four most popular steelhead patterns in the province," reports Lingren, with his information grounded in the sales records kept by Harkley & Haywood Sporting Goods store in Vancouver where, says Lingren, "Welch spent most, if not all, of his working life as a salesclerk . . ."

Harkley & Haywood Sporting Goods was an institution in downtown Vancouver, thriving for more than 60 years before closing up shop in 1982. To this day, Harkley & Haywood bamboo rods and Harkley & Haywood fly-tying hooks occasionally come up for auction. With both Welch and his wife tying flies professionally, the store—which was also famous for its prodigiously stocked gun rack—sold not only the well-known British Columbia patterns of the time, but also its own exclusive flies, whose dressings were guarded secrets, even to the famous Roderick Haig-Brown. Lingren notes that when Haig-Brown was working on his book *The Western Angler*, "During his research he learned that places like Harkley & Haywood in Vancouver considered the make-up of many local fly patterns to be trade secrets and wouldn't give him pattern listings."

Luckily the Cliff's Special—and the store's other top-sellers, such as General Noel Money's patterns—could hardly be kept secret, their dressings being easily deciphered, and this attractive fly remains as viable now as it was half a century ago.

Conway Special (recipe on page 246)

Dan Conway (1866–1941) was a well-known Seattle fly tier who had emigrated from his native Ireland, probably before the turn of the twentieth century. His best-known pattern is the Conway Special, which he adapted from his Yellow Hammer, a popular steelhead fly in western Washington from the 1930s into the 1960s. By all accounts, Conway tied outstanding flies, but the story is best told by one of his fly-tying students, none other than Enos Bradner. In *Northwest Angling*, Bradner wrote:

> Dan learned to dress a fly when he was a boy in Ireland. Although he had his left hand amputated in his mature years he lost not a whit of his skill and could dress a truly beautiful fly with the one good hand and an iron hook for the other.
>
> Dan's brogue was as thick as a Dublin fog especially when loosened with a drop or so of "reel oil," and the flies he made were the most perfect that I had ever seen. One of his favorite patterns was a teal and red, dressed wet, and the wings were cupped as evenly and perfectly as if they had been placed there by nature. He took an uncommonly long time to select feathers, it seemed to me, but when they went onto the hook they matched exactly. Each black stripe of teal feather fitted the stripes of the other in spacing and width just as if they had been drawn by a draftsman.
>
> "Never make a poor fly," said Dan. "You're trying to please yourself and you don't want anything second rate. If it ain't right tear it apart and start over again."
>
> Charley King and I learned to tie together and we never forgot some of Dan's firm-rooted principles.
>
> "Always make true patterns," he would keep saying. "Find out the exact dressing and stick to it."

For the wings on the Conway Special, Conway only used the primary feathers from a snow goose because, as Bradner explains, "The fibers of these feathers hung so closely together that the fly could be used day after day, and the wings would remain intact and not shred out as they would if made from domestic quill."

Conway, who taught many local anglers to tie flies and was always willing to share his knowledge, tied the Conway Special (so-named by anglers who bought his flies) in two shades: a light, bright yellow and an orange-tinged yellow; he insisted that the body hackle and the wool yarn used for the body match exactly even if that meant dyeing them in the same dye bath. By the 1940s, Seattle-area steelheaders were dressing the fly—which had originally earned its popularity as a sea-run cutthroat fly—with bucktail wings.[15]

Coquihalla Red and Coquihalla Orange (recipes on page 246)

Canadian artist and angler Tommy Brayshaw (1886–1967) embodied the edict of high ethical standards in steelhead fishing and steelhead flies as well as any of the esteemed masters of the golden age of our sport here in the Pacific Northwest. The variations within his elegant Coquihalla series of flies are many, and the name pays tribute to the ruggedly beautiful Coquihalla River, which rises from the Coquihalla Lakes and then plunges 3,400 feet in just 33 miles to meet the Fraser River near Hope, British Columbia.

Brayshaw's art spanned a variety of media, including finely detailed wood carvings of trout, but his paintings, often pastel and aquarelle drawings, are meticulous; his ethereal renditions of trout and steelhead are evocative and realistic. Yet art was an avocation for Brayshaw. Still, toward the end of his life, he was especially productive in his hobby owing to extensive demand for his art from friends and admirers, especially after, says fly-fishing historian Skip Hosfield, "his good friend, Roderick Haig-Brown, asked Tommy to draw the illustrations for a revised edition of *The Western Angler* he was preparing. Publication of that book in 1947 with its two color plates and many line drawings enlarged Brayshaw's artistic reputation and further extended it throughout the angling fraternity."

Brayshaw's carvings and drawings were always in great demand, but, as noted Oregon angler Hosfield (one of the founders of the Federation of Fly Fishers) explains, "He never promoted his work as a commercial enterprise. His originals were done as gifts to friends or done on special order for a nominal fee. The number of original drawings done by Brayshaw during his lifetime is estimated to be no more than a few hundred and they all reside in museums or private collections. . . . No print edition was ever made from Brayshaw originals during his lifetime."[16]

As evidenced by his alluring, complicated steelhead patterns, Brayshaw's artistic talents extended to his fly tying. Eminent angling historian Art Lingren, in *Fly Patterns of British Columbia*, explains that the English-born Brayshaw, ". . . preferring to catch his steelhead on classic-looking flies, often varied his dressings and incorporated many of the characteristics of traditional Atlantic salmon patterns. . . . The Coquihalla Orange—Dark [the most complex in the series] dressed in all its finery is a most beautiful example of the fly-tier's craft and by dressing the fly so elaborately, I believe, shows the high regard that some anglers such as Brayshaw have for the steelhead as a game fish."

Courtesan (recipe on page 246)

Syd Glasso's best-known fly is the Orange Heron, which in the span of half a century became iconic. It was but one of the beautiful flies he created with the old Scottish Spey flies as his inspiration, and like so many other Northwest steelheaders, I have tied them by the score, modified them unashamedly, and fished them enthusiastically.

But the Courtesan is my favorite of the Glasso flies. My affinity for this graceful pattern derives from its resemblance, more so than the other Glasso designs, to the flies developed in the mid-1850s on Scotland's River Spey. Today, fly tiers often debate what constitutes a Spey fly, yet they need not argue; by the truest definition, a Spey fly belongs to a unique class of flies that come from the local anglers on the Spey in the nineteenth century. Spey flies bear several characteristics that make them unique, but generally only when each of these characteristics is included in the fly, rather than just one of them. That one singularity is the application of soft rooster rump hackles tied in by the butt rather than the tip and then palmered over the body. In the 1800s, tiers commonly used rooster hackles as the body hackle on salmon flies, beginning with simple patterns called Palmers. Soft hackles from the rump (saddle or tail clump) were used infrequently in deference to stiffer, shinier, thinner-stemmed neck hackles, but they were occasionally found on salmon flies from throughout the British Isles. However, on only one river were these soft-fibered hackles dressed in the reverse way from normal, and that was on the Spey.

Over the decades, writers (primarily Americans) have often asserted that the low-slung wing of bronze mallard, thin bodies, and long-fibered hackles identified the true Spey fly, but the mallard wings of the genuine article were not always low slung and the hackles were not always long fibered. One class of Spey flies called the Heron flies sported those long-fibered hackles in the form of plumes taken from the back or breast of the grey heron (*Ardea cinerea*), but the Spey held no monopoly on heron-hackled flies nor on mallard-winged patterns. However, another component of the true Spey fly—whether hackled with heron or rooster rump (from roosters specially bred for the feathers as early as the 1860s)—was the prominent use of ribbing material and, critically, the application of at least one rib crossing *over* the hackle stem, and locking the feather firmly in place. The defining characteristics of a Spey fly included: a hackle (if of rooster rump, dressed in the reverse way from normal), locked in place by a counter rib; ribbing with at least two and frequently three different tinsels; and birth upon the River Spey for which the tribe of flies is named.[17]

The Courtesan, like other Spey flies from outside Strathspey (the name for the valley of Spey), are not Spey flies at all and are better termed Spey-style flies. But the Courtesan, with its soft-fibered brown rooster schlappen hackle, even though the feather is not wound from its butt end, harkens to those unique old flies so deftly dressed by the likes of the incomparable Geordie Shanks, John Cruikshank, and Charles "Schoolie" Grant.[18]

Cuenin's Advice (Cuenin's Fly) (recipe on page 246)

H. L. Betten—best known for his early twentieth-century wingshooting writing—listed Cuenin's Advice "among the favorites" for steelhead fishing in his chapter "Western Trout Fishing" in *Fishing Lake and Streams* (1946). This attractive pattern could pass for a Silver Demon, a fly created and popularized by C. Jim Pray in the early 1930s; the two dressings are nearly identical, and whether outdoor writer J. P. Cuenin (1882–1963) borrowed from Pray or simply arrived at the same color combination is unknown, but his fly dates to nearly the same time, the mid-1930s (the *Ferndale Express* mentions the fly in 1935). So too, one of California's well-known tiers could have invented and named the fly in honor of Cuenin, as doing so was (and is) common practice.

Cuenin, the "Rod and Gun" columnist for the *San Francisco Examiner* beginning in 1927, was born in New York and in 1907 reached California by way of New Jersey, Maryland, Virginia, and Florida. He found employment as a comptroller with the prestigious Hotel St. Francis, and having hunted most of the small game of the East, Cuenin found his favorite hobby in waterfowl hunting the Bay Area. In those halcyon days, San Francisco Bay and the wetlands of the Sacramento River Delta hosted spectacular flights of ducks, geese, and shorebirds. Peter B. Moyle, et. al., estimate the Central Valley's historical overwintering waterfowl population at more than 10 million birds ("Changing ecosystems: a brief ecological history of the Delta," February, 2010). But Cuenin also loved fishing, and the Eel was his favorite steelhead stream; he first fished there in the early 1920s.

Cuenin was no armchair outdoorsman. In addition to his frequent forays afield for fish and game, he was the National All-Around Casting Champion in 1931 and a national skeet-shooting champion. He was a member of the influential San Francisco Fly Casting Club, and later a member of the Golden Gate Angling and Casting Club, which formed in 1933. Cuenin was also a member of the Pacific Rod & Gun Club, which gave him an honorary life membership for his casting-competition accomplishments. He was a "bold and tireless leader" in the fight to create reasonable bag limits for fowl, wrote William T. Hornaday in *Thirty Years War For Wild Life* (1930), and he campaigned for a variety of other conservation causes, from commercial fish netting to strengthening water-pollution laws.

Moreover, as noted by the *Eureka Humboldt Standard* (April 6, 1953), Cuenin, who had fished from British Columbia to Mexico and from New England to Florida, took a break from his column to spend World War II "teaching Air Force pilots how to hit enemy planes." His obituary in the *Eureka Humboldt Standard* says that he taught some 10,000 American pilots how to shoot.[19]

Cummings Special (recipe on page 247)

The North Umpqua tumbles steeply westward from the Cascade Mountains, hemmed in by a precipitous conifer-clad gorge. Come October, the deep, verdant canyon of the upper river warms reluctantly and when finally the day reaches a pleasant temperature, keep a jacket at hand, for the evening chill settles over the river sooner than on the famous pools down below. But the enchanting upper river is also lonelier in autumn, and my longtime fishing and hunting partner, Forrest Maxwell and I used to prefer it then. One October week we stayed at Eagle Rock and had the entire campground, quiet and sylvan, to ourselves. On our last evening there, we opted to fish out the evening light near camp.

Wading into a lively tailout I'd never before cast flies upon, I approached a narrow reef running laterally down the river, and thought it best to swing a fly across the gliding run on the far side. The first cast was just a short flip, 6 feet of line, a leader, and a Cummings Special—a North Umpqua classic beautifully designed in the 1930s by North Umpqua Lodge owner Clarence Gordon and his guide, Ward Cummings (1892–1978). I watched the fly come around, easily visible in the evening light, and much to my surprise, a steelhead ascended from the depths on the far side of the submerged reef, just a few yards from where I stood. Mesmerized, I watched the fish turn on the fly. A spirited battle ensued, and when the fish, a 9-pound hatchery steelhead, finally came to hand, I killed it cleanly.

Only then did I notice an onlooker above me on the highway embankment. The young man was beaming with excitement about watching my encounter with that steelhead from start to finish. He told me he had always dreamed of fishing the North Umpqua, and with college now behind him, he had packed his car and driven all the way across the country. I tried to explain to him how meaningful it was to me to catch that steelhead on a Cummings, one of the iconic patterns from this long-revered river; I think he understood. Forrest, having fished out a run above me, came upon us just then, and we invited the young man to dinner at our camp.

Forrest's organizational system made sense only to him, but after substantial rummaging about in the bed of his pickup, he reemerged with two large paper grocery sacks, a tub of butter, and a giant cast iron skillet. One sack contained farm-fresh Walla Walla sweet yellow onions; the other held a small fortune in chanterelle mushrooms. We filleted the steelhead, skin off, and wrapped one fillet for our guest's ice chest; the other we cut into 3-inch sections. We sliced up three big onions and a king's ransom worth of chanterelles. Into the skillet went copious amounts of butter with all the onions and mushrooms. Next came salt and pepper, and finally, as the onions and mushrooms reached the halfway point, we added the steelhead filets and still more butter. By then, giant October Caddis, attracted to our big Coleman lanterns, were swarming; dozens ended up in our dinner, but we hardly cared.

I've been enthralled and sated by many delicious camp dinners, but few have been so memorable as this dinner. I hope it was equally so for our young friend, whose name, regretfully, I have long forgotten.

Dave's Mistake (recipe on page 247)

In the mid-1980s, McNeese's Fly Shop in Salem, Oregon, had reached its zenith; under the tutelage of the irascible, puerile, boisterous, and artistically gifted David McNeese, a small cadre of fly tiers—myself, Forrest Maxwell, Brad Burden, Al Buhr, and a few others—learned to dress steelhead flies in what was just beginning to be recognized as the McNeese style. All of us would go on in the ensuing years to extrapolate on the fly-design concepts and tying techniques we learned from Dave, and our combined efforts began to change the way classic patterns were dressed and the way new patterns were designed.

The historical record speaks for itself: one of the hallmarks of a McNeese–style rendition of a classic steelhead pattern is the use of dyed golden pheasant crest feathers for the tail; we dyed them in myriad colors, and even bleached them so we could dye them pink and bright purple and blue. But an examination of all the literature on steelhead flies up through the 1970s is unlikely to reveal a single fly dressed with a tail of dyed golden pheasant crest. These tails—prominently on display for the first time in the plate of hair-wing flies dressed by McNeese for Trey Combs's *Steelhead Flyfishing*—are commonplace now. Those peaceful days at McNeese's, though we hardly realized it at the time, changed the game; the basic hair-wing steelhead fly was now elevated to the realm of artwork.

One day, in 1987 I think, I walked into the shop to start my shift at 10 a.m. Shockingly, McNeese had arrived well ahead of me. He was in an excited state and speedily dressing steelhead flies. More than a dozen were already sitting on the table. Upon my inquiry, he told me, hardly looking up from his work, that he was supposed to have completed an order of two dozen Del Coopers by that morning for a customer who would be swinging by to pick them up. Dave had a patented "is-every-one-here-a-moron-except-me" look, which he shot my direction when I said something to the effect of, "Umm, Dave, those aren't Del Coopers; Del Coopers have a purple body and bright red hackle, not the other way around."

After a few seconds it dawned on him that I was right and that he had wasted 90 minutes tying a red-body fly with purple hackle. The ensuing creative cuss words would have made a sailor blush; it was all the more amusing because he hated to admit I might be right about anything. There was nothing to be done but start anew, and together Dave and I finished the order in time. The new red-body flies went into the fly bins under the name I jocularly suggested: Dave's Mistake. That summer the pattern accounted for a number of steelhead on the local river, still more come autumn on the Deschutes, and demand remained steady for the balance of Dave's days owning the fly shop.

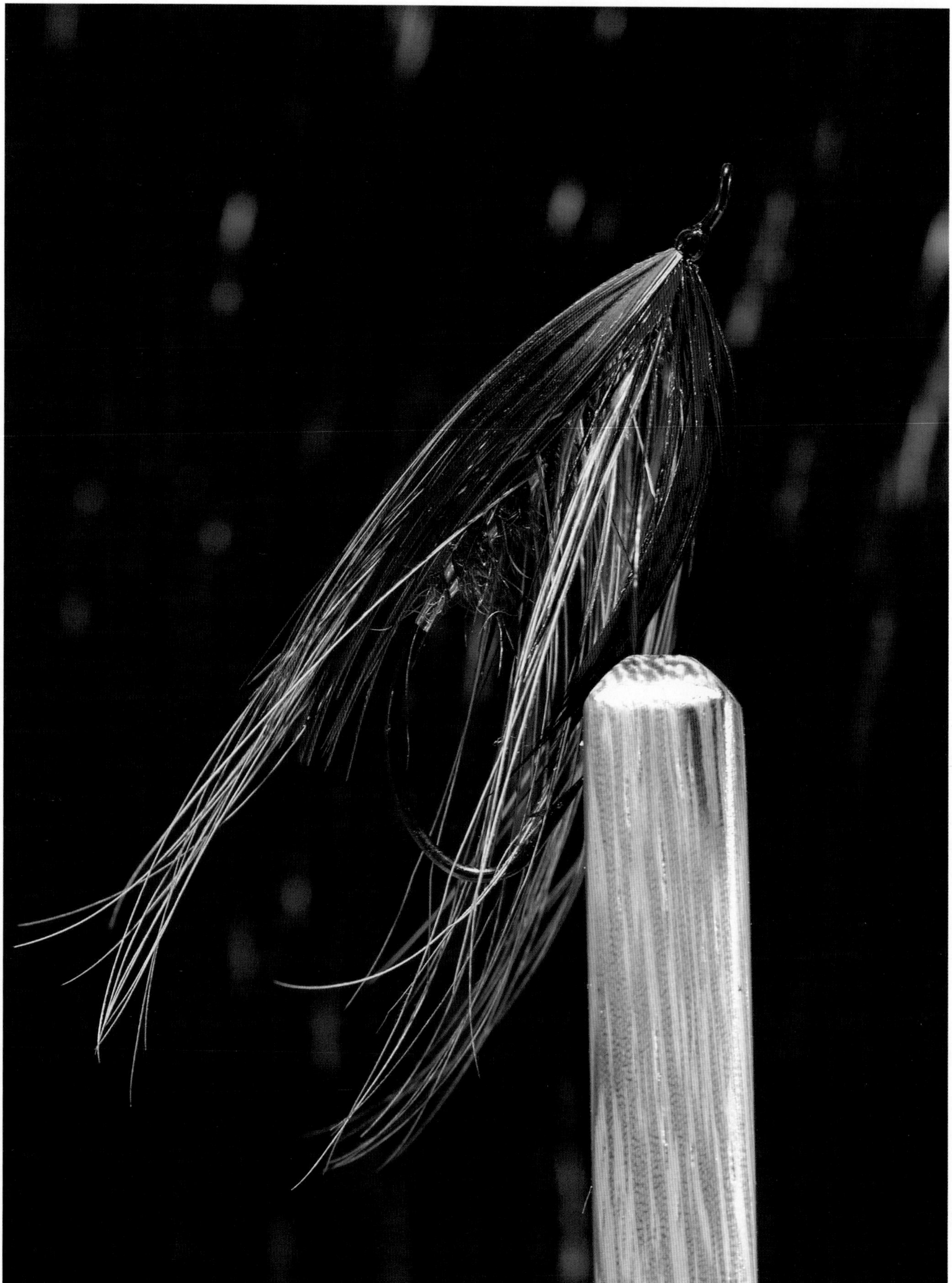

Deep Purple Spey (recipe on page 247)

Walt Johnson: affable, talented, artistic, visionary, conservationist, pioneering steelhead angler. He was all those things, yet remained humble throughout his life, even as his beloved North Fork Stilly fell into severe decline at nearly the same time that steelhead fly-angling ethics began devolving. In private to me, he lamented the arrival of strike indicators and anglers using them who seemed unfettered with any notion of fair sport on his home river. Yet when engaged in conversation with them or with anyone else, he was sincere and selfless.

Walt was also the Sasquatch of the Stilly, a moniker he learned to like, even though it came from sad circumstances. After the death of his wife June, Walt—understandably depressed—took solace in the arms of a mistress: his beloved North Fork of the Stillaguamish. For a time, as he grappled with the reality of life without June, Walt shied away from even his close angling friends, and it is said that if he were seen fishing a favorite run on the Stilly, he would vanish seamlessly into the riparian woods like the legendary Sasquatch. So too, he told me, in the 1970s before he was the Sasquatch of the Stilly, the Elbow Hole colony had disbanded; the pioneering steelheaders were aging, the Stilly's steelhead runs were shrinking, and the men could not defend their summer cabins from thieves and miscreants. Then in the 1980s, newcomers arrived, a new breed of steelhead fly fishers bent on instant gratification. They learned to recognize Walt's vehicle and thereby they tried to ferret out the river's best water; he learned to meld into the landscape, vaporize into thin air.

Long before, however, Walt had perfected his beautiful steelhead flies, and among his own favorites was his Deep Purple Spey. He had met Syd Glasso in the late 1940s; Glasso had been invited over to fish with Al Knudson, Walt's close friend. Walt then fished with Glasso on the Olympic Peninsula in the 1950s, just when Glasso was developing his beautiful Spey-style flies. Walt admired the style and quickly lent his considerable skill to the design of his own Spey-type flies. The first of these was his Deep Purple Spey. He had already embraced George McLeod's Purple Peril, and he told me, "In those days one of the best kept secrets a few of us shared was the use of gentian violet dye. This was available from the local pharmacy in crystal form."

The genesis of the Deep Purple Spey began with Walt's original purple fly, his Violet Nymph, and his admiration of Glasso's Spey-style patterns. Ever the theorist, Walt told me that he found the Violet Nymph successful under virtually all conditions, and he "concluded that the ultra-violet in the spectrum combined with the effect of light refraction produced a subdued color as viewed by the fish under bright light and clear water conditions, so the steelhead would accept it willingly. Also, the color being dark had the added advantage of showing up well even in turbid water and dim light."

With such theorizing in mind, and inspired by the Glasso flies, Walt tinkered with the dressing of his Violet Nymph, and "from these humble experiments," he told me, "my first effective Spey-type fly was born."

Del Cooper (recipe on page 247)

Mike Kennedy was perhaps the most prolifically successful steelhead angler ever to cast flies over Oregon and Washington Rivers. He took his first steelhead at age 14 on the Rogue, he loved the North Umpqua, he pioneered the steelhead fly fishing on the Kalama and Wind Rivers, and he fished just about every steelhead-bearing stream in Oregon, where he was born in 1910. He may well have been among the first to take winter-run steelhead on flies in the river I have called home waters since the early 1980s, the North Santiam. "Mike spent his last two high school years living with and working for Harry D. Hobson, a Lyons, Oregon, rodmaker," records Trey Combs in *Steelhead Fly Fishing and Flies*, ". . . whenever possible the work bench was left for the North Santiam River that flowed practically at the Hobson back door."

In those days, the North Santiam had no summer-run steelhead; in fact, no such runs occurred upstream of Willamette Falls at Oregon City because before flood-control dams were built on all the major Willamette tributaries—the McKenzie, the forks of the Willamette, the North Santiam, and the South Santiam—the falls formed an impassable barrier for upstream migration of anadromous fish during low water. Once the dams were built and flows controlled, the Willamette Valley floor was no longer subject to pervasive winter flooding followed by severe summer shrinkage of flows. The valley's 40 to 50-plus inches of annual precipitation occur primarily as rain in the winter and spring; summers are dry. So prior to the installation of the dams, the low flows of summer actually created a more formidable barrier at Willamette Falls to migrating fish than did the heavy winter flows. Winter steelhead, and salmon, could navigate the falls at high flows, but a summer run of steelhead never evolved above the falls.

So if Mike Kennedy did indeed find success fishing flies for steelhead on the North Santiam in those two years living in Lyons, he would have been fishing for winter-run natives. The run of these long-distance migrants—from the Pacific Ocean to the Mehama-Lyons area by way of the Columbia, Willamette, Santiam, and North Santiam—is substantially reduced from its historical size. The dams were built with no fish passage, locking away valuable spawning habitat, and the Willamette itself was polluted even before the impoundments were completed in the 1950s and 60s.

In the early 1970s, the Oregon Department of Fish and Wildlife began a program of seeding the North Santiam and other Willamette tributaries with summer-run steelhead smolt. The annual runs soon burgeoned, creating a new summer steelhead sport fishery. We enjoyed outstanding fishing in the 1980s, good fishing in the 1990s, and somewhat inconsistent success in the new millenium. I don't think Kennedy—known as Mr. Steelhead—ever fished the summer run on the Santiam, but he left his mark nonetheless with his lovely Del Cooper fly, named for a well-known Portland angler and fly tier (Del Cooper, 1908–1979); by the late-1980s, the fly had become one of the favorite hair-wing patterns for our river.

Deschutes Demon (recipe on page 247)

The Deschutes River rumbles big and bold, muscling its way down a massive cleft in the high desert; that the railroads were able to penetrate the canyon well more than 100 years ago is a testimony to American ingenuity and fierce competition between industrial barons. Leon Speroff tells the story captivatingly in *The Deschutes River Railroad War* (2006). When the dust had finally settled from the battle between James J. Hill's Great Northern Railroad and Edward H. Harriman's Union Pacific Railroad, anglers could ride the train from Portland to the Deschutes. By 1916, Union Pacific inaugurated late-night departures from Union Station that reached South Junction, at river mile 84, around dawn the next day. As advertised by the railroad in the *Morning Oregonian* that year, anglers could opt to be dropped anywhere along the line within the Deschutes River canyon by previous arrangement with the conductor.

Such ready access to this otherwise intimidating and largely inaccessible river canyon ushered in newfound popularity for the Deschutes and its fertile fisheries for trout, steelhead, and salmon. But more than a decade prior, a few pioneering fly fishers were discovering the autumn fishing for what, at the time, were considered a "steelhead salmon" or "salmon-trout." In early September, 1903, Edward R. Hickson (circa 1853–1935), "an enthusiastic disciple of the 'immortal Izaak' . . . repaired to the Deschutes on Sunday for some sport with the steelhead salmon, or trout, as some wiseacres choose to call these salmon" ("Fisherman in the Deschutes Loses All His Tackles," *Morning Oregonian*, September 10, 1903).

By the time Hickson reported the carnage of his tackle at the hands of these so-called salmon to the *Morning Oregonian* a few hours after he left the water, his fishing tale had reached proportions only an angler could evince. He estimated one fish at 50 pounds, and battled three more such brutes before running out of flies and light by which to cast. That 50-pound fish would be about double the weight of even the largest steelhead he could have hoped to encounter, but those big brutes—many of them steelhead bound for Idaho—feel like a behemoth twice their size when they smash a swung fly and dash for the heavy currents of the careening Deschutes. Even today the Deschutes attracts visiting steelhead from numerous rivers, including Idaho's Clearwater, long revered for its fall run of huge fish that can reach well over 20 pounds. Hooking a heavy Clearwater steelhead in the Deschutes—much closer to the sea than the Clearwater—is always an unforgettable experience.

A year before his memorable tackle-busting Deschutes experience, Hickson, in the company of Maurice Fitzmaurice (1854–1936; editor of the *Condon Times*), landed several 6- to 12-pound steelhead on the Deschutes and in doing so said the *Morning Oregonian* (September 10, 1903), "exploded the idea that the steelhead at least will not rise to a fly."

The two men, both Irish immigrants, pioneered Deschutes steelhead fly angling, and the torch was carried, a couple generations later, by Portland tackle dealer Don McClain and his wife Lola, proponents of floating lines, skated flies, and Deschutes steelhead. The Deschutes Demon was their most popular fly, though Don claimed his wife's Deschutes Skunk—similar to the standard Skunk but with dark-brown deer body hair topped with white bucktail for the wing—was a better producer.

Donnelly Coachman (recipe on page 247)

In the latter half of the nineteenth century, oversize popular trout wet flies developed in the East and in Great Britain served as the first steelhead patterns when the fly-angler's pursuit of the great seagoing rainbows was in its infancy. But by the late 1880s, furtive efforts at dedicated fly designing for steelhead were underway. In most cases, early steelhead flies created by West Coast tiers relied on the old classic trout flies as templates. Among the most popular of these trout patterns, which had come west to California not long after the forty-niners no doubt, and to Oregon probably around the same time, were the Coachman, Professor, Grizzly King, and the Hackle flies, all of English origin; by the 1880s, America's Eastern trout anglers were producing countless wet flies, among them the Parmachene Belle, a Henry Wells pattern, John Haily's Royal Coachman, and the ubiquitous Scarlet Ibis, sometimes called a Red Ibis.

With these flies, along with a few others, already accounting for "salmon-trout," as steelhead were then known, in the rivers of the San Francisco Bay Area and northward, the 1890s ushered in an explosive era of steelhead fly design, and it seems there appeared as many versions of the popular Coachman and Royal Coachman as there were anglers tying flies in California. The Coachman-style fly remained popular well into the twentieth century and into this angling culture came Roy Donnelly in the 1920s. In 1919 he had moved west from Tennessee, and by the 1940s he was a well-established professional fly tier hailing from San Pedro, near Los Angeles. Donnelly cut his steelheading teeth on the far-away Klamath River and fished it ever autumn for many years. And like virtually every well-known tier in the state, he attached his name to a version of the Coachman, and the Donnelly Coachman became, probably, his most famous contribution to steelhead fly tying.

Drain's 20 (recipe on page 247)

Humble and self-effacing almost to a fault, Wes Drain was the paragon of steelhead fly tiers in Washington; his streamlined, intricate, beautiful flies redefined the genre, and perhaps the most striking of them was his Drain's 20. Using this fly, Drain bested a state-record 20-pound, 7-ounce Skagit River steelhead on Friday, February 4, 1949—hence the pattern's name—a benchmark that stood for 20 years. The following Monday, Enos Bradner broke the story of Drain's angling feat in the *Seattle Times* in a story titled, "Drain takes 20-pound Steelhead on Pet Fly."

By the 1940s, a who's-who of the North Fork Stillaguamish gang began fishing for winter steelhead on flies on the Skagit, and thereafter the Stilly and Skykomish—a much more complicated task than tempting the relatively easy summer-run fish, for winter brought not only higher, colder flows, but also steelhead more locked into reaching the spawning grounds immediately and less prone to pouncing on flies. The idea of taking winter steelhead on flies had first been proposed to the North Fork regulars by rod-builder Don Holbrook, but Enos Bradner, according to what Walt Johnson told me in 1996, "ridiculed the idea as a hopeless endeavor, and he would have no part of it." Still, many of the others were game to confront the new challenge, with Ken McLeod among the first; Johnson told me, "Ralph Wahl, Judge Ralph Olson, and Al Knudson all fished the Skagit with good results" and were soon joined by Walt and Wes Drain, along with half a dozen or more others. If Sergeant Wes Drain was a tad late joining the Skagit winter steelheading party, it was because he had been busy fighting in the European theater in World War II.

The original Drain's 20 makes use of exotic feathers: a tail topped with yellow toucan breast feathers and an underwing of red cock-of-the-rock. Toucans, of which there are several species bearing yellow breast feathers, and cock-of-the-rocks, of which there are two species, are endemic to various parts of Central and South America, and the use of their feathers need not be encouraged in fly tying, although they remain available to some extent in the materials trade. Flies dressed with substitutes serve just as faithfully provided the angler wielding them fishes just as faithfully. Toucan substitutes include yellow-dyed cul-de-canard; the small white feathers from the neck band of a ring-neck pheasant, dyed yellow; and small feathers from a yellow-dyed hen cape. For the red cock-of-the-rock used in this fly, try substituting Golden Pheasant flank or rump dyed cerise or fluorescent red (dyed skins are generally available from materials dealers).

Evening Coachman (recipe on page 245)

In retrospect, it seems the members of the North Fork Stillaguamish steelheading colony in the 1940s and 50s—those anglers and their friends who built summer cabins and camps at the Elbow Hole and nearby—never considered that they *couldn't* catch Stilly summer-runs on dry flies. They realized, almost as an afterthought, that a steelhead pattern skating along the surface—on it, in it, or near it, depending on the whims of the water during each swing of the fly—and trailing a subtle wake often tempted fish to rise as surely as a wet fly.

Even before that, the Stilly regulars dead-drifted standard trout dry flies in large sizes for steelhead. For example, in the 1990s, Walt Johnson told me he had good luck on the Stilly fishing an "enlarged version of the Badger Bivisible . . . a turn or two of red hackle in front of this fly seemed to make it appealing to the steelhead . . . this was before riffle hitches and downstream waking flies became popular." I have one of his modified Badger Bivisibles, and it is expertly dressed with densely applied high-quality badger hackle for the body and two turns of bright red hackle as the face. The fly is tied on a light-wire Partridge salmon hook, size 6.

In fact, George McLeod's Purple Peril—one of the most popular wet flies of them all—was first tied as a dry fly, with purple hackle standing out at right angles rather than swept back. Johnson, in discussing the influence of Syd Glasso's flies, once told me in those years—the 1940s and 50s—most of the anglers he knew (and Walt knew them all) "used bucktail, hairwing, and spider-type patterns, along with dry flies."

I think it would have actually surprised the Stilly regulars of the 1930s and 40s to learn how infrequently dry flies were tried on other rivers bearing runs of summer steelhead. Walt's first dry-fly fish was a splendid hen of more than 10 pounds, taken on his version of a White Wulff, fished dead-drift as he stalked upstream through boulder-studded pocket water below his property near the Deer Creek confluence. He took the fish—after a tremendous battle—on a 7½-foot Powell bamboo rod. Walt loved fishing dainty tackle and was expert in quickly subduing steelhead even on what he called his "midge rods." He told me in no uncertain terms that too many anglers take too long to land steelhead.

Walt was keen to fish dry flies on the riffles and runs he knew so well on the North Fork, and he developed several flies specifically for such work. Chief among them was his Evening Coachman, developed in the early 1950s. A more beautiful steelhead dry fly has never been conceived.

Fall Favorite (recipe on page 248)

Famous Eureka tackle dealer Lloyd Silvius (see Brindle Bug, page 49) is often credited with the Fall Favorite, but whether he invented it or simply modified and popularized it is uncertain. Trey Combs, in *Steelhead Fly Fishing and Flies*, says Silvius invented the fly in 1946 specifically for the Eel River, and that the bright little pattern became so popular that it "would have to be counted in any 'ten best' list regardless of the steelhead region; it is a standard from the Skeena [British Columbia] to the Russian [California]."

Another possible inventor of the fly is Butch Wilson (1880–1951). Roy Patrick, in his *Pacific Northwest Fly Patterns* (1970), attributed the Fall Favorite to Wilson, and Jim Adams, longtime California angler and prominent dealer in rare books and tackle, said likewise to Sean Gallagher when interviewed for Gallagher's 2013 book, *Wild Steelhead*. Moreover, Adams said that Wilson tied the fly as follows: Tag, silver; tail, golden pheasant tippet; butt, red chenille; body, gold tinsel; hackle, red; wing, orange. The pattern described by Adams is similar to the Nite Owl, another pattern attributed to Silvius. Certainly the possibility exists that Silvius, tying these flies as Optics, made them popular even if he didn't originate the dressings.[20]

In his days as one of the preeminent West Coast fly tackle dealers in California, Silvius tied the Fall Favorite as an optic in the style popularized by his forerunner in the Eureka fly shop scene, C. Jim Pray. The optics as Pray designed them in 1940 sported heads of large split-brass beads with painted-on eyes and pupils. They amounted to a pioneering effort to find ways to get flies down to late-fall summer-run steelhead and winter-run steelhead on the Eel River and were often called Eel River Optics. Pray and others designed many different patterns as optics, but the Fall Favorite—though popularized as an optic by Silvius in 1946—garnered regionwide popularity as a standard hair-wing fly, rather than an optic.

Combs's remarks about the pervasiveness of the Fall Favorite, published in 1976, held true through the 1980s, giving this simple but eye-catching pattern a reign of nearly 50 years. But like many of the popular hair wings of the twentieth century, even the Fall Favorite fell into relative obscurity as other styles of flies began expanding—the curmudgeon in me might say diluting—the pool of patterns available to steelhead anglers by the 1990s and into the new century. Today, while the Fall Favorite remains well known at least in name to many steelhead anglers, its former widespread use has dissipated, and its sphere of influence has retreated back toward its home waters of Northern California, where anglers on the Klamath, Eel, and Trinity still give it occasional play.

Faulk (recipe on page 248)

Similar to the Orange Shrimp, which was ubiquitous in western Washington in the 1930s and 40s, the Faulk—created around 1923—is perhaps not only the forerunner to that fly, but may also be the first bucktail-wing pattern used on the steelhead waters of the state. Emil Nathaniel Faulk (1888–1961), who had come west from Nebraska, lived in Aberdeen, where he was instrumental in founding an angler's club around 1918, according to the *Sunday Oregonian* (June 30, 1918). He and his fellow club members would have been among the pioneers of fly fishing for a variety of species on the Olympic Peninsula, and artist Roger Moore notes that "Emil fly fished all of the steelhead waters on the western slope of Washington's Olympic Peninsula, but his favorite was the Bogachiel River." By the 1930s, Faulk was so respected as an angler that he hosted Prince George of Denmark on a fishing trip on August 20, 1939, as the *Centralia Daily Chronicle* reported a day earlier.

The most revolutionary characteristic of this otherwise simple standard hair-wing fly was the way Faulk left the clipped butt ends of the bucktail protruding at the front as a kind of head. This arrangement would become far better known when Harry Lemire's Grease Liner gained widespread popularity a few decades later, but it was a clever addition to a 1923 fly, invented at a time when the bucktail patterns had recently been introduced on the Rogue River in southern Oregon and the steelhead streams of Northern California. As Trey Combs pointed out in *Steelhead Fly Fishing and Flies*, "No doubt the stubble at the head helps to give it a more erratic action."

Fool's Gold (recipe on page 248)

Don Holm, an outdoor editor for the *Oregonian* newspaper in Portland, once wrote a piece about the new fiberglass fly rods that had rapidly replaced bamboo as the most common rods in the sport, as they could be obtained inexpensively. He subsequently received a letter from Mike Kennedy and printed it in its entirety in his column of February 26, 1970:

> Dear Don: Having been one of the silent majority who has read with interest your fine columns for the past couple of years, I find it is uncomfortable to remain silent any longer.
>
> My interest was reawakened by recent reference to bamboo rods and their glass counterparts. Needless to say, anyone in your position is subject to rebuttal, no matter what you say. I quite agree that glass rods do provide suitable tools for a great many anglers. I also agree that for a great majority they may even approach the point of being just a bit better—better in that they require almost no real care or "love." They also cost less than good bamboo. I might also point out that a poor bamboo rod is perhaps the worst atrocity ever foisted upon a poor unsuspecting fisherman.
>
> However, when it comes to good bamboo fly rods, you have arrived at a point of comparison with other materials that just isn't possible. To date no glass rods that I have ever seen or used under actual fishing conditions could even remotely be compared with any of the some 60 fine rods I have in my collection. The difference is in that extra "kick," or series of vibrations that always follow the power stroke and tends to destroy that much desired smooth power flow. This extra kick not only robs you of extra distance but it also makes for an arm-weary condition, not evident in good bamboo rods.
>
> Being an amateur rod maker, I think I have some knowledge of what does make the difference between a fly rod and a "fine rod." In fact, I have two Powell rods in my collection that are so good I have to keep them locked in a closet just to keep them from going fishing all by themselves.

Kennedy died in 1993 as a 70-year steelheading veteran who had probably caught more steelhead on flies than anyone else. So keen on well-made bamboo rods was Kennedy that when his ashes were scattered in the North Umpqua River, so too were the ashes of his favorite rod. Among his many fly patterns created for steelhead, some well-known and others forgotten, his Fool's Gold is one of the most striking.[21]

Freight Train (recipe on page 248)

Kaufmann's Streamborn, opened by brothers Lance and Randall Kaufmann in Tigard, Oregon, in the mid-1970s, developed a prolific mail-order business, and many fly anglers, myself included, always looked forward to each new issue of their catalog. Beyond the broad array of rods and reels and flies and all the other accoutrements of the sport, the catalog, as the years passed, promoted the Kaufmanns' burgeoning travel business. The brothers Kaufmann realized that a fly shop could also be a travel bureau for exotic fly-angling destinations and they marketed that idea in full color in the pages of the catalog. So too, they promoted steelhead and trout fishing on the famous Deschutes River, and Randall spent considerable time there running fly-fishing schools. He designed his Freight Train during those years, and then added a series of additional similar patterns, such as the Coal Car, Flat Car, and Signal Light.[22]

Those fly names derive from the railway along the river's west bank; all Deschutes anglers are keenly aware of it. But the story of how those tracks got there is compelling, and brilliantly told by Leon Speroff in *The Deschutes River Railroad War*. Work on two competing lines, one on each bank, began in 1909, but several years before—in the absence of rail access to the massive and precipitous canyon, steelhead fly fishing on the Deschutes was essentially pioneered by ". . . a pair of sportsmen of Hibernian [Irish] origin, residing at Moro, Sherman County," wrote John Gill in the *Oregon Sportsman* (April, 1914). Gill reported that "Chinook and other salmon run up the Deschutes in great numbers, and are caught by fly tackle within a few miles of the Columbia," and he recalled the two Irishmen telling him "of their success with fine tackle—gray flies tied by themselves on hooks not bigger than No. 8—with which they caught large silverside salmon in the vicinity of Free Bridge."[23]

The two Irishmen, who had reached Oregon in the early 1880s and homesteaded sheep ranches south of Fossil, were Edward R. "Ned" Hickson (circa 1853–1935), who at various times was treasurer of Moro and a Sherman County deputy sheriff; and his buddy, Maurice "Mossy" Fitzmaurice (1854–1936), a "big, blustery Irishman" who bought the *Condon Times* in 1908, and for 12 years served as mayor of that small, isolated town, and who also owned several hotels around the state.[24] Both men had brought their sheepherding expertise from Ireland, and arrived in the remote, sparsely settled high plains above the John Day River. Said the *Morning Oregonian* (January 7, 1922), "Mr. Fitzmaurice, like many another successful citizens in that section, went there years ago with a pack on his back and herded sheep for a time. Some of these pack-burdened newcomers developed into sheep kings, but Mr. Fitzmaurice preferred the newspaper business."

In 1902, if not earlier, the two adventurous anglers, according to the *Morning Oregonian* (September 10, 1903), using flies of their own making, "exploded the idea that the steelhead at least will not rise to a fly," and in so doing quietly pioneered what would become, by the 1960s or 70s, Oregon's most popular summer-run steelhead fishery. But in those early days, even after the railroads provided ready access to the canyon, the aforementioned John Gill realized, "We have much to learn about the fishing on Deschutes, but no river in the state looks more promising."[25]

General Money No. 1 and No. 2 (recipes on page 248)

The wild wonders of British Columbia—the superb fishing, abundant game, sylvan forests, tempestuous coastline, majestic snowcapped ramparts—must have been too glorious to resist, too tempting, for a 50-year-old English sophisticate who had served his country and pursued his passion for angling and shooting across the globe. Noel Money, injured in the Second Boer War (1899–1902) and then decorated with both the King's and Queen's Medals, first visited the Campbell River in 1913. A year later, having sold his estate in Herefordshire in the west of England, he returned to British Columbia with his wife and two children, purchased land, and began construction of Qualicum Inn. World War I interrupted his plans, as he reenlisted to serve England in the Middle East, where he attained the rank of brigadier general; but upon the conclusion of that conflagration, he returned to his beloved Vancouver Island.

General Money had followed in the footsteps of his father; Captain A. W. Money, family patriarch and expert in guns and shooting, had first ventured to America in the 1880s, and in 1890 moved to Oakland, New Jersey, with his family to help set up the E. C. Schultz Powder Company. The eldest of his two sons, Lieutenant Noel Money, Imperial Yeomanry, then retired his commission to join his father in the United States as secretary of the firm, which sold out to DuPont in 1903. Captain Money returned to England, though he had been greatly admired and was sincerely missed by shooting enthusiasts on the East Coast. While the captain's youngest son Harold sought his fortune in the rubber business in Ceylon, Noel bought the home in Herefordshire, where he enjoyed plentiful shooting. But one trip to fish for Tyhee salmon convinced him to move halfway around the globe, to the comparative wilds of coastal British Columbia.

There, on the Stamp and Ash Rivers and other waters, the well-traveled outdoorsman would decide that the summer-run steelhead, as a sport fish, was superior even to the long-regaled Atlantic salmon. In 1939, Noel wrote to author Harold Smedley, who was assembling his book, *Fly Patterns and Their Origins*, saying, "In some of the big rivers on our West Coast, we have a run of these big trout starting in May and going on to October. This fly fishing, I consider the best in Canada, except for Atlantic salmon in the East, but our steelheads are better fish than salmon—much more lively and jump more."

With his Atlantic salmon pedigree firmly in pocket, it's no wonder that Noel Money—whom Roderick Haig-Brown in *The Western Angler* called "the finest and most experienced fly fisherman in British Columbia"—developed some of the prettiest flies yet designed specifically for steelhead; the best-known of his patterns are his General Money No. 1 and General Money No. 2, though several other of his patterns enjoyed popularity in Canada well through the twentieth century.

Money's Prawn Fly, the simplest of his patterns, was a standard British Columbia fly for those few anglers who began pursuing winter steelhead on flies in Money's time; Money was a pioneer in fly angling for winter-run fish and began doing so at about the same time Ken and George McLeod were learning to catch winter fish in Washington in the 1930s. Money's Golden Red, dating to the 1920s, is nearly contemporaneous with the similar Golden Demon (Money had fished Oregon's Rogue River in the 1920s, but whether that has any connection to the similarity of the two flies is unknown). It is among Money's most alluring patterns and is dressed as follows: Tip, silver oval tinsel (fine); tag, yellow silk; tail, a topping with red hackle fibers over; body, gold oval tinsel; hackle, hot orange; wing, bronze mallard and a topping.[26]

Golden Demon (recipes on pages 248–249)

"What are more delightful than one's emotions when approaching a trout stream for the initial cast?" asked the incomparable Nash Buckingham. Those emotions must have run deep for Zane Grey (1872–1939) when he first visited the Rogue River in southern Oregon in 1919. He was enthralled, and having already amassed a fortune from his prolific writing and moved into a Southern California mansion, he embarked on annual expeditions to Oregon to fish his beloved Rogue for fall steelhead. He built his now-famous fishing cabin at Winkle Bar (at the time, a remote part of the river). His writings championed steelhead angling in the West and on the Rogue, and eventually he found the Rogue growing too crowded for his tastes, so he moved to the North Umpqua. His exploits there became fodder for intrigue, legend, and even scandal. His novels, many of them adapted to Hollywood movies, sold spectacularly, the best known of them being his wildly successful *Riders of the Purple Sage*, which, owing to Grey's formulaic, aureate style, garnered him the unflattering nickname "writer of the purple prose" from critics.

Having earned the means by which to travel the world in search of gamefish, Grey discovered the angling riches of New Zealand in the mid-1920s, and visited often, occupying a base of operations at Otehei Bay Lodge on Urupukapuka Island. From New Zealand waters, Grey boated numerous world-record fish. And somewhere herein begins the story of the Golden Demon, though the tale is really one of prologue and epilogue and little in between. Grey discovered the Golden Demon in New Zealand, and sent samples to Joe Wharton, well-known tackle retailer in Grants Pass. The fly's originator remains unknown, but as a steelhead fly, it quickly became popular on the Rogue and beyond.

Portland's Bunnell sisters were perhaps the first to dress the fly commercially. Irene and Ardath Bunnell started a professional fly-tying company in Portland in the early 1920s, following in the footsteps of San Franciscan Martha Benn, the first female commercial fly tier on the West Coast. The July 27, 1947, edition of the *Sunday Oregonian* carried a story about the Bunnell sisters, and Ardath recalled, "It was in 1923 that we made our first Golden Demon. It was copied from a sample received by Joe Warden [Wharton], the 'father of Rogue River fishing,' from the late sportsman-author, Zane Grey, who was in New Zealand on a fishing trip. So far as I know, I believe my sister Irene and I were the first to produce this beauty in the United States."

To this day, if you know whom to ask in the Rogue Valley and beyond, you can find examples of 1930s-era Golden Demons that local tiers dressed for steelhead; sometimes the vintage examples have wings of bronze mallard, likely emulating the originals. But as steelhead anglers were keen to use more durable hair rather than feather in the wings of their flies, the typical Golden Demon soon sprouted wings of bucktail at the behest of Grey himself. In an article titled "North Umpqua Steelhead" in the September, 1935 issue of *Sports Afield*, Grey recalled, "I had Wharton make a pattern after the New Zealand Gold Demon, adding hair and jungle cock."

Naturally, the Golden Demon spawned myriad progeny, the first of which was the Silver Demon, the brainchild of C. Jim Pray, who was also largely responsible for spreading the fame of the Golden Demon. Soon came the Black Demon and eventually even a Copper Demon. They are lovely patterns, all of them, and when artistically rendered, the tinsel bodies lacquered for durability in the style of old, they remain among my favorite fishing flies.

Golden Edge Orange (recipe on page 249)

The astute, widely admired Washington steelhead angler, Harry Lemire (1932–2012), continued to expand his fly-tying repertoire until his final days. By then, the grand old master was routinely confounding awestruck audiences with his ability to dress exquisite full-dress Atlantic salmon flies of the Victorian era in hand, without need of a vise.

So too, his legendary casting ability never waned, and in a heartfelt obituary penned for *Northwest Fly Fishing* (November/December 2012), Oregon-based Don Roberts recalled that ". . . to see it in person was something else. It's hard to describe such deft economy of movement, his casting stroke seemingly effortless, both sinuous and serene, as the line soared on a long glide path over the water. Taken together with his extemporaneous fly-tying skills—look, Ma, only hands—it was enough to give one an inferiority complex. But competition and frail egos (mine) didn't count. Lemire wasn't built that way. His quests were personal. Quiet. Unassuming. Inward."

As early as the mid-1990s, Harry had expressed to me, in person, that he was bothered by recent trends in steelhead fly fishing. By then, the gentle art had been corrupted by strike indicators, flies without soul, and anglers obsessed with body counts: the number of fish landed trumped the manner in which they were taken. Harry said as much to others over the next two decades, as Roberts wrote:

As gentle as Lemire was, he was not without a hard-edged opinion or two. While on his last fishing trip with guide Dean Finnerty on an Oregon coastal stream, Lemire remarked that over the years, fly fishing had become "diluted." So-called improvements in tackle, equipment, and flies had "diluted our sport," Lemire insisted. Strike indicators, weighted Glo-Bugs, and the like had turned fly fishing into "drift fishing with a fly rod." Finnerty duly noted that this was "troubling to fly fishermen like Harry."

As well it should have been, for Harry had followed in the footsteps of the legendary North Fork Stilly anglers, the men who had, beginning in the late 1920s, deciphered the summer-run fish, and then the winter steelhead, of the rivers north of Seattle. Among those fishermen were a few who elevated steelhead fly tying to newfound artistry: Wes Drain, Ralph Wahl, and Walt Johnson. Lemire embraced the mantra that steelhead deserve beautiful flies; in fact, he came to embody that edict. His Golden Edge Orange ranks among his prettiest flies. He tied an equally alluring companion pattern called the Golden Edge Yellow, which is identical except for a body of bright yellow silk floss.

Golden Girl (recipe on page 249)

The preeminent British Columbia fly-angling historian, Arthur Lingren, produced two editions of *Fly Patterns of British Columbia*, one of several titles he has released through Frank Amato Publications. The original edition found a waiting audience in 1996, and then in 2008, Lingren again demonstrated his grasp of historical research methodology in an expanded edition timed to coincide with the hundredth anniversary of the birth of Roderick Haig-Brown, the pioneering, British-born angler who fell in love with the waters of British Columbia and penned some of fly angling's most poignant and powerful words. Lingren's expanded volume was subtitled *The Roderick Haig-Brown Centenary Edition* and it is replete with captivating details about Haig-Brown and other prominent fly designers of British Columbia.

Of the Golden Girl, Lingren informs the reader that Haig-Brown devised this fly chiefly for winter steelhead; he wanted a simple fly dressed in shades of red and orange that would bear some resemblance to the ornate featherwing Atlantic salmon flies he knew so well from his British upbringing. "The pattern Haig-Brown developed," explains Lingren, "was a combination of the slim-bodied Red Sandy and the golden pheasant tippet-winged Durham Ranger without many of the frills."

Lingren notes that the original dressing had a tail made from the small red feather of the Indian fruit crow (a South American bird of the Cotinga family), but that eventually Haig-Brown opted instead for a golden pheasant crest feather (a "topping," to use the Atlantic salmon parlance) for the tail. Indeed, the topping-tailed version is the familiar pattern, though the fly looks nothing short of riveting when the golden pheasant crest tail is itself topped with a layer of fruit crow feathers or substitutes, such as small scarlet-dyed hen neck feathers or likewise dyed golden pheasant throat feathers. In later versions, Haig-Brown also included a tag of orange silk, which is made all the more lustrous if underlain and tipped with flat tinsel. As evidence to that variation, Walt Johnson (in the 1990s) supplied me with copies of steelhead fly recipes submitted to the Washington Fly Fishing Club in the 1950s and 60s, including a page of patterns submitted by Haig-Brown.

For the Golden Girl, Haig-Brown specifies a tag of orange silk, and says of the fly, "This is primarily a winter steelhead fly. Have also taken cutthroats and summer steelhead on it in sizes down to No. 8." The other flies he included are the Quinsam Hackle, Silver Brown, and Stickle-Back.

Gray Hackle Yellow (recipe on page 249)

The simple Hackle flies, as well as the somewhat related Palmer flies, date back to the earliest days of fly fishing in Great Britain, and while their original form was corrupted over time, they remained popular well into the twentieth century. Even today among trout fishers, we find the occasional adherent to derivations such as the Gray Hackle Peacock. Perhaps the earliest description of Hackle flies appears in *The Angler's Guide: Being a Complete Practical Treatise on Angling*, 1815, wherein author Thomas Frederick Salter explains, "Artificial flies are called dub flies when the body is principally made of wool or mohair, when chiefly made of feathers they are called hackle flies." Further, Salter says, "Hackle-flies, artificial flies, whose bodies are slender and chiefly made of the hackle-feather. If they have not wings they are palmers, if with wings, they are generally called palmer-hackles."

Hackle flies were dressed in as many color combinations as possible when spiraling a hackle over a thin body, and by 1905, Francis Henry Buzzacott listed 21 different Hackles in his *The Complete Camper's Manual*. Among the popular versions in North America were the Gray Hackle Yellow and the aforementioned Gray Hackle Peacock, both of which Ray Bergman included in *Trout*, saying, "Although this fly is very old, it is a good basic design with either peacock herl, yellow floss silk, or fluorescent body. This last, a recently developed material, is brighter than silk. The tie is simple. It consists of only the body and hackle, which is grizzle or grizzly, also called barred or Plymouth Rock."

In California, Oregon, and Washington, the Gray Hackle Yellow was an early favorite for trout, so naturally it followed the path of other famous trout flies, such as the Parmachene Belle and Royal Coachman, and became a favorite for steelhead, particularly on the Eel, Klamath, and Rogue Rivers, where anglers began adding a wing of brown bucktail in the first half of the twentieth century.

Grease Liner (recipe on page 249)

I always relished my conversations with the late Harry Lemire, and I envied those members of the Northwest Atlantic Salmon Fly Guild in Seattle, of which Harry was a member, who enjoyed more frequent opportunity to see the great steelheader. But long before that club formed, I was fortunate enough to receive a few of Harry's steelhead dry flies in the mail; I carried on a correspondence with him and mentioned that his Grease Liner was the dry fly that first ignited my interest in using skated flies for steelhead on the Oregon waters I frequented. I wasn't alone: many steelhead enthusiasts owe Harry a tip of the cap for the same reason.

As his friend Rocky Hammond wrote in a posthumous homage to the Washington-based Lemire in *Northwest Fly Fishing* (January/February 2013), "Here was a man who developed the first steelhead dry fly specifically designed to be waked, the Grease Liner. That was in 1962 and today it is still a standard and a model on which many floating patterns are based. Lemire continued to develop numerous steelhead patterns, such as the Thompson River Caddis and others that most of us carry in our fly boxes."

Like most waking/skating flies, the Grease Liner is effective in broken water, but I prefer dry flies for use on glass-smooth surfaces because the experience is so visual; perhaps nothing in steelhead angling can trump the excitement of witnessing a fish attacking a waking fly on the surface of a mirror-flat tail-out. Such assaults can take many forms, from a subtle troutlike sip to a toilet-flush whirlpool to a cannonball splash. Steelhead are never without intrigue and at times become entirely nerve-wracking. I'll not forget the North Umpqua fish that attacked a skated fly seven times on a single swing without ever hooking itself—after that incident I had to sit down on a boulder to calm my frayed psyche.

Green-Butt Black (recipe on page 249)

Art Lingren is the expert chronicler of British Columbia fly-angling history and in fact has spent many years serving as the official historian for the British Columbia Federation of Fly Fishers. The province's fly-angling legacy could hardly be entrusted to more capable hands: Lingren's research is thorough, his methodology sound. His writings reflect his diligence and his passion, perhaps nowhere more evidently than in his beautiful and detailed 2008 *Fly Patterns of British Columbia, The Roderick Haig-Brown Centenary Edition*. Lesser known, especially south of the Canadian border, are Lingren's elegant steelhead flies. It was he, in 1984, who first rendered the famous British-born General Practitioner, originally designed for Atlantic salmon, in all black. Black General Practitioners garnered near-instantaneous acceptance on the steelhead coast and, were soon followed by Purple General Practitioners ("GPs").

And while Lingren's color variation on an Atlantic salmon fly may be the best known of his flies, many steelhead fly fishers who love fishing GPs don't realize who invented the black version or that Lingren's Black GP helped spur the popularity of the original Esmund Drury General Practitioner throughout the realm of steelhead some 20 years after Bob Taylor had first introduced the original GP to the American West.

But Lingren's original patterns conceived exclusively for steelhead earned a place in the arsenal of many British Columbian fly anglers in the 1980s. Of the various steelhead flies he has designed, the As Specified series and his unassuming Black Spey may have enjoyed the most widespread use, but my own favorite is his Green-Butt Black. Lingren actually dresses two versions of the "Black," one without the green butt, and one with it, and he admits, "I find no difference as to whether the fluorescent green butt is there or not; both flies work equally well."

Green-Butt Skunk (recipe on page 249)

There is nothing easy about photographing the North Umpqua in all its seasons—its tepid summers, vibrant autumns, sodden winters. Plunging steeply westward off the Cascade Mountains, the river slices through a rugged, sylvan gorge, where forested steeps rise precipitously from the shadowy banks. A nemesis to photography, the high ridges block the sun, especially as the North Umpqua enters its showiest season, October, which paints riparian bigleaf maple in yellow and understory vine maple in flame, and even more so when winter and early spring arrive, draping many runs and pools in daylong shade. To photograph this river well, one must know it intimately, know when the sun will peek through where, and know where the leaves first turn and where anglers will occupy photogenic pools—and most of them are—at the right times.

Dan Callaghan (1931–2006), a native Oregonian and Salem-based attorney, was the acknowledged master of capturing this scenic river on film; he knew its every twist and turn, and understood its every mood. The North Umpqua was his home river, no matter that he lived three hours away; he and his wife, Mary Kay, frequented the river all the way back to the founding days of the Steamboaters club (1966), of which he was an original member. In his later years, Dan could often be found driving his distinctive van with vanity plate CABIN 1 (referring to his usual accommodation at Steamboat Inn), and the last time I saw him on the river, he was standing on an embankment above his van, camera mounted on a tripod, waiting for that perfect moment when the setting sun sent a shaft of light onto a glassy tailout reflecting golden maples. I left him to his work because I had precious few casts remaining before nightfall enveloped the North Umpqua, but in retrospect I wish I had stopped and chatted, for Dan, who was a regular at McNeese's Fly Shop, was always amiable, inquisitive, informative, and sincere.

Many of Dan's fabulous images of the North Umpqua are preserved in a limited-edition coffee-table-quality book titled, appropriately, *Dan Callaghan's North Umpqua* (2008), and his photographs appeared in numerous magazines. Yet his most enduring legacy may yet prove to be his modification of the Skunk: he added a bright green butt to the fly and the Green-Butt Skunk was born. Subsequently it garnered immense popularity throughout the Northwest, reaching the kind of rare longstanding acclaim enjoyed by such iconic flies as the Purple Peril, Thor, and Skykomish Sunrise.

Headrick's Killer (Killer) (recipe on page 250)

Lifelong Washingtonian Frank Headrick (1908–2011), designer of this lovely pattern, was among the cadre of anglers who, beginning in the early 1940s, became so enamored of the wonderful fishing for summer-run steelhead on the North Fork of the Stillaguamish River that they purchased cabins on the river, most of them at the famous Elbow Hole downstream from Deer Creek and the Oso General Store. Headrick's cabin was flanked on the west by Walt Johnson's place—Walt told me he had been the first to buy a summer cabin on the river, while Ken McLeod had been the first to buy property there—and on the east by Enos Bradner's cabin. Bradner, on his way to regional renown for his outdoor writing in the *Seattle Times*, would become longtime fishing partner to Headrick, and together the two would begin chasing rumors of outstanding fall steelheading on the tributaries of the Upper Columbia—and they would substantiate those rumors, too.

Says Trey Combs, in *Steelhead Fly Fishing*, "The little colony on the North Fork of the Stillaguamish marks the birthplace of steelhead fly fishing in Washington . . ." and while there were certainly furtive, and later dedicated efforts at fly angling for steelhead prior to this time, it would be this group of anglers, converging in one place, that would form the wellspring for nearly all of the state's inroads and ingenuities into this genre of angling. To overstate the profound influence of the North Fork Stilly gang—Johnson, Headrick, Bradner, Wahl, Hosie, McLeod, Knudson, and the others—is impossible. These pioneering anglers, through discourse, discussion, debate, and determination, forged much of the steelhead fly-fishing methodology and the steelheading culture we embrace today.

Francis "Frank" Headrick outlived all his old steelheading friends; he finally succumbed to old age at almost 102 years in 2011. He was a 70-year member of the Washington Fly Fishing Club (WFFC), and upon his death (no services were held at his request), the family asked that remembrances be sent to the WFFC Foundation, P. O. Box 639, Mercer Island, WA 98040, and donations sent to Project Healing Waters Fly Fishing.

Hellcat (Headrick's Hellcat) (recipe on page 250)

Frank Headrick's Hellcat, created by the prominent Washington angler in the early 1950s, earned a permanent spot in my Wheatley fly box one regal autumn evening.

As the years passed and my seasons on the local river accumulated, I increasingly limited my fishing to the conditions I liked best. I quit fighting the high water and troublesome wading of early summer where once I had eagerly gone astream when the first rush of summer fish arrived in late May. I also quit fighting the crowds of summer evenings, light though they were, and shifted most of my fishing to weekday mornings, when only rarely would I encounter another fly angler. Though for many seasons I had sought to expand my knowledge of the river, after a while I realized fewer than a half dozen of the myriad pools and runs I fished were truly my favorites.

I found myself in a comfortable pattern: I would leave home just before dawn on weekdays between late June and early September and fish two, sometimes three pools, and then be back at my desk before 10 a.m. The fishing could persist through September, but each year, around the 10th, the dam on the upper river began spilling water, thereby spoiling the best sport—from my perspective.

One early September day, I was reading a letter from Walt Johnson wherein he discussed flies prominent in the 1940s and 50s. One was the Hellcat. I'd never tied one. I opted to heed Walt's opinion and dressed a pair of Hellcats that night, eager to swim them at the first opportunity, which proved to be the next evening when I broke my usual morning routine and headed for a favorite pool.

The sun, dipping low, pleasantly warmed my face; a zephyr fluttered the yellowing maple leaves; each cast boomed out satisfyingly over the glassy currents. And on what I had determined to be the final swing at the lowermost extent of the fishable water—the final swing of my summer season—the fly came around and suddenly stopped in that familiar interlude before a weighty steelhead exerts its might and the battle begins.

I landed a gorgeous buck of 12 or 13 pounds, a wash of crimson on his gill plates. I admired him briefly, carefully removed the Hellcat, and slipped the fish back under the lustrous surface. Only then did I notice that a raft with four people had pulled over opposite and above me to watch the engagement; as if sensing the finality of my season, they remained silent and gave me my space to sit down on a moss-covered cobble and watch the evening envelop my river.

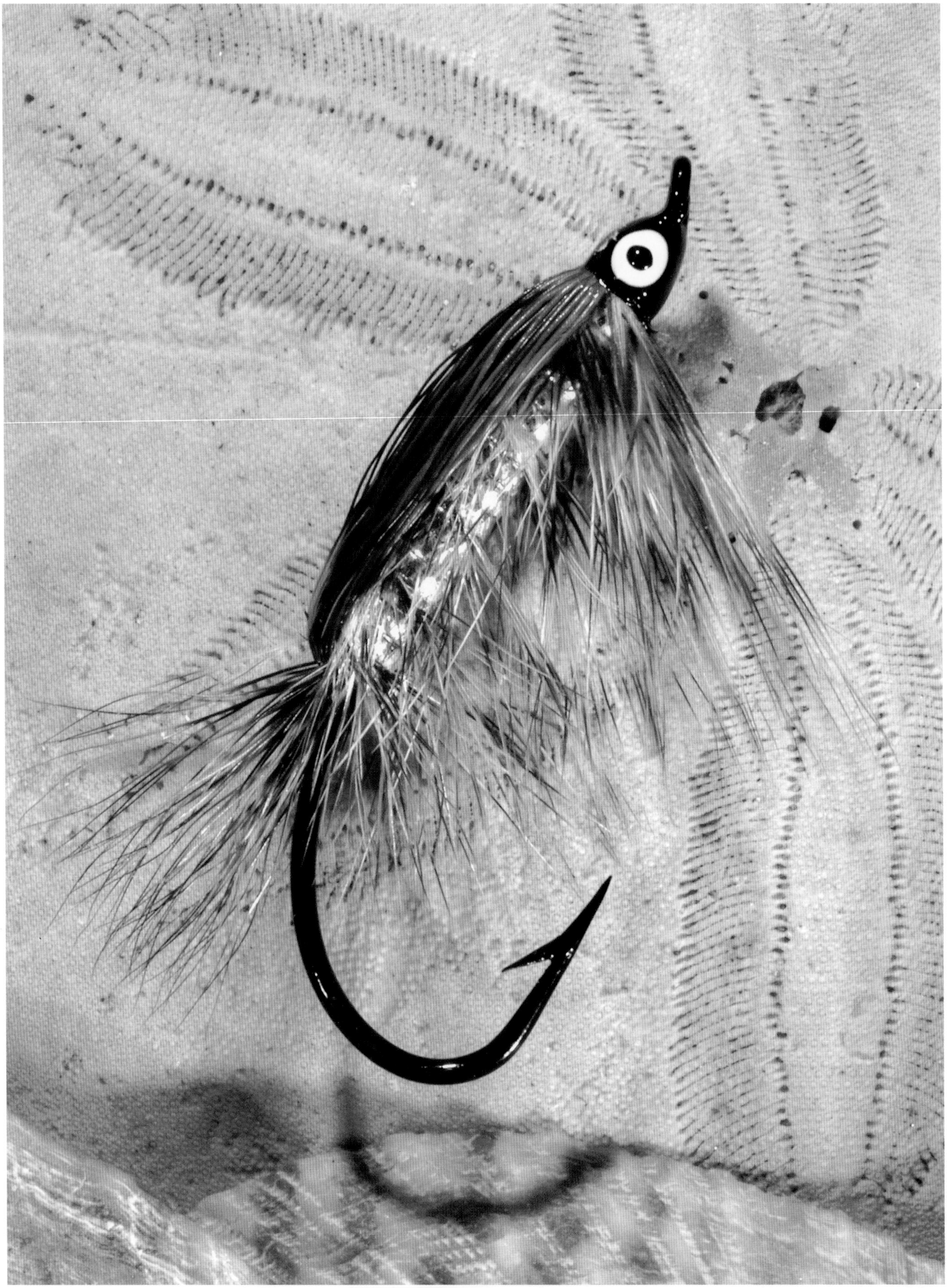

Horner's Silver Shrimp (recipe on page 250)

Sometime around 1990—I've forgotten exactly when—a lithe, bespectacled, ivory-haired old gentleman came into McNeese's Fly Shop in Salem, Oregon, for the first time. He was intelligent and inquisitive, a terrific storyteller and an astute listener; he was contemplative and analytical.

His name was Woody Sexton—the legendary tarpon guide from the Florida Keys—and he had decided to retire to western Oregon. He served as a fitness instructor in the US Navy during World War II, and then headed for California where he attended college, hung out with the likes of Bernie Henry (a respected gunsmith) and Jack LaLanne (the fitness guru), felled timber, and fished religiously. In the late 1950s, he and Jim Adams loaded gear into an aluminum boat and hauled it to the Florida Keys, where Woody carved a niche as a fly-fishing guide. The wonderful writer Jim Harrison reported in the early 1970s, "Sexton . . . is willing to chase tarpon upwind and uptide, and the amount of power he gets into the pole is appalling. The skiff leaves a wake . . . This requires the kind of physique and conditioning that leaves the joggers and exercise buffs hiding in any available closet . . . Sexton gives the impression of being hyperintelligent, cranky and totally physical."[27]

Woody spent his off seasons out West, and until 1966 annually employed himself cutting redwoods in Northern California, in the early days with a two-man jack-saw. When it comes to cutting giant redwoods with a two-man jack-saw, pansies need not apply; in fact, mere mortals need not apply. When I met Woody, he was in his 70s, and he habitually parked a half-mile from the shop, which he visited often, just so he could swiftly walk up the hill on High Street. During those off seasons, he also hunted chukars in Idaho and fly fished for steelhead in California and on Idaho's Clearwater. These two topics gave Woody and me ample conversational fodder. One weekday morning the subject was tidewater steelheading on the lower reaches of California rivers: being an old Humboldt County hand, he was well versed in this topic, and from Woody I learned much about the so-called shrimp patterns that had been popular in the mid-twentieth century. They were fished with active retrieves, often on sinking lines, Woody explained.

One of those flies, the prototype really, was Horner's Silver Shrimp, created by San Franciscan Jack Horner for the Eel River in 1938, and it spawned myriad variations. Horner was a widely traveled angler, but "is best remembered for his narrow escape on California's Smith River. In late December 1964, Jack Horner was in his truck-bed-camper along a gravel bar near the mouth of Rowdy Creek. He awoke in the middle of the night to a foot of water in his camper. Within a few hours he was forced to the roof of his truck. At day break he was spotted and rescued moments before his rig was washed down river, never to be found. The rains continued and when it was all said and done, it had become the Christmas Flood of 1964, California's most devastating flood on record" (from Horner's biography on the Rivers of the Lost Coast Website).

Woody was no stranger to the Smith, the Eel, and all the other great rivers—and angling characters—of the Lost Coast, and it was to his beloved Humboldt country that he quietly retreated when cancer began exacting its terrible toll on him. He passed away there in 2003.[28]

Hoyt's Killer (recipe on page 250)

The old Black Gnat wet fly found ample popularity as a trout fly in the American West even before the dawn of the twentieth century, and so unsurprisingly it found its way into the steelheader's arsenal. It benefitted from the eventual conversion to a bucktail rather than quill wing, rendering it the once-popular Black Gnat Bucktail.

But of course fly tiers are keen to tinker, and the Black Gnat Bucktail, like many other old flies, became a template for various steelhead patterns, among them Clyde Hoyt's Killer. Hoyt was a regular on the North Fork Stillaguamish, and his two flies—Hoyt's Killer and the Hoyt Special—enjoyed a measure of popularity. The Hoyt Special is Hoyt's Killer sans wing. Various sources differ on the wing material for Hoyt's Killer; Combs lists "natural brown deer body fur." Terry Hellekson says "Coastal blacktail deer hair." However, Walt Johnson once gave me a pattern recipe list assembled by Frank Headrick, and therein Headrick specifies "mule deer body hair."

Naturally, any steelhead fly that earned popularity, even in measured doses, was likely to find itself subjected to variation, and so it was with Hoyt's Killer: it functioned as the forerunner to the McLeod Ugly, a George McLeod pattern coined in 1962, which served its inventor faithfully on British Columbia's Kispiox and on his local steelhead streams in western Washington. Hoyt and Ken McLeod (George's father) roamed the Stilly together by the late 1930s and found consistent success on both summer- and winter-run steelhead. In those days, the Seattle sporting goods stores would place steelhead freshly caught by anglers out for their customers to view, and Hoyt regularly had his catches on display.

Ken McLeod and Hoyt were not entirely wedded to the fly for winter steelhead fishing, and on January 16, 1942, the *Seattle Times* reported that the duo accomplished quite a feat on the Skykomish when they both took limits of three fish: "They took them all in one hole. In the first five casts, the two anglers declare, Hoyt hooked five fish, landed two. Then McLeod stepped in and got his limit of three fish in four casts. After that, Hoyt stepped up to the plate again and finished out his limit."[29]

Improved Governor (recipe on page 250)

Perhaps the last in a long line of renovations to an old English trout fly called the Governor, the Improved Governor was once ranked alongside the Parmachene Belle, Benn's Martha, and California Coachman as one of the best steelhead flies for the Eel River. So said Al M. Cumming and Allan Dunn in *California Sportsman* (1911), a promotional publication produced by Southern Pacific Company.

By the time the original Governor found its way to the United States, it was subjected to substantial variation and the most famous version became the Governor Alvord, apparently devised by Thomas Gold Alvord (1810–1897), lieutenant governor of New York from 1865–66 and longtime assemblyman from that state. This version, too, was further modified, and Terry Hellekson, in *Fish Flies: The Encyclopedia of the Fly Tier's Art*, credits the steelhead version to Martha Benn, the skilled fly-tying daughter of famed San Francisco fly maker John S. Benn. Hellekson says Martha Benn created the Improved Governor in 1915, but the fly was already in general use on the Eel by that time, according to the above-mentioned *California for the Sportsman* (1911) article.

Later, probably in the 1930s, famous fly dresser C. Jim Pray replaced the feather wing with bucktail (Martha Benn had first used bronze mallard as the wing). Such was the typical fate of featherwing steelhead flies after early steelheaders discovered that the sturdy hair wings were more durable in the face of rigorous currents, repeated long-distance casting, and in particular, toothy steelhead that tore up flies much more quickly than the diminutive brook trout of the East for which many American trout flies were invented.

Bucktail flies had already been introduced for trout on the West Coast by around 1910, if not earlier, and by 1912, Walter Backus, well-known angler and casting champion from Portland, had promoted them for Oregon waters. On the Middle Fork of the Willamette River, his bucktails met with success, and he wrote in the *Sunday Oregonian* (June 20, 1912), "That popular fly, the yellow bucktail proved to be the best killer . . . they all fell for that queer-looking fly with the deer hair wing."

Within a decade or so, steelhead anglers would begin not only converting standard featherwing flies to bucktails, but also creating new flies that specifically called for bucktail wings. With influential tiers and tackle dealers such as Jim Pray leading the way, bucktails would come to dominate the steelheader's fly wallet by the 1930s.

Juicy Bug (recipe on page 250)

In the late 1890s, E. McDonald Johnstone, in *Shasta: The Keystone of California Scenery*, observed, "Rogue River Valley seen from Table Rock is a perfect picture, a magnificent composition, where light and shade, relief and repose, the sublime and the pastoral, are beautifully blended. . . . Some day this valley will hold half a million people."

Happily that day has yet to arrive, and the view from atop the Lower and Upper Table Rocks on a clear early morning remains breathtaking, though earned at the price of fairly rigorous hiking. Save for more people and well-maintained Bureau of Land Management trails and trailhead facilities, little has changed at the two landmark promontories just north of the Rogue River since Johnstone's visit. By then, with the Rogue Indian Wars more than 40 years past and the Rogue Valley burgeoning with agrarian industry, these verdant lands had been tamed. (For an overview of the conflicts between white settlers and Native Americans in the Rogue River country, see *The Rogue River Indian War and Its Aftermath, 1850–1980*, by E. A. Schwartz, 1997.)

The river itself, however, still coursed wild and free and was just then beginning to attract attention for its fabulous fishing. Into this angling wilderness—figuratively—was born Isaac "Russ" Tower in 1885, son of Coos Bay pioneer Dr. Charles W. Tower.

The elder Tower had arrived in Empire City (the city of Coos Bay did not exist until 1944, when Empire and Marshfield merged by vote) in 1862 in such poor health that he had to be carried from the ship. Upon recovery, having learned his surgical skills as a surgeon in the Civil War (Massachusetts Volunteers), he graduated from Willamette University Medical Department (in Salem) and started his practice in 1870; he ran a drug store from 1874 until 1880, and founded the *Coos County Record* newspaper in Marshfield in 1874. Son Russ developed a penchant for outdoor pursuits, especially duck hunting, but also fishing. He first fished the Rogue in 1925, having cut his angling teeth on the forks of the Coquille and the streams draining into Coos Bay.

Like his father, Russ became an institution in the community: in 1909 he and his brother Jay opened The Gunnery, an auto supply and sporting goods store, and that same year, Russ broke ground on a new auto dealership for the Buick Line. In 1914, he opened Tower Motors, selling both Buicks and Fords, which in those days were shipped from Portland via steamer, primarily the famous *Breakwater*.[30] Tower Motors remained in Tower family hands for decades, and the business forges on to this day, more than a century after its founding—a remarkable story of community continuity. So too, the original Tower home, where Dr. Tower lived in the late 1860s and early 1870s, remains intact as a bed and breakfast and is listed on the National Register of Historic Places.

Today, most residents of Oregon's so-called Bay Area know little of the Tower family and its significance to the community, but the steelhead fly-angling fraternity has hardly forgotten Russ Tower's contributions in the form of his still-popular Rogue River fly patterns, including the Juicy Bug, co-created with Tower's friend and fishing partner, Ben Chandler, a Marshfield banker and an avid hunter and angler.[31]

Jungle Dragon (recipe on page 251)

In his *Seattle Times* outdoor column, Enos Bradner explained, "This pet pattern of Bill Hosie is perhaps typical of the flies that are being developed in the Northwest for migratory fish. It has the flash of silver, a bit of red, and the appeal of the jungle cock. It is more somber than the customary steelhead fly. It therefore works well in heavily fished waters as a change from the usual bright bucktail fly."

William Hosie, a federal labor conciliator by trade, was a member of the Washington Fly Fishing Club (WFFC), and during the 1950s, he directed the popular fly-fishing and fly-tying classes offered by members of the club at the Central YMCA in Seattle; Hosie himself taught the tying courses, and eventually passed that torch on to Roy Patrick, the founder of Patrick's Fly Shop. Meanwhile, he found ample time to pursue his passion of catching steelhead on flies, and once landed a truly giant summer steelhead on the North Fork of the Stillaguamish, where typical summer fish weighed 3 to 6 pounds, with 8-pounders fairly common. Hosie's behemoth, taken on the then-ubiquitous Orange Shrimp pattern in July, 1951, weighed 14 pounds and was the largest Stilly summer fish of the season. So remarkable was the catch that the *Seattle Times* (July 30, 1951) ran a photo of Hosie posing with his magnificent steelhead.

The aforementioned WFFC and the North Fork Stilly are inextricably linked: the club formed in 1939 when a rift developed between some of the fly anglers and gear anglers in the Steelhead Trout Club. Fly fishers such as Enos Bradner, Ken McLeod, Letcher Lambuth, and Dawn Holbrook had pressed the Washington state game commission to set aside a mile of the North Fork Stillaguamish as fly-only water in the mid-1930s, and the proposal was adopted. But after intense backlash from gear anglers, the new law was reversed. When fly anglers in the Steelhead Trout Club urged the membership at large to pressure the commission into again adopting fly-only status for this short stretch of the Stilly, they met substantial resistance from their fellow club members. Consequently, they split off and formed the new club, which remains active in steelhead conservation and management issues to this day.

There are two variations of the Jungle Dragon: the pattern given by Enos Bradner in his "Brad's Fly of the Week" column in the *Seattle Sunday Times*, August 19, 1959, differs from the recipe collected earlier by the Education Committee of the WFFC, and reconciliation seems impossible at this point. Both may be correct: Bradner knew Hosie well, but Hosie himself probably supplied the dressing to the club, so perhaps he modified his own pattern—hardly surprising where steelhead tiers are concerned. Walt Johnson, one of the original members of the Washington Fly Fishing Club, supplied me with copies of some of the original pattern listings that had been collected for the club's bulletin, and this is the source for the WFFC dressing of the Hosie Jungle Dragon listed in the Appendix.[32]

Kalama Special (recipe on page 251)

Every time you launch a single-hand cast 90 or 100 feet across a broad steelhead river, you can thank Maurice "Mooch" Abraham (1867–1936), the legendary Portland outdoorsman who invented the double haul. Born in southern Oregon to parents who achieved wealth in business and real estate, Abraham developed a keen interest in hunting and fishing at an early age. He moved to Portland around 1880 and worked for clothier Fleischner–Mayer. When his father died in 1901, Maurice—who had garnered the nickname "Mooch" in his childhood—inherited an estate worth $150,000. Not long after, he married Madge Carlon, herself an outdoorswoman, and, as Jack W. Berryman wrote, "During the first decade of the twentieth century, Mooch and Madge were one of the most stunning outdoor-oriented couples in the greater Portland area."[33]

Flush with his inherited wealth and embarking on a new business venture selling carpeting and furniture with his sister's husband, J. G. Mack, Abraham took full advantage of the region's outstanding fishing and hunting. He accumulated ". . . more guns in his rack than any other sportsman in the city . . ." and both taught and competed at shooting. He accomplished a remarkable feat in 1907: hunting the Columbia at Deer Island, using .20- and .28-gauge double-barrel shotguns, Abraham killed 50 ducks with 50 shells, killing each bird that came, rather than selecting his shots by passing on difficult marks (*Morning Oregonian*, November 27, 1907).

Their financial fortunes faltered, however: Abraham and his brother-in-law had formed J. G. Mack, but by 1917, the company was in trouble, and when it failed, it took most of their accumulated wealth with it. Already closely associated with the various sporting goods stores in Portland—including Backus & Morris—Abraham started a fly-tying business to earn income. By then he had already engaged in competitive fly casting at a new casting grounds at the east end of the Hawthorne Bridge. Abraham and Backus helped found Portland's first fly-casting club, and by the 1920s, Mooch was mentoring many of the city's fly anglers.

Famously, he coached Marvin Hedge to a trout distance-casting championship in 1934: with Mooch's double-haul technique Hedge broke the previous record by nearly 25 feet and awed the crowd in St. Louis. So too, Abraham would prove a vital influence on iconic Oregon steelheader Mike Kennedy. Abraham may have pioneered steelhead fly fishing on the Kalama River,[34] but it was Kennedy who converted Mooch's favorite sea-run cutthroat fly into a steelhead fly and used it to such effect on the Kalama that it became mistakenly known as the Kennedy Special.[35]

Kispiox Special (recipe on page 251)

Karl Mausser's 33-pound world-record steelhead from British Columbia's Kispiox River, caught in 1962 on a Kispiox Special, was—fittingly—landed on a leader tied for him the night before by George Mcleod, the pioneering Washington steelheader who, along with Enos Bradner and Ralph Wahl, opened the way for American fly fishers to seek the monster steelhead of this famous Skeena River tributary. The trio of McLeod, Wahl, and Bradner first ventured to the Kispiox in 1955, and on that highly successful adventure, McLeod broke the world record for fly-caught steelhead with a fish of more than 29 pounds; it fell to his Skykomish Sunrise, perhaps the single most iconic fly in the history of steelhead angling.

McLeod's massive steelhead eclipsed the previous record, a 28-pound fish from Oregon's Deschutes River (though likely a Clearwater River, Idaho, fish, as most of the truly monstrous steelhead taken in the Deschutes are temporary strays on their way back to their natal waters much farther up the Columbia and Snake River system). The record steelhead from the Deschutes had fallen, in 1946, to Nevada politician Morley Griswold (1890–1951), who had served a brief stint as governor of that state.

Griswold's record stood for nearly a decade before McLeod broke it with his leviathan from the Kispiox. The Kispiox and her sister Skeena tributaries would come to dominate the record books for giant fly-caught steelhead. Mausser had first ventured there from his home in Burlingame, California, in 1957, and he returned again in both 1960 and 1961. Those first three trips afforded rather meager results, but he was hardly dissuaded and the 1962 record steelhead fell to a fly he and fishing partner Roy Pitts had designed on his first trip to the famous river.

Knudson White Streamer and Knudson White Marabou (recipe on page 251)

An affable pioneering steelheader of remarkable skill and innovative vision, Al Knudson (1901–1980), did not name these flies the Knudson White Streamer and Knudson White Marabou; he humbly and simply called them White Streamer and White Marabou. His name was attached to the two patterns by later writers to preserve the lineage of these groundbreaking flies in a modern world with thousands of fly patterns. At least that's what I think each time I write about the two white giants of Knudson's litany of interesting and effective flies.

Best known for his days in Washington as one of the original members of the Elbow Hole colony on the North Fork of the Stillaguamish from 1943 through the 1950s, Knudson actually spent most of the 1930s living in southern Oregon. But he took his first fly-caught steelhead on the Stilly in 1927 and later that same year, his first winter steelhead on a fly from the South Fork Stilly. The latter feat was especially noteworthy at a time when local anglers scoffed at the idea of taking winter fish on fly tackle.

His huge white streamers patterns were equally noteworthy, predating by many decades the gargantuan flies that would supposedly revolutionize fly fishing for winter-run steelhead. Moreover, Knudson was the first to apply marabou to steelhead fly tying, and he explained that genesis to author Trey Combs, saying, ". . . one day while walking down the street [in Klamath Falls], I picked up a fluffy white feather that had blown in front of me. . . . I noticed it had a very lively wiggle and would make a very good streamer fly. . . . when I got home I sat down and tied up my first marabou streamer though this feather was really an ordinary white chicken feather."

That was the mid-1930s when Knudson first tied the new fly for trout, but he soon up-sized it for Rogue River steelhead; upon moving back to Washington and embracing winter steelhead angling there, Knudson began tying the streamer on huge hooks. His hackle-wing version is built from as many as five *pairs* of soft white neck hackles. The stems of these feathers are spread apart slightly at the tie-in point so they are partly tented, a trick that requires practice.

Lady Caroline (recipe on page 251)

Sprinkled among the many flies whose popularity with steelhead anglers has waxed and waned since the 1880s are a precious few with pure, unsullied British Isles pedigrees. Chief among them is the best-known of the old Spey flies, the Lady Caroline. The River Spey, gathering from the Monadhliath and Cairngorm ranges of the Scottish Highlands and meeting the North Sea at Moray Firth not far from Fochabers, after a 107-mile run, has long ranked among the most famous salmon rivers in the United Kingdom. Its rich angling history is replete with famous anglers enjoying (and paying handsomely for) prestigious opportunity to fish renowned pools on famous estates under the guidance of celebrated gillies.

Like all the famous Atlantic salmon rivers, the Spey generated its own salmon flies in the nineteenth century, but unlike most other rivers, the Spey also produced its own unique style of fly, and by the 1880s, any learned salmon angler understood the term "Spey fly." The style was defined by a unique method of applying a body hackle to otherwise rather plain and somber-colored flies: the hackle, taken from the rump of roosters often bred specifically for these plumes, was tied in by its butt end (or "root"), rather than by its tip, and spiraled over the body of the fly. It was then locked down with a rib. So too, the flies were thin of body, made from simple wool yarn or dubbing; wings were strips of brown mallard or turkey tail. A few of the old Spey flies, including the Lady Caroline, retained the basic body style and wings but used heron hackles rather than rooster hackles.

Originally popularized on the steelhead coast by transplanted Englishman Roderick Haig-Brown, the Lady Caroline takes its name from Lady Caroline Gordon-Lennox, daughter of Charles Gordon-Lennox, the 6th Duke of Richmond and Gordon. The Gordon-Lennox family had its Scottish home at Gordon Castle, Fochabers, and each autumn they journeyed there from England, with salmon fishing on the Spey being among the chief recreations. They hosted many famous guests, among them countless anglers, but the family members themselves enjoyed tutelage in salmon fishing from the learned Geordie Shanks, head gillie at the castle for nearly five decades. Lady Caroline herself, among Geordie's favorite charges, was an expert angler, and in fact, the vanguard of woman anglers on a river that would produce more well-known female salmon fishers than any other in those glorious days.

Lady Coachman (recipe on page 251)

The most prolific and popular steelhead fly of the opening decades of dedicated angling for the seagoing rainbow was the American offshoot of the Coachman, the Royal Coachman; the pattern spawned countless variations. One such fly in the Royal Coachman family was designed in bejeweled intricacy by Walt Johnson, the longtime guardian of Washington's North Fork Stillaguamish. Walt first tied this pattern in 1958, and for decades thereafter, he told me, it ranked among his favorites, particularly for dark, cloudy days and for the last light of evening.

Like his friends and contemporaries Wes Drain and Ralph Wahl, Walt wanted his flies to be functional but also artistically designed and rendered. Among them, from the 1940s through the 1960s, those three men produced several dozen gorgeous patterns. Most are little known, but a few earned lasting repute, and I think Walt's Lady Coachman is among the prettiest. Walt was an early proponent of fluorescent materials, such as those used in this pattern, and he explained to me in private correspondence, "Wes Drain was the person who first introduced fluorescent Gantron material to the fly anglers of our area. He initially received [this material] from Eugene Burns of San Francisco, and it was a product of the Firelure Corporation. This was the body material Wes used on his beautiful Drain's 20 pattern."

Firelure Corporation was based in Bakersfield, but its distribution center was in San Fransisco; Burns (a graduate of the University of Washington) was its president, with one of the partners John Gantner, who had used fluorescent dyes in clothing manufacture, hence the name Gantron for the fluorescent-dyed wools and flosses the company began marketing on the West Coast. Trey Combs, in *The Steelhead Trout*, confirms that Wes Drain was the first of the Washington tiers to enroll in the "Gantron Program" set up by Firelure. The Gantron fly-tying materials became especially popular with Walt and his contemporaries, the Stillaguamish River regulars.

With my own tying so profoundly influenced by my close association with David McNeese in the 1980s and 90s, I like to substitute cerise-dyed golden pheasant crest for the tail, which lends a graceful curve to this already-elegant dressing. Walt generally dressed this fly on light-wire hooks. He liked the Partridge Wilson, but in later years, also used the Alec Jackson Spey hook. His dressing, however, is easily adaptable, with a few minor changes in proportions, to heavier-wire hooks of all sorts.

Lady Godiva (recipe on page 252)

The year 1949 was a watershed time for steelhead fly fishing in Washington and throughout the realm of the great seagoing rainbow: in the winter of that season, fly anglers succeeded in the until-then unthinkable task of beaching three winter steelhead weighing more than 15 pounds.

Steelhead ascending the cold, swollen rivers of winter were no easy mark for fly casters for two reasons: first, as has always been the case, winter steelhead—whether by their nature or by virtue of cold water—are less aggressive than their summer-run brethren. And second, the fly lines, rods, and flies available to modern steelhead anglers were decades away from development at the time pioneering Washington anglers undertook their first furtive efforts at tackling winter steelhead in the 1920s, entering the realm that until then was the domain of gear anglers. Ken and George McLeod had no integrated sinking-tip heads to confront cold, swollen flows; Don Holbrook had not the advantage of 15-foot rods made from high-modulus graphite; Al Knudson could not open his fly box and select a contrivance rigged on a metal tube or an articulated hook and weighted with a big lead dumbbell or heavy metal cone. No, these stalwarts fished with cane rods and dressed the lines of the day with graphite to help them sink. As they experimented with winter steelhead, they modified their gear and their tactics, and soon, some of them—George McLeod chief among them—began developing new fly lines that would revolutionize not only steelhead angling, but also fly fishing in general.

But such advancements were in their infancy on January 1, 1949, when George McLeod bested a 17-pound 3-ounce Skykomish river brute on, appropriately, his Skykomish Sunrise. Then on January 29, Judge Ralph Olson set a new fly-rod record with an 18-pound 4-ounce Skagit River fish taken on his beautiful Lady Godiva pattern; that record lasted but a week, because Wes Drain then broke the 20-pound threshold by 7 ounces with a magnificent steelhead from the Skagit that took a new fly he would coin the Drain's 20 in celebration of the feat.

The Minnesota-born and sadly short-lived Olson (1902–1955), a popular judge in Bellingham who eventually earned appointment to the Washington Supreme Court, had been one of the early proponents of fly angling for winter-run steelhead—having caught the bug from his longtime friend and fishing partner, Ralph Wahl—and his smartly designed flies served him well for both winter and summer fish. Of the handful of patterns he developed, the Lady Godiva is his best known. Its companion was the Orange Wing, which Olson preferred on bright days, dressed as follows: Tag, silver embossed tinsel; tail, orange swan or goose; butt, orange chenille; body, yellow wool; rib, silver tinsel; wing, orange over white polar bear.

Sadly the lovely Lady Godiva has fallen into obscurity now, but the decades-old words of outdoor writer Enos Bradner deserve a willing audience today: "As the Judge has had such good luck with this fly on the Skagit, we hope some of the steelhead clan will try it on a few of the other good winter streams."[36, 37]

Lady Hamilton and Lord Hamilton (recipes on page 252)

Ralph Wahl (1906–1997) was an artist with a camera and with a fly-tying vise. His black-and-white photography spoke volumes, even when unaccompanied by words; his steelhead flies were captivating and innovative.

A native of Bellingham, Washington, Wahl owned and managed the J. B. Wahl department store (founded by his father) from 1937, when his father died, until his retirement in 1971. He developed an interest in photography while still a teenager, and during the 1940s his photos began to appear in magazines and other publications. Even the pages of *Sports Illustrated* once carried a Ralph Wahl photo; titled "Going Home," the photograph, in Paul O'Neil's story, "Excalibur: The Steelhead" (March 11, 1957), showed a fly angler trudging through snow dragging alongside him a very large steelhead.

On the nearby Skagit River, in 1936, Wahl took his first steelhead, and two years later beached his first winter steelhead, joining Ken and George McLeod and a handful of other winter steelhead fly-angling pioneers who in the mid-1930s proved that fly fishers could routinely take winter-run fish on the Skagit, Skykomish, and Stilliguamish Rivers. Wahl developed new patterns prolifically, and his Lord and Lady Hamilton are his best known. To help sink the flies for winter fishing, he built up underbodies of wool yarn on these flies and then coated them with Tester's Clear Dope; after layering on the floss body, he would then add another coating of Clear Dope, and yet another after adding the tinsel rib. (In his excellent book, *Tie Your Own Flies* [1966], Roy Patrick provided detailed instructions on how Wahl tied his Lady and Lord Hamilton.)

Wahl's photography would find a larger and increasingly appreciative audience when, in 1971, he released his first book, *Come Wade the River*, featuring excerpts from Roderick Haig-Brown's *A River Never Sleeps*. Then, in 1989, Wahl's *One Man's Steelhead Shangri-La* celebrated—in pictures and in prose—his decades of idyllic steelhead angling in a secret lagoon on the Skagit River, at the mouth of Day Creek. Intriguingly, Wahl was not the pioneering angler at the Shangri-La pool: Bob Dahlquist actually discovered the pool while duck hunting, and upon seeing fish swirling in the still water, he convinced fellow high school buddies George McLeod and Park Johnston to further explore the possibilities and the trio soon found they could strip-retrieve flies for sea-run cutthroat, Dolly Varden trout, and steelhead.[38]

Just a few years after Wahl died, his sons donated his entire collection of photographs, writings, and recordings to the Center for Pacific Northwest Studies at Western Washington University, where it remains "as a permanent remembrance of one of the Northwest's true pioneers in winter-run steelhead fly fishing and an artist who captured through his camera lens the thrill, beauty, and grandeur of being close to fish and rivers" ("Pioneers & Legends: Ralph E. Wahl [1906–1996]" by Jack W. Berryman in *Northwest Fly Fishing Magazine*, Summer 2004).

Max Canyon (recipe on page 252)

In 1976, fly-fishing-addicted school teacher Doug Stewart decided on a change of careers: he opened Stewart's Fly Shop in Portland, joining a small cadre of other entrepreneurial anglers who founded fly shops in western Oregon and southwest Washington at about the same time, largely by happenstance, between 1975 and 1977. These influential shops became institutions: The Greased Line Fly Shoppe (Mark Noble) near Vancouver, Kaufmann's Streamborn (Lance and Randall Kaufmann) in Tigard, McNeese's Fly Shop (Dave McNeese) in Salem, and The Caddis Fly Angling Shop (Bob and Kathy Guard) in Eugene. Stewart's, like all of those shops, would last more than three decades, and all contributed profoundly to the fly-angling culture of the Pacific Northwest.

Perhaps Doug Stewart's most enduring contribution is his fetching Max Canyon, a pattern he developed in 1970 for the Deschutes River, combining the basic color schemes of the Brad's Brat and the Skunk. The fly not only gained popularity on the Deschutes, but also set the trend for flies designed specifically for this famous river. It would provide the basic model for many variations sporting its characteristic two-tone body: a bright-colored butt section and a black or purple fore section. This style had long been popular throughout the Northwest, but Stewart's fly led to a brief resurgence in the development of color combinations. Among the many Deschutes flies of such description is Randall Kaufmann's Freight Train, which, like its progenitor the Max Canyon, derives its name from Deschutes River manmade and natural affectations, respectively.

Seeking our own variations among the legion, anglers like myself arrived at dark-winged versions of Stewart's fly, the first being Larry Piatt's Dark Max (mine was dubbed the Black Max). And Marty Sherman, one-time editor of *Flyfishing*, honored his friend with a lovely hair-wing fly simply called the Stewart, dressed as follows: Tag, gold flat tinsel; tail, golden pheasant tippet; body, black wool yarn ribbed with gold flat tinsel; hackle, black hen; wing, black hair with a topping of orange hair.

McGinty Bucktail (recipe on page 252)

The origins of the McGinty are opaque, and I'll leave it to other researchers to decipher the conflicting accounts of its genesis, but it seems to date to around the turn of the twentieth century. Obviously modeled after a bee, the McGinty quickly became a standard trout pattern and continued to enjoy the limelight for decades.

Eventually the spritely McGinty fell out of fashion. Or perhaps the influential Gary LaFontaine drove a stake into the heart of this cleverly designed, once-ubiquitous wet fly. The brilliant and articulate LaFontaine seems to have fallen victim, as many a scholar has, to confusing correlation with causation, and then to redoubling the problem with a dose of confirmation bias: he found a McGinty to be especially effective one day after a thunderstorm had passed, and deduced that trout only took bees after rainstorms. It seems thereafter he only fished the McGinty after rainstorms.[39]

LaFontaine reasoned that bees out gathering nectar sense an approaching summer storm and head back to the hive. Many of them don't make it and are caught by the storm, some of them being deposited on the water, where they become potential trout food. Taking up the question of bees as trout food after contemplating LaFontaine's theory, the astute Iowa-based fly-angling writer, Jene Hughes (1945–2014), remarked in his story "Bees: The McGinty and Its Progeny" (*Northwest Fly Fishing*, September/October 2013):

> That all may well be true. It probably is.
>
> But after reading LaFontaine's original account and of the origin of his theory about thunderstorms—which I had already heard repeated—I reacted with one of my more common responses to research and the ensuing speculation: "Huh! Really?"
>
> It makes sense that thunderstorms affect bee activity and behavior, but the notion that an unfortunate bee that, for whatever reason, takes a swim would routinely be shunned by trout seemed unlikely. Why would fish wait until bees are numerous? Bees don't appear in hatches any more than hoppers or crickets do.

Hughes went on to conduct his own research, and eventually concluded, "My casual experiment established, for me at least, two facts about bees and the McGinty. Fact number one: trout won't just eat bees, they'll hammer the hell out of them. While thunderstorms may increase the action, just as wind brings more hoppers into play, storms are by no means a prerequisite."

Steelhead anglers, of course, are unburdened by theories on the reasons trout eat particular foods, and like many turn-of-the-century trout wet flies, the McGinty soon found itself swimming the riffles of the Eel and Klamath and Rogue. Before 1910 it had found its way west as a trout fly, even if its acceptance was uneven; in 1921, the *Morning Oregonian* humorously remarked, "Personally we incline to a professor, or a blue upright, but have at least one friend so odd that he bespeaks the McGinty. In 12,000,000 trout doubtless there will be a fish as odd as he."[40]

By the 1930s, the McGinty was a steelhead standard, and by the time it reached the rugged, sylvan canyon of the Rogue, it often bore a wing of bucktail (or sometimes squirrel), and thereafter became the McGinty Bucktail (or Bucktail McGinty). At least two Portland newspapers mention the fly, including the *Morning Oregonian*, which ran a story with the quote: ". . . excellent catches [of steelhead on the Rogue] were made on Royal Coachman, either plain or bucktail, on Stone flies, McGinty and other flies that had plenty of yellow on the body" ("Angling Results Show Wide Range," November 1, 1935). Another mention of the fly is found in "Oregon's Angling Setup Hits New High for 1937," the *Oregonian*, July 16, 1937.

Interestingly, the McGinty's decline as a steelhead fly seems contemporaneous with its diminution in trout fishing. By the 1970s, it could scarcely be found in the fly wallets of steelhead anglers, and while I might posit explanations for its demise, I'd again risk confusing correlation with causation.

McLeod Ugly (recipe on page 252)

George McLeod caught his first steelhead before he was 10 years old—hardly surprising considering his father, Ken, was one of a small cadre of pioneering anglers who popularized fly fishing for steelhead in Washington. To be sure, anglers in Washington had been taking steelhead on flies prior to the 1920s when Ken McLeod (1898–1987) devoted himself to the pursuit, but such feats are poorly documented and scattered. The elder McLeod had little to go on—so new was the idea of fly fishing for steelhead in the rivers of northwest Washington that he simply had to figure things out on his own, which he did to eventual fanfare from fellow anglers in the area, and by the time Ken helped found the still-active Steelhead Trout Club in 1928, he was already regarded as one of the top steelhead anglers in the area.

Ken McLeod was not strictly wed to the fly, especially in his early days, but fly fishing for the grand gamefish would become his favorite method, a love he would instill in his son, George. So too, Ken did not tie flies, but his friend—local fly tier and competitive caster E. B. George, who had come to Seattle by way of California and Oregon—insisted on teaching young George the art of fly making. Before long, George agreed. Having brought the idea of using bucktail flies for steelhead with him from the south, E. B. George—no doubt almost inadvertently—launched the plethora of bucktail styles that would spring from the tying vices of many local fly dressers, and chief among them was the young George McLeod. He and his sister, Mary, tied flies commercially; when George headed off to Europe in World War II (where he flew 30 missions as a bomber pilot), Mary ran the business.

George McLeod is best known for his Skykomish Sunrise and Purple Peril—two quintessential steelhead flies—but on the Stillaguamish River and other streams, his McLeod Ugly enjoyed substantial popularity. Its progenitor was Clyde Hoyt's Killer; Hoyt had arrived at the idea of employing black flies on the North Fork of the Stillaguamish when the river was turbid, as explained by Enos Bradner in the *Sunday Seattle Times* ("Double the Fun of Fly Fishing," April 23, 1961). McLeod's son Ken James McCleod told me in 2013 that his father George dressed two versions of his pattern, one with black wings (the better-known of the two), and one with wings of natural gray deer hair or bucktail, called the McLeod Gray Ugly.

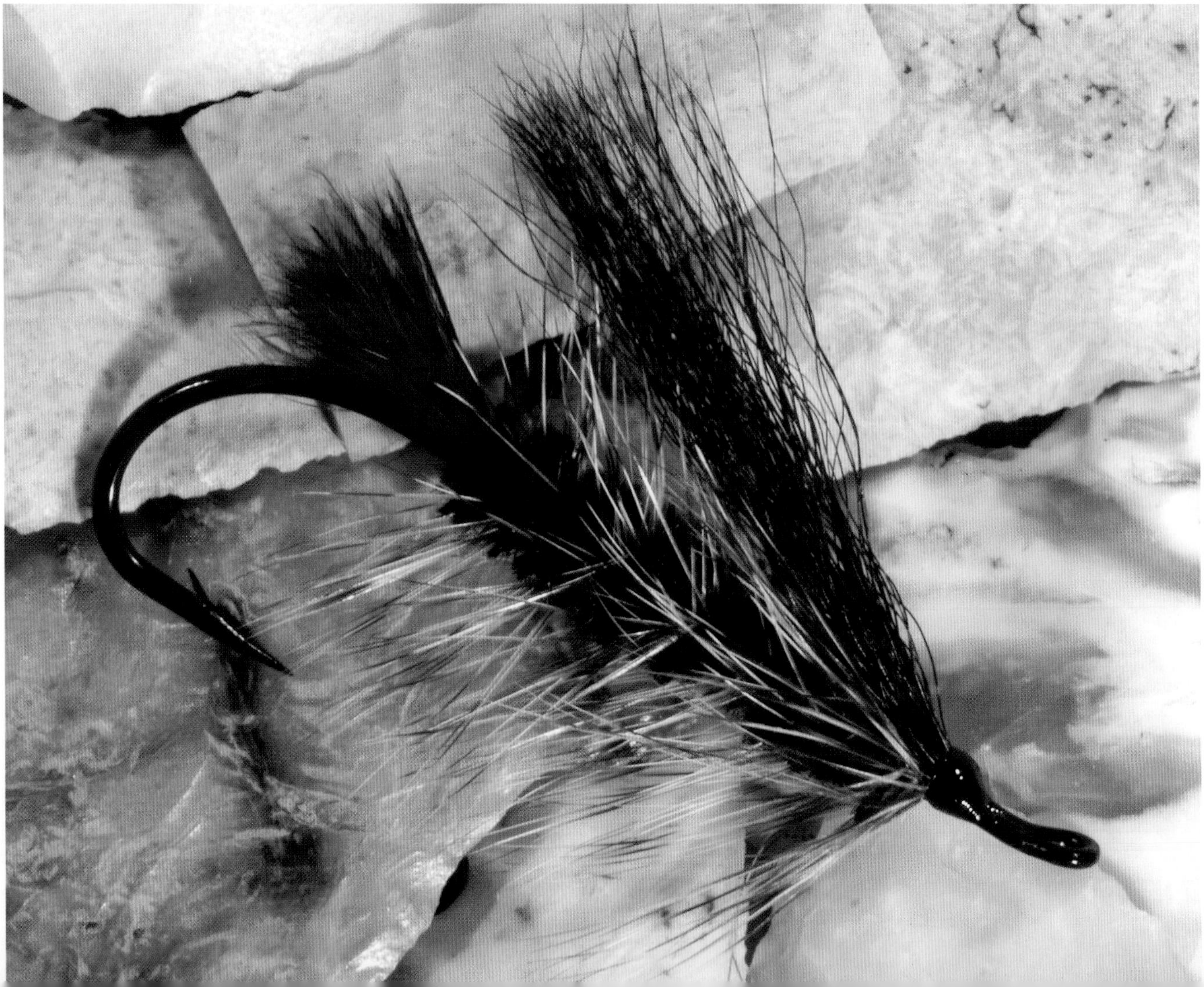

Migrant Orange (recipe on page 252)

Walt Johnson's fly dressing ability always amazed me; more so, his fly design concepts. His palette comprised a broad range of fly styles—hair wings, Spey types, featherwings, skaters, dead-drift dries, and others that defied ready classification. He was the archetypal example of the steelhead fly tier who considers functionality while adhering to the notion that the flies we fish for steelhead should represent the artistry inherent to the craft. His flies were intelligently conceived and expertly dressed. Each was an ornament, and fittingly, he often sent flies to his friends carefully packed in little jewelry boxes that had once held fine watches, bracelets, and necklaces; to each hook he would attach a tiny tag by string bearing the name of the pattern, written in Walt's hand.

Walt, in his humble manner, once said to me, "I have always attempted to create patterns that appeal to the fish as well as look respectable [to the angler]." He did so for dozens of original patterns, and his Migrant Orange, which enjoyed its first widespread public exposure in the color plates of Trey Combs's *Steelhead Fly Fishing and Flies* (1976), is among my favorites. Originally, he used fluorescent orange-dyed bucktail for the wing, but eventually he switched to acrylic hair of the same shade. In either case, he topped the wing with a strand of fluorescent red-orange wool yarn, and the resulting fly is one of his most striking. I have a pair of Migrant Oranges tied by Walt, and I also still have the little necklace box in which he sent them to me, along with three other of his original patterns, including his little-known Golden Spey. As usual, he attached tiny paper tags, tethered by string, to each fly, with the fly names written out. But on the outside of this particular box, he also wrote a short note, an equivoque: "John, set your feet!" He knew I'd be thrilled to open the lid to reveal the marvels inside; he also meant that if I were to fish any of these flies—and he hoped I would—I'd better set my feet firmly on the river bed and hold on tight.

Night Dancer and Patriot (recipes on pages 252 and 253)

Nearly fifty years have passed since Frank Amato Publications launched its first magazine, *Salmon-Trout-Steelheader*, the brainchild of Frank Amato himself. Eminently approachable; keenly articulate; gracious, urbane, and affable, Amato crafted his publishing house in part by being willing to listen to nearly any proposal. When I went to him in the late 1980s with an idea for a book that would encapsulate some of the offbeat Northwest fly-fishing pursuits I was undertaking—surfperch on the beaches and night-fishing the jetties for rockfish, for example—Frank was enthusiastic and receptive. The result was *Northwest Fly Fishing, Trout & Beyond*, which has been in print since 1991. Far more impressive however, are the Amato books that have become angling classics, especially Sheridan Anderson's *Curtis Creek Manifesto* (1978) and Trey Combs's *Steelhead Fly Fishing and Flies*.

Frank himself is a dedicated steelhead angler, and a champion for the fish and their habitat. For decades he has been a fixture on Oregon's Lower Deschutes River, and upon the river's swift runs and boulder-studded tailouts, he has perfected his own favorite patterns, the beautiful Night Dancer being perhaps the best known. Originally, Frank named this fly the Queenie, and under that name he introduced the fly to Combs on the Deschutes River. Combs, impressed by the lovely and productive fly, felt the name was hardly befitting, and queried Frank about it.

Recalling the conversation in *Steelhead Fly Fishing*, Combs says, "Months later as I was preparing my first trip to British Columbia's Sustut River, Frank sent me a small package that contained several examples of the Patriot, and a fly he called the Night Dancer, a pattern I recognized as the Queenie from our days together on the Deschutes. I liked the new name."

The companion fly to the Night Dancer is the Patriot, and Frank has spent many years deciphering which pattern he prefers to fish under varying conditions. I like to underlay the Patriot's yellow floss body with a layer of flat silver tinsel, starting at the front, winding the tinsel carefully rearward in edge-to-edge turns, forming a short tag, reversing directions, and wrapping the tinsel back to front. This silver underbody brightens the yellow body considerably when the fly is wet.

Nite Owl (recipe on page 252)

World War II seems to have inadvertently created the opportunity that led now-legendary Eureka tackle dealer Lloyd Silvius (see Brindle Bug, page 49) to turn his love of fly angling and fly tying into his business. He had come to California from Colorado with his family as a young child in 1907, and there he developed an affinity for fly fishing. He found work as a baker for the well-established Log Cabin Bakery in Eureka before finally opening his own establishment in 1938. But World War II brought heavy industry to Eureka when Chicago Bridge and Iron Company (CBI) was tasked with building floating dry docks for the Pacific Theater of Operations, and the town transformed almost overnight. CBI became the largest employer in the area and prompted Silvius and his wife, Leona, to seek employment with the company.

The economic boon was short-lived, spanning the duration of the war and not much beyond. So when employment at CBI came to an end, Silvius made a momentous decision to turn his passion for fly fishing and fly tying into his business, and he opened Lloyd Silvius Tackle Shop. By that time, Silvius had already invented many different flies, and one of his standards was the Nite Owl. Originally this pattern was coined the Silvius White Bucktail, and he created it around 1930, making it one the earliest bucktail steelhead patterns. Trey Combs, in fact, says that the "Nite Owl was the first popular hair wing steelhead fly where the more durable material is called for in the original," and his assertion on that count would be difficult to disprove, although one or two old Washington patterns might predate even the Nite Owl in this regard.[41]

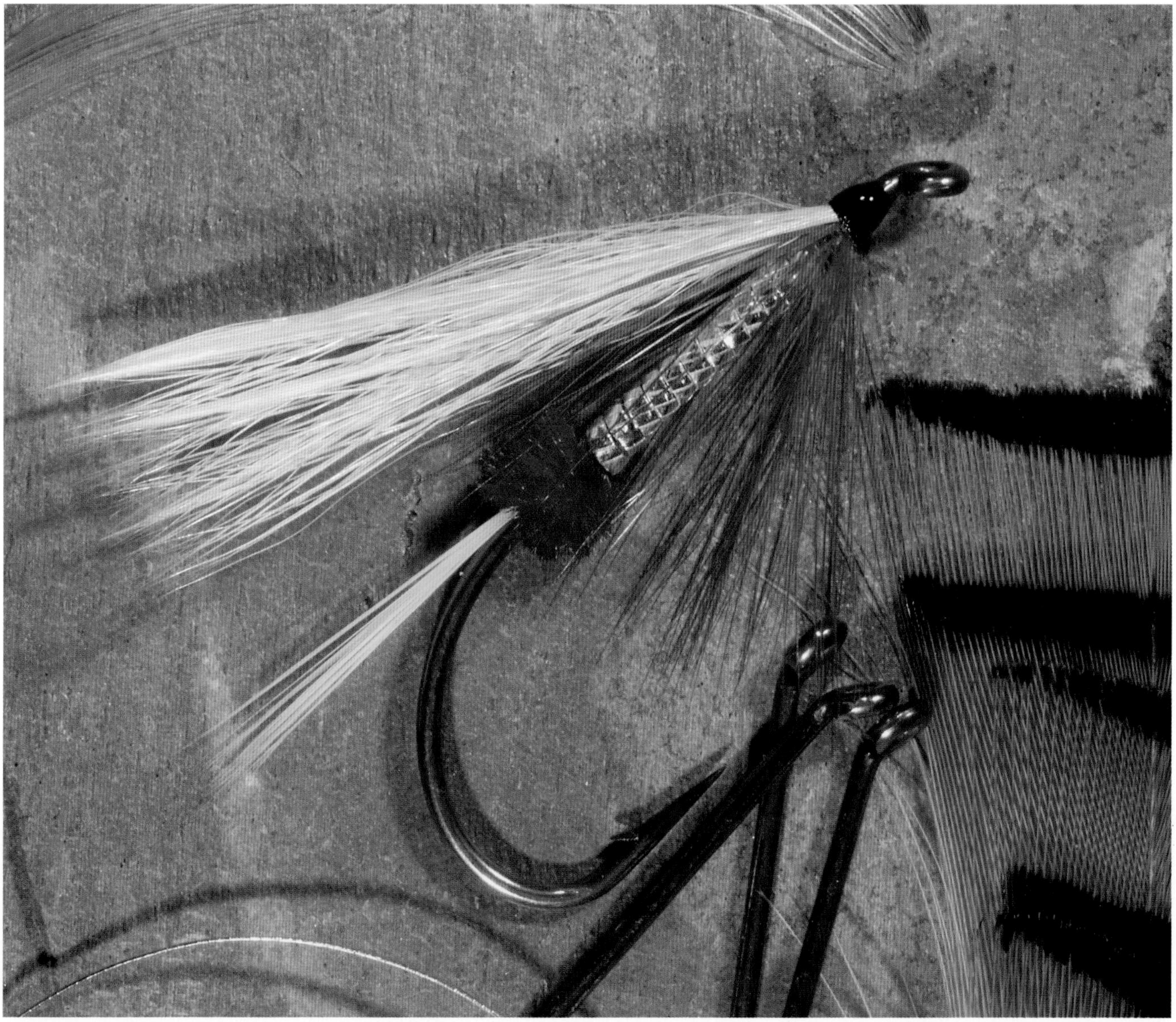

Orange Heron (recipe on page 253)

Myths and misconceptions surround Syd Glasso's gorgeous Orange Heron, perfected in the early 1960s when Glasso resided on Washington's Olympic Peninsula. The fly is now much adored—and frequently adorned in components never found on the original. For example, there is simply no historical basis for "tenting" the wings on the Orange Heron and the other hackle-wing flies invented by Glasso and his friend and protégé Dick Wentworth; though nowadays almost universally touted as the "proper" way to dress the pattern, this is revisionist history, and while I don't know the source of the tenting, Wentworth insists that he and Glasso did not tent their wings. Much associated with Wentworth, the late Doug Rose likewise told me unequivocally that Glasso did not tent the wings on his hackle-wing flies, and in the lovely Glasso flies owned by Dave McNeese (most if not all of which were lost in two separate unfortunate events—a shoplifting incident and a basement flood), the wings were laid low against the body in knife-edge fashion and not tented.

Moreover, while this fly helped spawn the widespread misuse of the term "Spey fly," Glasso was conservative in his use of the term; for some of his patterns, he drew upon the Spey flies for a basic foundation, having procured a copy of Eric Taverner's *Salmon Fishing* (1931) to study the concept of Spey flies. Indeed, in "The Olympic Peninsula," a story he wrote for the *Creel* (bulletin of The Flyfisher's Club of Oregon) in 1970, Glasso explained, "I like Spey type flies for winter steelheading and have used them for over twenty years. The style is over a century old, they're easy to tie and they look seductive in the water. The fish take them solidly and that's enough for me." Note that Glasso called them "Spey type flies" and not just "Spey flies."

One interesting aspect about the construction of this fly—and an element contributed by Wentworth—is that the floss is actually split into two strands with a bodkin and then the dubbing material is incorporated into the floss and wound forward to form the front third of the body. In addition, the wings are made more secure by capturing a few fibers under the thread wraps (they can also be tied reverse-wing style, an arrangement that makes them impossible to pull out).

Thanks to feathers given him by David McNeese around 1980, Glasso began occasionally using hooded merganser flank for the collar on his Orange Heron and other patterns; these striking brown/black-barred plumes perfectly complement this regal fly. In a letter circa 1979, Glasso thanked McNeese for sending a batch of hooded merganser flank feathers, acknowledging that these lovely feathers would make wonderful adornments to his flies; included with the letter was a Green Heron—hardly a well-known fly from Glasso, but proof that he was constantly tinkering with his color combinations. It joined a Glasso White Heron also in Dave's possession at the time, but sadly this letter and the Green Heron succumbed to a flood that buried Dave's basement tying den at his Salem, Oregon, house in the late 1980s or early 1990s.

Some learned steelhead enthusiasts might debate that the Orange Heron dates to the early 1960s rather than the 1950s, but on this count, Wentworth is the authority: until he supplied Glasso with feathers from a heron in the early 1960s, Glasso called this fly the Orange & Gray, with long-fibered barred grizzly for the hackle instead of heron. Misconceptions and revisionism aside, the captivating Orange Heron—inspiration for innumerable variations—is, today, one of steelhead angling's best-known flies.

Orange Shrimp (recipe on page 253)

I once asked Walt Johnson if he recalled which fly beached his first-ever steelhead. "I certainly do," he replied slyly, "Would you like to see it?"

Naturally I answered in the affirmative, and Walt disappeared up the stairs to the tying den in his lovely home on the North Fork Stillaguamish. He quickly returned with a little glass container holding a single fly, slightly worn, but well tied. It was an Orange Shrimp, and had bested a Stilly summer fish in 1938.

Surprisingly, the once-ubiquitous Orange Shrimp—perhaps the most popular Washington steelhead fly of the 1930s and early 40s—is of uncertain origin. It inspired numerous variations, many of them works of the legendary steelheaders who frequented the North Fork of the Stillaguamish beginning in the late 20s and early 30s, and reaching a zenith from 1943 through the 50s. Its most popular variant is the Polar Shrimp, in which the orange wool yarn body of the Orange Shrimp is swapped for fluorescent orange chenille, and gleaming white polar bear hair replaces the white bucktail for the wing (at least that was the preferred wing of Johnson and his fellow Stilly enthusiasts).

Likewise, fluorescent-orange-dyed hackle became a popular addition to the Polar Shrimp, and Walt Johnson told me that by the mid-40s, with Wes Drain at the point, the Seattle-area steelhead tiers eagerly adopted fluorescent dyes and fluorescent-dyed materials. These days, this simple pattern, oft imitated in form and color, is rarely to be found in the fly wallets of steelhead anglers, but it surely hooked as many or more steelhead from the Stilly in the 30s and 40s as any other fly.

Orleans Barber (recipe on page 253)

Renowned fly tier of Williamson River, Oregon, fame, E. H. Polly Rosborough, who lived for a time near California's Klamath River, once undertook the task of researching the origins of one of the Klamath's most famous and popular steelhead flies, the Orleans Barber. Until (and even after) Rosborough published his findings in a delightful story in the Spring 1984 issue of Dick Surette's *Fly Tyer* magazine, other writers had simply noted that the fly had come from a town barber in the tiny, remote community of Orleans deep in the Klamath River's canyon.

"It took considerable research and letter writing to come up with the data and history of the Old Barber, but finally the right contact was made in 1982 with an elderly lady in Northern California [Zelma Franzoni, 1909–1984] who had known him as a very close friend over a period of many years," Rosborough reported. The barber was Hungarian-born John Borisa (1885–1962). Having been employed at the Saint Francis Hotel Barber Shop in San Francisco, Borisa, along with friend Little Johnny Shoemaker, "got the wanderlust and landed in Orleans which, at the time, was about as far out in the sticks as one could get." That was 1928 or 1929, Rosborough reported. When Steve Hauser, one of Borisa's former well-to-do customers from San Francisco happened upon him during a fishing expedition to the Klamath, he set up the barber with a nice shop in Orleans, reputedly telling Borisa, "I always have to have a regular shave and haircut, and you had better be here to take care of it."

Borisa became an expert fly tier, and the fly that would become known as the Orleans Barber was designed for a specific purpose: "to coax jumping steelhead to strike." Borisa's talent for tempting jumping steelhead (which are notoriously lockjawed) on his fly blossomed into a traveling business when the river was at low flows and the steelhead moody. He would drive up the river with plenty of Orleans Barbers ready for sale, and upon spying other anglers having little luck in the falling water, would put his skill on display. Invariably, when he hooked fish, the onlooking anglers became interested in how he had done it. Sales of his special fly were always forthcoming, and the fly's fame soon spread as far away as Eureka, where the esteemed tackle seller C. Jim Pray tied and sold them.

In 1941, after his friend Shoemaker had returned to San Francisco and his good friends the Franzonis (he was godfather to three of their children) had moved to Trinity, Borisa "became very lonely and moved to Happy Camp some fifty miles upriver from Orleans" and set up a nice barbershop in his home. Borisa, born in 1885 in Hungary, died in 1962 in Siskiyou County, though minor legend and likely fading memories suggested he lived to age 99 and died in 1982.

Rosborough concluded his story by relating, as explained to him by an elderly friend of Borisa's from many years prior: "But at 99 years of age, he had the best fishing in years with a San Francisco friend. Going ahead of the others, he put his fish in the boat, lay back to rest and never woke up. You can be certain John Borisa, 'The Orleans Barber,' died a very happy man." Without benefit of genealogical data we enjoy today, one can hardly blame Polly for embracing the legend that Borisa lived to age 99 and died in his fishing boat, having just landed his last steelhead.

Pacific King (recipe on page 253)

For many years, starting in 1946, the opinionated but knowledgeable Roy Patrick owned and operated Patrick's Fly Shop in Seattle, where he was an institution in the sport. The shop was a gathering place and attracted a who's-who of Seattle area anglers. Walt Johnson, the famous steelheader of North Fork Stilly fame, once told me that, at times, just getting a ranting Patrick to slow down enough to take your money and complete a purchase was something akin to pulling teeth. But Patrick had a knack for fly-tying materials and stocked an impressive array of offerings, including stores of exotic feathers and furs, many tucked away in mysterious enclaves in the shop.

Patrick wrote a nifty little fly-tying instructional book in 1956, titled *Tie Your Own Flies*, with a foreword by Claude Kreider, the author of *Steelhead* (1948). Some years later he followed with a self-printed pattern guide called *Pacific Northwest Fly Patterns*. Both books include what may have been his personal favorite creation, the Pacific King. He first devised this fly as a trout pattern for the Sierra Nevada high country in California, and then later found it useful as a steelhead fly, tied on larger hooks, in Washington. In classic Roy Patrick hauteur, he wrote, in *Tie Your Own Flies*, "The fly comes by the name 'Pacific King' honestly. In time it will be classed as one of the best flies used anywhere."

Despite such imperiousness from Patrick, the Pacific King never really took hold, though it enjoyed a measure of popularity among his customers and converts. But its inventor taught many hundreds of people to tie flies, and he was said to be a patient and highly effective instructor despite his hubris. For many years his shop was a focal point for Seattle-area anglers. And from those impromptu fly-shop gatherings sprung countless innovations in steelhead flies and fly tying.

Parmachene Belle (recipe on page 253)

At the end of September, 1921, reported the *Blue Lake Advocate* (October 1, 1921), "A steelhead trout, measuring 34 inches in length and 18 inches in girth and weighing 14-1/4 pounds, was hooked and landed after a fight of 20 minutes by Joseph Gephart of Eureka at Fernbridge Sunday. The fish, which is the largest caught on a fly in Eel River for the past five years, has been entered in the 'biggest fish' contest being conducted by *Field and Stream* sporting magazine. It was caught on a No. 10 Parmachenee Belle fly and was on display Monday at Sam Wells' sporting goods store on F street, Eureka."

It was hardly the first giant Eel River steelhead to fall to the beautiful Parmachene Belle, but the 1920s were the twilight for the classic old Eastern and British featherwing wet flies that opened the doors to fly angling for the great seagoing rainbow of the Pacific Coast. Many steelhead anglers, by 1930, were relying primarily on indigenous flies and while the Belle, along with the Red Ibis and Royal Coachman and other fancies, still had its adherents, the Pacific Coast originals were more popular. To be sure, many of the early steelhead flies designed by local anglers were minor variations of the Parmachene Belle, Coachman, Royal Coachman, and others, but the shift to river-specific and steelhead-specific West Coast flies was well underway, and the reign of the bucktail flies was imminent.

Today the Parmachene Belle is hardly ever found on a steelhead river or for that matter even on a New England brook trout lake or stream closer to its birthplace. Its diminution is unfortunate because the fly ranks among the most fetching American classics. It was the brainchild of Henry Parkhurst Wells (1842–1904), a Rhode Island patent attorney by trade and an ardent angler, and it first appeared in print in *Fishing With the Fly* (1883) by Charles F. Orvis and Albert Nelson Cheney; Mary Orvis Marbury's *Favorite Flies and Their Histories* (1892) includes a number of endorsements for the fly submitted by regional experts. Wells had invented it for Maine's Rangeley Region lakes and named it after Parmachenee Lake,[42] itself named for Parmaginnie, son of the Indian chief Metalluk. (A rare and stirring account of Metalluk was penned by Fred C. Barker and appears in his 1903 book, *Lake and Forest as I Have Known Them.*)

No doubt the Parmachenee Belle's popularity in New England quickly spread, and whether imported by reputation or physically by means of anglers or tackle coming to San Francisco, it became one of the first steelhead flies. Wells himself, in a failed pursuit to catch king salmon on flies in Oregon, caught steelhead on his fly in Oregon's Clackamas River, though they were emaciated kelts, unsporting and unimpressive. California tiers soon made their own variations, which were often minor: black ostrich in place of peacock for the butt; yellow floss instead of mohair for the body. When slightly more significant renovations were made, the Belle garnered new names—fly pattern evolution at work—and steelhead fly tying was born.[43]

Polar Shrimp

(recipe on page 253)

Trey Combs in both *Steelhead Fly Fishing and Flies* and *Steelhead Fly Fishing* credits the Polar Shrimp to Clarence Shoff, the longtime tackle dealer, and notes that, "The Polar Shrimp first gained widespread publicity on California's Eel River in 1936. . . . According to the late Jim Pray, the first of these flies he saw were supplied by Shoff Fishing Tackle Company in Kent, Washington."

Clarence Shoff (1894–1975) was an innovative fly tier and a cagey businessman; Shoff Tackle, founded in 1922, is still in business. Shoff hired and trained several women to tie flies for the firm; he sold flies and goods at both the wholesale and retail level, and his reach extended well into California. Shoff invented the clipped-deer-hair mouse fly (and casting lure), for which he sought a patent in 1930; the patent was granted a few years later (for details, see www.fishinghistory.blogspot.com).

In the Winter 1983 issue of *Fly Tyer* magazine, founded by (and in the early 1980s still owned by) Dick Surette, Washington-based freelance writer Les Johnson contributed a story titled, "Knudsen's Cutthroat and Shoff's Polar Shrimp." He explained, "Hitting the roads for weeks at a time [Shoff] sold flies and hand-tied gut leaders at fishing camps on the banks of rivers from Washington to California. Being a totally gifted and smitten angler, it was not uncommon for Clarence to set up his vise at a fishing lodge and tie custom orders well into the night, then, rise early to fish a few hours on a noted pool before heading out to the next stop along his route."

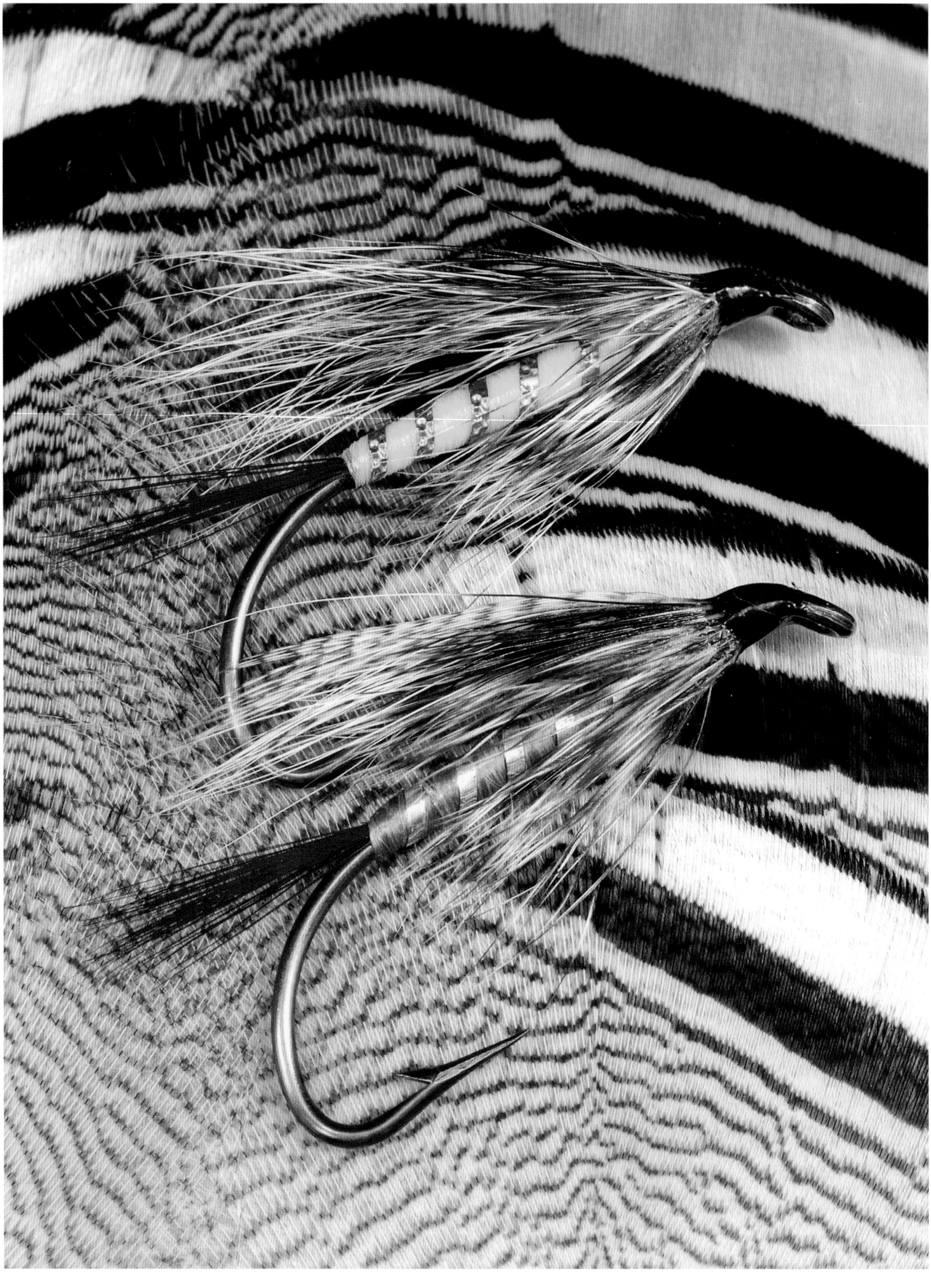

Professor and Grizzly King (recipes on pages 253 and 249)

Among the first flies fished for steelhead, the Professor and the Grizzly King were originally designed as trout flies by the multitalented brothers John and James Wilson of Scotland early in the nineteenth century. John Wilson (1785–1854), who used the pseudonym Christopher North, was a writer, a sportsman, and a professor at the University of Edinburgh. He created the Professor, while his younger brother James Wilson (1795–1856), a zoologist, created the Grizzly King. Both patterns enjoyed considerable popularity in their native land and throughout the Americas.

In *The Rod and The Gun* (1840), James Wilson describes the Grizzly King, explaining, "The Grizzly King is a hackle par excellence. . . . His wings are broad and burly, formed of any undyed feather, bearing narrow natural bars of black and white, and he bristles with many stripes from head to heel, his dark green body being wound about with gray or mottled hackle. And terminated by a fiery tail, turned up in what naturalists call an ensiform—that is, somewhat after the fashion of a sword."

In the same book, James Wilson describes the Professor as having "wings usually composed of mallard wing, barred by nature in the usual way, and varied in the ground-color by being dyed by art, lighter or darker, as may be deemed advisable. His body is formed of Paisley yellow flos [sic] silk, its texture rather tight and slim in form. It is not always advisable to try to hackle him, although he may sometimes be so slightly either with red or black about the shoulders, but his prevailing character is that of clearness, quietness, loveliness, and originality of composition, with a good deal of sarcastic sharpness about the barb, especially to bunglers who don't understand the nature of the Kirby bend."

Steelheaders in the Northwest could hardly hope to match such eloquence in describing their flies, but as far back as the 1920s, they were keen to modify the popular Professor and Grizzly King by replacing featherwings with hair (or using both). Through the 1930s, both the original dressings and the hair-wing styles were eminently popular on the Rogue River in southern Oregon, and on this brawling river, the two old Scottish trout flies would remain popular among steelhead anglers through the 1950s.

Protein Buck (recipe on page 253)

Ed Haas (1916–1987) lived a singularly remarkable existence. Later in life—having previously earned his living as a bartender, bookmaker, chess hustler, and stock investor—he retreated to the Salmon Mountains in remote northern California, in the Klamath River drainage, and tied flies for a living. Reclusive and cynical, Haas "was an eccentric genius, a definitively literate man, who was an acknowledged expert on many subjects, ranging from philosophy, to international economics, to the metals market, to nutrition. He read for about four hours a day, including writings in Latin and Greek, and had a library containing more than 25,000 books."[44]

In his small cabin deep in the woods—with no electricity or piped water—where he could escape interference from everyone, Haas perfected his fly-dressing techniques, and during the 1970s and 80s when he was tying commercially, his steelhead flies set a new standard for excellence. He was the consummate professional fly tier; he guaranteed his flies for durability and if one was damaged by any means, he would simply replace it. More significantly, many would argue that Haas tied the most perfect steelhead flies of his or any other era. Each was flawless, impeccable. They were superbly crafted, and while he generally stuck to the known patterns, he added his own flair in logically determined design elements. Early in his commercial fly-tying career, he took suggestions from the famous California tier and angler Andre Puyans about proper proportions and design. Based on his idea of what type of hair performed best under what specific water conditions, Haas even tied the same patterns with at least two different options for wings.

Haas used the reverse-wing method of attaching a fail-safe hair wing, but even here he added his own innovation: he would wedge the butt ends of the hair, and the thread holding them in place, in between the two wires that formed the return-loop on the Seeley and Mustad hooks he preferred. He laid on his flawless chenille bodies over a foundation of varnish, and when he used a tinsel rib, he wound it so tight that only a razor blade could remove it. He locked in his hackles with thread. He tied most of the standard steelhead patterns, but also created his own; the best known of his originals is his Protein, or Protein Buck.

Purple Angel (recipe on page 253)

Fully possessed of social graces befitting his English heritage and upbringing, hook designer Alec Jackson surprised me in 1991 with a lovely gift. Knowing from Alec's writings that Washington's Bob Stroebel—the Old Blue Herron, as Alec dubbed his mentor in steelhead angling—had devised the lovely Purple Angel, I had asked him for some background on the pattern; not a week passed before one out of only a hundred of Alec's elegantly presented "West Riding Press Steelhead Fly Pattern Cards" appeared in my mailbox. The heavy cardstock cover protected a double-matted, mounted Purple Angel, expertly dressed by Alec, and on the inside of the cover was a smartly written story about the fly's originator.

It seems Oral Dudder, who once owned a fly shop in Washington, took an interest in teaching Bob Stroebel to fly fish as a positive influence in the life of a rowdy urban teenager. But the young Stroebel's "introduction to the gentle craft was far from gentle and anything but pleasant," relates Alec. What Dudder planned as an introductory fishing trip, Stroebel saw as "an opportunity to partake in cigarettes, whisky, and wild, wild women," and he had no intention of picking up a fly rod. The result was a knockdown brawl in which Dudder gave Stroebel a sound thrashing. "Not wishing to take another whipping," reports Alec, "the kid decided to make the best of bad situation and pick up a fly rod."

Over the decades, says Alec, that once headstrong kid developed into perhaps the finest steelhead angler he has ever known, and he explains Stroebel's nickname: "Among his friends, Bob Stroebel is known as 'The Old Blue Herron' because of his fishing skills, wading prowess, and ability to melt motionless into the river's landscape. When The Old Blue Herron develops the ability to stand in a river's current on one leg, like the wily bird he is named after, I will then spell his name with but one 'r'." (From personal correspondence with Alec Jackson, and also from his article "Steelhead Flies, The Purple Angel," *Fly Tyer*, Spring 1985.)

Purple Peril (recipe on page 254)

One of the most popular steelhead flies of all time owes its existence to a propitious accident. The auspicious chain of events that led to the development of the Purple Peril started long before the groundbreaking fly actually derived from the tying bench of George McLeod, son of the legendary Washington steelheader, Ken McLeod, who was not a fly tier himself, but who seized upon the serendipity of having a steelhead-addicted young son who tied flies. At age 12, in the early 1930s, George learned to tie flies from E. B. George, a competitive caster who had moved from Southern California to Seattle, and brought bucktail flies with him to Washington, reputedly being the first to introduce them there.

George soon began to sell flies to local tackle shops (including the Oso Store at the mouth of Deer Creek), and his venture expanded to the point that he taught his younger sister, Mary, to tie flies, and, he notes, "between us we developed quite a little business." World War II interrupted George's fly-tying business, but Mary carried forth with it while her brother flew 27 bombing missions over Germany in a B-17 (two of his best friends, also aviators, were killed in the Pacific). But not long before the war, George developed the Purple Peril, and its genesis is best explained by him:

> Kind of an interesting history on the Purple Peril, my Dad used to do a lot of dry fly fishing for summer-run in the North Fork of the Stilly . . . One of his favorite patterns was the Montreal, which was a claret color, sort of a wine color. I ordered the claret Montreal hackles from M. Schwartz and Sons in New York, fly material suppliers, and by mistake they sent me purple hackle. I tied up some purple bucktail dry flies, and lo and behold they turned out to be really a killer on dark days especially for dry fly. Most of the fishing being done was with wet patterns, I tied it in wet bucktail, Purple Peril, and it also turned out to be a real good taker. . . . I remember Walt Johnson telling me one day on the river that the Purple Peril was the best pattern color that ever came out."[45]

Real good taker indeed: the Purple Peril soon became one of the most popular patterns on the North Fork Stillaguamish and its repute quickly spread from the Stilly's hallowed riffles throughout western Washington, and then beyond—to the upper Columbia River and down into Oregon and up into British Columbia. By the 1980s, when imported foreign-tied flies increasingly dominated the bins at fly shops, the Purple Peril was among a handful of steelhead bucktails (often tied with fox squirrel for the wing) almost universally found in the store selections. Not only was the fly popular, but it was also the inspiration for North Fork Stilly regulars, such as Johnson, to experiment with—and become obsessed with—the color purple in steelhead flies.

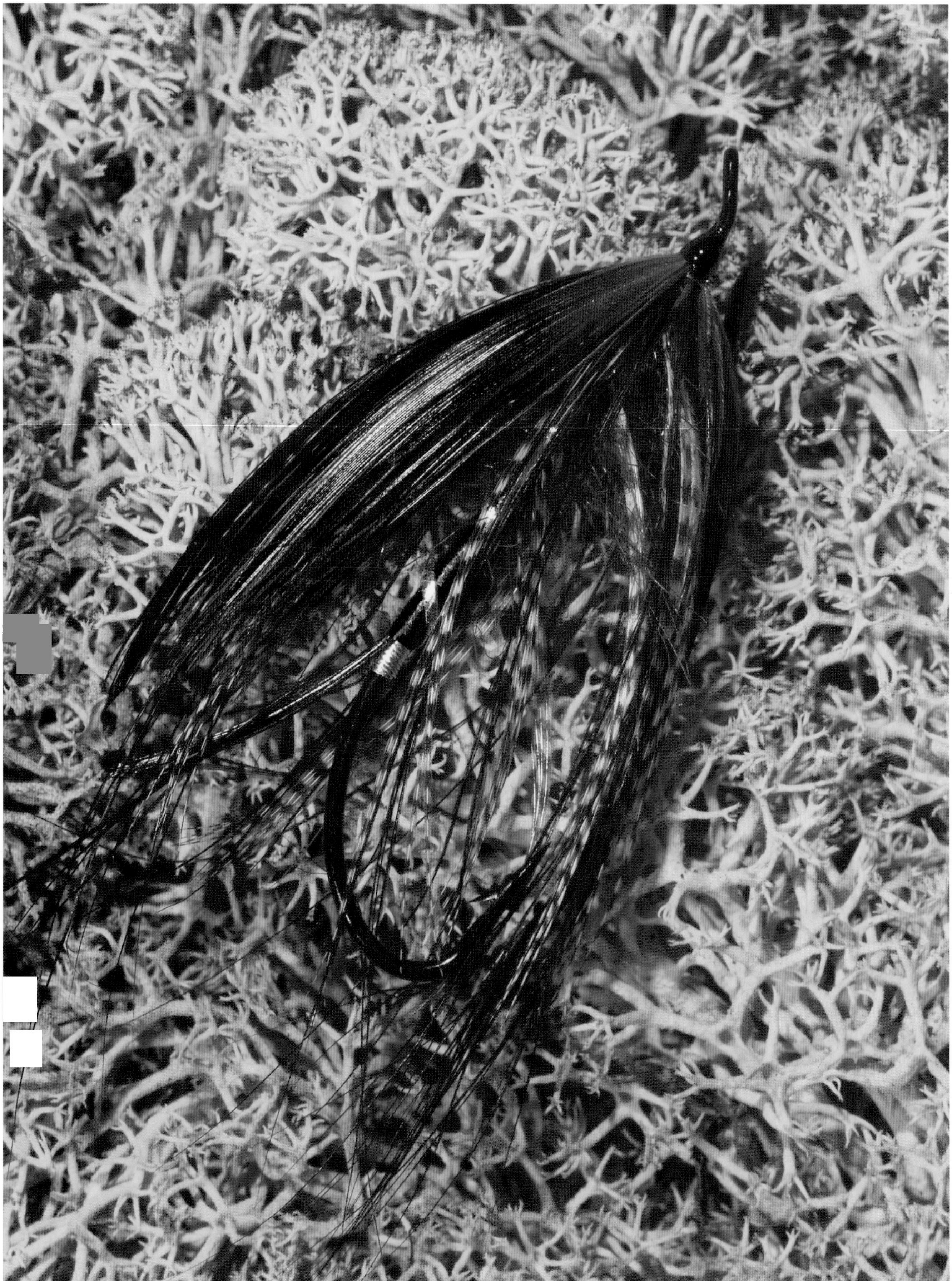

Quillayute (recipe on page 254)

The graceful and beautiful flies designed by Syd Glasso and Dick Wentworth in the 1960s have inspired countless variations; they were unlike anything the steelhead fly-tying community had seen and gained a modest following among other skilled fly tiers in northwest Washington. When, in the 1970s, author Trey Combs teamed up with publisher Frank Amato on the release of *The Steelhead Trout* and *Steelhead Fly Fishing and Flies*, a much wider audience became enamored of the unique Glasso and Wentworth patterns.

Unfortunately, the popularity of the Glasso and Wentworth patterns—including the Orange Heron, Sol Duc, and a host of others, such as Wentworth's Quillayute—sped far ahead of the facts surrounding these flies, and by the time the internet became a powerful tool for disseminating information, fly tiers, anglers, and writers began postulating all sorts of details with no basis in reality. For example, arguments have ensued on fly-fishing web forums over the exact and correct dressings of these flies when in fact, Glasso and Wentworth, as virtually all fly tiers do, routinely varied their own dressings. Just at the time such debates were becoming commonplace, one erudite Olympic Peninsula angler, the late Doug Rose, took the logical but until-then-unprecedented step of simply asking his friend Dick Wentworth about the origins and characteristics of the flies. Glasso mentored Wentworth in steelhead fly tying and fishing, even though the two never actually tied flies together.

Rose told me personally about the variation in the Glasso and Wentworth flies, and then later wrote on his blog that "the recipes for these flies are far from sacrosanct. . . . most of the literature describes the Sol Duc with a tag, golden pheasant crest tail, and the body hackle from the second tinsel turn. . . . that wasn't the way Dick tied it the day I watched him. 'We used to tie with what we had,' Dick says."

Among Wentworth's own contributions, which Glasso was keen to adopt for his own tying, was the use of heron hackles in place of the grizzly hackles he had first used on his Orange & Gray, the precursor to the now-ubiquitous Orange Heron. Wentworth also conceived the idea of splitting his orange floss into two strands, inserting dubbing in between them, and then creating the bodies of his flies from that combination. The two men were highly successful anglers, and Walt Johnson—one of the Seattle-area anglers who embraced Glasso's tying style—once told me that Wentworth was "one of the best waders I have ever seen, and I will always remember the day I witnessed him wade across the Quillayute directly below the confluence of the Sol Duc and Bogachiel Rivers. This is a feat I would not attempt and doubt very many other anglers would either."

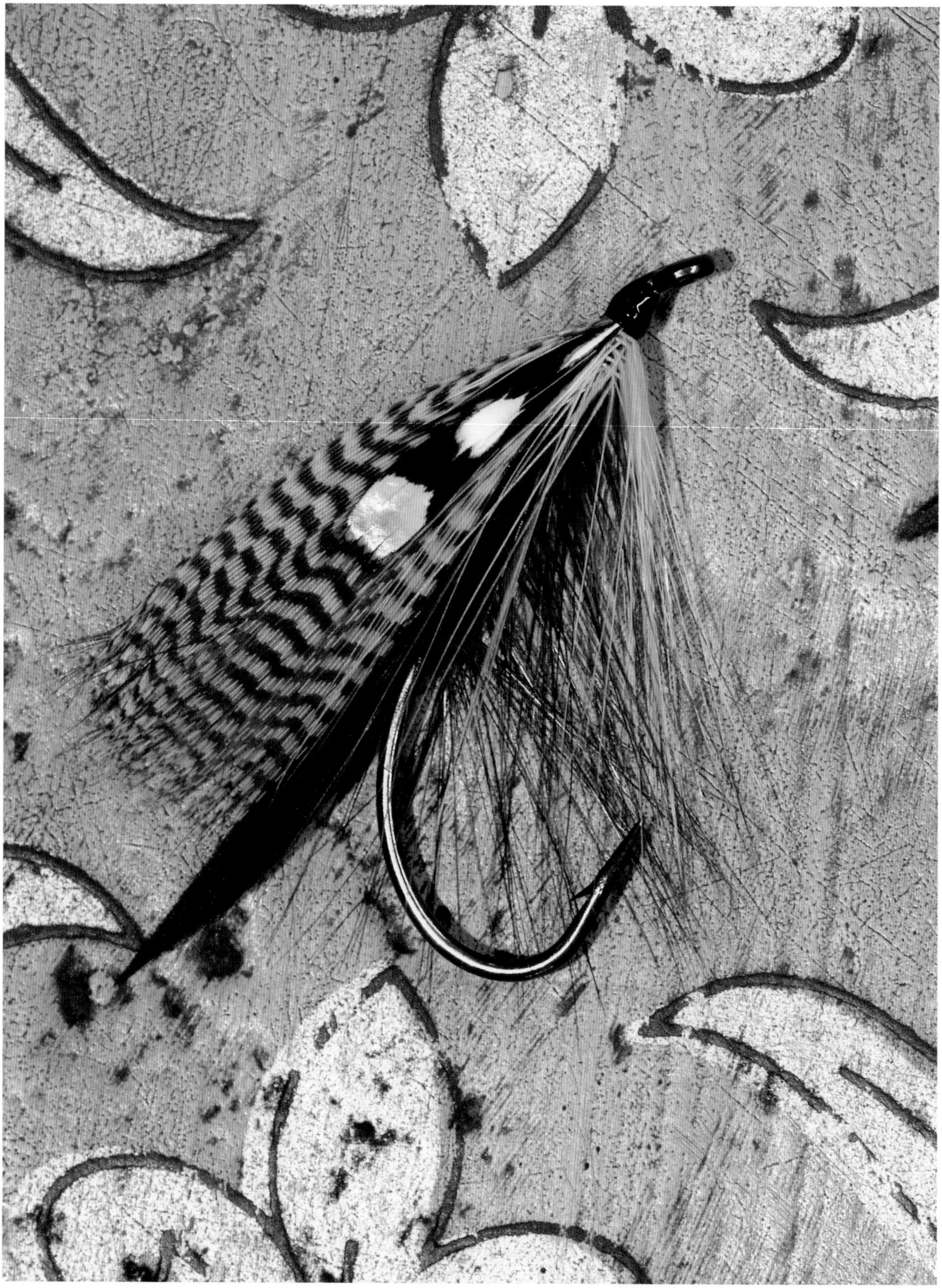

Railbird (Benn's Railbird) (recipe on page 254)

John S. Benn's Railbird possibly takes its name from the feathers he used for the wing, these coming from the flanks of the Clapper Rail, a secretive, long-billed, long-toed relative of the coot, endemic to saltwater marshes in California, but now classified as endangered in the state.

However, without examples of John Benn–tied Railbirds to furnish proof that he used rail feathers, one other reason for the fly's name remains viable. In horse racing, which was popular in California in Benn's time, a railbird is a racing enthusiast who sits on or near the track rail to watch a race or workout. Joseph D. Bates, Jr., whose research was typically first rate, says in *Streamer Fly Fishing* (1950), "This popular pattern was first tied about 1900 [by Benn] with wings of railbird flight feathers," but he goes on to mention a possible alternative to the fly's name. After noting that "there is reason to believe that the above historical facts are true," Bates records the following:

> Mr. A. J. McLane . . . writes about the Railbird Steelhead fly as follows: "One of the old-time patterns developed in or about 1915. . . . Jim Hutcheson . . . was fishing the Breakwater Pool on the Eel River, taking some nice steelhead on the Kate. Several friends, working the same piece of water, were doing very badly, and they asked Jim what fly he was using. Being in a Puckish frame of mind, he replied that the fly was a "railbird," local argot that referred to people who sat in front of the cigar store. He passed out samples and one fellow wanted some extras sent to Martha Benn. . . . Fly tying materials were hard to get in those days, so Martha improvised, making the fly as near to the original as she could. It was none too close, so she dubbed it the Humboldt Railbird.
>
> Still, the original Railbird dates to much earlier than 1915, so it seems Martha Benn devised and named an alternative pattern to her father's original, and the entire episode hardly settles the matter of how the original fly derived its name.
>
> It's also possible Benn obtained the feathers not from the native rails, but from the Water Rail, a species found in Britain, or some other of the world's numerous species of rail. Benn obtained tying materials from around the globe. The *San Francisco Call*, June 9, 1907, in a story about Benn, reported, "He has bluejays [sic] sent from France, woodcock wings from Japan, jungle cocks from India, grouse and partridge from the heaths of Scotland and the golden pheasant from the Black river in China."

Already subject to devastating market hunting in the nineteenth century, clapper rails remained a game bird in California until 1913, when passage of the federal Weeks–McLean Act, precursor to the stronger 1918 Migratory Bird Treaty Act, protected them. By that time these coastal-marsh birds were approaching extinction in the state. Likely Benn found his supply of clapper rail feathers shrinking as the birds became increasingly scarce, and so he began making the wing of the Railbird from gray mallard flank, which became standard—at least for a while.

As fly tiers are keen to tinker, the Railbird was subjected to variation, and by the 1920s the so-called Humboldt Railbird and later the Bair's Railbird (designed by C. Jim Pray for his friend Fred Bair of Klamath Lodge) appeared on the Eel and other waters. In 1928, Clark C. Van Fleet was called to business in Eureka, where he remained for a year; in *Steelhead to a Fly*, he noted, "During the year of my residence in Eureka, and for a great part of previous yearly visits, I stuck religiously to but one pattern, the Humboldt Railbird." The Humboldt Railbird (as per Van Fleet and Combs) is dressed as follows: Tail, yellow quill segment, golden pheasant crest, or magenta quill segment; body, magenta wool yarn palmered with magenta hackle; hackle, yellow; wing, teal flank; cheeks, jungle cock.

Red Shrimp Spey (recipe on page 254)

The legendary Sasquatch of the Stilly, Walt Johnson, was among the first of the Seattle-area steelhead fly-fishing addicts to explore the steelhead-bearing tributaries of the Upper Columbia River in central Washington, and in 1997, he told me the story of how he created his beautiful Red Shrimp Spey, one of the best-known of his original patterns. Walt had spent several winters venturing out to the Olympic Peninsula to fish with Syd Glasso, especially noteworthy since few anglers could ever claim to have spent much time on the water with the man who brought us the Orange Heron and other iconic steelhead Spey-style patterns. Walt embraced the revolutionary Spey-style patterns, appreciating the soft, long-fibered hackles, and soon expanded the genre to include several of his own designs, quite different from those created by Glasso, whom Walt was always quick to credit.

One of these Walt Johnson originals, the Red Shrimp Spey came about in the late 1960s. One autumn day, Walt recalled:

> Enos Bradner called Ralph Wahl and told him that he was down on the Grande Ronde [in southeastern Washington] chukar hunting and planned to fish the river when he was through hunting. He told Ralph and I to come join him. . . . but a cloudburst hit the area and put the Ronde out, so Bradner called back and cancelled. Ralph inquired if I would still like to go fishing, or back to work. My choice was obvious, so he suggested that we go up and try the Upper Columbia at the mouths of the Entiat and Methow. This was before Wells Dam was built and the river was still free-flowing in that area. . . .
>
> The fishing proved spectacular.

While on the river, they met Ray Olsen from Chelan, a regular on these waters. Olsen used a simple red palmer-style fly with no wing. With Olsen's fly as the inspiration, Walt created a Red Shrimp that sported a red body, red hackle, and a dyed-red hair wing. One season in the mid-1960s, using the new shrimp pattern, Walt took a 15-pound steelhead on the first day of the season and then another 15-pounder on the last day of the season.

But with the beautiful flies created by Syd Glasso as inspiration, he would soon alter the dressing to arrive at this beautiful Red Shrimp Spey. "Having fished with Syd Glasso for several winters," Walt said, "I had become indoctrinated into his Spey flies, so this prompted me to tie the Red Shrimp" as a Spey-style fly.[46]

Rogue Red Ant (Red Ant) (recipes on page 254)

By the time John S. Benn died in 1907, his legacy was unfolding over an increasingly broad geographic area. Fly anglers targeted steelhead on the Klamath River and their furtive efforts had already proved successful on the faraway Deschutes River in north-central Oregon. But southern Oregon's Rogue was beginning to steal the national spotlight. A writer for the *Rogue River Courier* (April 23, 1909), only about 20 years after Benn had opened the doors to Eel River steelhead fly fishing, opined, "In that queen of all streams, our beautiful Rogue river, which is a grown up mountain brook, the finest fly fishing on the American continent may be had. Nova Scotia, New Brunswick, Maine, Canada and the famous Restigouche are completely outclassed . . . our steelhead trout rise as freely and fight as fast and furiously as the celebrated 'Ouinaniche' or land-locked salmon of Maine and Eastern Canada, and are much larger fish . . . All this with an environment wild and picturesque as any to be found . . ."

By then, traveling anglers from San Francisco and Portland and beyond—even as far away as New York City—were journeying to the Rogue for autumn fishing, and by 1910 the Medford Hardware Company was selling fly-fishing tackle along with locally developed flies, imploring anglers via ads in the *Medford Mail Tribune* to "Catch steelhead on our special Rogue River trout flies." Joe Wharton, who opened a tackle store in Grants Pass in 1907, was a rising star, soon to be synonymous with Rogue River steelheading.

Wharton seems to have invented several different patterns and to have had commercial fly tiers supply them in quantity. His Turkey and Red was one of his early specials for the Rogue and may have helped spur the popularity of red flies in general, including the Rogue Red Ant, which comes in two forms: an original, modified from an antiquated English trout fly, and a further modification by legendary Portland angler Mike Kennedy, a prolific inventor of steelhead patterns.

EDGAR SEALEY
& SONS, LTD.
REDDITCH, ENGLAND
Highest Quality
2

Rogue River (recipe on page 254)

I'm not sure the genesis of the two patterns known as the Rogue River and the Rogue River Special can ever be resolved: their roots are obscure and their variations are legion. The Rogue River Special (see page 149) may have been invented by tackle dealer Frank Colvin; then again, some version of it may come from Joe Wharton's trailblazing outdoor store in Grants Pass, Oregon. The two flies differ substantially; the Rogue River Special, with minor adaptations, would evolve into the Umpqua and Umpqua Special (the "Special" is an Umpqua with the addition of jungle cock cheeks). The Rogue River, meanwhile, has essentially faded from memory and is rarely used, even on its home waters.

Both flies seem to date to the 1920s, but probably not earlier than that, because in the 1910s, the few fishing reports from the Rogue that survive—some reporting on the steelheading exploits of Wharton—mention the most popular Rogue River flies of the period: Royal Coachman, Professor, Silver Doctor, and a few others. So the special patterns for that river, which would arrive by the dozens if you count all the variations, had not yet blossomed. But as word of the Rogue and its outstanding steelhead fly fishing spread across the country in the pages of sporting magazines and—significantly—the writings of Zane Grey, the wild Rogue would come into its own; by the 1950s it could probably claim more fly patterns than any other steelhead river.

But before all that—in the opening two decades of the twentieth century—the local anglers, as well as adventurous steelheaders from California and Portland, such as Jim Backus (casting champion and outdoor writer), fished the Rogue with the flies that had earned the respect of fishermen on the Eel and Klamath to the south. And even in those glorious days, steelhead anglers debated the merits of the various flies in language that is familiar today, as seen in the *Rogue River Courier*, October 26, 1915:

> The big fellows are taking the fly in great shape, and little preference is shown to the exact kind of fly. . . . B. F. Skillman put his trust in the "Professor," and brought in seven big fellows, all taken on that fly, to prove his judgment. But then Joe Wharton duplicated the catch and used the "Royal Coachman," "Abbey," "English Admiral" and "Silver Doctor" indiscriminately, thereby proving to his entire satisfaction that it is not the fly, but the man. Fishing on the same riffle with Wharton was Dr. Dillingham, and the six great steelheads that were landed by him were all taken on the "Royal Coachman," which, according to Dillingham, is the real thing in a trout lure.

Wharton's family had migrated across the country from Massachusetts to settle near Roseburg, Oregon. In his early 1920s, he had moved southward a short distance and in 1898 became head clerk at George Riddle's Grocery in the settlement of Doe Flat. Later, he moved still farther south to Grants Pass, where he became county clerk until 1907, when he opened Joe Wharton Sporting Goods, ". . . putting in a complete line of Guns, Ammunition, Fishing Tackle, Cutlery, Sporting Goods and other allied lines."[47]

Wharton's—a pioneering sporting goods store in still-remote southern Oregon—became the focal point for steelhead anglers in the Rogue Valley. Innovations aplenty emanated from the store, which no doubt, like most tackle shops, hosted regular impromptu gatherings of intrepid anglers. Wharton (1873–1952) ran the store for 45 years, even while serving as mayor of Grants Pass from 1941 until 1947.[48]

Rogue River Special (recipe on page 254)

The name Rogue River Special comprises perhaps two dozen different patterns invented by probably two dozen different fly tiers between the 1920s and 1950s. But the original may have been the brainchild of Frank Colvin (1882–1974), a native of the Gold Beach area who operated a sporting goods store there for many years. However, Trey Combs, in *Steelhead Fly Fishing*, notes that "Wharton's '#1 Special' became the Rogue River Special," so it truly is difficult to pin down the originator of this fly. Colvin seems a likely candidate. Certainly he may have taken his lead for the design from the "#1 Special" and then perhaps coined the name "Rogue River Special."

Born on Hunter Creek, south of Gold Beach, Colvin never attended school, yet learned reading, writing, and arithmetic from his mother and from Jimmie McMonies, an old homesteader with whom young Frank lived part time. In the early 1900s, Colvin worked for R. D. Hume, the self-proclaimed "Pygmy Monopolist"[49] in the salmon hatchery business, a trade that would soon lead him to Bonneville on the Columbia River. "Returning to Curry County in 1910," recalls his son, Edsel, "Frank worked at many different jobs. He was a cook at the Gauntlett place, a timber faller, a fence builder, and finally a rancher, after purchasing a 160-acre farm from Phil McManus about 2 miles up Hunter Creek."

In 1921, Colvin purchased the Gold Beach Confectionary, and after a few years converted it to a sporting goods store, which he operated (at various locations after a highway project claimed the original site) until 1949. During those years, explains Edsel Colvin, Frank gained widespread acclaim as an angler, and "fishermen from all over the world came to Gold Beach and the world-famous Rogue River, and most of them sought out Frank for advice. He won many trophies and prizes in national fishing contests and had articles written about his fishing expertise in national magazines and books. If he had a desire to be remembered for anything, it would be fishing, which occupied a major portion of his life."

Colvin was not a fly tier, but he was a fly designer, and according to Syl MacDowell, author of *Western Trout* (1948), who visited Colvin at his store, Frank "was the originator of several widely used artificial-fly patterns."

Edsel Colvin recalls his father telling him he was the inventor of this popular fly, and says his father had the store flies "tied by a woman named Stella McDonald and then later by two ladies, the Bunnell sisters . . . I worked in Dad's store and remember that we pretty much sold just three different flies—the Rogue River Special, Red Ant Bucktail, and Royal Coachman Bucktail. They were always double hooks (we kept what we caught!) in size 10 and size 8. They sold for 25 cents or $2.50 a dozen."[50]

The Rogue River Special in its myriad permutations—forerunner to the Umpqua Special—was ubiquitous for decades on the Rogue. Asserting that Colvin was the originator is perhaps contestable: one of his versions was sometimes called Colvin's Rogue River Special, and, as Joseph D. Bates, Jr. reported in *Streamer Fly Fishing in Fresh and Salt Water* (1950), ". . . when the description of the pattern was published in *Field and Stream* magazine more than twenty fly dressers sent in supposedly correct versions, no two of which were exactly alike."[51]

Royal Coachman Bucktail (recipe on page 255)

Anglers in Northern California, on the Eel and Klamath, and on Oregon's Rogue, realized by the early 1920s that hair-wing flies—bucktails to use the parlance—outperformed the featherwings that had faithfully served the first two generations of steelhead fly fishers from the 1880s through the opening two decades of the twentieth century. The bucktails were more durable; they could withstand the demands of long-distance casting and hold up to the sharp teeth of hard-fighting steelhead. Moreover, the anglers of the day decided these bucktail versions proffered a technical advantage, as explained by Joseph D. Bates, Jr., in *Streamer Fly Fishing in Fresh and Salt Water* (1950):

> . . . the turbulent rivers of the Western coast have caused a rather different type of bucktail to be more popular. Flies of the streamer type rarely are used in Western rivers for steelhead and salmon, because it has been found that the bucktail variety is more serviceable on the fast rivers. This is partly due to the savage strikes of the big steelhead and salmon. Their teeth tear the feathers and give the streamer a relatively short life. It is also due to the fact that the stiffer wings of bucktails can be dressed at an angle of about 35 to 40 degrees from the head of the fly. This angle of dressing makes it possible for the wings to open and shut in the swift current, giving greater action to the fly in that type of water.

The first bucktail steelhead patterns were conversions from featherwing flies, so by the second decade of the twentieth century, such popular old flies as the Coachman, Royal Coachman, McGinty, and a host of others were gaining popularity as bucktail patterns for trout and—on the Rogue, Eel, and Klamath, at least—as steelhead flies. By 1912, bucktail flies for trout were being sold as far north as Portland by Backus & Morris, downtown at 223 Morrison Street, and touted in the firm's advertisements in the *Morning Oregonian*. Walter Backus was an expert angler from Portland; his angling forays took him as far afield as the Rogue, and he wrote on angling topics for the Portland newspaper. And while Backus talks of using standard flies of the day for Rogue River steelhead—Professor and Silver Doctor—he was an early proponent of bucktails for trout. By 1912 he was also advocating using flies for "salmon-trout" on the Nehalem and Salmonberry Rivers in northwest Oregon—rivers that only had winter steelhead, essentially making him a pioneer in fly angling for winter-run fish.

Sawtooth (recipe on page 255)

Lots of steelhead flies are named for their originator, or for people honored by their originator; many others carry descriptive names or the names of rivers. But few flies derive their name from well-known steelhead pools or runs. The Sawtooth is one pattern that does take its name from a specific place, an intriguing bedrock-bound run on the North Umpqua River.

Sawtooth is aptly named: downstream from historic Mott Bridge and upstream from the mouth of Steamboat Creek, at the upper end of the famous North Umpqua Camp Water, the river squeezes between bedrock on both sides, flowing deceptively smooth and deep. The long narrow glide, upstream from Sweetheart and Hayden's Run, is not as placid as it may appear, as any careless wader is apt to discover, and one jagged section of the reef is notorious for sawing through tippets. The tailout is essentially the garden spot in Sawtooth, but the run is deep throughout, so when a fish rises to a swung fly—and more than a few fish here have fallen to a skated Muddler or other dry fished by intrepid steelheaders—it has made a major commitment, and one for which this legendary river is justifiably renowned: its fish have a propensity for rising from considerable depths to assault feathered imposters. So too, the tailout is adjacent to the nefarious tippet-cutting Sawtooth reef.

The Sawtooth fly comes from no less an angling legend than Ray Bergman, author of *Trout*. Prompted by Clarence Gordon, who had established North Umpqua Lodge and was eager to draw in high-end customers, Bergman visited twice, apparently in the early or mid-1930s, and fell in love with the river and its steelhead. So smitten was he with the North Umpqua, that Bergman included a chapter called "Steelhead of the North Umpqua" in *Trout*, and therein he admits, ". . . the Sawtooth Pool had fascinated me from the beginning . . ."

Bergman also devised a companion fly to his Sawtooth, and named it for the nearby Surveyor Pool on the North Umpqua. The dressing is as follows: Tail, white and brown bucktail; body, rear half red tinsel, front half yellow chenille, with red tinsel continuing through the chenille as a rib; hackle, grizzly and brown mixed; wing, red and white bucktail.

Scarlet Ibis (Red Ibis, Red Fly) (recipe on page 255)

Among the earliest of the flies dedicated to steelhead angling, the Scarlet Ibis—more frequently called the Red Ibis or Red Fly by the California anglers who employed it—has its origins in the East. It enjoyed considerable popularity as a trout fly (and also as a bass fly) by the 1890s, and was among the standards in the fly wallets of California fly casters, though not so popular as the Coachman, Professor, and a few others.

Some claim this fly was the first dedicated steelhead pattern, but this claim comes with a caveat: likely before the Scarlet Ibis was ever cast by silken line and cane rod and gut leader, it served as part of a trolling rig intended to target steelhead and salmon in tidewater reaches of California rivers, possibly beginning at Tomales Bay, the mouth of Paper Mill Creek (now called Lagunitas Creek). A 1909 story in the *San Francisco Call* describes the tactic, which by then was widely used: ". . . attach a No. 3 or No. 4 red ibis fly on a small swivel, allowing to run free on the line which carries a running sinker and ends in a Wilson double steelhead hook baited with worms or salmon row, with a piece of fresh shrimp on the fly." An 1893 story in that paper—evidence that the technique was by then well established—describes the rigging in even more complexity, advocating the "ibis fly for shrimp, a No. 3 coachman with a silver body for worms, a No. 5 double hook for clams, a No. 7 double for canned roe, and above that and last a silver spoon coppered on either side."

Soon enough the Ibis earned its place among the earliest flies cast for steelhead on the Eel River, as well as other waters, and while its champions were few when compared to the ardent adherents to the Coachman clan, this lovely bright pattern was among the handful of inaugural steelhead flies.[52]

Silver Admiral (recipe on page 255)

Inventive and observant, at times indelicate and even scurrilous, entertaining and garrulous—Ernest Herbert "Polly" Rosborough (1902–1997) could certainly endear himself to people when he wanted to. He is legend in Southern Oregon's Williamson River country, though a transplant by way of Arkansas birth and a wide-ranging upbringing that ultimately landed him in Northern California, whereupon his coworkers in a box factory in Bray dubbed him Polly because of his incessant talking, like a parrot. After a few years he moved to Oregon's Klamath Basin and embraced the Williamson and Sprague Rivers, before a temporary move back to California, which gave him the chance to encounter steelhead on the Klamath River; soon Polly was back in Oregon, near the banks of the Williamson, which enthralled him. Upon the enigmatic Williamson Polly vented his most ebullient and innovative efforts to devise new flies and fly-tying concepts, but he was keen to design steelhead flies as well.

Completely self-taught, Polly tied flies commercially. Retail-outlet orders for his famed patterns were so voluminous that he brought in partners in the production-tying business, first teaming up with Klamath Falls angling legend Dick Winter, among the most engaging and humble men ever to set feather to steel, and then coaching several local women to tie his flies. Polly likewise taught the late Jerry James—like Winter, both highly skilled and always unpretentious—to dress his flies. James would later open a fly-angling museum at his home in Grants Pass.

One of the earliest members of the Federation of Fly Fishers, Polly was often recognized for his accomplishments, and he received the federation's Buszek Award in 1975. At the suggestion of Skip Hosfield, Polly authored the widely read *Tying and Fishing the Fuzzy Nymphs* (1965), and later released *Reminiscences From Fifty Years of Flyrodding* (1982). His trout flies are still in use today on the Williamson and other waters, testifying to Polly's innovative, effective designs. Without question, Polly was a trout angler first, but he was also an adroit commercial fly tier for most of his adult life, and while he may not have spent much time in pursuit of steelhead, that hardly detracts from the simple beauty of his steelhead patterns. Among them, I think his Silver Admiral, a color conversion of the old Admiral, is the most fetching.

Silver Ant (recipe on page 255)

When Isaac "Russ" Tower first visited the Rogue River in the late 1920s, he must have fallen under its spell: by the time he wound up his reel for the last time, not to mention put away his golf clubs (he once "shot his age" by scoring a 72 at age 72) and shotguns (he once teamed up with a buddy to bag a record 100 snipe in a day), the lifelong Coos Bay resident, iconic local businessman, and keen sportsman had become a Rogue legend. He was kind, genial, gracious, and intelligent. So too, he proved himself a shrewd businessman. Just three years after returning from Harvard with a law degree, he procured the Buick, and then the Ford dealerships for the Coos Bay area in the form of Tower Motors, which still exists after more than a century. But in those days before he first fished the Rogue in 1927, Tower had also proven himself a witty adventurer—along with his mischievous best friends—and the local newspapers reported some of their exploits, and occasionally gave voice to Tower's humor:

> John D. Goss took a bath yesterday that he had not bargained for. He and George Goodrum, Ray Kaufman and Russ Tower were up Haines Inlet duck hunting. Goss was standing in the front of the boat when the craft lurched suddenly. He went in head first and was finally fished out, the wettest individual you ever saw. He was taken back to camp, a fire built and some old clothes furnished while his suit was drying. Meanwhile the others went out and secured 19 birds. The *Coos Bay Times*, December 07, 1908

> They were tellin' how well they could shoot and Judge Goss recalled a duck hunt in which he had brought down five birds with one shot.
>
> "Talk about shootin'," began Russ Tower, "I saw Capt. Harris do a mighty neat piece of work one day last week. His wife was puttin' out the washin' and she was complainin' about the pesky birds makin' dirt marks on damp clothes with their feet.
>
> "They're thick as bees 'round here," says she. "There's seven of 'em sittin' on the clothes line this blessed minute."
>
> "I'll fix 'em," says Cap. takin' down his shotgun, which he always keeps loaded with fine birdshot. He tiptoed to the door, took aim, and—
>
> "Killed every one of them sparrows," broke in Goss.
>
> "You're wrong," corrected Russ Tower, calmly; "he never teched 'em, but when his wife took in the washin' she found she had three pair of openwork stockings and a fine peek-a-boo shirtwaist." The *Coos Bay Times*, January 08, 1909

> R. K. Booth, Ray Kaufman, John D. Goss, and Russ Tower have returned from the Glasgow Gun Club where they attempted to display their artistic ability by giving the club house a thick coat of verdant green paint. When they got home, the other members of the club expressed doubt as to whether there was more green on the club house than on the garments of the industrious quartette. The *Coos Bay Times*, May 16, 1910

Tower, best known for his Silver Ant and for the Juicy Bug (which he devised with the help of fishing buddy Ben Chandler), played baseball for the local club in Marshfield, and on one important occasion—a hugely attended July 4, 1907, contest against rival North Bend—he literally saved the game. It seems someone forgot to bring the baseballs. But Tower came to the rescue and cycled down to the boat landing, procured the services of Jasper O'Kelly and his speedy new taxi boat, *Bonita*, and shot across the bay to Marshfield.[53] There, Tower ran from the docks to his new sporting goods store, grabbed a bunch of balls, ran back to the boat, and motored back to North Bend. Deducting the time needed to go retrieve the balls, it took just 22 minutes—a new record for the round-trip between the two landings. Moreover, playing shortstop, Tower led his team, going three for four at the plate, with two doubles and a stolen base in a losing effort.[54]

Silver Demon (recipe on page 255)

C. Jim Pray of Eureka, California, (see the Black Demon on page 36 or the Carter Fly and Carter's Dixie on page 55) remains to this day—among pansophic anglers—one of the most influential and highly regarded figures in steelheading lore. Said Ted Trueblood in a 1973 piece for *Field & Stream*, "I believe Jim Pray originated more good steelhead patterns than anyone else—the Optic series, the Red, Black, Cock Robin, and Orange Optics; the Thor, Carter, Silver Demon, and Black Demon—plus adapting many old wet-fly patterns to steelhead and West Coast salmon fishing."

Reputedly, Pray's Silver Demon originated both from the Golden Demon and the Cains River series of streamers that had been used in New Brunswick by Chicagoan Fred Pete in the 1920s. By 1935, the Golden Demon—having been introduced to the steelhead coast by Zane Grey in the 1920s and tied and sold by the thousands by Pray—ranked among the most popular steelhead flies. In that year, Pray introduced his beautiful silver-bodied variation, with its signature tail of barred wood duck, and in 1936, as reported by Joseph D. Bates in *Streamer Fly Fishing in Fresh and Salt Water* (1950), Pray sold 1,300 Silver Demons compared to 200 of the well-established Golden Demon.

In mounting the tail of barred wood duck, cut a slip of fibers twice the width of the actual tail and then gently fold the slip in half lengthwise. Pinching the slip between your left thumb and middle finger, with the fold in the feather upward, use the soft-loop technique to secure it to the hook. If the fly is to carry a rib of oval tinsel, start the tinsel from the far side of the hook to avoid canting the tail with the first turn. The tinsel-body flies, such as the Golden Demon and Silver Demon, are rendered nearly indestructible with a coating of varnish over the body, but this step requires drying time so you must tie the fly in stages: complete the tag, tail, body, and rib; then tie off the thread at front and carefully brush varnish or thick head cement onto all sides of the body, being mindful not to allow the cement to seep into the tail. Rotate the fly in hand or in the vise to make sure the cement sets up evenly and then allow it to dry completely before adding the hackle and wing.

Silver Hilton (recipe on page 256)

The well-known Silver Hilton hails from the Klamath River, but its popularity spread throughout the Pacific Northwest, and it remained a favorite into the 1980s. Even a tentative biographical sketch of the Henry Hilton who invented the fly has proven elusive. Nonetheless, Hilton seems to have come to Humboldt County from Central California; in a story titled "Cooks and Cookhouses" in the *Times-Standard* for August 23, 1974, Andrew Genzoli, gathering his information from local citizens, reported, "In 1926 Scotty and Hilda Shifflet were the cooks at the cookhouse at Korbel. In 1927, Henry Hilton came from Merced to cook there and Hilda Shifflet went to Riverside to cook. In 1928 she married Henry. They now live in a mobile home in Yuma, Arizona."[55]

Korbel is a small unincorporated settlement on the Mad River named for the Korbel family of California Champagne fame. After acquiring the Arcata and Mad River Railroad, the Korbel brothers extended the line to the North Fork of the Mad River and started a sawmill there in 1883, naming the town North Fork (it was renamed Korbel in 1891). In 1902 they sold their Mad River properties to the Northern Redwood Lumber Company. The mill shut down in 1933, and presumably with it, the company cookhouse, and Hilton's location thereafter remains murky, but he still lived in the area, perhaps at his cabin on the Klamath River, jocularly named Red Rat's Haven.

George Burdick, author of *Klamath River Angling Guide* (1989), explains:

> Located downstream from Bluff Creek was a cabin that gained fame as Red Rat's Haven. It was referred to by many names, including Hilton's Cabin, and was occupied by Henry Hilton, the inventor of one of the Klamath River's most enduring fly patterns, the Silver Hilton. This cabin was known to have provided lodging to many of fly fishing's colorful characters during the 1920s and 1930s. The Silver Hilton pattern was invented here in those early years of steelhead fly fishing. . . . Many early flies and fishing ideas for angling with a fly rod were bandied about in the cabin called Red Rat's Haven before being put to the test in the river the following morning.

Burdick records that the original Silver Hilton had a tail of red hackle fibers, but the mallard flank tail has long been regnant among today's fly tiers almost since the fly's inception. Further, reports Burdick, "There are two versions of how the fly was named. Local fly historians say it was because of the silver tinsel wrap, however, two of the octogenarians I interviewed said it was named for Mr. Hilton's graying temples, which were quite striking . . . an original Silver Hilton tied by Henry Hilton (which I photographed) had no tinsel wrap."

Hilton put Red Rat's Haven up for sale in 1956, according to the Eureka *Times-Standard* (June 6, 1956); his classified ad says he needed to sell quickly because was moving. Perhaps he was headed for retirement in Arizona.

Skunk (recipe on page 256)

Possibly the most widely used steelhead fly of all time after its popularity throughout the Northwest from the 1950s through recent times, the Skunk was designed by Mildred Krogel of Roseburg (1906–1983) sometime in the 1930s. She created the fly for her husband, Lawrence, says North Umpqua legend Frank Moore (an ardent fan of this ubiquitous pattern), and, according to the *Fisherman* (Volume 6, 1955), in the 1940s one newspaper reported, "Local tackle stores sell a large fly designed especially for the steelies [on the North Umpqua]. Called a 'skunk fly,' it is entirely black except for a facing of white hackles."

Trapping skunks and selling the hides represented a major share of the household income for the Krogels (and of course it supplied tying material), and both Lawrence and his two sons, Don and Clete, were actively involved in the business before the skunk fur market collapsed "once furriers had to correctly identify the silky black fur, which was being sold under various exotic names" (as per Bob Wethern in *The Creel, North Umpqua Edition*). Thereafter the father-and-sons team focused on their firewood business, and also spent lots of time fly-fishing, while Mildred augmented the family income through the sale of fishing flies. She did so until 1941, when she developed an allergy to feathers, and by then her flies—tied by the hundreds of dozens each year—were sold at the outdoors stores in Roseburg and the resorts along the river.

By the 1960s, the fly had spread throughout the land of steelhead, from the waters of Northern California and Southern Oregon, into British Columbia, and all the way out into eastern Washington. It changed much along the way, but retained the simple black-and-white pattern. Fenton Roskelley—outdoor writer for the Spokane newspapers for more than half a century—noted in 1969, "Fly fishermen probably will catch more Steelhead from the Columbia River and its tributaries in the Inland Empire [eastern Washington] this fall on the Skunk and Fall Favorite flies than all other fly patterns combined. . . ."[56]

At some point, the original Skunk lost some of its character when the white-over-black wing fell out of fashion. I'm not sure when and how this happened. The original wing may have fallen victim to large-scale commercial fly tying that blossomed in the 1980s; perhaps eliminating one step and one material saved time and money, or perhaps it was accidental—a simple misinterpretation of the pattern. Either way, I don't ever recall seeing a properly tied Skunk from the big commercial fly producers. Roy Patrick (*Pacific Northwest Fly Patterns*, 1970) lists the proper wing (black and white) for the Skunk, and Harry Lemire tied the proper wing on his Skunk that appeared in the plates of *Steelhead Fly Fishing and Flies*, although the dressing listed in the text does not list the wing that way. How the correct dressing for the wing disappeared from the written record thereafter is puzzling.

Then again, the originator, too, varied her dressing of the fly, as did subsequent local tiers. Dale Greenley, a native of the North Umpqua, told me, "Don's mom [Mildred Krogel] used whatever material she had on hand that was close to the right color: yarn, chenille, and maybe even floss. Many of the flies in the local shops had almost as much brown in the wing, from the bucktail, as they did white. . . . I don't remember ever seeing one, but Joe [Howell] recalls seeing Skunk flies in a local hardware store that had a couple of strands of small white chenille laid over the top of the body from the base of the tail to the hackle. Somebody was apparently tying a closer imitation of a skunk."

Skykomish Sunrise (recipe on page 256)

The rise of the Skykomish Sunrise was meteoric, and the decline of the steelhead fishery for which it was named equally quick. Almost as soon as Ken and George McLeod, of Seattle, introduced the colorful fly to their angling friends in the late 1930s, the Skykomish Sunrise skyrocketed in popularity, and soon the pattern topped nearly every list of recommended steelhead flies for Washington and beyond.

The fly's story begins in 1928, when Ken McLeod (see the McLeod Ugly on page 118), George's father, along with two fishing partners, purchased a small parcel of land on the North Fork of the Stillaguamish at the mouth of Deer Creek. More than a decade later, Walt Johnson would be the first of the Seattle cadre of fly anglers to buy property and actually build a cabin at the Elbow Hole, but Ken McLeod and his buddies Joe Husby and Harold Pemberton paved the way. Here, in these waters once fertile with steelhead, salmon, and trout, young George McLeod became a fly angler; he hooked his first steelhead above the Elbow Hole at age eight, and was thereby hooked himself on the pursuit of these magnificent fish. He and his father helped pioneer the craft of luring winter-run steelhead to a fly, and among the patterns they used was the Skykomish Sunrise.

Ken largely left the fly-tying duties to his son and to his daughter, Mary. And while driving to the Skykomish River one January morning, George and Ken were awed by a vibrant sunrise, which inspired George to design this iconic fly. Trey Combs, in *Steelhead Fly Fishing* wrote that the Skykomish Sunrise "is simply the most popular steelhead fly pattern in the history of the sport." A day or two after George designed the pattern, his father fished it on the Skykomish and caught 7 steelhead, including a chrome-bright buck of nearly 14 pounds, his largest to date. The new fly earned its wings just as George would earn his in flight school before flying 27 B-17 bombing missions over Germany in World War II.

The Skykomish Sunrise would gain even loftier status in the 1950s and 60s as it racked up an impressive tally of *Field and Stream*–scoring steelhead, largely from the Kispiox River, including George's 1955 world-record steelhead, which weighed in at more than 29 pounds. The fly remains a favorite today, even if it's more popular at the tying bench than on the end of a stout tippet. Originally George McLeod dressed the fly with the hackle standing out at nearly dry-fly angles from the hook; more popular these days is the swept-back hackle. Naturally, slight variations are legion, but the Skykomish Sunrise is so well designed that major modifications have never superseded the original.[57]

Sol Duc (recipe on page 256)

While the iconic Orange Heron is the best known of Syd Glasso's beautiful steelhead flies developed during the 1950s and 60s, the elegant Sol Duc may have been his favorite. Longtime *Seattle Times* writer Enos Bradner called the Sol Duc Glasso's "pet pattern," and also noted—in 1961 well after Glasso perfected this fly—that the pattern is properly tied with ". . . wide yellow hackle, stripped and wound Spey fashion, with the longest fibers at the rear. Wings, four hot-orange hackle tips."[58]

Of note, these key elements of the Sol Duc and the later Sol Duc Spey are largely forgotten and thus poorly understood. Many contemporary tiers dress these hackle-winged Glasso flies with two, rather than four feathers, and also place emphasis, even pride, on "tenting" the wings even though Glasso and protégé Dick Wentworth never did this. Glasso and Wentworth (see the Quillayute, page 139) dressed the wings so they laid low along the fly's body, on edge. Four feathers created a more substantial presence than two. Capturing a few hackle fibers under the thread wraps used to mount the wings in place helps secure them. You can make the hackle-tip wings nearly indestructible by tying them in reverse: tie the hackles facing forward and then fold them carefully back and tie them down so they stay low along the body. These reversed wings cannot pull out, yet when dressed in the normal manner, with attention to detail—including trapping a few fibers under the thread wraps—they are amply able to withstand the rigors of fishing.

Glasso was a skilled fly tier who dressed complex Atlantic salmon flies. And he studied the old Spey flies from the River Spey in northeast Scotland. By the middle decades of the nineteenth century, Speyside tiers had developed two branches of their unique flies—those dressed with heron hackles and those dressed with hackles taken from a rooster's rump at the base of the tail, what we might call schlappen today. By the 1860s, the characteristics required of these cock hackles—thin stems, long fibers, less webbing in the fibers than typical for a rooster rump hackle—were so well defined that the birds were being specially bred at key estates on Spey and also at Goodwood near London, the seat of the Duke of Richmond and Gordon, who also owned Gordon Castle on the Spey.

Unlike any other Atlantic salmon fly in the world, Spey flies were dressed with the cock's hackle tied in by its butt end and wound up the body, rather than by its tip end.[59] This unusual concept meant the longest, fluffiest fibers of the "Spey cock" hackle adorned the rear of the fly—and as Bradner recorded in the *Seattle Times*, Glasso dressed his Sol Duc with the longest fibers at the rear. But he did this by feather selection rather than by reversing the hackle. Without benefit of selectively bred roosters to supply the hackles for his Sol Duc and Sol Duc Spey, Glasso would search through hundreds and hundreds of yellow hackles (schlappen for the Sol Duc Spey, and either schlappen or neck hackles for the Sol Duc) to find those few that would work well on his flies. Little has changed in that regard: feather selection is everything in fly dressing, and tiers willing to search through plumes tirelessly will find the hackles that make the Sol Duc and Sol Duc Spey so seductive both in and out of the water.

The Sol Duc Spey was dressed with the longest-fibered yellow schlappen for the body hackle, and usually a black feather from the heron's shoulder (substitute dyed-black pheasant rump or dyed-black blue-eared pheasant rump). The third fly in the Sol Duc series was Glasso's Sol Duc Dark: Tag, silver tinsel; tail, golden pheasant flank fibers; body and hackle, as per Sol Duc; rib, silver flat and silver oval tinsel; collar, teal flank; wing, golden pheasant flank. Walt Johnson, who was inspired by his friend Glasso's fly designs, tied an all-yellow version of the Sol Duc.

The Soule (recipe on page 256)

As Trey Combs, in *Steelhead Fly Fishing and Flies*, reports, "The Soule pattern has been credited to [John] Benn though there is some confusion as to who 'Soule' was. I believe that Harold Smedley in his book, *Fly Patterns and Their Origins*, erroneously credits Henry H. Soule, an outdoor author who died in 1889."

Combs is correct, and there need be no confusion over the origin of the fly's name, for it honors one of Eureka's preeminent citizens of the late 1800s and early 1900s, Charles Parsons Soule (1851–1922), an ardent angler, according to E. Oliver Putnam in a story titled "Fishing Facts of the Redwood Realm" in *Outing* magazine (April, 1919). Soule was born and educated in Maine, but in 1867 his family moved west. Upon moving, 17-year-old Soule found work in the banking business in 1868, and would forge a substantial career in that industry, largely in western Nevada. Soule, a Mason, was elected as a Republican member of the Nevada 10th General Assembly for a term from 1879–1880. Finally in 1889 he relocated to Eureka and cofounded two banks, the Bank of Eureka and the Savings Bank of Humboldt County; he served as president of the former and vice president of the latter. In 1904 he was elected president of the Humboldt Chamber of Commerce, an organization he helped develop in 1892, and he continued to actively promote the region (as per Leigh Hadley Irvine's *A History of New California*, 1905). This lovely little John S. Benn variation on the Parmachene Belle, virtually unknown today, enjoyed considerable popularity on the steelhead streams of California and was listed by author H.L. Betten as "among the favorites" for steelhead as late as the 1930s ("Western Trout Fishing," in *Fishing Lake and Stream*). Little could be done to improve the beauty of the Parmachene Belle, and indeed the only major modification Benn made was to make the hackle all red instead of red and white.

Spade (recipe on page 256)

Bob Arnold's unassuming little Spade is a steelhead fly designed to meet a specific need. Namely, Arnold wanted a fly for low, clear water and dour summer steelhead on his home river, the North Fork Stillaguamish. In his 1993 book *Steelhead Water*, Arnold explains, "What I wanted was a fly with no bright colors or flash of tinsel. Most flies of the day were red or orange, intended for dirty water."

He desired a simple, somber fly that would behave properly in the water, and to circumvent the fact that he had no size 8 Sealy hooks (which he would have preferred), he dressed the fly small for the size 6 hooks he did have on hand. "What I concocted belongs to a long tradition," he realized eventually, admitting, "If I didn't know it then, I know it now. There's not much new to be uncovered. The English soft-hackled nymph and wet fly . . . were important antecedents to Spade. So were the Oregon and Washington steelhead flies—Burlap, Brindle Bug, Boss, and Comet series."

Moreover, the Spade led Arnold to an epiphany in the summer he devised it, when renowned Canadian steelheaders Jerry Wintle and Bob Taylor were there with him. He learned how to "work" a fly, a tactic that can take several forms, and at times motivate a steelhead to strike. He recalls the episode in *Steelhead Water*:

> Bob Taylor and I watched Jerry [Wintle] hook and play a fine fish just before dark in the Elbow Hole. . . . Afterward I saw him whisper something to Bob. I was highly curious. What did he tell him—what secret? I had to know.
>
> "What did he say?" I asked Bob, as soon as I had a chance.
>
> "Tell you later," he promised.
>
> Back in camp, drinking a beer, I cornered him. "What's Jerry doing? What's his trick?"
>
> "He's working his fly."
>
> "What do you mean 'working it?' How?"
>
> "If you watch closely at the end of the drift he lets his rod tip bob up and down. And he'll release or else take in a few feet of line. Not a lot. It isn't necessary to work the fly much. Even if you are watching closely it's easy to miss seeing what he's doing."
>
> "He's a sly one, all right," I agreed.[60]

The Spade gained a loyal following, primarily in Washington where it was born, and it enjoyed a measure of popularity until fairly recently. Alec Jackson, nearly 30 years ago, began rendering his friend's pattern in the distinctive Alec Jackson style, with a body made by spinning ostrich and peacock with wire and tinsel; other variations are legion. The Spade is not often seen nowadays, but that fact hardly renders its tale less interesting. Rather it only testifies to what Arnold himself observed in *Steelhead & the Floating Line* (1995): "Flies have their period of vogue, then slipslide into oblivion." While Arnold's simple, somber Spade has not yet fallen into oblivion, its inventor keenly understands the likely path for all but a few of the classic steelhead flies.

Spectral Spider (recipe on page 257)

Walt Johnson was a thinker and a tinkerer, an accomplished artist at the vise and a skilled angler who, increasingly beginning in the 1970s, enjoyed the challenge of landing North Fork Stillaguamish summer-run steelhead on the daintiest of tackle. He pondered deeply how fish see colors in various light and water conditions, telling me many years ago that he had "always admired the late Preston Jennings and his studies on the theory of light refraction and its prismatic effect on our flies as viewed by the fish in its window, and I have attempted to create patterns incorporating his principles."

Walt's beguiling Spectral Spider, perfected in the early 1970s, was one of his few patterns on which he used synthetic materials rather than natural furs and feathers. He was exacting in his selection of materials and graded feathers carefully for particular uses, avoiding substitutes for rare feathers and using synthetics sparingly. "Maybe I am too fussy," Walt once wrote me in the early 1990s, "as I will use some synthetics if they provide the results and appearance I strive for."

The beautiful blending of colors in the Spectral Spider (Walt was an early proponent of the Spider-style flies for steelhead) made it a winner for sea-run cutthroat, for which he originally designed the fly, but a chance encounter with a huge steelhead on the North Fork convinced him of the fly's efficacy for larger game. He lost that fish, which he estimated at nearly 20 pounds, but thereafter this kaleidoscope-like fly became one of his favorites for steelhead. He sometimes added a collar of dry-fly-grade grizzly hackle under the mallard collar to make the fly float, or almost float.

Steelhead Bee (recipe on page 257)

McNeese's Fly Shop in Salem, Oregon, in the days when it was owned by David McNeese, was renowned for its specialty materials for Atlantic salmon flies and fanciful steelhead flies. The freezer in the backroom was stuffed with feathers, skins, and whole birds—some of the stuff was legal to own and sell, some wasn't. McNeese was a materials junky: he loved dealing in and owning rare materials.

But even beyond the questionable legality of some of the materials in the shop, there was a seedy underside to the laden stores of fine and exotic feathers: the iconic shop, at various times, was infested with feather-eating moth larvae. We battled them almost nonstop, and their origins have been the subject of some debate among myself, Dave, and one or two others, but the bugs were damaging and difficult to control.

In addition to all those beautiful feathers, Dave was proud of his collection of valuable flies, tied by the continent's leading tiers. When the feather-eating bugs became especially wretched, I begged and pleaded with Dave to remove his prized fly collections from the shop. I finally decided to press the matter.

Dave's friend, the mischievous Al Buhr, walked in one day when I was cleaning out drawers to assemble collectible flies for Dave to remove from the shop. I told Al of my concerns, parading as an example an original Steelhead Bee that the famous author and angler, Roderick Haig-Brown, had given a young McNeese in person years before. Of all his collectible flies, it was his favorite. He cherished it.

Never one to miss a chance at a good practical joke, Al hatched an insidious plan: rummaging through the shop, we found an antique hook like that used by Haig-Brown. With Al at my shoulder offering suggestions, I dressed a Steelhead Bee in the rattiest form possible. Al examined it, then took scissors and a bodkin to it, leaving little but the disheveled skeleton of an antique-looking fly. We then opened a filthy tying-table cabinet and swept dead moths and feather dust into the box that had held the original Bee, which we secreted safely away. Dave was due back about then, so we put the box back in the drawer where I had found it.

When Dave arrived, I told him Al wanted to see that Haig-Brown Steelhead Bee, and Dave went right to the drawer where it had been kept, produced the box, and handed it to Al without taking the lid off. In a perfect ad-lib, Al opened the box, and stood there staring, mouth agape. After a long few seconds, acting stunned, he handed the box to me. I took one look and unleashed a curse-riddled "told-you-so" speech on Dave, who then snatched the box from my hands for a look. Instantly panic registered on his face; then he was crestfallen as the tears welled up in his eyes.

Al and I let him suffer for a bit, but finally relented. I don't know about Al, but I almost feel bad about that episode to this day. Almost.

Steelhead Caddis (recipe on page 257)

To paraphrase Doug Rose, an Olympic Peninsula guide, angler, author, and cognoscente who died in 2013, Bill McMillan is a singularity. As Rose once wrote on his blog, "There are plenty of celebrated fly fishers in our region—not a few who seemingly view being a 'celebrated fly fisherman' as their life's work. But Bill is the only angler I know who is a great and innovative steelhead fly fisherman, who has created flies that have become part of the fabric of Northwest steelheading, who has written a classic fly fishing book, and who is also one of the sport's most passionate and articulate advocates for wild fish."

McMillan, typically quiet and unassuming, but passionate and outspoken as a crusader for wild steelhead, has lived up to such accolades for several decades. Not only has he carried the torch for the Northwest's iconic gamefish and shouldered the heady burden of being the steelhead's greatest ally, he has also inspired like-minded efforts by both individuals and organizations.

In 1985, McMillan authored the influential *Dry Line Steelhead and Other Subjects*, and thereafter his diligent work on the behalf of wild steelhead continued unabated. In 2006, McMillan—a trained biologist as well as the 2009 Wild Steelhead Coalition Conservation Award winner—authored an extensive, eye-opening, and frankly rather depressing report titled *Historic Steelhead Abundance: Washington NW Coast and Puget Sound*. As Rose succinctly reported, the paper ". . . is elegantly conceived, exhaustively documented, and persuasively-argued. It is also a ringing indictment of what passes for fish management in the state of Washington."

McMillan next teamed up with his son, John, to produce what I consider one of the most important works ever penned about anadromous fish, the rivers in which they live, and the larger ecosystem. The beautifully detailed book is titled *May the Rivers Never Sleep* (Frank Amato Publications, 2012), and in light of not only this significant book, but also McMillan's decades-long advocacy for wild fish, his handful of well-known fly patterns seem almost insignificant. But they are part of the man, part of his legacy, and as Rose pointed out, part of the fabric of the Northwest's steelhead fly-angling cultural history. Among them, the Steelhead Caddis—conceived as it was for dry lines and summer fish—is my own favorite. Among his other flies is the colorful Winter's Hope, dressed on a large, heavy-wire hook for winter steelhead: Body, silver flat tinsel; hackle, silver doctor blue, then purple; wing, two yellow and two orange hackles; topping, golden-olive calf tail.

Stillaguamish Sunrise and Stillaguamish Sunset

(recipes on page 257)

Capturing the fancy of steelhead anglers everywhere, George McLeod's Skykomish Sunrise—perhaps the most famous steelhead pattern of them all—was a near-instant success in Washington after its introduction in 1939. By then, McLeod, not even 20 years old, had already embarked on a successful commercial fly-tying enterprise; his youngest sister, Mary, also tied flies and helped George fill orders. But World War II intervened in dramatic fashion for the McLeod family: George became a B-17 bomber pilot and flew 27 combat and 3 relief missions in the European Theater. While he was gone, Mary minded the store, so to speak, and continued to tend to the fly-tying business.

After the war, George continued to excel at designing and selling flies, and while others tried their hands at designing variations of the Skykomish Sunrise, it was George who proved most adept at capturing the spirit of that venerable pattern in his Stillaguamish Sunrise and Stillaguamish Sunset. These two flies, along with McLeod's Skykomish Sunrise and Purple Peril, were among the standard steelhead flies in the McLeod's "Ketch-em" flies lineup; alongside them were standards of the day such as Enos Bradner's Brad's Brat, Dan Conway's Yellow Hammer, Clyde Hoyt's Killer, and the long-popular Orange Shrimp. In addition, McLeod also dressed another variation on the Sunrise/Sunset theme called the Steelhead Special; the pattern is as follows: tag, silver tinsel; tail, red and yellow hackle fibers; body, yellow chenille; rib, silver tinsel; hackle, red and yellow; wing, red over yellow bucktail.

The McLeod Tackle Company branched out into lines, leaders, and more, and George became instrumental in the development of new fly lines. In fact, George and his father Ken, working with Leon Martuch and his fledgling line company Scientific Anglers, were responsible for the invention of sinking fly lines (and sinking-tip lines), which were an instant hit among salmon and steelhead anglers in the Pacific Northwest. Whereas the revolutionary Scientific Anglers floating lines were called Air Cel floating lines, George suggested the name Wet Cel for the new sinking lines and the McLeod Model Wet Cel sinking lines were born.[61]

Surgeon General (recipe on page 257)

Contrived by Robert P. Terrill, the Surgeon General has several variations, and the original is frequently confused with the similar Del Cooper, invented by Mike Kennedy. The characteristic that distinguishes the two patterns is the throat of natural guinea on Terrill's fly. So too, the Surgeon General calls for the hackle and tail to be fluorescent red; Kennedy used standard bright red for the hackle and tail on his Del Cooper. Kennedy's fly was named for Portland Oregon's Del Cooper, a fly tier, locally well-known angler, and tackle expert who died in 1979. The Del Cooper seems to predate the Surgeon General by less than a decade, and confusion over the two similar flies is common; in *Flies of the Northwest* (Frank Amato Publications, 1998), for example, the Surgeon General is actually credited to Del Cooper.

Born in Nebraska in 1908, and Stanford-educated in the late 1920s, Terrill moved to Portland in 1937 to take a position as a professor of economics at Reed College, but after the outset of World War II, he was tapped for a federal government position, in the division of special research in the State Department, where his duties, according to the *Oregonian* ("Acting President of Reed Leaves," July 21, 1942), were "concerned with investigating the economic aspects of problems arising from the war." After the war, he continued in federal service, landing a stint as an economic advisor in Brazil, whose petroleum resources were coveted by both private and federal interests in the United States.

In 1962, Terrill retired to the central Oregon coast, at the small community of Gleneden Beach, a few miles south of Lincoln City. While on vacation there from Washington D.C. in November, 1956, Terrill's wife, Dorothy, caught her first steelhead, a 9-pound winter fish from the Siletz River. Even during his years away from Oregon in the service of the federal government, Terrill remained interested in fly fishing—especially with Paul Young rods.

Terrill created his Surgeon General in those mid-1970s retirement years, and Trey Combs, who listed several obscure variations of the fly in *Steelhead Fly Fishing and Flies*, further reported, "It is the hottest new steelhead fly to appear in several years and has won a wide following in Oregon and Washington."

Indeed, by the 1980s, the Surgeon General had proven itself attractive to both fish and fishers. Throughout that decade and into the 1990s it was among the most popular of the steelhead flies we sold at McNeese's Fly Shop in Salem. Within the shop and for our customers, David McNeese himself set the standard for continuing to differentiate between the still-popular Del Cooper and the Surgeon General, insisting that when tied for the sales bins at the store, the latter fly had to be dressed with fluorescent colors and with that distinctive guinea fowl throat.[62]

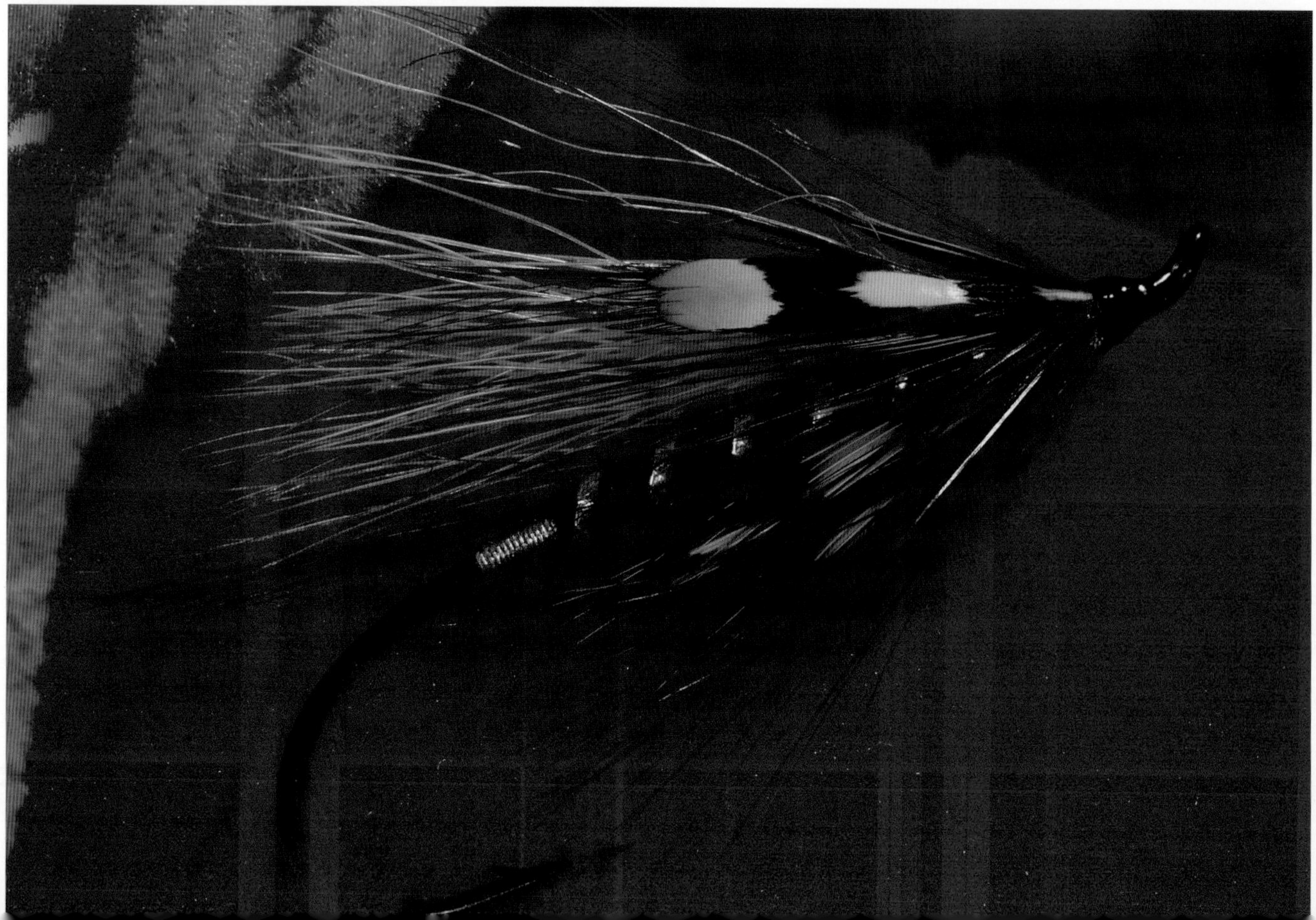

Thor (recipe on page 257)

In the late 1930s when William Bayard Sturgis (1885–1951) was crafting his influential book *Fly-Tying*, he knew that C. Jim Pray was the preeminent authority on steelhead flies and fly fishing, and so Sturgis consulted Pray in gathering patterns for the book. So beautifully dressed were the flies Pray sent Sturgis, a resident of Monterey far to the south, that the author chose to depict them on a color-plate frontispiece.

At the time *Fly-Tying* was published in 1940 by Charles Scribner's Sons, the Thor was vying for popularity with the Golden Demon on the Eel and other waters of Northern California. It was all because of the story of a remarkable feat by the fly's namesake: the Eureka-based fisherman Walter Thoreson had, on Christmas Day, 1936, taken the first-ever *Field and Stream* prize-winning steelhead—a spectacular 18-pound winter fish, as stunning for its size as for the time of year it was boated. Under the right conditions, Eel River anglers realized, winter steelhead could be coaxed into taking flies. Pray himself described the origins of the Thor— unnamed when it bested the 1936 record fish on the Eel—to Sturgis:

> At the close of the day of tying, I was about to throw out some left-over material on the table. A piece of red chenille, an orange hackle, some white Buck-hair, and a Rhode Island Red saddle hackle were part of what few pieces remained. So, I tied these into a fly on a No. 6 hook, and Walter Thoreson, of Eureka, later on in the Fall took the first prize-winning Steelhead of the nation on this fly. He also established a record that afternoon that I have never seen equaled. He took his limit of five Steelhead and they averaged a little over twelve pounds each—the largest weighing 18 pounds. Using the first four letters of his last name, I therefore christened this fly the Thor.

Umpqua Special (recipe on page 257)

In probably the finest tale I have read involving the Umpqua Special, the fly itself is but a footnote to a captivating story of a first encounter with a North Umpqua steelhead. It is an episode familiar to countless anglers who have cast the hallowed waters of this most famous of steelhead rivers. From the magnificently clear and startlingly swift currents, to the treacherously difficult wading, to the river's electrifyingly powerful steelhead, to the will-testing patience and determination required for success, Syl MacDowell, in *Western Trout*, captured the essence of the North Umpqua:

> Old Man Gairdnerii torpedoed that red, yellow, and white Umpqua Special when I was teeter-tailing on a wet rock with deep, fast water and treacherous bedrock bottom all around me. I had made a precarious wade to reach that position. In so doing I had ignored warnings against fishing from such billy-goat perches. The ideal casting position is on an open bank, with a few hundred yards to caper along with a hooked fish, rod gripped overhead and reel whirring.
>
> I should have remembered. That steelhead reminded me of my mistake in a hurry. A blur of action, a burst of uncontrollable force, and we parted company all too soon. Away went fish, fly and leader tippet.
>
> Until then I had fallen into dogged, almost despairing angling, mechanically going through the moves of casting thousands of times over, without eagerness or expectation. Who wouldn't, after long, eventless months of it, reaching from one season into the next?
>
> But now I had, at least, the needed stimulation. I had hooked one. From this time on I tried with tremendous zest. Everything else was neglected—gainful pursuits, meals, everything. I talked, lived, and dreamed steelhead. Nothing else was important.

The colorful, attractive Umpqua Special—an offshoot of the Rogue River Special—is of uncertain pedigree, though some have said that the reclusive Vic O'Byrne (1890–1951) may have had a hand in originating the pattern. He had a small, remote cabin 2 miles up Cougar Trail from Clarence Gordon's lodge, and one evening appeared at the camp, when Jack Hemingway was there, "dressed to the teeth," as Hemingway later recalled in his posthumously published *A Life Worth Living: Adventures of a Passionate Sportsman* (2004). He partook in libations and, rather mysteriously, drowned on his way home later that night. An Irish immigrant and World War I veteran whose lungs had been damaged by gassing, O'Byrne apparently had moved to the west for his health and the fishing, and may have been the first to introduce two-handed rods to the local rivers, first the Kalama and then the North Umpqua.

What research I have done on O'Byrne suggests that he first came to America through Hawaii and then settled in Los Angeles before moving north to San Francisco in the early or mid-1930s. His name appears on the passenger lists for arrival in Hawaii; in 1942 he filled out a World War II draft registration card with a stated address as: "c/o Trust Department, Bank of America, San Francisco," but the 1940 census lists his residence as Douglas County, Oregon; the *Oakland Tribune* (May 18, 1939) references a story that came over the wire from Roseburg about Victor O'Byrne "of Los Angeles" landing a 25-pound North Umpqua Chinook salmon on a fly rod (I believe this feat occurred after he had moved to the Northwest). Even Hemingway's memory of O'Byrne may have been flawed, as he recalls meeting O'Byrne in 1948 and says that O'Byrne drowned that evening; yet O'Byrne actually drowned in 1951. Moreover, as noted in *The Creel: North Umpqua River Edition* (ed. Bob Wethern), O'Byrne was fastidious in manner and dress, so being "dressed to the teeth" would have been quite typical for him.

Whether O'Byrne devised this fly is uncertain; I suspect credit really goes to Frank Colvin for the dressing, though not the name, but O'Byrne's story is an intriguing part of North Umpqua lore. Wistfully, this iconic pattern is no longer fashionable on the North Umpqua and rarely seen. Yet it remains as effective as any newcomer and more elegant than most; it deserves a resurgence on the waters where it was born.

Van Luven and Myers Buck (recipes on pages 257 and 252)

Peter J. Schwab, the famous Northern California angler, named this fly to honor its co-inventor, his steelheading mentor Harry Van Luven (1867–1930), of Portland, Oregon. Van Luven frequented the Rogue, and Schwab told author Joseph D. Bates, Jr., (*Streamer Fly Fishing in Fresh and Salt Water*) that Van Luven "tied six of the 'red flies' every night in his little cabin near Ennis Riffle on the Rogue River, and it was the only fly I ever knew him to use." Van Luven and one of his fishing partners, Jack Myers, arrived at the final version of their Red Fly—still known only by that name—by what Schwab called a "simple process of elimination starting with the great Royal Coachman." By the time Schwab gave the fly its name in the late 1920s, Myers and Van Luven had been fishing the Rogue for years, sometimes in the company of casting champion Walter Backus, also from Portland. In 1922, Van Luven landed a 15-pound Rogue River steelhead, no doubt on his Red Fly.

At the same time they were fishing the Red Fly, which had evolved from a featherwing pattern to a bucktail, the duo came up with a yellow version they simply called the Yellow Fly. Later, this fly was named the Myers Buck, or Myers Bucktail. The Van Luven, of course, resembles Jim Pray's Thor, which became popular in the late 1930s, but the resemblance is entirely accidental, and the famous Eureka fly shop owner graciously acknowledged Van Luven's precedence, telling Bates, "Harry Van Luven tied a fly very closely resembling this pattern probably earlier than I tied the Thor. It was essentially the same except that it had a silk body instead of chenille and it was spiraled with oval silver tinsel."

Harold Smedley, in his lovely and informative book, *Fly Patterns and Their Origins*, opined that these two flies can be improved by making the tails and wings from polar bear hair, and adding "a thin topping of brilliant yellow polar to finish." Given my own proclivity for such improvements, I think Smedley, a casting expert and champion from Michigan, was well ahead of his time with regard to such modifications.[63]

Van Sant (Van Zandt) (recipe on page 258)

On the heels of steelhead fly fishing's founding fathers—John S. Benn, John Butler, and a few others, who had journeyed north, arduously, to reach the Eel River as early as the mid- to late 1880s—came an influential crop of local anglers on the Eel. Indeed, the local sportsmen probably began casting flies on the Eel for "salmon-trout," even before the "Three Johns" (Benn, Butler, and Gallagher) and other San Francisco anglers—still content to explore the fertile anadromous-fish runs on Bay Area streams much nearer their home city—ever ventured north.

Among the Humboldt County locals was Josh Van Sant, Jr. (erroneously at times spelled Van Zandt or Van Zant, and sometimes spelled Vansant in the family's genealogical records), son of Joshua Van Sant (1834–1913), who served Eureka in a variety of capacities, including a lengthy stint as county undersheriff. The elder Van Sant, who seems to have sought fortune in the gold fields of the American River in 1850 after moving west from Maryland, was demonstrably a fisherman: one day in September, 1864, he gifted a rod-caught salmon to the editors at the *Humboldt Times*. His son Josh Van Sant, Jr. (1861–1950) was also a sportsman, as well as a photographer who opened a studio in downtown Eureka for a time; Josh was best remembered as owner of the city's Empire Theater (later the Rialto) and Margarita Theater. The *Eureka Humboldt Standard* (August 16, 1958) recalled, "The late well-known Eurek-an Joshua Vansant first operated the theater shortly after it was built at the turn of the century. His widow, Louise, now 90, still lives at 2434 D Street. 'It's been so long ago, and I haven't thought of the theater for years. I can't remember too much about it,' mused the elderly Mrs. Vansant. 'But I do remember we had wonderful crowds and fine performances in the old days,'."[64] The pattern bearing his name harkens to the earliest days of steelhead fly angling, and not surprisingly, many of these early patterns dedicated specifically to steelhead resembled the most popular trout wet flies of the day, especially the Scarlet Ibis (Red Ibis), Royal Coachman, and Parmechene Belle, three imports from the American Northeast that would serve as templates for myriad variations. The Van Sant, which resembles the Scarlet Ibis save for the body material, is a good example of one of these variations.

"As a rule the steelhead flies have some red in their make-up," reported Edward Cave in *Recreation* magazine in 1915 ("Salmon and Steelheads in Northern California," Issue 3, 1915). He continued: "In fact, the eastern angler finds himself pretty much at sea among the popular flies used by these California anglers. For instance, he finds the scarlet ibis tied with a peacock herl body, like the coachman, and called the Van Sant, and the same fly but with jungle-cock wing, the Josh Van Sant."[65]

Weitchpec Witch (recipe on page 258)

Weitchpec, the accepted Anglicization today for the Yurok Weitspus or Wechpues, is a tiny unincorporated village on the lower Klamath River, but more significantly it has always been the center of the Yurok world, or as Theodora Kroeber wrote in the foreword to her husband A. L. Kroeber's book, *Yurok Myths*, "Weitspus, the village, is at the junction of the Klamath and Trinity rivers; it is as well at the Center of the World."

Indeed, of the many unique and complex cultures that evolved on the West Coast over the course of over 10,000 years, none were more intriguing nor—thanks in part to Kroeber—more studied than the Yurok. Like many coastal cultures along the Pacific, the actual Yurok world was quite small geographically. Kroeber, who studied the Yurok people and recorded their mythology in spectacular detail, explained, "The Yurok land consists of two lines, each stretching a scant fifty miles. One is a straight hilly coast, the other the Klamath River, winding only in short bends. The two lines meet at a sharp angle at Rekwoi [a major Yurok village about 1 mile above the current town of Requa], at the mouth. The upper end of the line of river is Weitspus, where the Klamath, which previously has been flowing south, turns with an impressive sweep to the northwest, and the Trinity comes in. . . . Upstream on the Klamath the alien neighbors of the Yurok were the Karok."

Fittingly, the translation of the word Wechpues is "confluence," and the village carrying the name, so central to Yurok history and culture, is present-day home of the Yurok Tribal Office and Community Center. Moreover, beginning in 2010, the Yurok tribe partnered with Portland-based Western Rivers Conservancy to create a salmon sanctuary and ensure the survival of anadromous fish runs on the Klamath River. The backbone of this effort is Blue Creek, a vital cold-water tributary on the lower Klamath and a lifeline for migrating salmon and steelhead.

The attractive fly named for the Yurok village is of uncertain pedigree. George Burdick, author of *Klamath River Angling Guide* (1989) repeats Trey Combs (*Steelhead Fly Fishing and Flies*) in noting that the fly was created in 1949. Burdick says it may have been devised by Henry Hilton—inventor of the Silver Hilton—who had a cabin about four miles upstream from the village.

Wells Special (recipe on page 258)

Around 1917 Sam Wells moved to Eureka, then the epicenter of steelhead fly fishing, with the famous Eel River nearby. Having worked as a salesman at the renowned Golcher Bros. sporting goods store in San Francisco, Wells must have decided he wanted his own shop, and in Eureka—a destination for anglers of all kinds—he found clientele keen to embrace his attention to fine tackle. For many years, he had flies dressed in Ireland and sent to him for sale in his shop at 315 F Street; he imported English reels, Scottish lines, and many other "High Class Necessities." In *Steelhead Fly Fishing and Flies*, Trey Combs includes a 1940 letterhead from Wells stating that he had imported Irish-made flies for 18 years and listing some accoutrements available in his shop. Combs says Wells devised the exquisite Wells Special around 1920, which would coincide with Wells's early years in Eureka. I have not discerned for certain when Wells moved to Eureka, but he is listed in the *Crocker–Langley San Francisco City Directory* up through 1916, but not in 1918 or 1920. In at least one of the directories he is listed as a salesman for Golcher Bros.

Wells had been a champion caster and member of the San Francisco Fly Casting Club, and won the club's 1914 distance-casting competition as reported in the September, 1914 issue of *Forest & Stream*. He garnered great acclaim on the Eel and other waters, where among his fishing partners was Milt Carson, son of the great lumber magnate, William Carson.

The fly has long since fallen into obscurity, and the well-traveled outdoor writer A. J. McClain explained why in a February, 1949 piece for *Field & Stream* titled "The Western World":

> For quite some time after steelhead fishing got under way, the flies used were largely Atlantic salmon or trout patterns, in many cases being variations of both. The Wells' Special typifies this pioneering, and likewise typifies the "salting out" process that struck many of the originals. In the beginning the fly came from England under the name of Kate. Minor changes were imposed, and anglers fished with a California version of the Kate, now called the Wells' Special. After kicking around in California it went to southern Oregon, where it had minor successes; but because it was one of the few steelhead patterns requiring "marrying" of the wing, it dropped out of circulation.

Whitesel's Wine (recipe on page 258)

By the early 1920s, Southern Oregon's Rogue River had equaled if not surpassed the famous Eel and Klamath Rivers in California as the premier destination for anglers in pursuit of steelhead. And while astute anglers from throughout the Northwest and California were well aware of the Rogue's excellent fall fishing for steelhead by the time Zane Grey first visited in 1919, the famous "writer of the purple prose" essentially put the Rogue on the map for the rest of the country with his writings, including two books, *Tales of Freshwater Fishing* (1928) and *Rogue River Feud* (1929), as well as magazine pieces, such as "Shooting the Rogue" in the *Country Gentleman*, May, 1926.

But another important factor was in play even before Grey set eyes on the Rogue: the state of Oregon, in a wise management decision, curtailed commercial fishing for steelhead on the Rogue while such harvest of the Northern California rivers had burgeoned into a massive industry. On March 9, 1911, in a story titled "An Asset for Oregon," the *Medford Mail Tribune* presaged the future of the Rogue:

> The best fly fishing stream in California has for many years, been the Eel river, which flows through Humboldt county. It has for years enjoyed the reputation in California that the Rogue had in Oregon—of furnishing the finest steel head angling in the state, and was a mecca for the money spending sportsmen of the coast.
>
> The glory of the Eel, however, is about to depart. That a few Portuguese and others too lazy to work, may make a comfortable living, the Eel river is to be commercialized, and steel head seining is to be permitted.
>
> A law recently passed by the California legislature, sanctions the seining and sale of steelhead below tide water from October 23 to February 1. As the Eel is a small stream, and the big run of steel head comes during this period, when the fish go upstream to spawn, the extermination of the steelhead in the Eel is but a question of a few years. In addition to this regular steel head season, fishermen are allowed to keep and sell all steelhead taken in nets after September 17.
>
> Now that the people of Oregon have closed the Rogue to commercial fishing and the governor of Oregon has kept it closed, and the legislature of California opened its streams to commercial fishermen, the Rogue will soon have the national reputation as the only exclusively angling stream on the coast and will attract hither thousands of anglers from all parts of the country, including those who formerly annually visited the Eel.

Soon anglers flocked to the Rogue each fall, and the river quickly developed its own culture on the strength of the angling feats and flies of local men such as Joe Wharton, Al Knudson, Russ Tower, Bob Savage, and Frank Colvin, among others; so, too, came the well-to-do traveling anglers, some of whom built cabins, houses, and lodges on the Rogue. Among them were Fred Burnham, Fred Noyes, and of course, Grey. With the river's rich culture and excellent fishing still at hand in the middle decades of the twentieth century, it's easy to see how the great steelheader from Portland, Mike Kennedy, became enraptured by the Rogue. Named for his Seattle-based friend, Jack Whitesel (1908–2003), Whitesel's Wine is among Kennedy's most attractive flies.

Witherwox Special (recipe on page 258)

"The fall steelhead were running last month in Oregon's famed Rogue River," reported Virginia Kraft in the days when *Sports Illustrated* and its readers still took an interest in outdoor pursuits. Kraft continued:

> Fresh from their dark, mysterious feeding places in the sea, they plunged in pink-and-silver splendor through the Pacific surf at Gold Beach into the broad, flat estuaries of the river. As they surged toward distant inland spawning beds, anglers came from all over the country to intercept them. With Silver Doctors and March Browns fishermen worked Pierce Riffle above the town of Grants Pass and cast Witherwox Specials and Golden Demons from the gravel bars below it. (From "Steelheads on a Rough River," *Sports Illustrated*, November 15, 1965.)

The Witherwox Special is a Rogue River original: the Rogue may be the only place it's ever been fished. The Witherwox Special's pedigree is pure and its lineage—no doubt the Royal Coachman family—uncluttered. Named by its inventor, Hally Witherwox (1895–1980), better known as Hal, this lovely little pattern should instill confidence in an angler anywhere on the steelhead coast. Hal Witherwox and his wife Bea ran Black Bar Lodge, on the Rogue about 9 miles below Grave Creek, during the 1950s; they managed the property for owner Tom Orderman, a Portland attorney, beginning shortly after he purchased it in the early 1930s, and helped oversee the construction of the lodge. During the 30s, Hal and Bea hosted Orderman's friends and business associates, some of whom were journeying downriver to visit Orderman's friend, the famous writer Zane Grey, at his place on Winkle Bar. In the 50s, Hal and Bea began catering to anglers, running the lodge as a commercial operation.

To this day, Black Bar Lodge still exudes the grace of a lovely old fishing lodge from those halcyon days when adventurous souls from around the world came to the Rogue's slippery bedrock to swing flies like the Witherwox Special, cast with silken lines by split-can rods.[66]

Yellow Hammer (recipe on page 258)

I often wonder how the one-armed fly tier from Seattle, Dan Conway, arrived at the name for his Yellow Hammer, which is almost identical to his better-known Conway Special. Perhaps the name is straightforward: it is yellow, and it hammered the steelhead for several decades.

To posit another (perhaps unlikely) possibility, note that the northern flicker—a large, familiar woodpecker—is ubiquitous throughout the continent. In the West, we have the red-shafted flicker, named for the underside and edges of the tail and flight feathers, which are a flashy shade of red. In the eastern half of the continent lives the yellow-shafted flicker, nearly identical except that those red feathers are yellow. Quite some time ago, these two attractive and gregarious birds were lumped together under the name northern flicker. Throughout much of the yellow-shafted flicker's range, and especially in the American South, the common parlance for the bird is "yellow hammer" or, more precisely, "yaller hammer."

In the South, especially in Tennessee, there is a popular old fly called the Yallarhammer: so named because anglers tied it with the quill from a yellow-shafted flicker. But the Yallarhammer and Conway's Yellow Hammer are unrelated. Still, the name of the western Yellow Hammer might come from the bird: as settlers moved west in the nineteenth century, they brought their parlance with them—and despite its red feathers, the western flicker was commonly called a yellow hammer. You can find examples of the term yellow hammer being applied to western red-shafted flickers in newspaper searches. One interesting example appeared in the *Morning Oregonian*, August 8, 1914, which reported on Joe Knowles undertaking a 15-day "nature man" test in the woods of southern Oregon. He used a bone from the "breast bone of a yellow hammer he had killed with a stone" to make a fishing hook. Knowles then made the "fly part of the hook" from partridge feathers, which would probably be ruffed grouse feathers as the grouse was often called a partridge in some parts of its range.

At any rate, Ken Binns, outdoors columnist for the *Seattle Times* in the 1930s, considered the Yellow Hammer a standard, touting its virtues alongside the Royal Coachman, Professor, and Jock Scott.[67] Conway tied it with quill wings (he preferred snow goose), but George McLeod, as explained to me by his son, Ken James McLeod, dressed the fly with bucktail, no doubt propelling the Yellow Hammer to longstanding popularity by making it easier to tie and offering it commercially. It was a standard into the 1960s, even earning a 12-pound summer fish for Phil Tucker of Lake Forest Park in June, 1967. The *Seattle Times* (June 11, 1967) carried a photo of Tucker with his fish—a large steelhead for the North Fork's summer run. A decade earlier, in the 1950s, Enos Bradner reported in the *Times* on Walt Johnson using the Yellow Hammer to take winter steelhead on the Skagit ("Peninsula Rivers Offer Best Steelheading," March 16, 1956), and he mentions the Yellow Hammer as one of the "early patterns used on the Stilly" ("Chart Gives Magic Hours For Steelhead Fishing," July 9, 1959).

According to Ken, "The Yellow Hammer had been tied by our family using fluorescent yellow-green chenille. Mary [George's sister, and also a fly tier] ordered yellow [chenille] in the 1960s, but they sent a bright greenish color, so we used it too."

CHAPTER V

Style Conversions of Classic Patterns

In this idyllic scene, an angler casts a long line over a broad tailout on a western Oregon steelhead river.

The joy of owning fine tackle is so great that it is often difficult to distinguish between basic needs and the urge to possess that which delights the sensitivities.

—Harold Blaisdell, *The Philosophical Fisherman,* 1969.

Classic steelhead flies lend themselves to a wide range of stylistic interpretations. Tiers render such expressions by altering the materials and the proportions of a standard dressing. Several of the old hair wings are formulaic: a tag, a tail of hackle fibers, a wool yarn or chenille body, a hackle, and a wing of bucktail or similar hair. So for example, a Del Cooper, a Polar Shrimp, a Purple Peril, a Skykomish, and a Killer are all basically identical except for the colors; so too, a Black Gordon, a Prince, and a Max Canyon adhere to the same basic concept (a butt of one color and a body of another). Change the colors, and you change the pattern. But change the materials while maintaining the colors, and only the style changes, not the pattern. Thus, classic steelhead flies, by their nature, leave ample opportunity for personal expression through variation.

As autumn's colorful foliage fades, an angler hooks a late-October steelhead.

My own steelhead fly tying was first shaped by the works of Ed Haas and Cal Bird, whose precise "brush strokes" with their methods, materials, and styles produced beautifully perfect flies in the tradition of the great mid-twentieth-century tiers; not long after, my fly-dressing style and techniques were profoundly influenced by David McNeese. His influence on the steelhead genre was monumental in the 1980s, and many classic steelhead flies dressed by tiers today bear the unmistakable marks of the McNeese style. One such characteristic is the use of dyed golden pheasant crest feathers—called "toppings"—as tails on steelhead flies, an affectation devised by McNeese. On that count, the historical record is clear: Prior to the McNeese's Fly Shop era, when Dave and his employees used these dyed-crest tails extensively, these toppings do not appear on steelhead flies. The entire body of steelhead fly literature bears this out.

In my opinion, the pursuit of steelhead with fly tackle should be imbued with artistry, both in the tactics we choose and the flies we employ. A steelhead is too fine a gamefish to be insulted with ugly flies; a simple classic steelhead fly—say a Brindle Bug or a Skunk —even when dressed by a novice tier is nonetheless an object of beauty worthy of the steelhead's majesty, for it is a fly with a pedigree, with a history deriving from the great anglers, rivers, and feats of our pursuit.

What follows here is but a sampling of classic flies dressed in the manner that I most enjoy fishing them. Again, you'll find recipes for them in the Appendix. They may take more time to construct, and feature affectations that have no bearing on their effectiveness, but they adhere to my personal ethos. The only critique I ever find offensive is the insinuation that any particular fly, no matter how regaled with rare feathers and how time-consuming to produce, is "too good to fish." The steelhead of the Northwest, as they grow increasingly rare, deserve our most sincere efforts to maintain the artistry and culture of our chosen method of angling for them.

Max Canyon and Black Max (recipes on pages 252 and 244)

Skykomish Sunrise and Al's Special (recipes on pages 256 and 243)

Cummings Special and Silver Demon (recipes on pages 247 and 255)

Black Prince and Icterus (recipes on pages 244 and 250)

Brad's Brat and Kalama Special (recipes on pages 245 and 251)

The Spawning Purple: Evolution of a Confidence Fly

The Spawning Purple provides an example of evolution among flies. Tiers tinker with past designs and alter their tinkerings to arrive at new patterns, and this was certainly the case with the Spawning Purple, my confidence fly.

The evolution of this fly began in the mid-1980s, a decade after Dave McNeese devised a new robust hair-wing fly for winter steelhead tied on size 2/0 through 4/0 heavy-wire hooks. McNeese envisioned a spin-off on the venerable General Practitioner, an English fly that had recently found its way to the West Coast and begun making occasional appearances on the North Umpqua (it would gain widespread acceptance after steelheaders in British Columbia embraced it). Conceptualizing—the ability to envision the finished product before ever setting thread to steel—is a hallmark of McNeese's wonderful ingenuity at the tying bench; he is an artist, after all, who is skilled with pen and paper, colored pencil, and other media. And those talents have ultimate expression in McNeese's steelhead fly designs. He melds colors and styles and materials with honed tying skills, taking inspiration from the works of Preston Jennings.

McNeese's big winter steelhead fly embodied his creative ability. It featured a tail of orange-dyed polar bear hair dressed long in the style of the General Practitioner. The body was orange seal's fur, loosely dubbed, with three glistening wings of purple-dyed polar bear hair tied in near the front of the shank. Wide purple hackle and natural guinea formed a two-part collar. McNeese named the pattern the Spawning Purple, and it proved both beautiful and effective. But it never achieved fame and McNeese tied only a few dozen copies, mostly for himself and friends (many years later he developed a renewed vigor for tying this and others of his old flies). Nevertheless, when he opened his fly shop in Salem in 1977, McNeese stocked the fly displays with a few dozen Spawning Purples, and in subsequent years Forrest Maxwell and I tied a few for the shop each winter. I always liked the Spawning Purple and decided to create a slimmed-down version for low summer flows.

First I substituted orange floss for the dubbed body, and purple marabou for the polar bear wings. Then I changed the tail to dyed-orange golden pheasant crest and added a throat of heron hackle. At the time, McNeese had a supply of hackles from the European grey heron (*Ardea cinerea*), which he had imported from England for sale in the shop (unlike feathers from the indigenous great blue heron, which are illegal to possess, the grey heron was not protected by the Migratory Bird Treaty Act). I added a pair of peacock secondary quill segments for the type of "strip wing" commonly seen on nineteenth-century Atlantic salmon flies from the Rivers Spey and Dee in Scotland. The

A mouthful of Spawning Purple.

A favorite fly—in the author's case, this Spawning Purple—is made all the more alluring when cast with a favorite bamboo steelhead rod.

floss work was tedious, so I switched to single-strand heavy thread called flat waxed nylon, which was available in fluorescent colors. I liked the fluorescent flame shade better than fluorescent orange, so that color became the standard.

I called the resulting pattern the Spawning Purple Spey, with the "Spey" part of the name coming from the heron hackle and the strip wings. That was—in retrospect—a mistake. By the truest definition, a Spey fly is a unique style developed on the River Spey in the nineteenth century; they are identified by both their style and their place of origin. But beginning with Syd Glasso in the 1960s, steelhead fly tiers began using the name freely. McNeese, myself, and a few others, however, bear some of the burden of having denigrated the term Spey fly. We (and others before us) began using it to name the numerous flies with long-fibered body hackles and strip-style wings we were designing in the 1980s; however, more significantly—and more unfortunately—we began publishing magazine articles featuring those flies. By the late 1980s and early 1990s, Northwest steelhead tiers were designing supposed Spey flies so rapidly that they couldn't hope to be cataloged. I suppose we can't be blamed for our exuberance, but in my case at least, by the time I realized my error, the floodgates were fully open, and it was impossible to stem the tide of mislabeling our flies and misrepresenting those beautiful old Scottish Spey flies.

In any event, the Spawning Purple Spey was born of my admiration of McNeese's Spawning Purple and named because

Battered, beaten, and even broken, this stash of well-used Spawning Purples testifies to a remarkable successful week of steelhead angling on a Snake River tributary.

I added heron hackle and strip wings. Soon, however, I found myself digging deeper into the dark, dusty corners of the fly shop for what few heron feathers remained in the building until they'd all vanished. I tried different types of feathers as a replacement for the heron, but none caught my fancy. So I dropped the heron hackle from the pattern but retained the name Spawning Purple Spey.

The fly proved its value on the river, fishing well and hooking steelhead. I enjoyed tying it and did so not only to fill the fly bins at the shop but also in demonstrations at shows or club meetings. Then people began asking why I called it a Spey pattern. I grew weary of the long explanation, so I finally dropped Spey from the name, in favor of Shewey's Spawning Purple, to differentiate from McNeese's earlier fly. That name was a mouthful, and few people used it. Now anglers simply call it the Spawning Purple, the same as the original pattern, though I still prefer to call it Shewey's Spawning Purple in deference to the McNeese original. The recipe is on page 255.

CHAPTER VI

Notes on Tying

To see the ideas of your brain materialize in the vise is the prime reward of fly-tying . . . the creation is the thing that gets you. It stimulates your imagination and ingenuity . . .

—Ray Bergman, *Trout,* 1938.

With a grasp of fundamental techniques, a working knowledge of basic materials, and a bit of practice, even novice fly tiers can dress elegant classic steelhead flies.

Illustrated Steelhead Fly-Tying Glossary

Bucktail fly: Originally "bucktail fly" referred to patterns (mostly streamer-type) flies with wings made from bucktail; the definition is looser now, and the term often refers to specific steelhead patterns with hair wings, even if those wings are made from some other type of hair. For example, the name Bucktail Coachman remains even if the wing is made from calf tail.

Burnishing: With floss and tinsel fly bodies, the smoother the underbody, the smoother and neater the finished body. Burnishing is a simple process of using a smooth tool (polished wood or smooth metal) to rub the underbody and smooth out thread ridges. The handles of many tying tools serve well for burnishing.

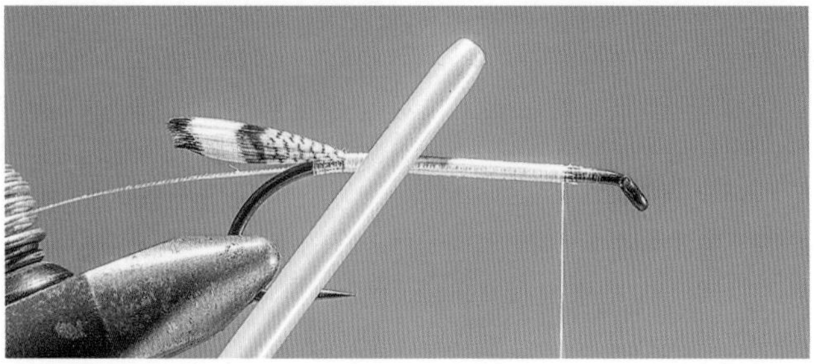

Butt: The rear end of the body of many steelhead flies, when formed with a few turns of wool yarn, chenille, dubbing, silk floss, etc. of a different shade than the body, is called the butt. This Purple Angel has a butt of fluorescent flame-red chenille.

Cheeks: Usually made from jungle cock "eyes" (neck feathers; see "jungle cock," page 202), cheeks adorn the front sides of the wing on many steelhead flies, trailing back along the wing or body.

Collar: The term collar is generally synonymous with the term hackle; it is the hackle feather wrapped in the standard fashion at the front of the fly, such as on this Skykomish Sunrise, which has a collar formed from one red and one yellow hackle. In some cases, a fly may have a hackle applied under the wing, or a hackle spiraled through the body, and a second hackle applied after the wing is tied in. In these cases, the second hackle (often duck flank or guinea) is usually called a collar.

Dubbing hook/Dubbing loop: A dubbing hook (top), or dubbing-loop tool, is a shepherd's hook–style tool used to create dubbing loops, which are doubled lengths of tying thread within which you spin dubbing materials. A dubbing loop more easily handles coarse furs that do not easily spin onto the thread. Below is the thread loop formed with the tool. The dubbing is then spun into the loop.

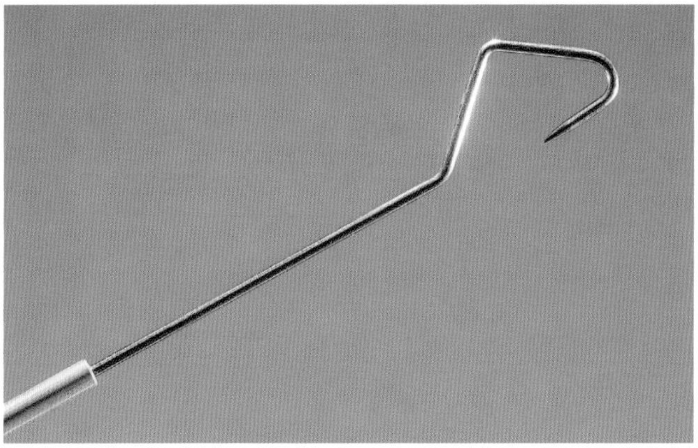

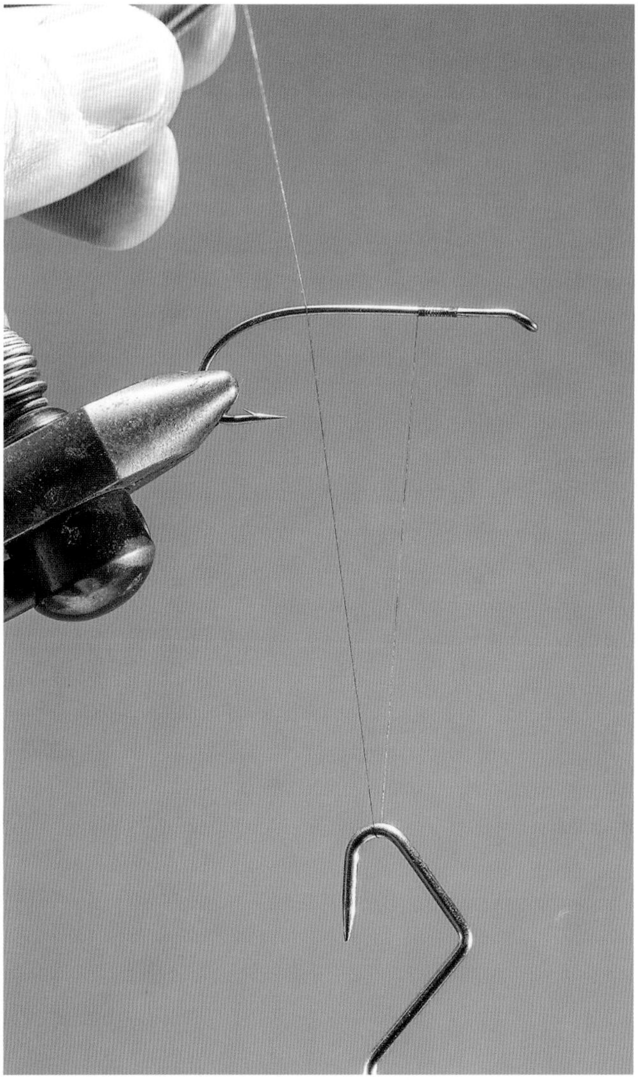

Folding (hackle): Folding is the act of preparing a hackle so that the fibers on one side are bent to the other side of the stem, effectively doubling the number of fibers on that side. Tiers use various techniques, including folding "in hand" (before the feather is attached to the fly), folding by hand after the feather is attached to the fly, and using scissors to fold the hackle after it is attached to the fly. In the top photo, the hackle has not been folded; the bottom photo shows the folded hackle.

Hard hair/Soft hair: Hairs used to make the wings on steelhead flies exhibit a wide range of characteristics; some are easier to work with than others. Soft hairs compress easily under thread tension and are simple to mount for the wing; examples include bucktail, skunk hair, and calf tail hair (from the base of the tail). The Yellow Hammer shown below is dressed with bucktail for the wing. Hard hairs are those that do not compress easily under thread tension and include squirrel tail and black bear hair, which is used on the Carter Fly shown at bottom.

Jungle cock: Jungle cock is the colloquial common name for the grey jungle fowl (*Gallus sonneratii*), a wild species of chicken endemic to India. Its attractive and unique neck feathers are frequently used as "cheeks" on steelhead flies, Atlantic salmon flies, traditional Maine featherwing streamers, and some classic trout wet flies. This Carson Coachman, sitting on a jungle cock cape, has cheeks made from jungle cock "eyes," as the small feathers are often called.

Married wing: A married wing is made by "zipping" together different colors of fibers taken from such quills as goose shoulder, turkey tail, duck or goose primary, swan quills, and others. Because the fibers on these feathers are edged with tiny Velcro-like hooks, they attach to each other easily. This Soule, a John S. Benn variation of the Parmachene Belle, has wings of white goose or duck primary with a strip of red married through the center of each.

Palmered hackle: When a hackle is wound through the body of the fly, rather than just as a collar at front, it is called a palmered hackle. This Conway Special has a palmered hackle of yellow rooster cape.

Quill wing/Strip wing: Flies dressed with strips of fibers cut from goose, swan, turkey, or other feathers, such as this General Money, are called quill-wing or strip-wing flies.

Return-loop eye: A return-loop eye (left) is the eye of a hook in which the metal loops around to form the eye, but then trails back down parallel to the shanks for a short distance. Such hooks are commonly used for steelhead flies, though ring-eye hooks (right) are also popular.

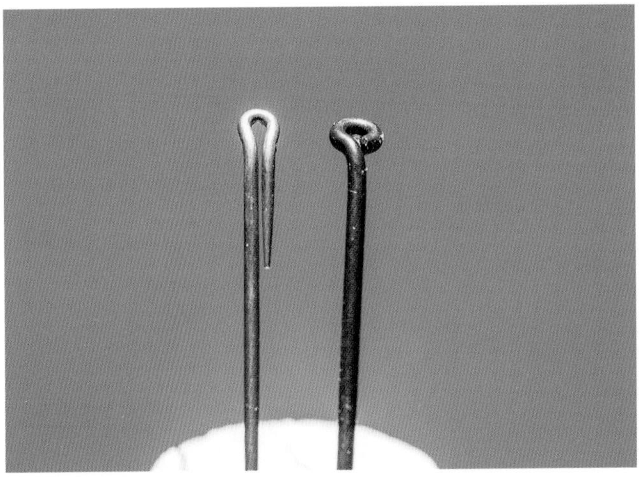

Rib/Ribbing: Spiraling over the body of a fly from back to front, the rib is usually made of oval or flat tinsel. This Boss, a type of Comet fly, has a rib of medium oval silver tinsel.

Spey fly: Characterized by a unique style of hackling combined with wings of bronze mallard or turkey tail strips, and usually multiple ribs, Spey flies are a unique type of Atlantic salmon fly developed on and named for the River Spey in northeast Scotland. They date back to at least the middle of the nineteenth century. Many contemporary steelhead flies emulate the Spey flies in some of their characteristics, though none are proper Spey flies. The Lady Caroline, shown here, is the most popular of all the old Spey flies.

Stacking/Stacked: Stacking is the technique of evening the tips of hair used for wings (and hackle fibers used for tails); it is generally done with a hair-stacking tool, which is usually a metal or wood tube within a tube or sleeve, such as those shown here.

Tag: The tag is a short length of tinsel (flat or oval), or sometimes silk or floss, located under the tail, and tiers typically create it before mounting the tail. Tags are sometimes referred to as "tips," but a true tip is usually a turn or a few turns of tinsel that extend behind the actual tag. One common technique to form a tag is to make a turn or two of the rib's oval tinsel under the tail before winding the rib, but longer tags require different techniques. These two flies show a tag of oval tinsel (front) and flat tinsel (rear).

Throat: Hackle fibers dressed only on the underside of the hook, rather than a full hackle feather wrapped as a collar, are the throat. See the guinea fibers on this Black Diamond, a Harry Lemire pattern.

Tip: A narrow band of tinsel (usually oval or flat) protruding beyond a tag of silk or floss. Sometimes tiers use the term "tip" interchangeably with "tag," but this is incorrect. This Drains 20 has a tip of silver tinsel.

Topping: In most cases, a topping is a golden pheasant crest feather crowning the wing, as in this Headrick's Hellcat.

The Soft-Loop Technique

Though not widely used, the soft-loop method of securing materials to the hook will help you obtain consistently satisfactory results with featherwings. It has many other applications as well, but because featherwings need to be compressed at the tie-in point without the actual wing folding or creasing, this technique is especially important to tiers of steelhead and Atlantic salmon flies.

The name is descriptive: rather than wrapping thread directly up and over the material you are attaching to the hook, you instead make a loose loop of thread completely around the material and the hook, and then draw the loop tight by pulling the bobbin upward. At the same time, you maintain a firm grip on both the material and the hook. In most instances, you will use your left thumb and left middle finger to grip the material in place on the hook while using your right hand to handle the bobbin (this would be reversed for a left-handed tier). The method requires proper technique and plenty of practice, but attention to detail leads to excellent wings. The following step-by-step tutorial shows the basic technique. In this example, large orange thread is used for visibility; finer tying thread yields much better results.

1. Pinching the wings (in this case, two matching slips of white turkey tail) between your thumb and middle finger, drop them down into position on the hook while sliding the bottom edge of your thumb and finger around the hook shank.

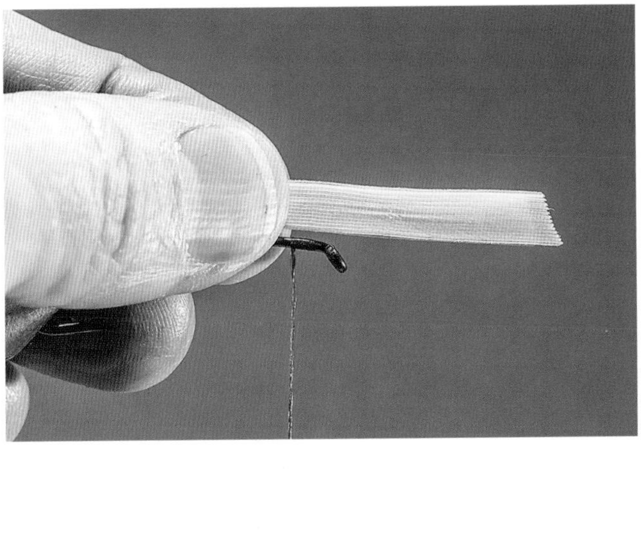

2. This step actually occurs *under the pads of your thumb and finger*, but here I have opted to show the thread for instructional purposes: when you have the wing positioned atop the hook shank, maintain a firm grip on the feathers and the hook with your thumb and finger, and then draw the bobbin up so the thread comes up across the feather *directly under* the pad of your thumb.

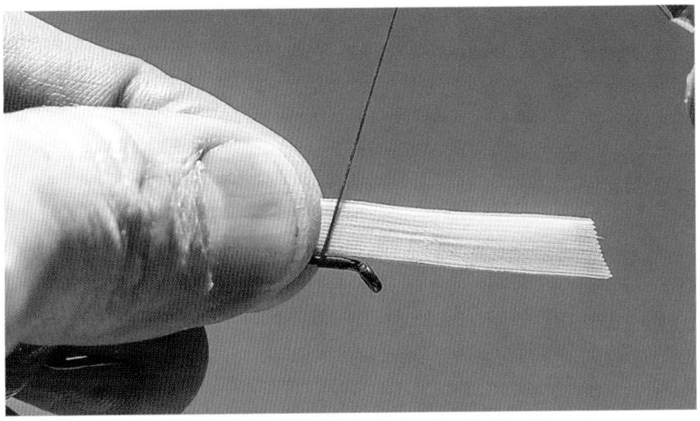

3. Here, the thumb, finger, and thread are properly positioned so that the thread is snugly held between the feather and your thumb.

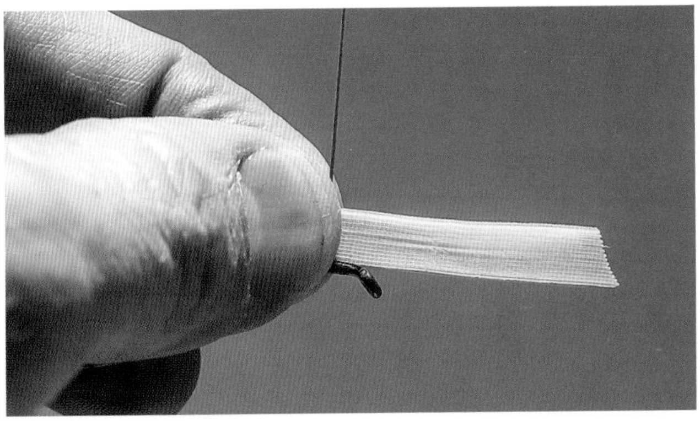

4. Now pass the thread over the top of the wing and slide it underneath the pad of your finger on the far side of the hook. Do not tighten the thread or allow the weight of the bobbin to tighten the thread.

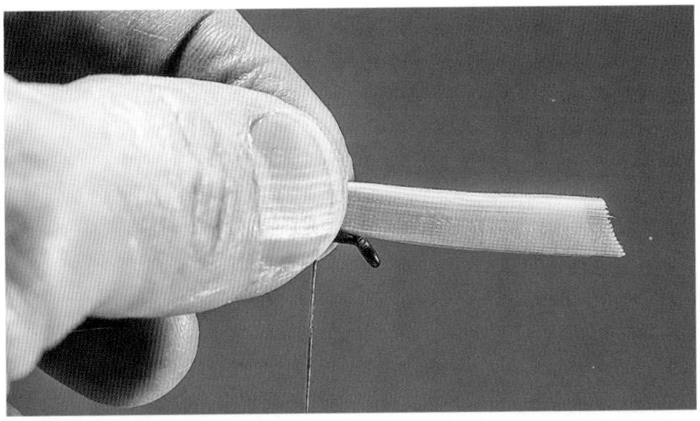

5. This photo shows the soft loop. The loop will not be visible when you tie it because it will be tucked between your thumb and finger. The near side and far side of the thread loop must be aligned with one another.

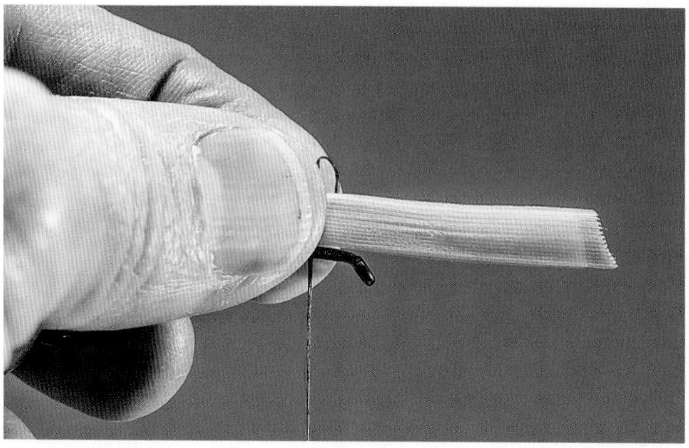

6. Again draw the thread up the near side of the hook between the pad of your thumb and the wing without releasing your grip. Slowly begin to tighten the thread by pulling directly upward with the bobbin. Some feathers can be "collapsed" into position with one loop, while others require two or three identical loops, each tightened progressively more.

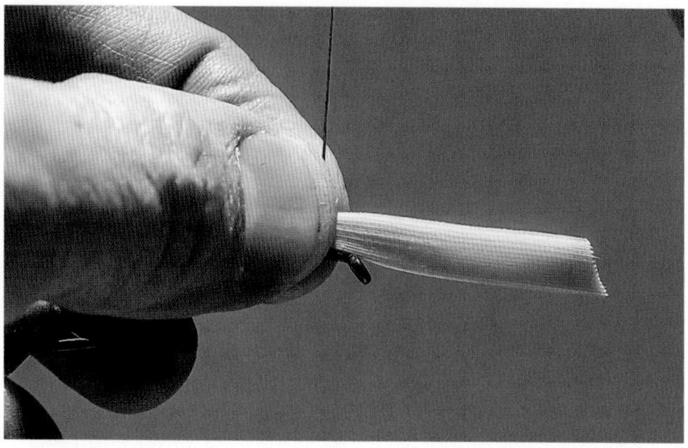

7. Maintain a firm grip with your left hand as you tighten the loop or loops, which will cause the quill segments to collapse and stack together.

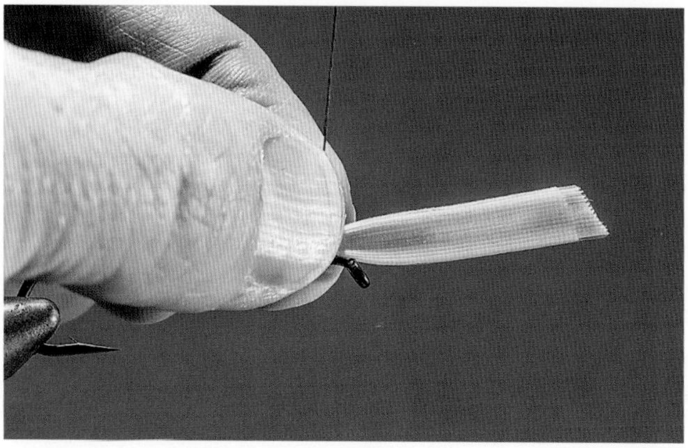

8. Notice that in this case, the near wing has creased along its center line. This is usually the result of improper grip, not maintaining the grip during the thread tightening, or improper loops.

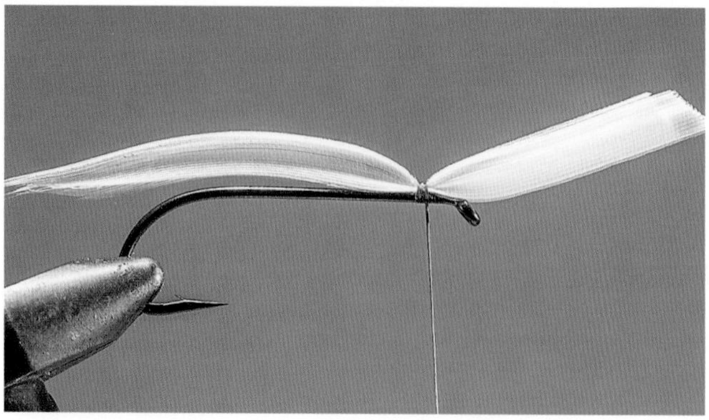

9. In this photo (with a finer, more effective thread), the wing slips have properly collapsed.

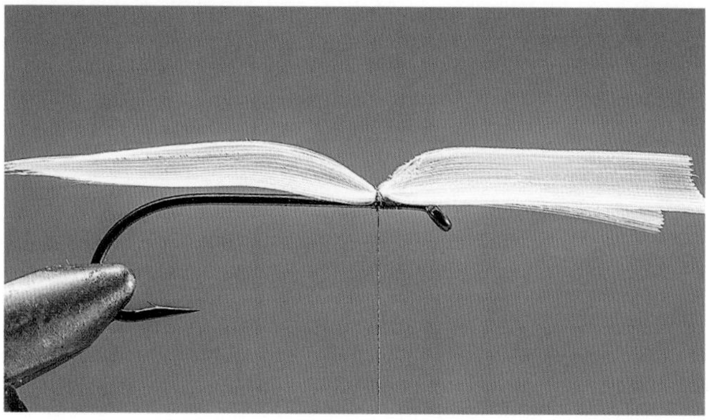

Tags

Increasingly since steelhead flies entered their truly artistic age in the 1970s, tiers have added tags to many classic patterns unadorned with such affectations by their originators. But the metallic glint or hint of color under the tail adds substantially to the elegance of many steelhead flies, so much so that these days I consider a fly lacking a tag to be incomplete. You can make tags with flat tinsel, small oval tinsel, or fine silk floss (or fine synthetic floss). The trick with tags—as with most tying techniques—is to use thread wraps purposefully and conservatively; in other words, use enough thread wraps to attach the materials securely but no more, for superfluous thread wraps tend to affect subsequent steps in building the fly.

As with most components of a fly, a variety of tying techniques can accomplish the same task. With tags of flat tinsel, I usually prefer metal rather than plastic (Mylar) tinsel because metal does not stretch and therefore maintains a uniform width as you wrap it on the shank of the hook, allowing for consistent results. With flat tinsel, the trick is to keep each wrap edge-to-edge with the previous wrap, but with no overlap. You can create smooth, practically seamless flat-tinsel tags by applying two layers of tinsel: first you wind rearward down the hook, and then you reverse directions and wrap forward, back toward the tie-in point. In most cases, starting the tinsel wraps from a tie-in point far forward of the actual tag position pays dividends because doing so prevents thread build-up at the front edge of the tag.

Finally, floss can be used to create showy tags, and so too can a combination of fine oval tinsel and fine-strand floss. In this latter arrangement, a few turns of tinsel protrude beyond the tag of floss and this tinsel segment is properly termed the "tip."

Oval-Tinsel Tag

Tags made from oval tinsel are different (see instructions below). The method I prefer requires time and persistence, but the results are excellent. A fine, multifilament, unwaxed thread is best. Carefully bind the gossamer oval tinsel down along the underside of the hook, making sure to keep the thread untwisted and thus flattened. This is accomplished by counter-spinning the bobbin several turns after each few turns of the tying thread, as the act of wrapping the bobbin round the fly continues to add a half spin to the thread with each pass (you can see this by tying most of a fly nonstop and then allowing the bobbin to hang free—it will spin of its own accord because of the twisted thread).

1. Using thread that flattens easily, attach a length of small, fine, or extra-fine oval tinsel at the front of the hook.

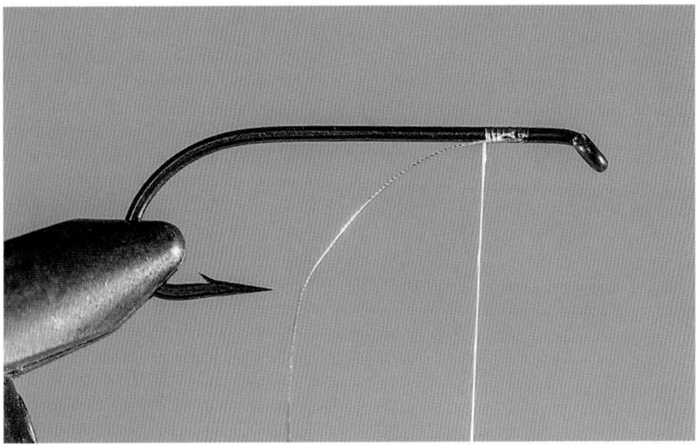

2. Bind the tinsel down along the underside of the hook shank, keeping it taut and using closely spaced thread wraps. Each style of hook will encourage a different placement for the tag, but generally it will occupy the point on the shank where the hook bend begins. Stop at that point.

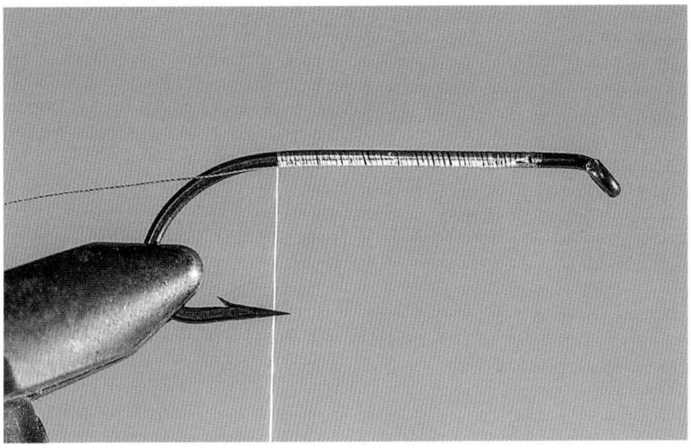

3. Be sure the thread is flattened by allowing the bobbin to hang and untwist of its own volition. Alternatively, use your thumb and fingers to gently spin the bobbin counter-clockwise to remove any twist in the thread. Then, using edge-to-edge thread wraps, bind the tinsel down along the bend of the hook to where the rear end of tag will be.

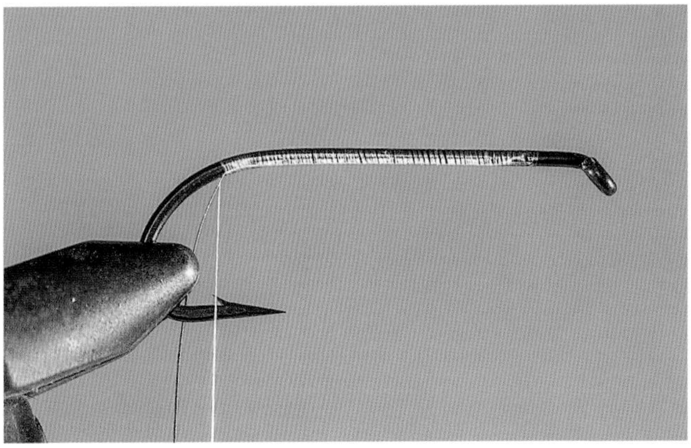

4. Again making certain the thread is flat and not twisted, reverse directions and wrap back up the bend of the hook with edge-to-edge (but not overlapping) thread wraps.

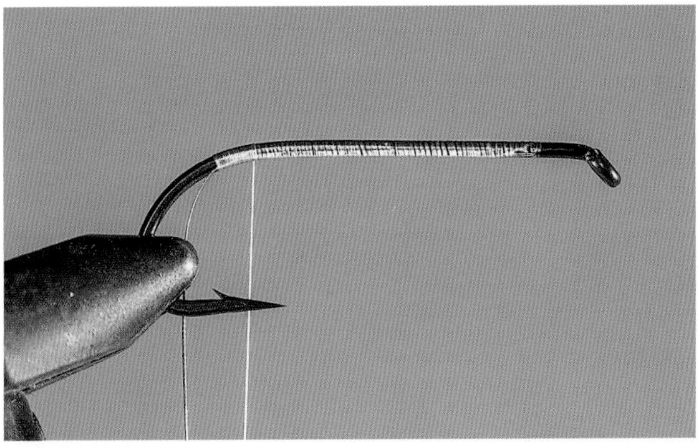

5. Wind the tinsel forward over the two layers of thread used to secure it, keeping each turn of tinsel tight up against the previous turn. Tie the tag end down directly against the last turn of the tinsel.

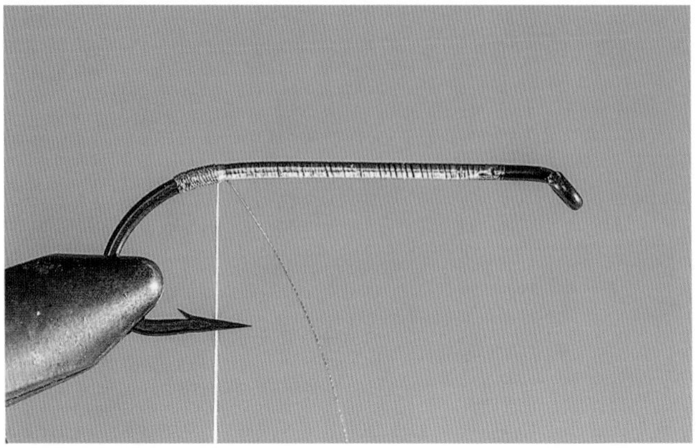

6. Bind the tag end along the underside of the hook, all the way back to the original tie-in point unless the fly will have a butt that will cover the tie-down and cut-off point at the rear.

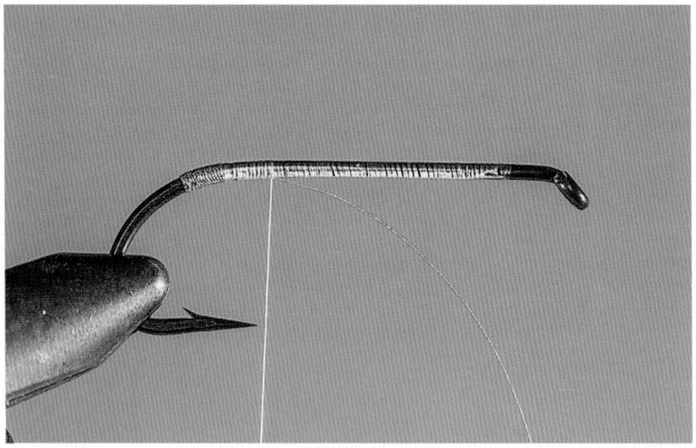

Speed Method for Tying Oval-Tinsel Tags

A much speedier but less tidy method of creating an oval tinsel tag is to simply hold the tinsel in place along the hook and then wrap back over it going forward. This method of applying a tag of oval tinsel does not deliver the superb results of the method described above, but it has an advantage in speed with just a little practice. The trick is to use the oval tinsel to bind itself as follows.

1. Bind the length of oval tinsel down along the hook shank, stopping when you reach the point where the front edge of the tag will be when it is finished.

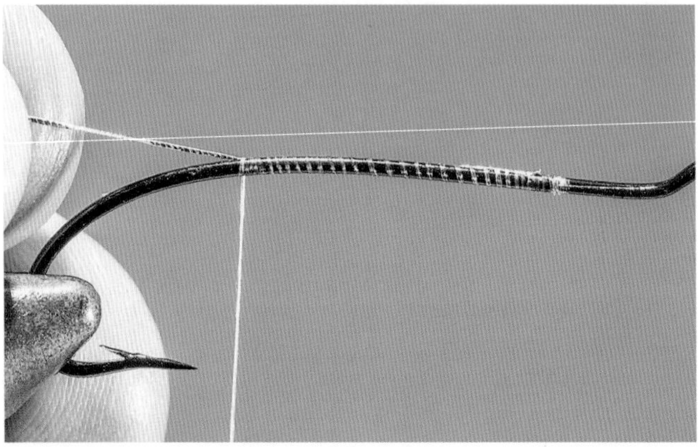

2. Pull the tinsel down along the hook shank with your left hand and press it against the hook with your left forefinger; then with your right hand pull the tag end back to your right. Maintain firm pressure with your left forefinger so the tinsel being held in place cannot move.

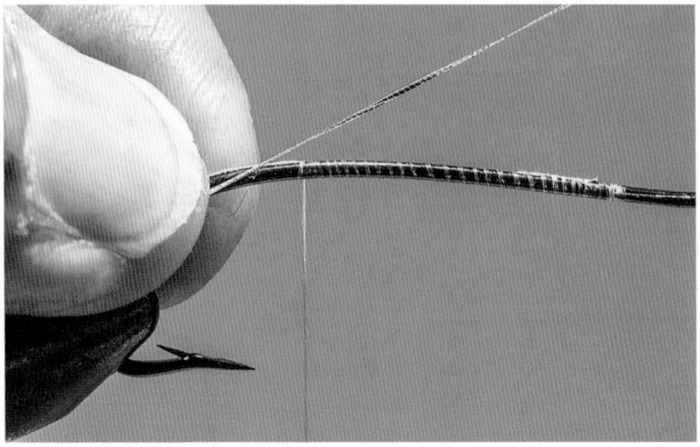

3. With your right hand, pass the tag end up and over the hook and double it over itself by slipping it between your left forefinger and the hook shank.

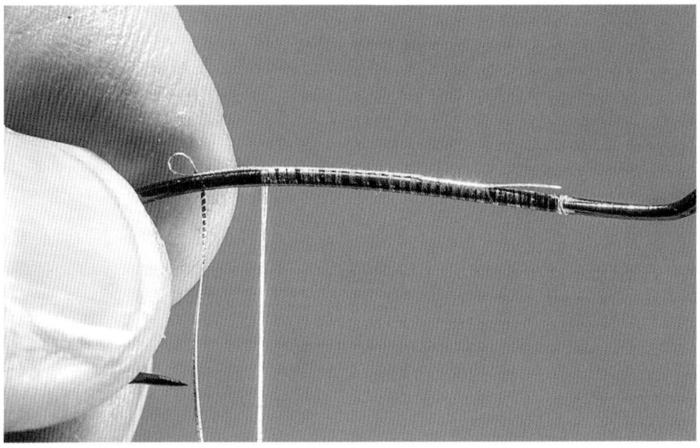

4. Once the tinsel is looped over the shank and over itself, pull it tight while still using your left forefinger to hold the tinsel in place against the hook.

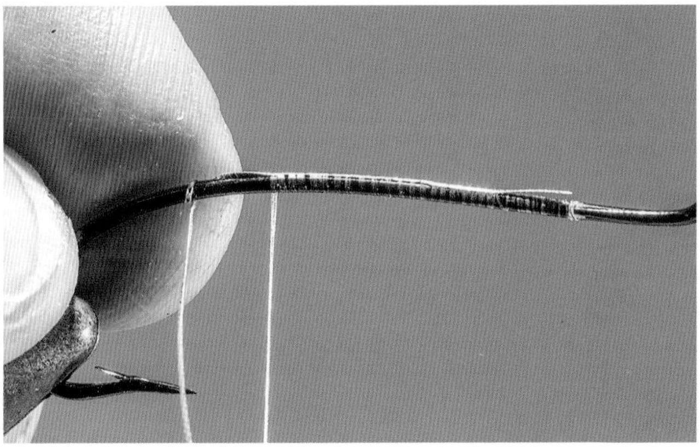

5. Make three or four such wraps so the tinsel doubles back on itself, progressing back toward the eye of the hook. Carefully pull these wraps snug while using your left finger or thumb to scoot them forward so they touch edge-to-edge.

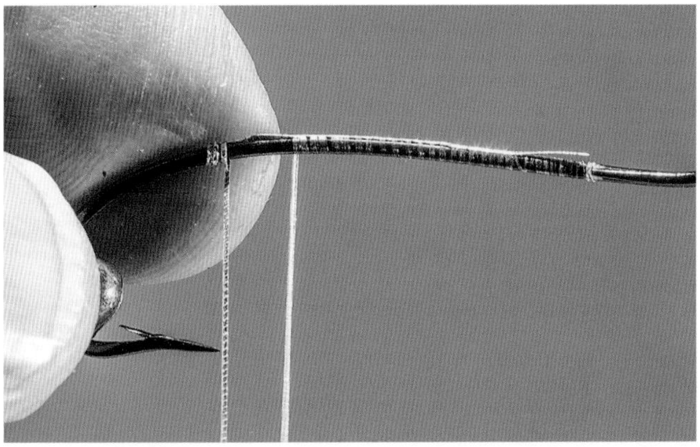

6. Continue wrapping the tinsel forward and pushing against the rear end of the tag with your left thumb or finger to eliminate gaps between the wraps.

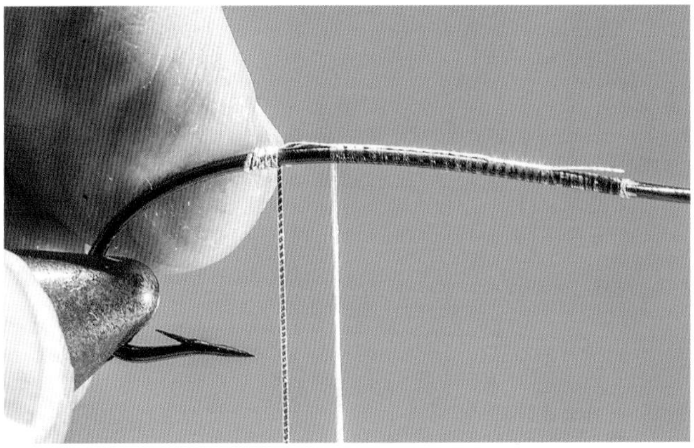

7. When you reach the point where the thread is hanging, tie down the tag end of the tinsel.

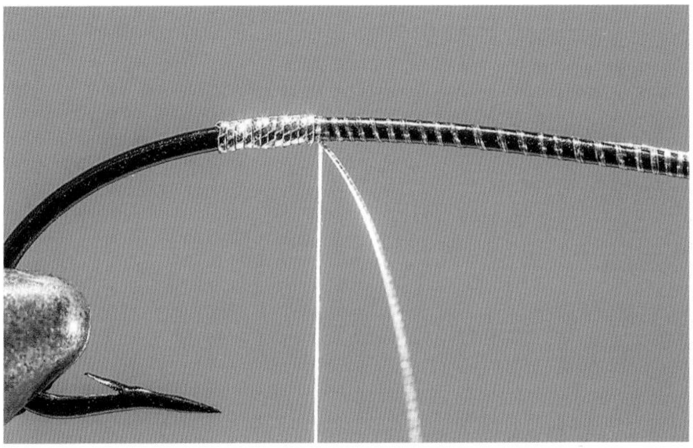

8. This top view shows the "X" pattern where the tinsel crosses over itself on the first wrap. A coat of head cement over the tag will aid in durability.

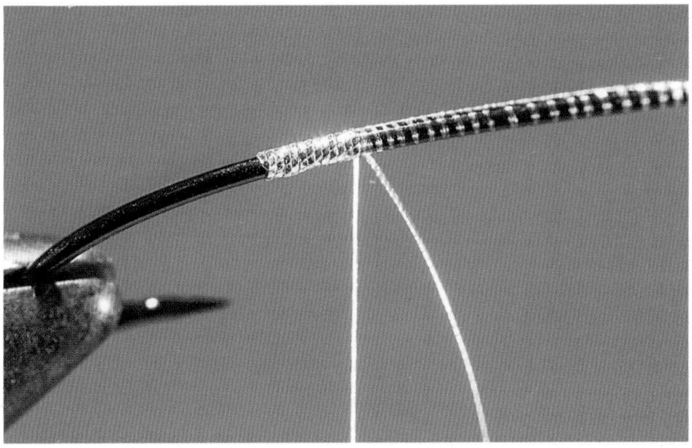

Oval Tinsel Tags on Double Hooks

On double hooks—rarely used for steelhead now, but commonplace on Oregon's Rogue River during much of the twentieth century—forming a tag of oval tinsel is an entirely different process than making such tags on standard hooks. For double hooks, bind the tinsel down along the hook shank as far back as the area that will be the front edge of the tag when it is completed. Wind the tinsel rearward (toward the hook bends) in tight edge-to-edge turns, and on the last turn, only go around the near shank. Then pass the tinsel between the two hooks, pull it forward under the hook and straight across the tag you have just formed. Pull it snug and tie it down at the front edge of the tag. The photo below shows the tag end pulled over the tag beneath the hook, locking it in place; the photo at bottom shows the last turn of the tag only passing over the near shank of the double hook and then passing between the two shanks.

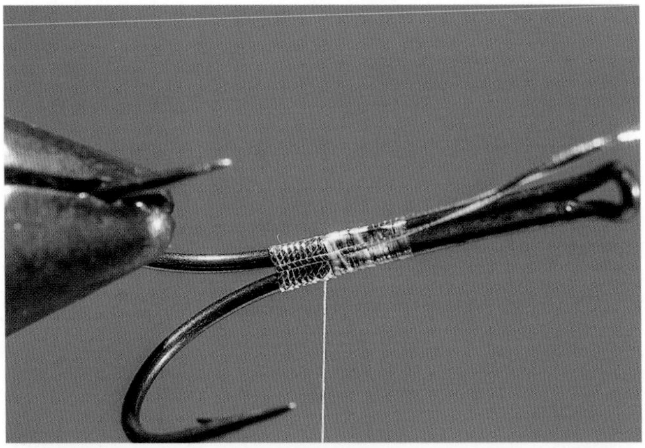

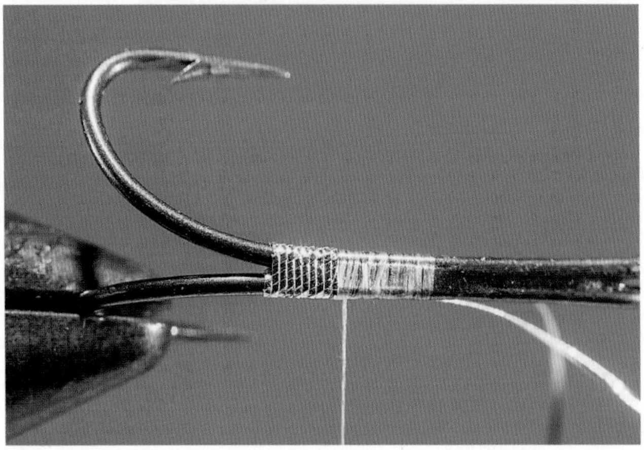

Tails

Most classic steelhead flies include tails made from any of several different materials. On the oldest patterns, which were mostly modifications of popular nineteenth-century trout flies, tiers often used segments of brightly dyed swan or duck quill or hackle fibers for tails; a few old steelhead flies sported tails of golden pheasant crest. By the early decades of the twentieth century, hackle-fiber tails were most common, and they remain so today, though many tiers now substitute dyed golden pheasant crests feathers to modernize their renditions of the classic patterns.

Hackle Fiber Tails

Many classic steelhead flies are tailed with fibers from large, dyed rooster neck or saddle hackles. Neat and attractive hackle fiber tails require attention to a few critical details. First, the best hackles for these fibers exhibit rich color and have a shiny upper surface, with barbules that, when made to stand at right angles to the stem, are of equal length for an inch or so along the prime part of the feather. Second, longer fibers are better than shorter, which means large capon rooster neck hackles (from the lower end of the cape) are generally better than saddle hackles. Third, when you remove the barbules from the stem—cutting them with scissors is best, though they can be stripped off by hand—be sure that the tips remain aligned with one another. The underutilized soft-loop technique is the best method for securing the hackle fiber tail to the hook because this method prevents the tail from rolling off to the far side of the hook as you tighten the thread.

1. Gently stroke the fibers on a large hackle so that they stand out at right angles to the stem.

2. Grip a section of the hackle fibers in your left hand while holding the tip of the feather firmly in your right hand.

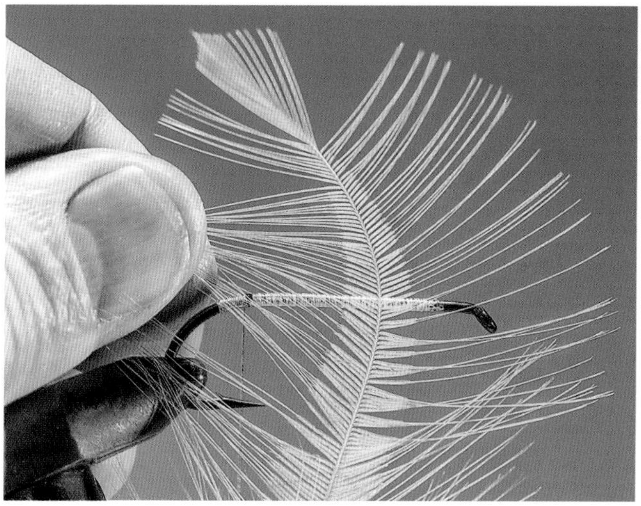

3. Holding the tip of the feather in your right hand, and maintaining a firm grip on the fibers in your left hand, strip the fibers from the steam in one downward pull.

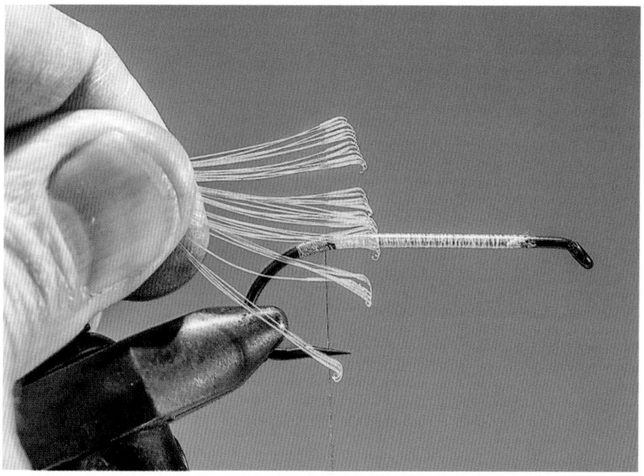

4. Alternatively you can cut the fibers away from the stem with sharp scissors.

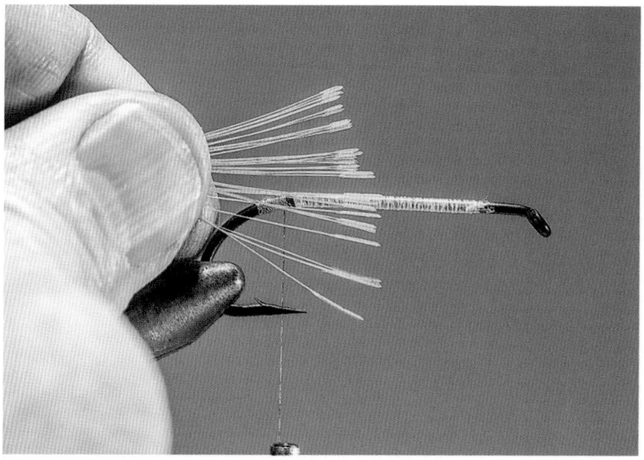

5. Carefully collapse the fibers into a single bundle. Switch to holding the bundle of fibers by the butt ends in your right hand so you can measure the length of the tail against the hook.

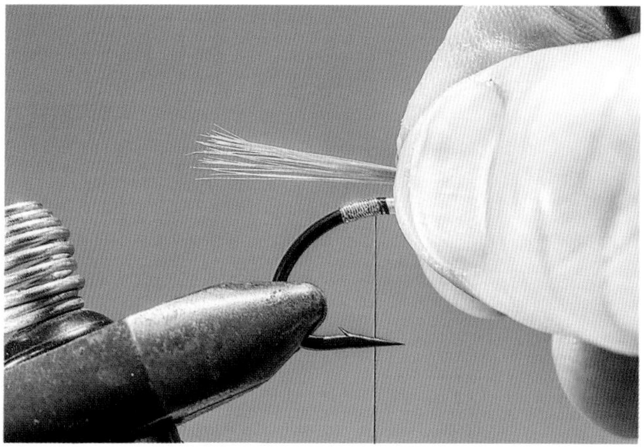

6. Holding the bundle of fibers in place, switch hands, using your left thumb and left middle finger or index finger to grip the tail and the hook.

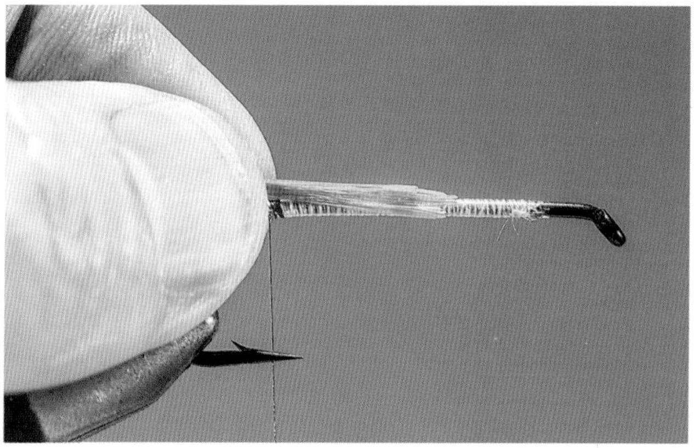

7. Use the soft-loop method (or careful standard thread wraps) to make three turns of thread to hold the tail in the proper place.

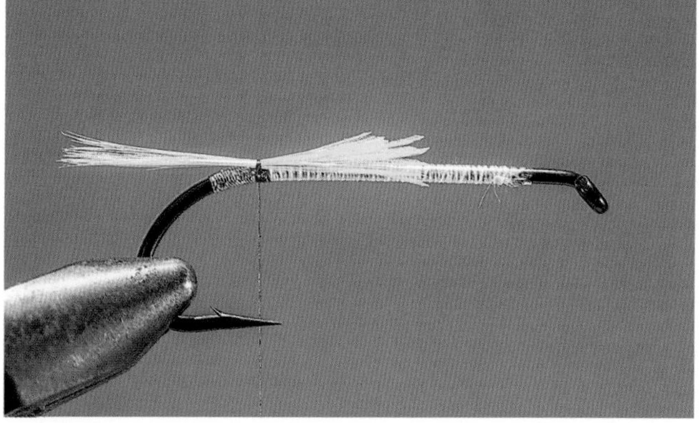

8. Check the alignment of the tail. If it is properly mounted, progress forward with the thread to bind down the butt ends of the hackle fibers.

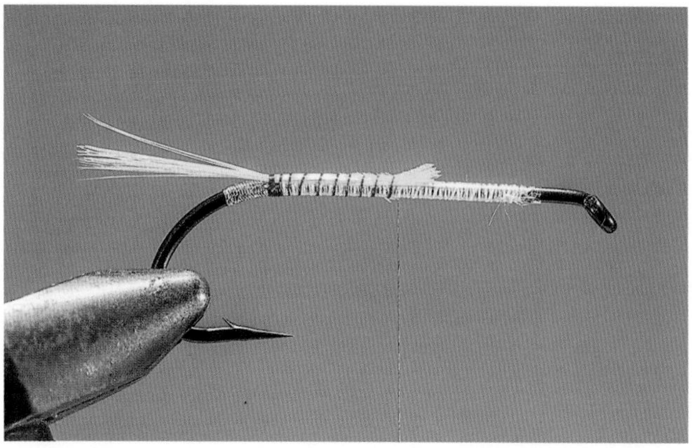

Golden Pheasant Crest Tails

Golden pheasant crest used as a tail has its roots in classic Atlantic salmon flies originating in the British Isles during the Victorian era. These slender, gracefully curved plumes were used similarly on a few old steelhead flies, the Golden Demon being the best-known of them. It was Oregonian David McNeese, however, who popularized their use on steelhead flies beginning in the 1970s. He dyed them in various colors commonly used on classic steelhead flies—shades of orange and red, primarily—as a more alluring option to the long-standard hackle fiber tails.

Dyed golden pheasant crest, because of the natural arc of the feather, is especially handsome when matched to hooks with long sweeping bends, such as the Partridge Bartleet, the Alec Jackson Spey hook, and McNeese's own Blue Heron hook. My own preference is to match the curve of the tail to the curve of the hook like a mirror image. Paying close attention to the length of the plumes and the angle of their arc, I choose feathers from the head of the golden pheasant that best accomplish this task. These feathers often tend to twist or curve to one side, which makes them more difficult to work with, so the ideal feather will be arrow-straight when viewed head on from the butt end or from directly above while held by the butt end. Finding crest feathers that are straight, properly curved, and of the ideal length for any given hook size can involve considerable searching, so tiers need to procure a fairly substantial amount of golden pheasants capes to assure a ready supply of prime tailing material.

While classic Atlantic salmon flies generally use but a single golden pheasant crest feather as a tail (often adorned with additional kinds of small feathers), my preference for steelhead flies is two, three, or even four feathers, all stacked carefully together to form the tail. The resulting density of color is wickedly attractive.

1. Select several crest feathers that are identical or nearly so, taken from the same part of the top of a golden pheasant cape.

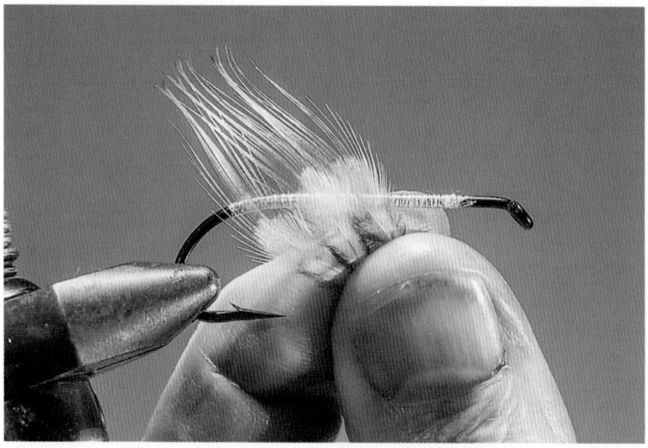

2. Near its base, each feather will exhibit a bit of fiber with a white-colored base. Carefully use your fingers to strip away these fibers from the stems.

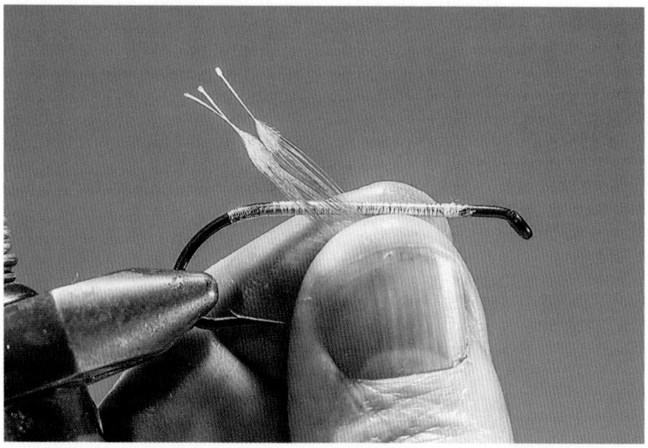

3. Stack the feathers together, making sure the tips are even. A bit of saliva helps hold them together as you continue.

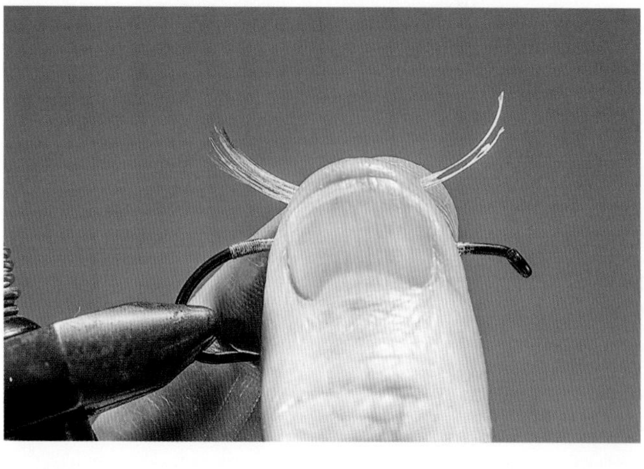

4. Using the same method outlined for hackle fiber tails, secure the stacked golden pheasant crest feathers to the hook, but make the tail slightly longer than you intend it to be when finished.

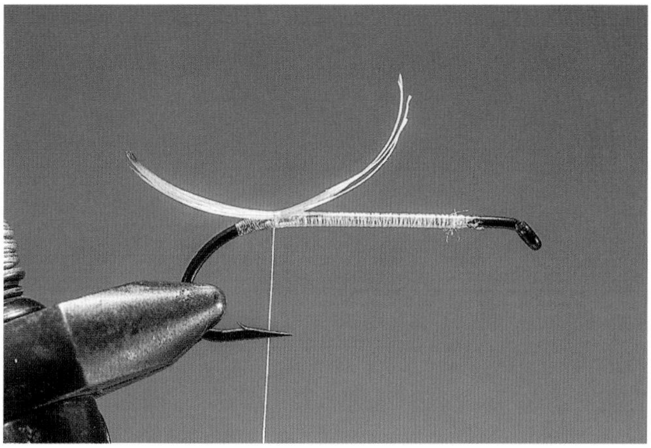

5. Now grasp the tail in your left fingers and the butt ends of the feathers in your right fingers. Gently pull upward and forward to place the tail in the proper position and gather the fibers along the top of the hook shank.

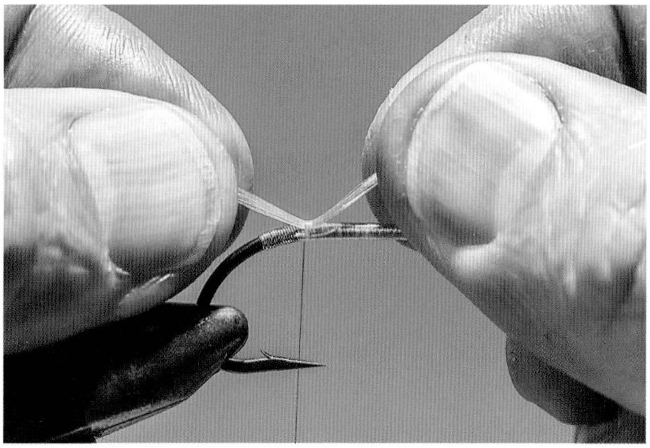

6. The tail should now be properly aligned and of the desired length.

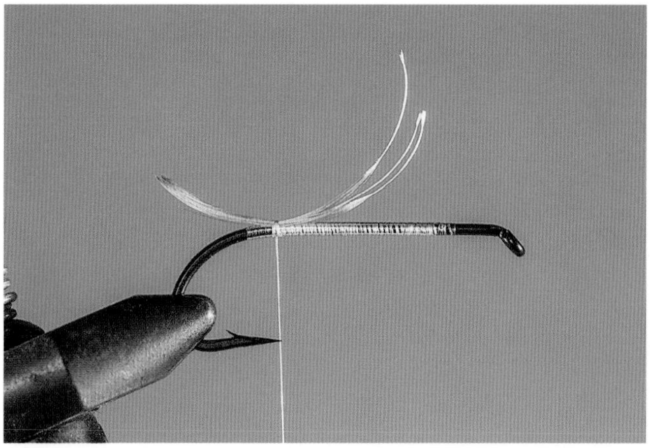

7. Bind the stems down by progressing the thread forward.

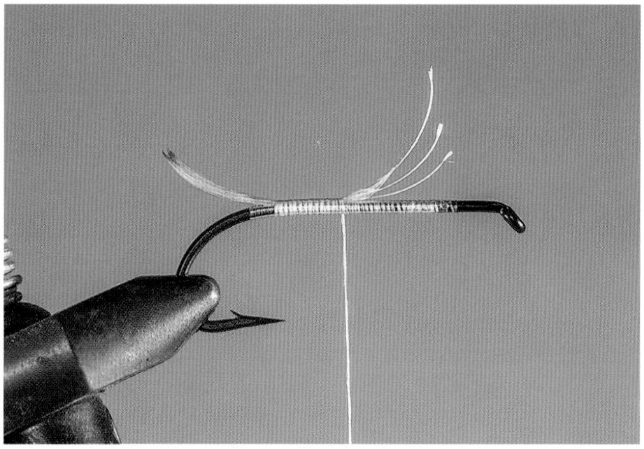

A beautiful native steelhead taken on a perfect October day.

Wood Duck Flank Tails

The most prominent use of black-and-white–barred wood duck flank for tails is found in the classic version of both the Silver Demon and the Black Demon. Creating these tails requires proficiency in the soft-loop technique, as the results depend on practiced execution of that method. In addition, wood duck flank feathers—like most feathers—behave better when clean and, in this case, steamed. Unless the flank feathers come right from a freshly harvested duck and are unsoiled, they should be steamed: use a stove-top tea kettle or plug-in electric steamer; with long tweezers or small tongs (so as not to burn your fingers), grasp individual feathers by their stems and hold them briefly over the steam. The steam revitalizes matted fibers and makes the feathers easier to work with. To begin the process of mounting the wood duck tail, be sure the thread is positioned at the front end of the tinsel tag; in securing the tail, all thread wraps will progress ever so slightly forward, not rearward.

1. Select a wood duck flank feather with relatively narrow black-and-white bars. Use a bodkin to carefully separate out a slip that is twice as wide as the actual tail will be when mounted on the fly.

2. Cut the slip away from the stem, being careful not to separate the individual fibers.

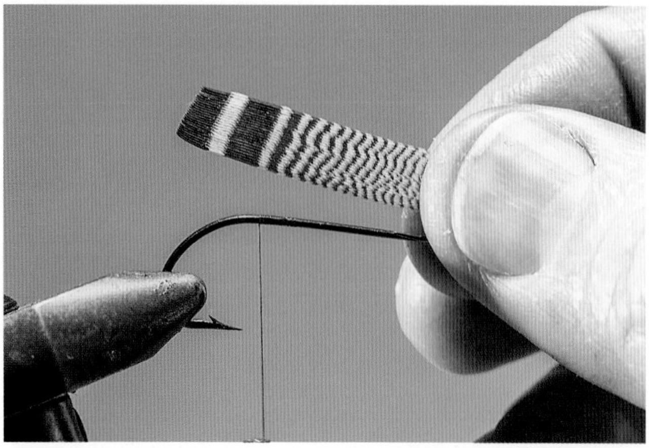

3. Gently fold the slip in half lengthwise in equal proportions with the shiny top surface of the feather on the outsides, being mindful that the slip does not split apart along the fold.

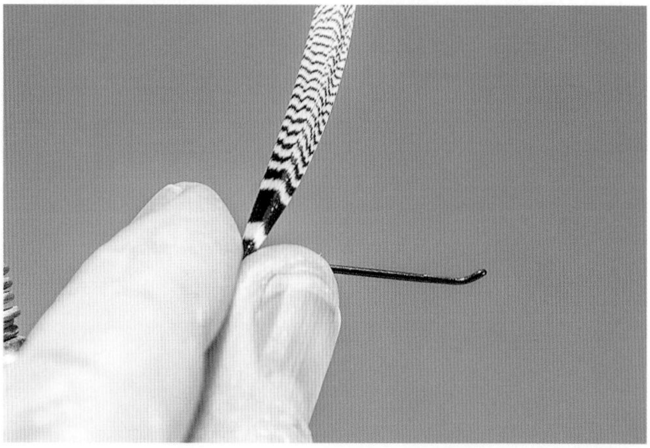

4. Hold the slip by its base in your right hand. Lay it atop the hook shank without releasing your grip on the feather so you can gauge the length of the tail. The fold is at the top.

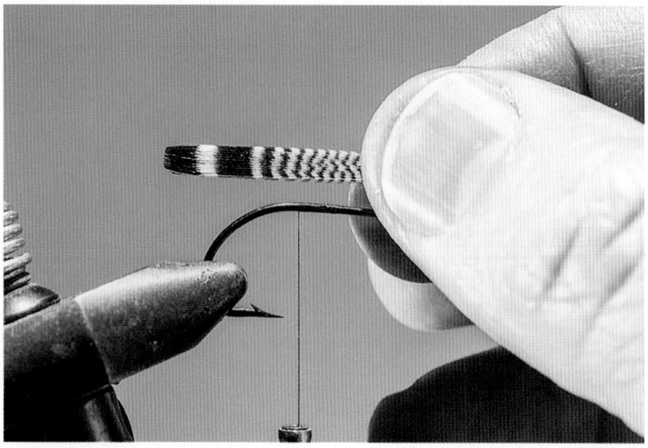

5. Holding the slip in place, switch hands, using your left thumb, and left middle or index finger, to grip the feather and a bit of the hook.

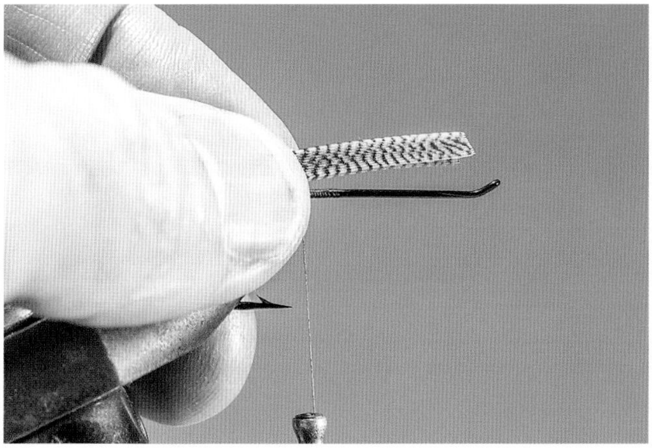

6. Maintain a firm grip on the feather and upper edge of the hook shank. With your right hand draw the thread upward, sliding it between your left thumb and the feather, and use the soft-loop technique to secure the tail to the hook.

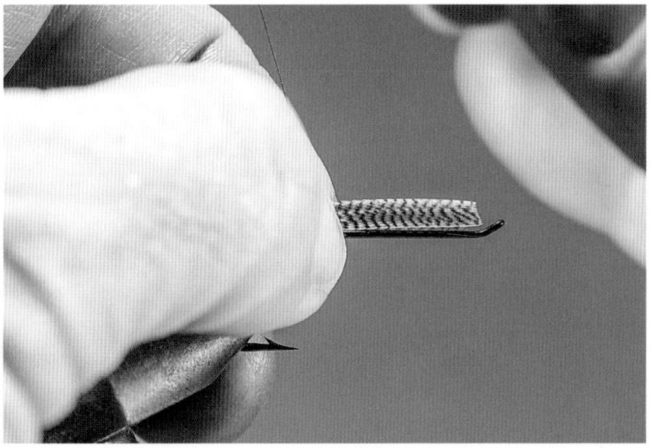

7. Repeat the soft loop twice more and then remove your fingers to check that the tail is properly positioned.

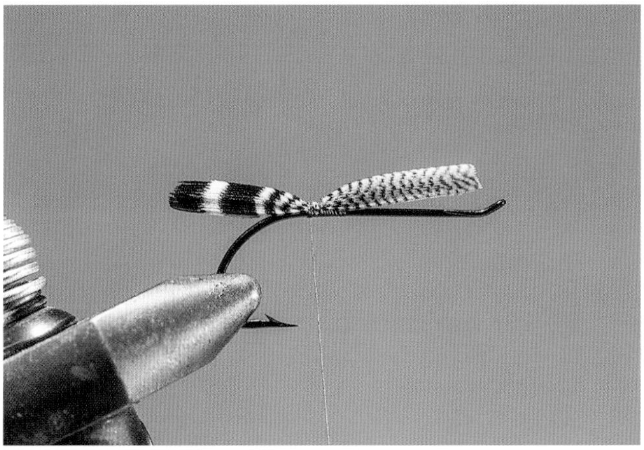

8. Bind the butt ends of the fibers along the top of the hook shank.

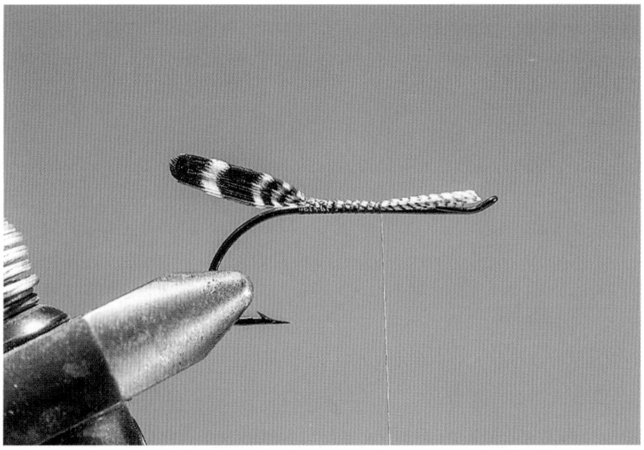

The author casts a long line across a clear, glassy steelhead pool. Such scenes beg for dry lines and classic patterns.

Bodies

In general, classic steelhead flies have simple, easy-to-use materials for bodies. Dyed wool yarn has long been popular, and chenille, available in many colors and several sizes, adorns many classic patterns. A few patterns feature bodies of flat or oval tinsel, dyed silk floss, or even dubbed fur. In many cases, body materials are interchangeable: for example, a Purple Peril might be dressed with a body of purple chenille, purple wool yarn, or purple dubbing. With the variety of choices available for tying steelhead fly bodies, tiers need to be proficient in an array of techniques.

Chenille and Yarn Bodies

Chenille and fine, strong wool yarn are among the most important body materials for steelhead flies. For most uses, small- and medium-size chenilles are best. Standard chenille has a "flow," meaning the individual fibers do not protrude straight out from the core, but rather at angles of less than 90 degrees. When you attach a length of chenille to the hook, be sure that the individual fibers angle away from the hook, not toward it: you can tell by gently running your thumb and finger along the length of chenille. In one direction the chenille will feel silky and smooth, and in the other direction it will feel somewhat rough. For specific directions for creating chenille and wool yarn bodies, see the tying procedures for the Skykomish Sunrise (page 233) and the Brad's Brat (page 236).

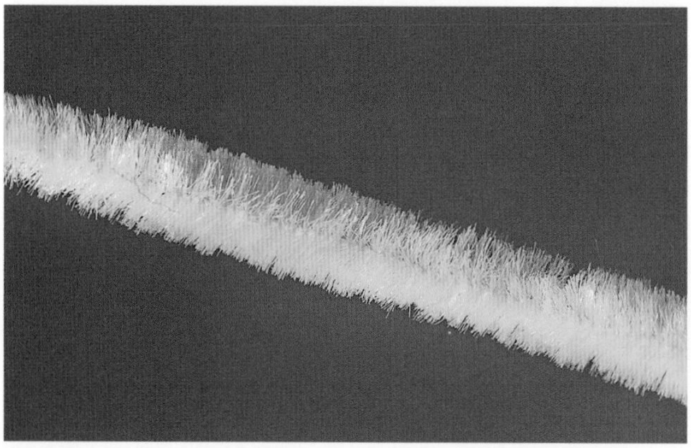

Figure 1

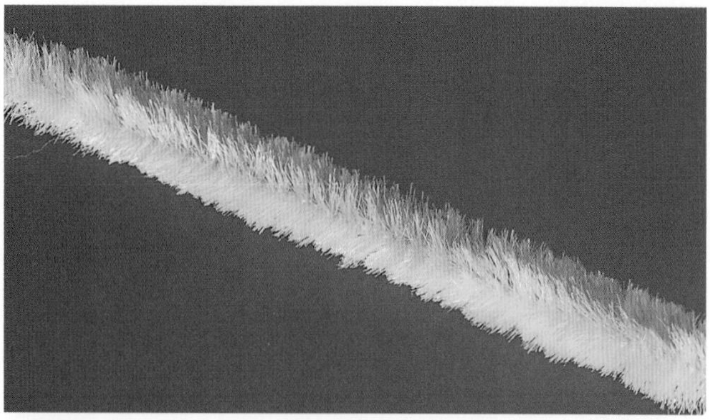

Figure 2

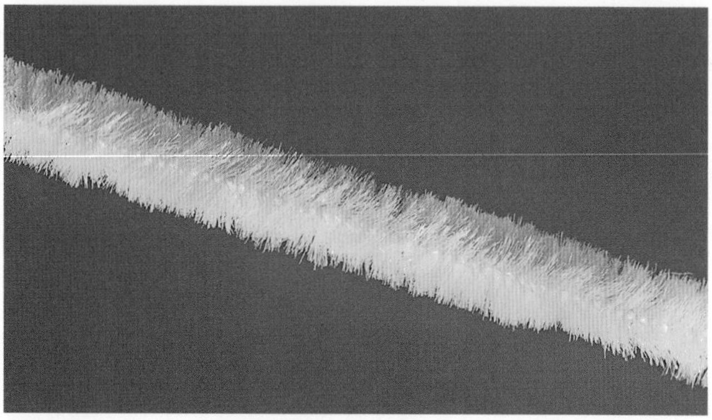

Figure 3

Figure 4

Although not immediately evident (Figure 1), chenille fibers have a directional "flow." If you gently stroke your fingers down a length of chenille, in one direction the fibers lay back easily and feel smooth (Figure 2), but when you stroke the chenille in the other direction, the fibers don't bend back as easily and so they feel a bit more stiff (Figure 3). In these photos, the lower end of the chenille as photographed would be attached to the fly. Figure 4 shows the cotton core exposed. Use your fingernails to strip away the fibers so you can then tie the chenille in by binding down the exposed core with the tying thread.

Dubbed Bodies

Some classic steelhead flies and many modern steelhead flies feature bodies made from dubbed furs. Among the traditionally popular dubbing furs is genuine seal fur, but legal sources of this material are scarce and dwindling as antique supplies are slowly used up. An excellent substitute for coarse fur from the harp seal is angora goat dubbing, which is packaged and sold by various commercial materials suppliers. Other furs are also appropriate for steelhead patterns with dubbed bodies, but in many cases—particularly coarse furs such as seal and angora—they are more easily applied with a dubbing loop than by simply twisting the fur onto the thread.

1. Using your fingers, lightly spin the fur onto the thread just enough that is stays in place. Below the dubbing, hook the thread with a dubbing-loop tool (aka dubbing hook).

2. Release more thread from the bobbin, and while holding the dubbing tool in your left hand, wrap the thread around the hook a few times so that the thread is now looped around the dubbing tool's hook.

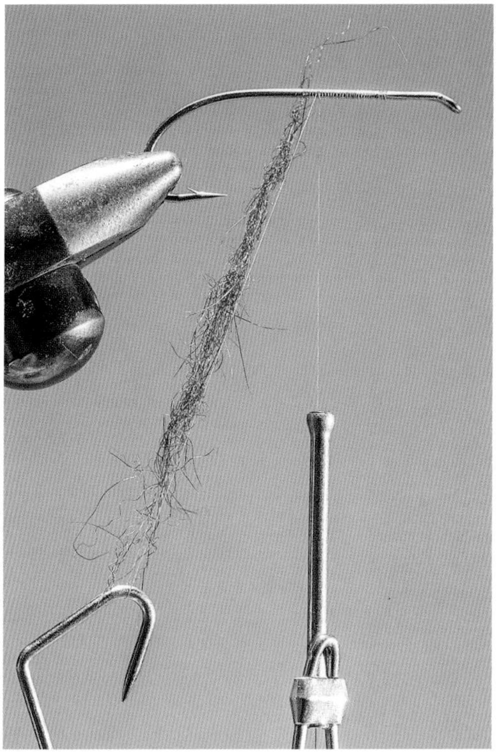

3. Wind the thread back so it closes up the thread loop as shown.

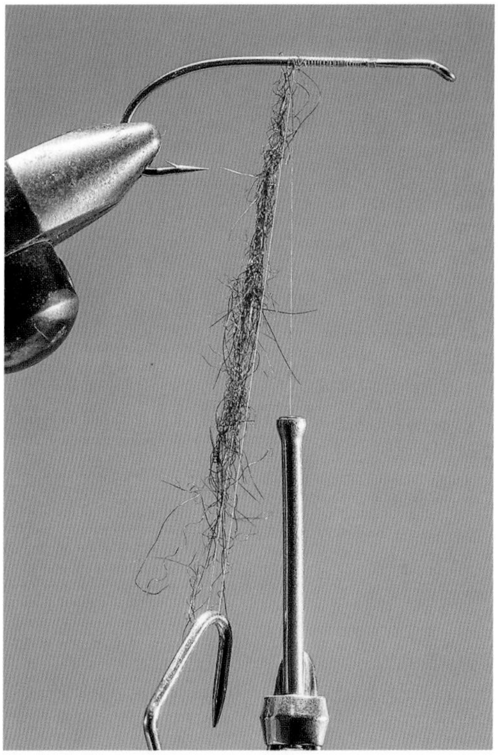

4. Wrap the thread forward to where the front of the dubbed body will be.

5. Spin the dubbing tool, twisting the thread and trapping the dubbing; the more you twist, the more compact will be the resulting dubbing "rope."

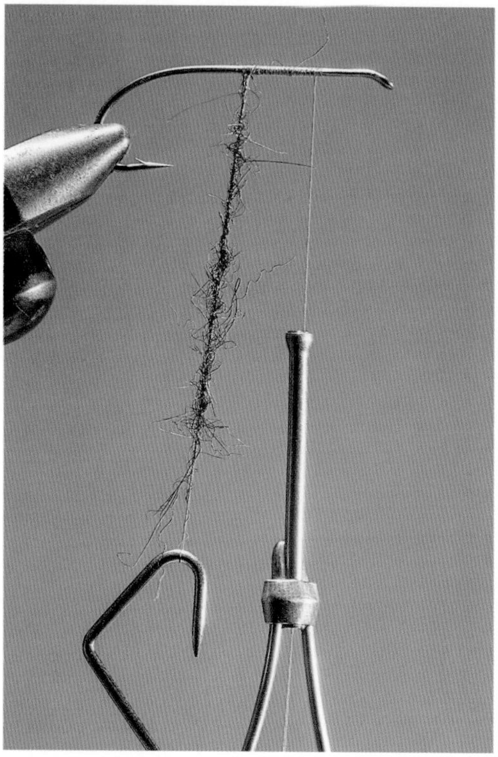

6. Rotate the dubbing tool so that the thread slides into the elbow notch, which must now face toward the fly, with the dubbing tool handle to the right and parallel to the hook shank.

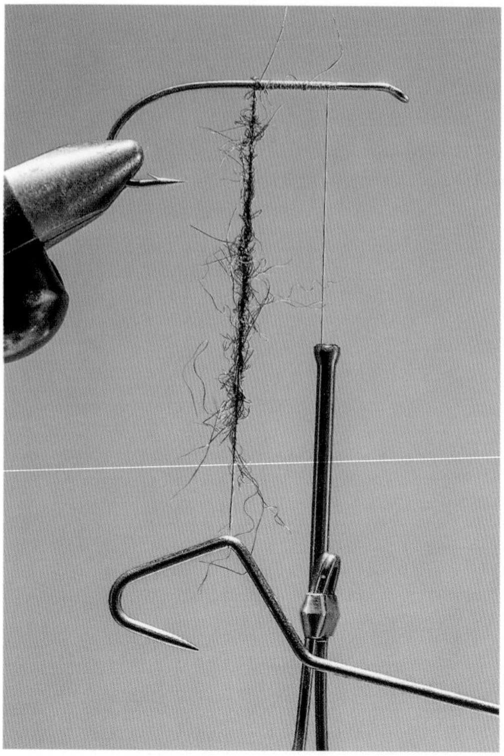

7. With the elbow notch of the dubbing tool facing the fly throughout, use the dubbing tool to wind the dubbing rope forward to form the body.

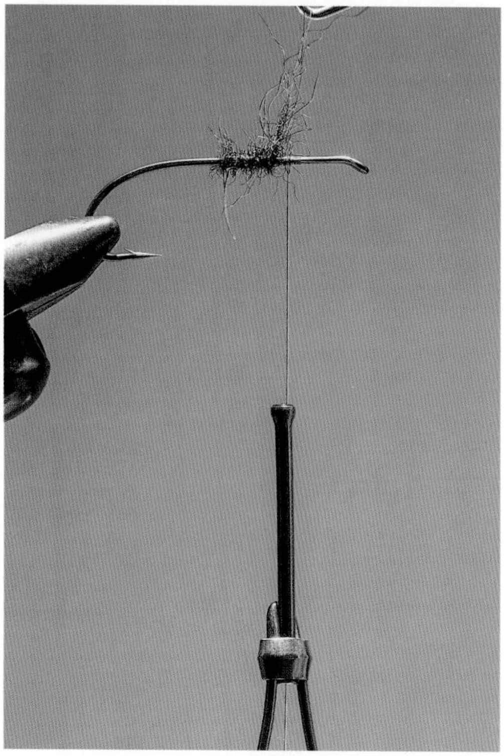

8. Tie down the dubbing rope, and then slide the hook out of the thread loop.

Tinsel and Floss Bodies

A few steelhead flies—most significantly the Golden Demon and Silver Demon—sport bodies made from tinsel. They can be dressed with either oval tinsel or flat tinsel, with the former generally being not only easier and quicker, but also, in my opinion, more alluring. In either case, tinsel bodies are only as perfect as what you apply them over: the underbody must be smooth and even for the body to be smooth and even. This is especially important with flat-tinsel bodies. In both cases, as you plan and then build the fly, use a thread that flattens easily. Thread twists as you tie, gaining a half twist for every turn of the bobbin, so keeping the thread flat requires that you counter-spin the bobbin after every 6 to 12 turns (depending on the demands of the tying procedure in question). You can see how the thread twists by making 15 or 20 turns of thread on a hook shank and then releasing your grip on the bobbin and allowing it to hang by itself; soon it will spin on its own as the thread untwists (and this is the direction you want to spin the bobbin to manually untwist the thread).

Creating smooth floss bodies also requires a smooth underbody. In addition, the highest-quality silk flosses make the smoothest, prettiest floss bodies, so when available, look for untwisted genuine silk floss. Many different synthetic flosses are available as well, and these expand the range of colors and textures you can use.

For both silk and tinsel bodies, burnishing the underbody creates a better surface over which to wind the body material. To do this, use an ultra-smooth wooden or metal tool and carefully rub the underbody to flatten out minute thread ridges. I use the wood handle on my Dennis Collier bodkin or the brass handle on my dubbing twister as burnishing tools. As a final consideration, some of my old friends from the Rogue River—chiefly the late Jerry James and Al Brunell—taught me many years ago to apply a layer of cement to the entire tinsel body to make it durable, or as Al used to say, "built hell for stout." Dress the tinsel body, tie off the thread with a few half hitches or a whip finish, apply a light coat of head cement or varnish to the entire body, and set it aside to dry before adding the hackle and wing.

Instructions for oval-tinsel bodies and floss bodies follow; for instructions on flat-tinsel bodies, see Lesson 3: Silver Demon (page 239).

Oval-Tinsel Body

1. After dressing the tag and tail, and maintaining an even thread underbody, return the thread to the front of the hook and attach a length of oval tinsel to the far side of the shank.

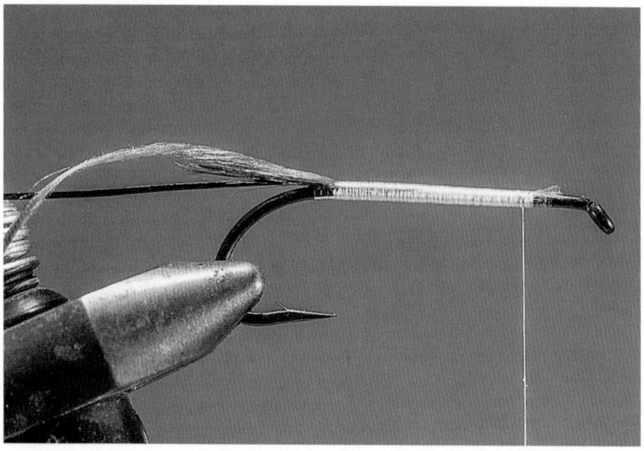

2. Bind the tinsel to the far side of the hook shank, progressing the thread rearward in a narrow spiral.

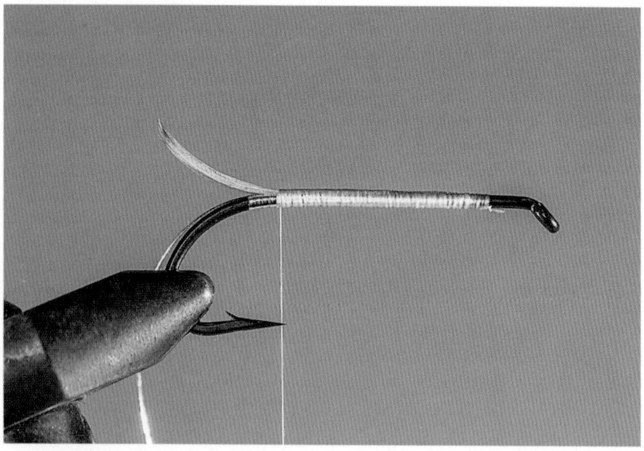

3. Return the thread to the front, again in a narrow spiral so each thread wrap sits edge-to-edge with the previous wrap.

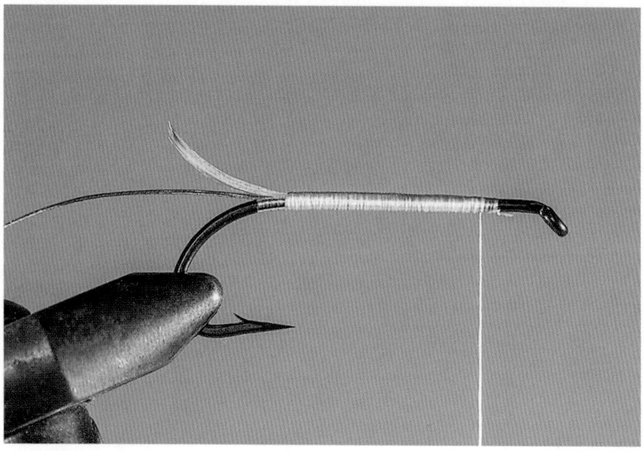

4. Select a smooth wooden or metal tool to burnish the thread wraps by gently rubbing the underbody to flatten thread ridges.

5. Here, the underbody has been briefly burnished. With flat tinsel and floss bodies, the smoother the underbody, the better. Oval tinsel is a bit more forgiving.

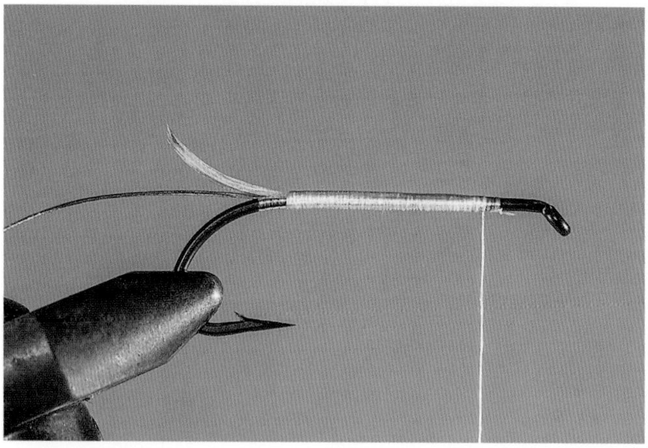

6. Begin spiraling the tinsel forward, each turn snug against the previous turn.

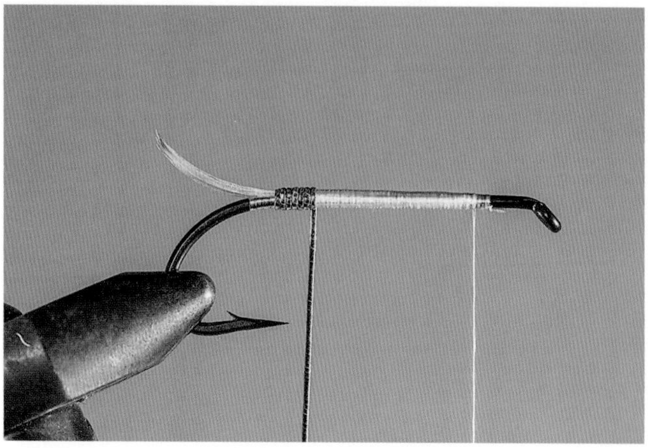

7. Complete the body, then tie off the tinsel at front, leaving ample room for the hackle and wing.

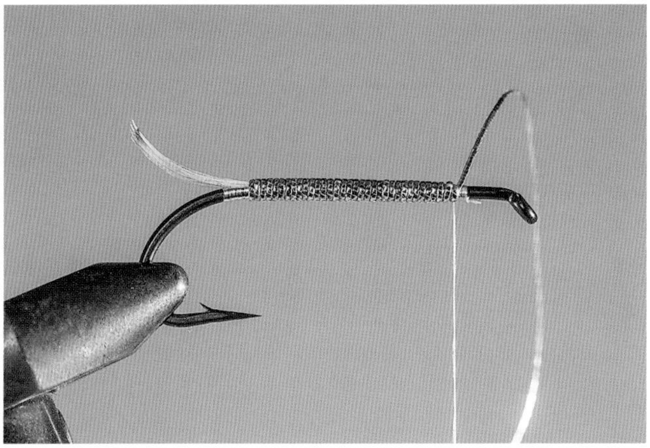

Floss Body

1. Build the tag and tail using a thread that flattens easily, and keep the thread wraps close together. Counter-twist the thread every 6 to 12 turns of the bobbin. Return the thread to the front.

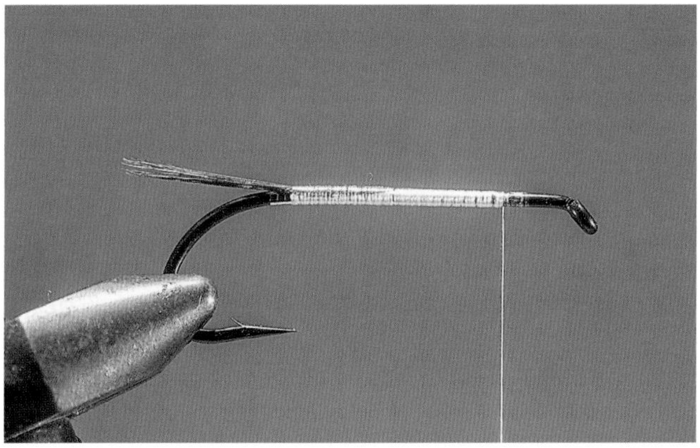

2. On the far side of the hook, secure the tinsel rib material, and then attach a length of silk floss.

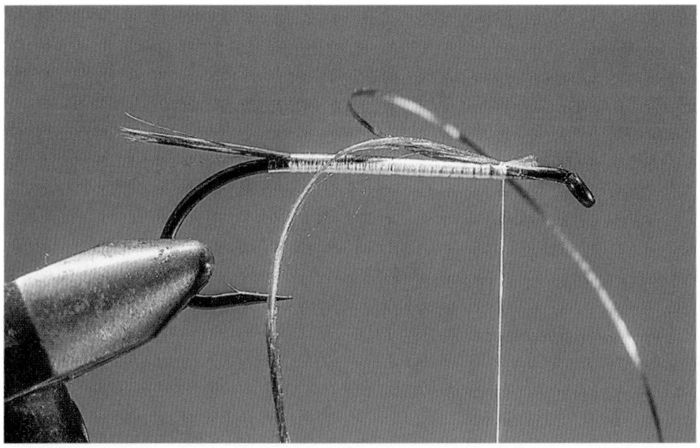

3. Bind the tinsel and floss down along the shank; as you wind with the bobbin, hold the tag ends of the materials in your left hand so they remain taut and in line with their tie-in points. Counter-spin the bobbin periodically. Upon reaching the base of the tail, reverse directions and wind the thread forward in edge-to-edge wraps.

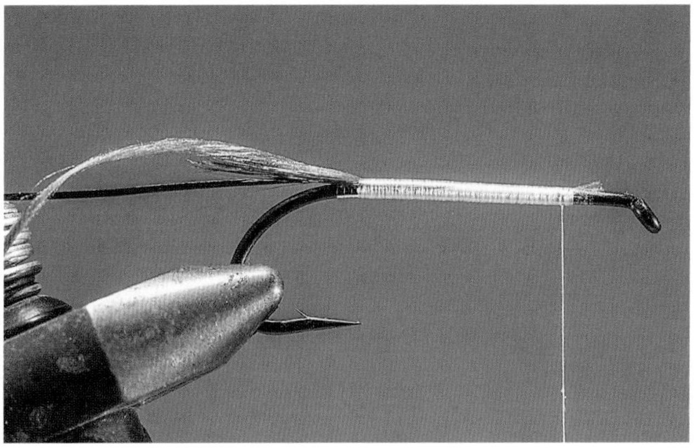

4. If desired, burnish the thread wraps as described previously. Begin winding the silk floss forward, keeping steady, even tension on it so it flattens out. Each wrap should lie edge-to-edge with, or slightly overlap, the previous wrap.

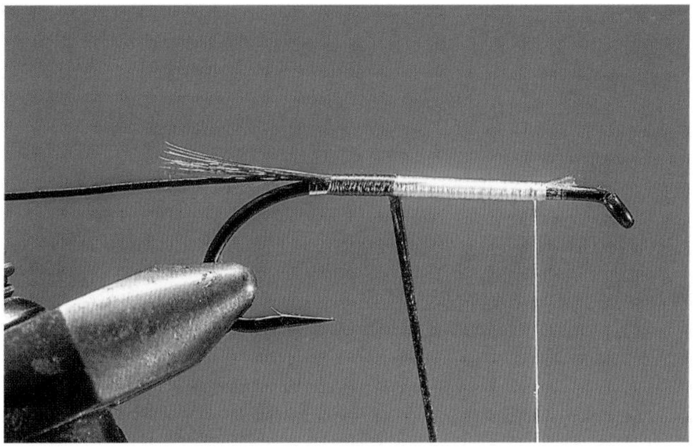

5. Finish winding the body and then tie the silk floss off at the front.

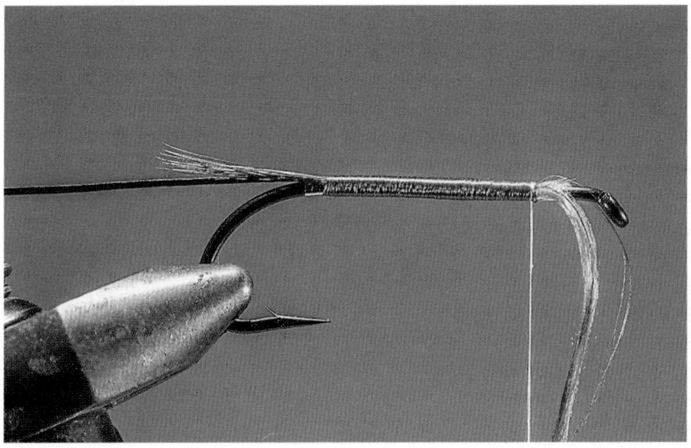

6. Spiral the tinsel forward to form the rib and tie off at front. This completes the silk body.

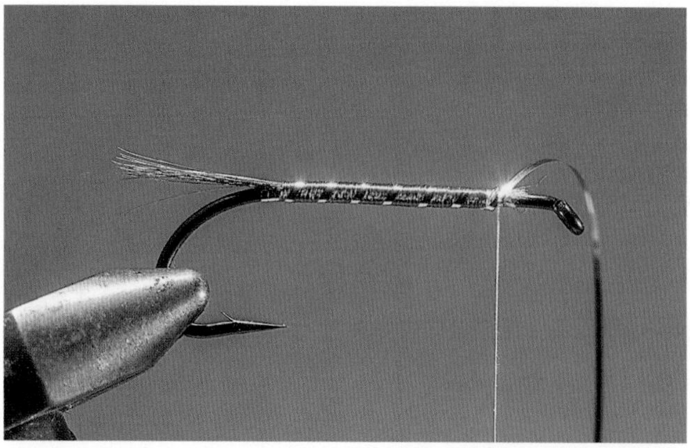

7. This technique is also used to make two-tone bodies in which the rear portion is silk and the front portion a different material, such as wool yarn, chenille, or dubbing. Here, the thread is switched to red so it will match the forward portion of the body, and then wound rearward to the midpoint of the hook.

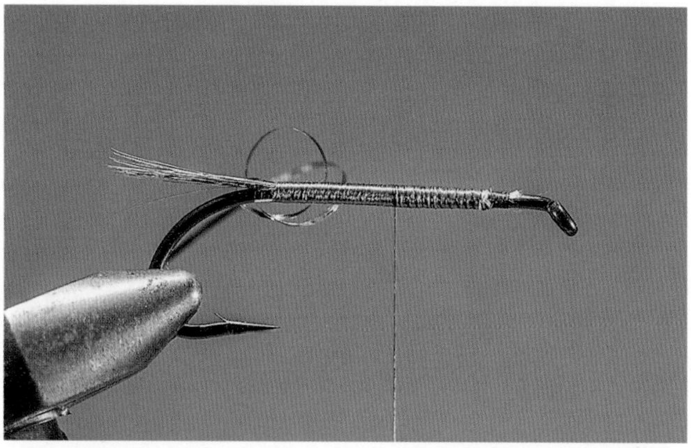

8. Form a dubbed body and then spiral the tinsel forward to form the rib.

Hackles

Tiers commonly use hackles from large dyed rooster capes on steelhead flies, although saddle hackles are often better on hooks smaller than size 2. Tiers prefer full capes and saddles over strung hackles because they provide a range of hackle sizes. Most steelhead patterns have hackles dressed wet-fly style so that the hackle fibers angle rearward toward the bend of the hook rather than standing out at right angles from the hook as would be the case for typical dry flies. Tie the hackle in by its tip and wind forward in tight spirals to achieve this swept-back appearance, but "fold" the hackle prior to wrapping it to make the finished product tidy and uniform. Folding a hackle simply means that the fibers on one side of the stem are bent 90 to 180 degrees so they align better with the fibers on the opposite side of the stem.

Of the several methods of folding hackles, the two techniques outlined here are easiest because the feather is already attached to the hook. This leaves both of your hands free to work. For both techniques, trite as it sounds, practice does indeed make perfect.

Scissor-folded Hackles

Scissor folding is actually simpler than it might seem upon an initial attempt. The tricks are to keep the hackle stem taut as you fold the fibers, and to make sure the scissor blade stays on the top of the stem, slightly on the shiny (front-facing) side of the hackle fibers so that they are forcibly bent to the back side of the stem. With proper technique, you will feel and hear the "tick, tick, tick" as each hackle fiber is broken down and bent backward by the scissor blade. If the blade is not aligned properly on contact with the hackle stem, you will not feel the fibers fold; re-align the blade and practice until it works—once you get it right, and see how easily this method folds the hackle, it will become your primary technique for doing so.

1. After gently stroking the fibers back to create a tie-in point on the stem, secure the hackle by its tip, shiny side facing the front when the feather is wrapped.

2. Be sure the hackle is well anchored and cannot pull out easily, and then cut away the tip of the feather.

3. Open your scissors 90 degrees and hold them at the joint.

4. Hold the butt end of the feather with your left hand, keeping it straight and taut. Run the sharp edge of the far blade along the top of the hackle stem so that it breaks down the fibers on that side and bends them rearward.

5. Once folded with the blade of the scissors, the hackles on the top edge of the stem are creased back so they align with the hackles on the opposite side of the stem.

6. Gently reinforce the fold by stroking the fibers from the stem out toward their tips with your left hand as you hold the hackle taut and upward with your right hand.

7. Use your left hand to pull the hackle fibers rearward as you wrap the hackle with your right hand.

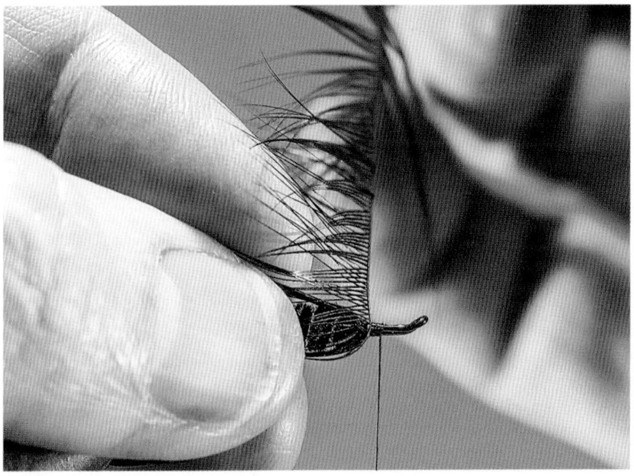

8. Depending on the fly and the desired look, make three to eight turns of hackle going forward, each turn edge-to-edge with the previous turn.

9. Securely tie off the hackle and then clip away the butt end of the feather.

10. Pull all the hackle fibers rearward and create a platform of thread on which to mount the wing.

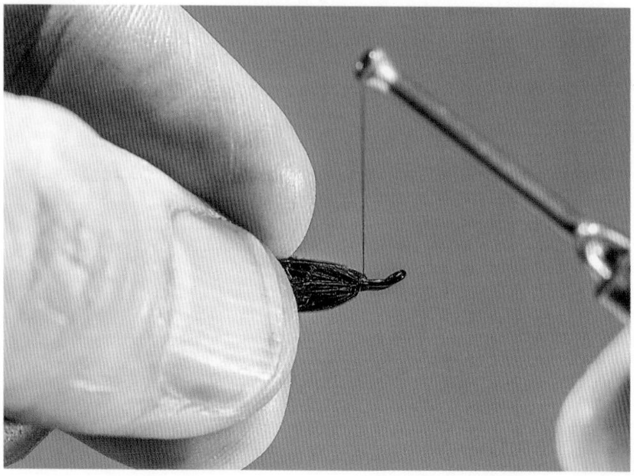

Hand-folded Hackles

Hand-folding is also easy and effective with practice, and it is essential for flies that require two hackles to be wrapped simultaneously, such as the famous Skykomish Sunrise where a red hackle and a yellow hackle are applied together. In this case, scissor folding is ineffective because one hackle gets in the way of the other as you attempt to fold them, so hand-folding is the best option. The example below shows two hackles being applied together to demonstrate the technique.

1. After stroking the fibers out to create a tie-in point on the hackle tips, lay the two hackles one on top of the other, both shiny sides facing up. You can also strip away the excess fibers from the stems as shown here.

2. Tie in both hackles together by their tips, shiny sides facing forward, and make sure they are securely attached so they cannot pull out easily.

3. Hold the hackle stems in your right hand so they are fairly taut. Reach around the feather with your left thumb and middle finger, and as you draw your fingers to the right, pinch the stem and drag the fibers backward so the fibers on the far side fold rearward.

4. Repeat Step 3 several times to make sure all the fibers are folded back.

5. Begin winding the hackles forward, and with each turn, use your left hand to keep sweeping and pulling the fibers rearward.

6. Tie the hackle stems off securely at the front of the collar.

7. Clip away the stems and prepare a base of thread on which the wing will sit.

Hair Wings

Though not nearly so popular for winging steelhead flies as it once was, bucktail is still regnant among aficionados of hair-wing classic patterns. Properly handled, bucktail makes beautiful wings. It is available in many dyed shades, along with natural white and brown; it is inexpensive; and it is easy to work with after you master a few simple tying tricks. These tying tricks address two primary challenges: stacking bucktail and mounting it securely.

Stacking bucktail (evening the tips) typically requires a large hair stacking tool. The single biggest hurdle is overcoming the urge to use too much hair. Cut a sparse amount of hair from the tail and then, holding the hairs by their tips in one hand, gently pull away the short hairs with the other hand. Then begin the stacking procedure by evening the length of the hairs by hand: simply hold the tips of the longest hairs with one hand and pull out the shorter hairs by their butts with the other hand, then lay them alongside the longer hairs farther forward so the tips of all the hairs are a bit more even. Next insert all the hairs into the stacker and tap the stacker on the desktop or your free hand as aggressively as possible. Remove the hairs, cut away a short length of the butt ends, and use the hair stacker again. Continue this process until the tips are even.

Calf tail is also commonly used on steelhead flies and can be troublesome to work with as well. With calf tail, the selection process is important, so if possible, remove calf tails from their packaging before purchasing: look for tails with minimally crinkled hairs. The hairs on the lower half of calf tail are easier to work with than the hairs from nearer the tips because they tend to be straighter and softer (so they compress more easily under thread tension). Once you select the straightest hair possible, calf tail stacks almost effortlessly and makes it easy to give your flies small, neat heads because it compresses under thread tension and is easy to mount with the reverse-wing method shown on page 228.

A variety of other hairs are commonly used on steelhead flies. Among them are the "hard" hairs, so named because they don't compress too much under thread pressure. These include squirrel tail and black bear hair. Fine-diameter polar bear hair, when available legally, is easy to work with, as are the softer hairs, such as goat and arctic fox tail.

Flush-cut Method

The two primary methods of securing hair wings on steelhead flies each have advantages. The flush-cut method, when properly executed, is quick and easy. A drop or two of cement in the tying process helps make these wings more secure, but they can be pulled out by force no matter how sound your technique in mounting them. That said, in all my years of fishing flies tied using this method, I have never had a wing come apart.

1. Build a platform of thread as a base on which to mount the wing.

2. Position the thread near the rear portion of the platform, in front of the last turn of hackle.

3. In your right hand, grasp the butt ends of the stacked hairs as shown and measure the proper length for the wing.

4. Switch the wing to your left hand, gripping it at the measure spot.

5. With sharp scissors, cut away the butt ends.

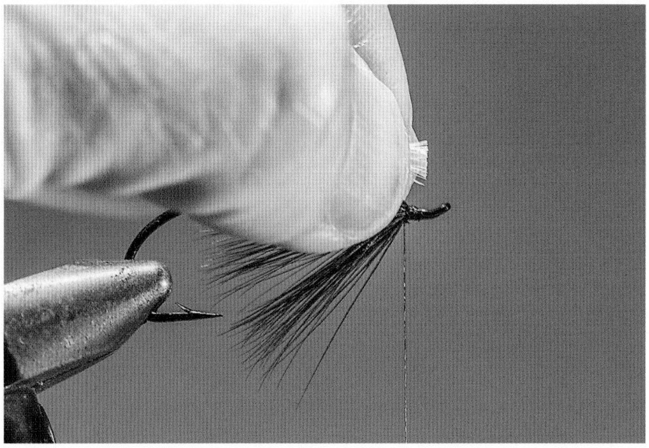

6. Place the wing on the platform from above and in front so that the bottom edge of your thumb and finger simultaneously push the hackle fibers out of the way. Make two or three firm thread wraps over the butt ends of the hairs.

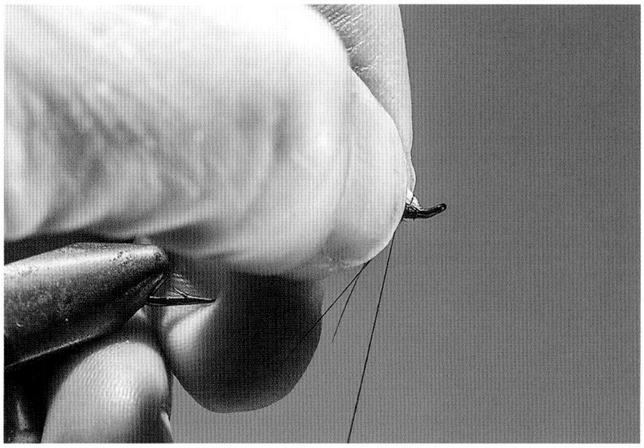

7. Remove your fingers and check the length and orientation of the wing.

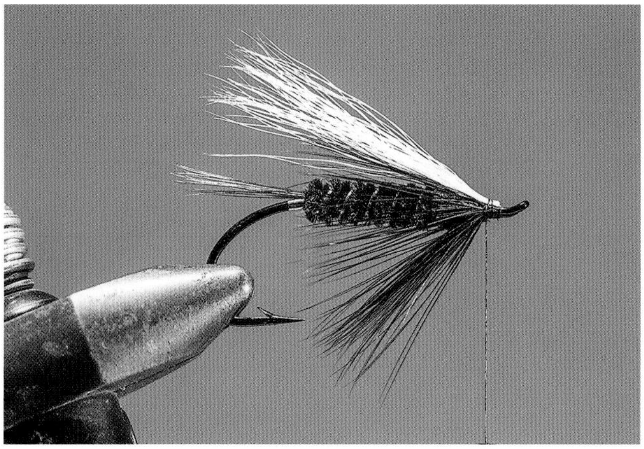

8. Bind the wing firmly, winding the thread forward and then rearward again. Finish the head (or if you're going to add jungle cock eyes, mount them first and then finish the head).

Reverse-wing Method

The reverse-wing method creates the most durable possible wing, and is especially effective for working with fine-diameter hairs such as squirrel tail and calf tail.

1. After attaching the tag and tail, measure the wing for the desired length and then attach it facing forward as shown.

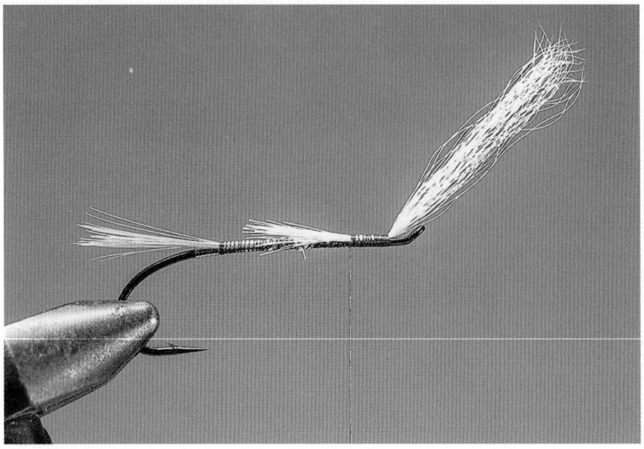

2. Bind the butt ends of the hair down by progressing the thread rearward on the shank, but before finishing, cut the ends of the hairs to three different lengths so there won't be an abrupt edge.

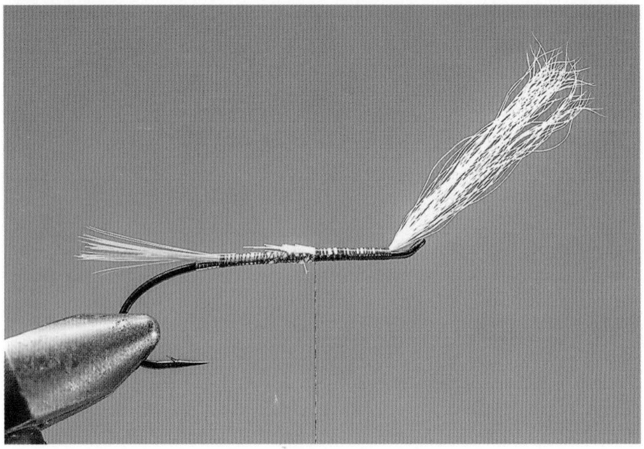

3. Finish binding down the butt ends. If the fly will have a rib, return the thread to the front and secure the rib and the body material. In this case (a Polar Shrimp), there is no rib, so tie in a length of chenille for the body.

4. Dress the body of the fly, but leave a gap to accommodate the hackle between the front end of the body and the forward tie-down point of the wing.

5. Tie in a hackle by its tip in the gap you have left.

6. Wrap the hackle to fill the gap, tie it off at front, and cut away the stem.

7. Pull the wing firmly back over the body of the fly and secure it in that position with the thread.

Mallard Wings

Mallard wings (often referred to as bronze mallard wings) are commonly used on the old original Atlantic salmon flies that originated on Scotland's River Spey in the 1800s. A few steelhead flies bear this style of wing as well. While fly tiers employ a variety of shortcuts and tricks to secure these wings in the desired tent shape (they have been described as looking like an upside-down boat), the standard method of reversing the thread to attach the far-side wing usually yields the best results. However, perfecting bronze mallard wings requires proper feather selection and a great deal of practice. Fly tiers who delve into the classic Spey flies must learn proper technique and feather selection. For particulars, see my earlier book *Spey Flies & Dee Flies: Their History and Construction* (2002).

Bronze Mallard Roof-style Wing

In addition to the standard method of tying bronze mallard wings on to the fly one at a time, first the far wing and then the near wing, you can also opt to tie them as a "roof" (a term borrowed from Atlantic salmon tying). This technique is especially useful for steelhead flies. In the case of steelhead flies intended for fishing, I prefer a two-layer roof as shown in these instructions. One good example of a classic steelhead fly with a roof-style bronze mallard wing is Tommy Brayshaw's beautiful Coquihalla Red (see page 60).

1. Select a pair of matching bronze mallard feathers. The feathers shown here have been cut in half to expose the best fibers.

2. From each feather, carefully separate out a section of fibers (called a "slip") that is about twice as wide as the actual wing will be.

3. With sharp scissors, cut away each slip from its feather stem.

4. Lay one slip directly over top of the other, with shiny sides of each feather facing the same direction, rather than back to back or front to front.

5. Carefully fold the slips lengthwise with your left hand, but do not squeeze them all the way together.

6. Switch the folded slips to your right hand and place them atop the fly so they are the proper length, but do not release your grip.

7. Switch back to your left hand and gently pinch the wing to the top of the hook using your thumb and middle finger. Use the soft-loop technique to secure them with several wraps of thread.

8. Remove your fingers and check that the wing is properly seated.

Jungle Cock Eyes

Jungle cock eyes are optional on most steelhead flies, but they add to the beauty of many patterns. Typically they are secured one at a time, and meticulously adjusted so that the eye on each side of the fly is the same length and orientation. However, attaching both eyes simultaneously using the method shown here works well on most types of flies.

1. Select two matching jungle cock eyes.

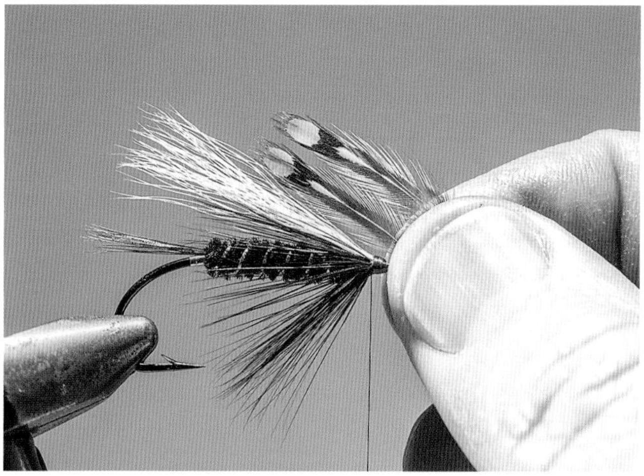

2. Lay the two feathers together with the shiny sides facing outward, and carefully strip away the fuzz from the stem below what will be the tie-in point.

3. Once the fibers are stripped away from the stems, lick the pad of your left thumb and left forefinger (or middle finger) to moisten them, and then grip the two jungle cock eyes as shown.

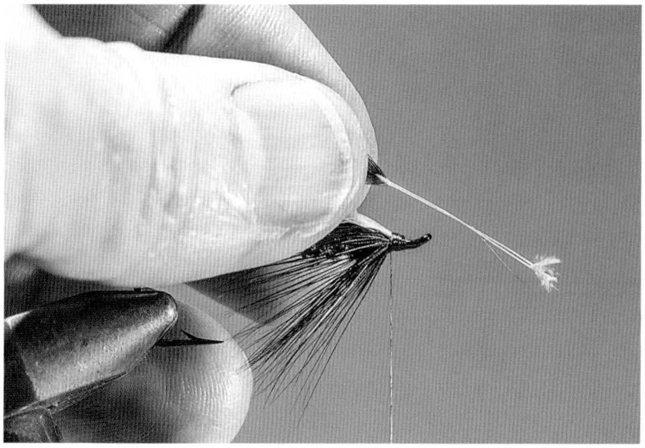

4. Relax your grip on the feathers as shown so that one jungle cock eye is stuck to your thumb and the other to your forefinger.

5. With the jungle cock eyes stuck to your thumb and forefinger, grip the front of the fly at the appropriate angle, positioning a jungle cock eye on each side of the wing.

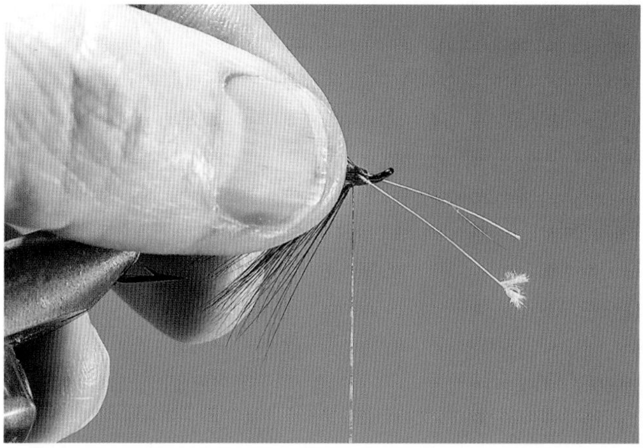

6. Without releasing your grip on the fly, make three wraps of thread—not too tight.

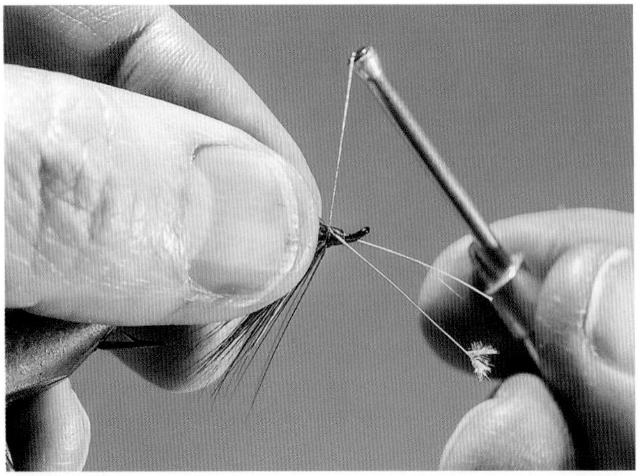

7. Carefully release your grip on the fly and check the position of each jungle cock eye.

8. Pull forward gently on each stem to seat the eyes under the thread wraps.

9. Secure the eyes firmly in place with additional thread wraps.

10. Some tiers prefer to double back the stems to secure them, thinking this will add durability, but I have not found that doing so makes any difference so long as the feathers are properly secured.

11. Finish the head of the fly and tie off.

Three Tying Lessons

Lesson 1: Skykomish Sunrise

1. Use the method outlined on pages 206–207 to create a fairly long flat-tinsel tag.

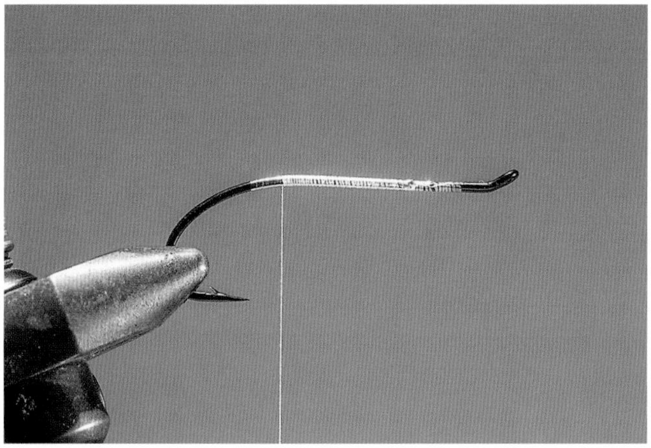

2. Use the method outlined on pages 210–212 to create a hackle fiber tail, but in this case the tail will be two colors, red and yellow mixed. Lay one hackle over top of the other as shown so that the hackle tips on the left-hand sides of the feathers are even in length.

3. Cut away the hackle fibers and mount them on the hook shank.

4. Progress the thread forward, binding down the butt ends of the hackle fibers.

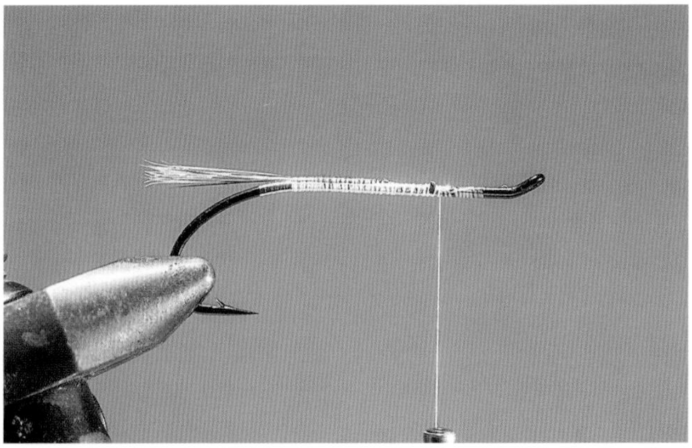

5. Attach a length of silver oval or flat tinsel on the far side of the hook.

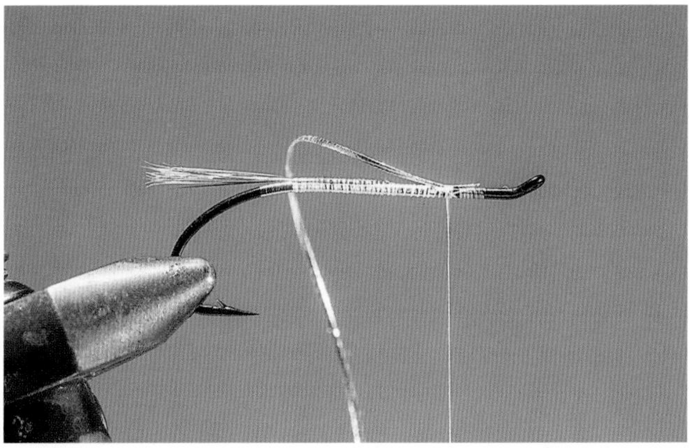

6. Form the body with red chenille. There are several methods for attaching it. One way is to attach the length of chenille at front after using your finger nails to strip just a few fibers away from the chenille's string core.

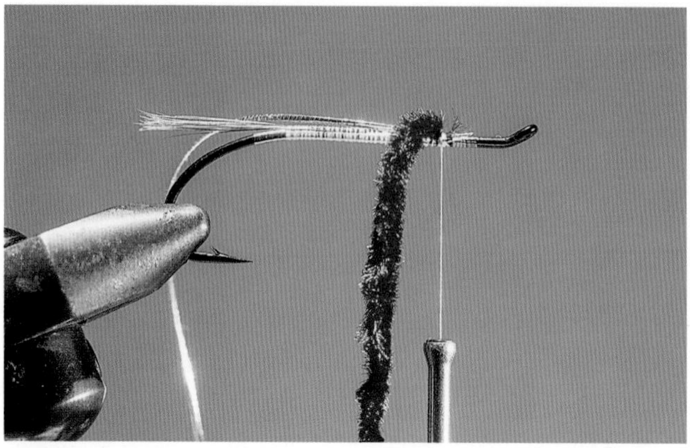

7. Next, bind both the tinsel and the chenille down along the far side of the shank.

8. As an alternative to step 6, you could strip away fibers from the chenille to expose a length of the core almost as long as the hook shank as measured back to the base of the tail. Tie this in at front as shown.

9. Bind the chenille core and the tinsel down along the hook shank.

10. If you wrap the tinsel forward without compressing the wraps up against one another, the result is an uneven-width body as shown here.

11. By using your thumb and forefinger to pull each wrap of chenille rearward to snug it up against the previous wrap as you make the wraps, the results are much cleaner.

12. In this example, the chenille wraps have been compressed as described in Step 11, resulting in a more uniform body diameter and shape.

13. To improve this uniform-diameter body, twist the chenille as shown here so it is rounder, and also compress the wraps as you wind the chenille forward.

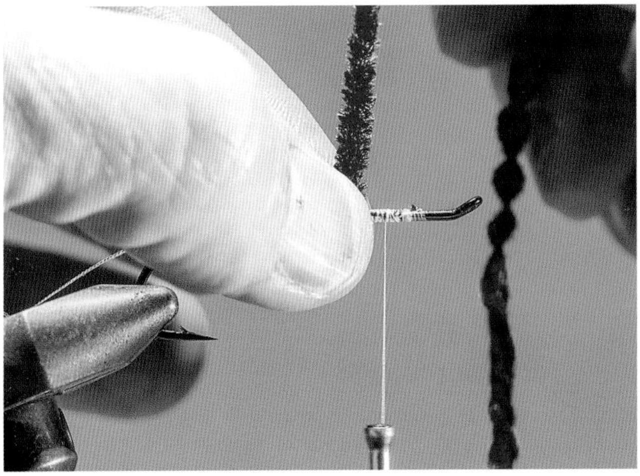

14. Finish the chenille body and secure at front by gently wiggling the thread side-to-side so it sinks down through the chenille fibers and seats over the chenille core.

15. Spiral the tinsel forward to form the rib and secure at front. Cut away the tag end.

16. Select a yellow hackle and a red hackle, matching them for size. Lay the red hackle over top of the yellow hackle and gently stroke the fibers downward so they stand out at right angles from the stems. Attach the hackles by their tips as shown.

17. Using the hand-folding method as outlined on pages 224–225, fold the fibers so they angle rearward.

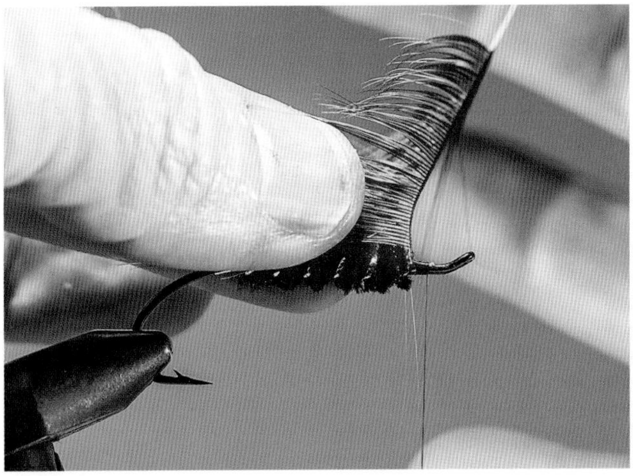

18. Wind both hackles forward at the same time, using your left hand to continue to stroke the fibers rearward.

19. Tie off the hackles and clip away the butt ends. Create a thread platform on which to mount the wing.

20. Using the flush-cut method as outlined on pages 226–227, add a wing of white bucktail or similar hair. Finish the head.

Lesson 2: Brad's Brat

1. Using the method outlined on pages 207–208 for oval tinsel tags, create a fairly long tag of fine gold oval tinsel. In this example, I used a fine white thread (UNI-Cord size 12/0) that flattens easily.

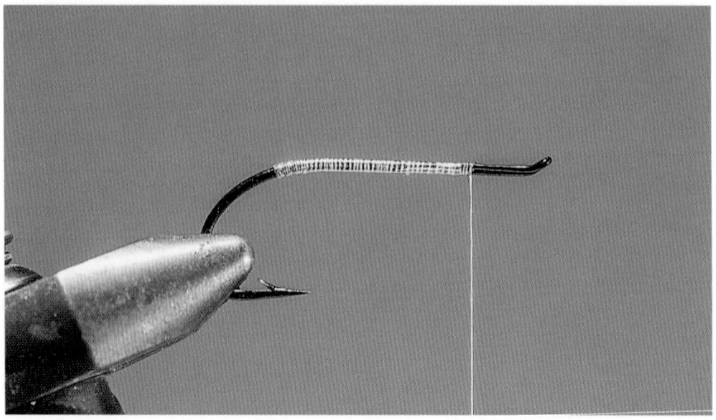

2. With the thread at the front of the hook, just behind the back end of the return-loop eye, switch to a fine red or orange thread (or black if you prefer). Wind the thread back to the front edge of the tag and attach a sparse bundle of stacked white bucktail hairs with about three thread wraps. Do not pull too tightly on the thread.

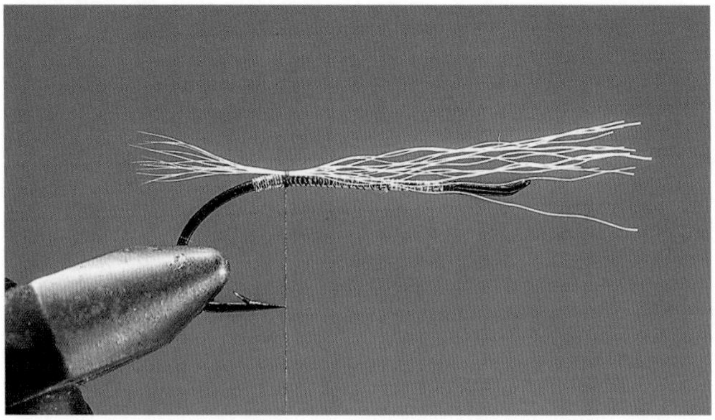

3. Over top of the white bucktail hairs, attach an approximately equal number of stacked orange bucktail hairs (alternatively, you can stack both shades of hair together and attach them as one unit for the tail).

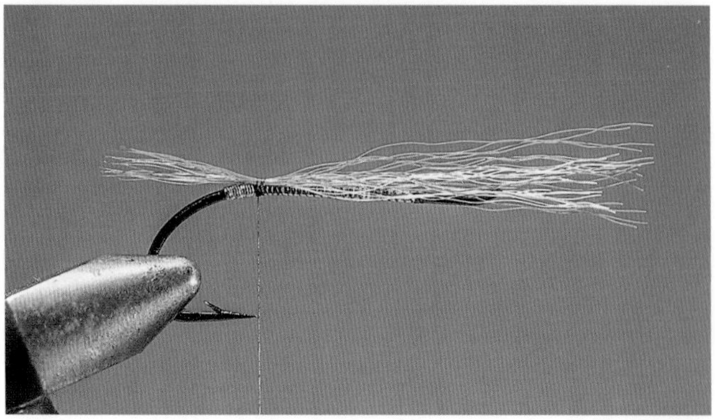

4. Bind the butt ends of the bucktail hairs along the top of the shank, progressing the thread forward. Stop when you reach the return-loop eye and make three tight turns of thread.

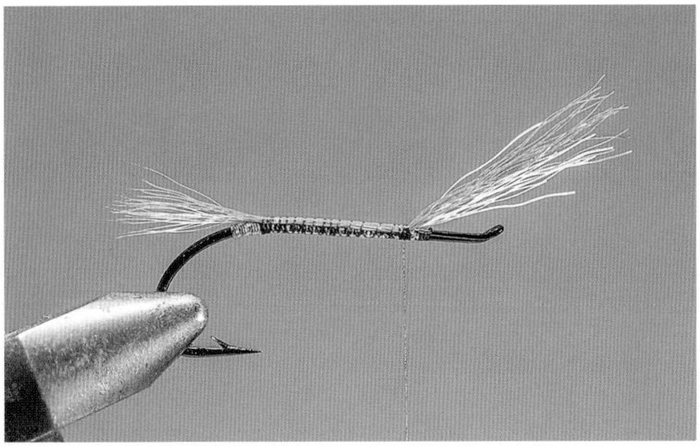

5. Cut the hairs off close to the hook shank, and then attach a length of small or medium gold oval tinsel (depending on hook size) and a length of bright orange wool yarn on the far side of the hook.

6. Bind the orange wool yarn and the oval tinsel down along the far side of the shank all the way back to the base of the tail, then wrap the thread forward again to the midpoint of the shank.

7. In close spirals, wind the orange wool yarn forward to where the thread is positioned and then capture the tag end with two or three turns of thread.

8. Carefully pull the tag end of the orange wool yarn forward while you make another thread wrap or two to secure it and then bind it down along the shank.

9. Cut away the tag end of the orange wool yarn and then attach a length of red wool yarn at that point. In this case, because the red yarn is smaller in diameter than the orange yarn, two strands are used so that the red half of the fly will be slightly thicker than the rear half.

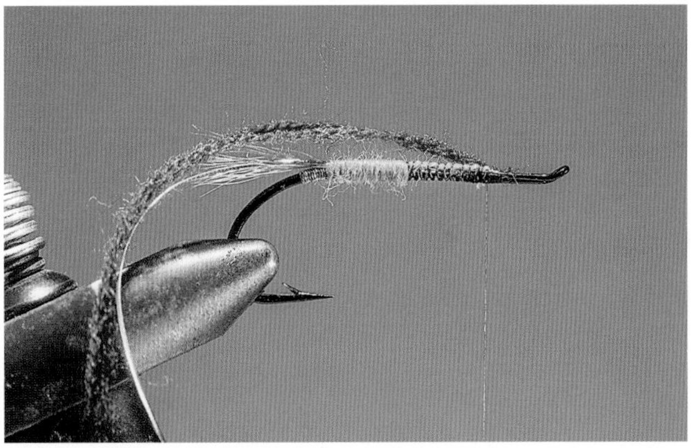

10. Bind the red wool yarn down along the shank and then return the thread to the front.

11. Wind the red wool yarn forward to form the front half of the body, secure it at front with two or three thread wraps, and cut away the excess. Leave plenty of room for the hackle and wing.

12. Spiral the gold oval tinsel forward to form the rib, but make the first turn under the base of the tail, tight against the back end of the body to prop the tail up at an angle as shown.

13. Make four to six turns of brown hackle. After tying off the hackle, create a platform of thread on which to secure the wing.

14. Using the flush-cut method, secure a sparse wing of stacked white bucktail.

15. On top of the white bucktail, secure an equal amount of stacked orange bucktail.

16. Using the method outlined on pages 231–232, mount a jungle cock eye on each side of the wing.

17. Completed Brad's Brat.

Lesson 3: Silver Demon

1. At the front of the hook, a short distance behind the eye, attach a length of fine silver oval tinsel. Using a thread that flattens easily, bind the tinsel down along the underside of the shank.

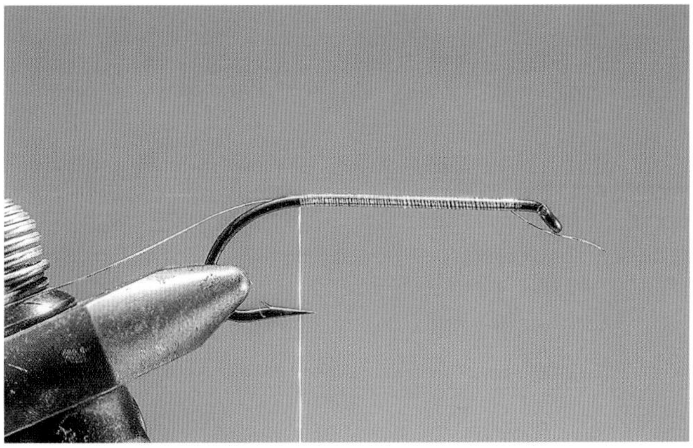

2. Form the tag from the silver oval tinsel (see pages 207–208), and secure it with three turns of thread up against the last turn of the tinsel.

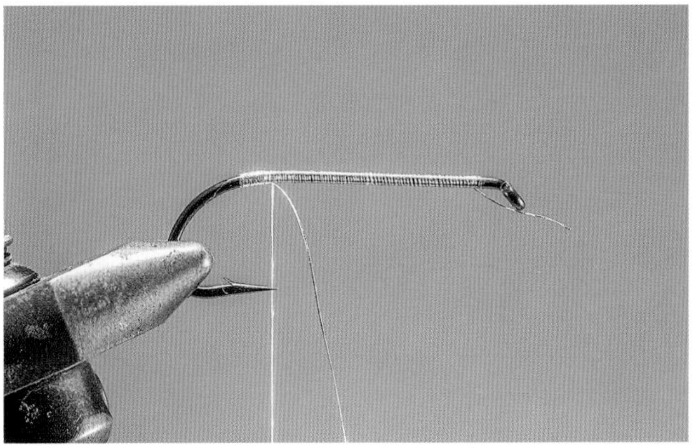

3. Gradually draw the tag end of the oval tinsel alongside the shank while progressing forward with thread wraps.

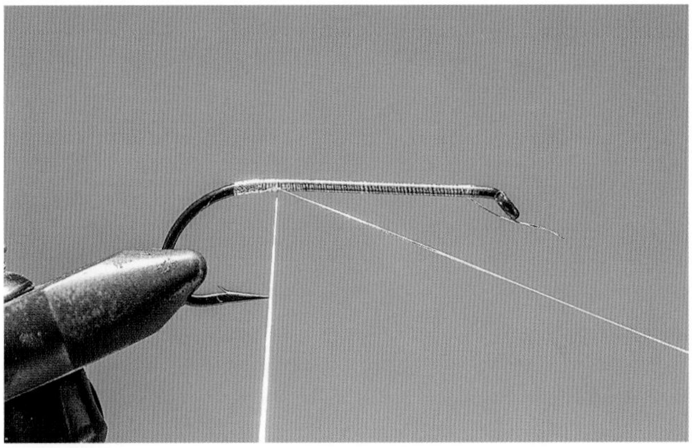

4. After binding the tag end of the oval tinsel down along the length of the underside of the shank, progress the thread back to the rear, add the tail of wood duck, return the thread to the front once again, and secure a length of medium or large silver oval tinsel.

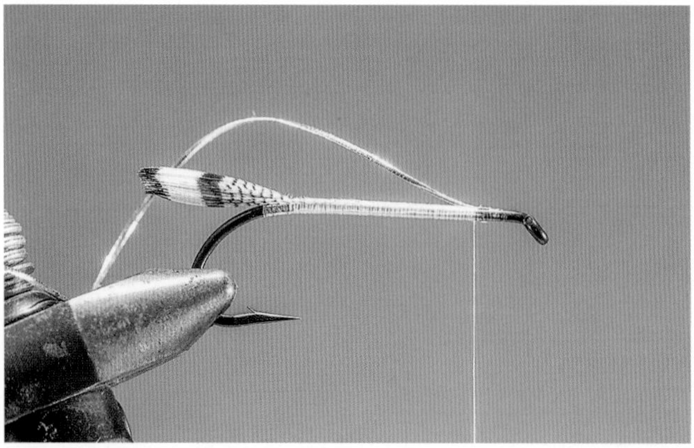

5. Bind the medium or large silver oval tinsel down along the far side of the shank with edge-to-edge thread wraps, and then return the thread to the front, also with edge-to-edge wraps.

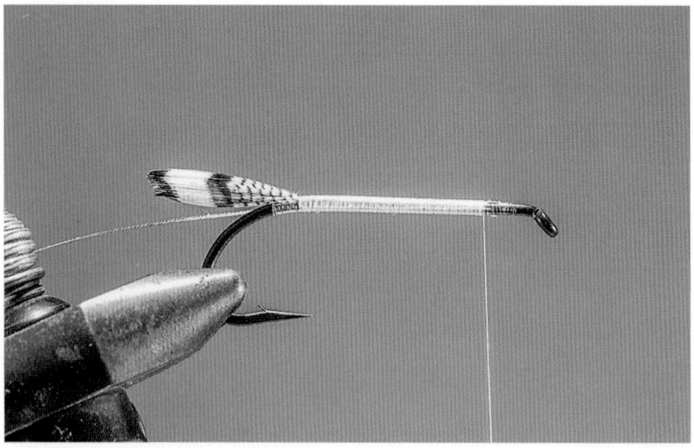

6. Gently burnish the thread underbody to smooth out thread ridges.

7. Switch to a finishing thread and then attach a long piece of flat silver tinsel at the front.

8. Begin wrapping the flat tinsel rearward, toward the tail, keeping each turn of tinsel edge-to-edge with the previous turn, but without overlapping.

9. Maintaining uniform tension on the tinsel throughout the process, wrap back to the base of the tail, then reverse directions and begin wrapping the tinsel forward.

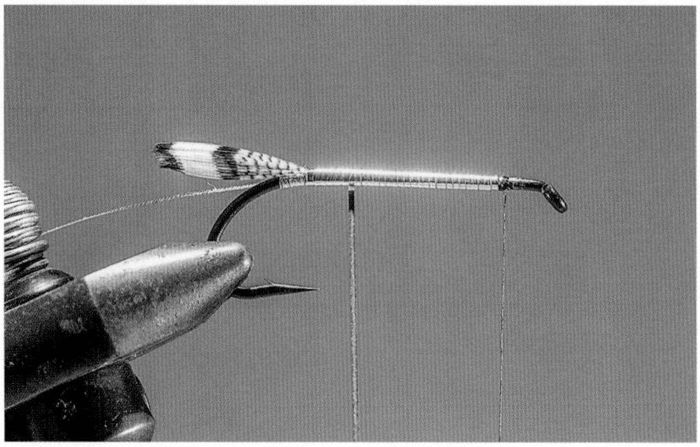

10. Tie off the flat tinsel at the front.

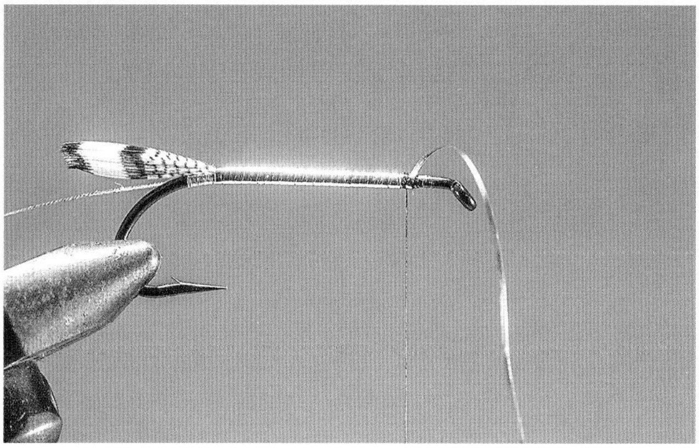

11. Spiral the oval tinsel forward to form the rib and tie off at front on the underside of the hook.

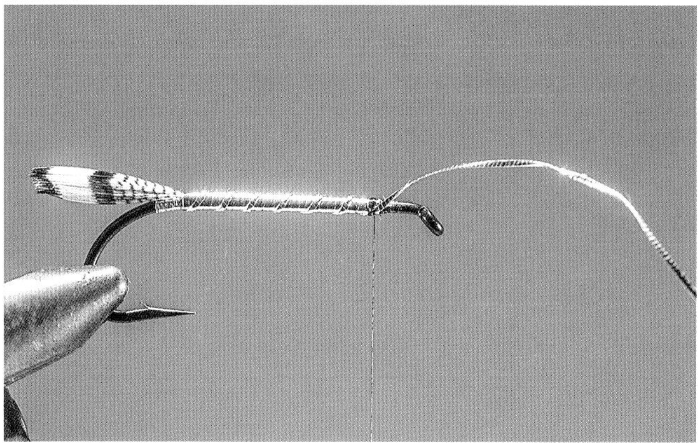

12. Add a collar of orange cock's neck or saddle hackle.

13. Add a wing of brown bucktail or similar and secure jungle cock cheeks. Finish the head. Note the orange thread band on this head, which is an affectation that the skilled tier Jim Stovall used to add to his steelhead flies.

14. Two coats of high-gloss head cement complete this Silver Demon.

FLY RECIPE APPENDIX

ADMIRAL

Unknown, named for Rear Admiral Eustace Baron Rogers, USN, 1855–1929 *page 27*

Tail: Red hackle fibers
Body: Red wool yarn
Rib: Gold flat tinsel
Hackle: Red
Wing: White bucktail

Note: The original was tied with quill duck or goose primary strips, but tiers began using white bucktail for the wing when the fly garnered popularity for steelhead.

AL'S SPECIAL

Al Knudson, 1930s *page 28*

Tail: Red hackle fibers
Body: Yellow chenille
Rib: Silver oval tinsel
Hackle: Red
Wing: White bucktail

ALASKA MARY ANN

Frank Dufresne, circa 1929 *page 29*

Tail: Red hackle fibers
Body: White silk
Rib: Silver flat tinsel (medium)
Wing: White polar bear
Cheeks: Jungle cock

BEKEART'S SPECIAL

Possibly Philip Bekeart, for whom the fly is named, or perhaps John Benn, 1890s *page 30*

Tag: Gold oval tinsel
Tail: Scarlet hackle fibers
Butt: Peacock herl
Body: Red silk floss
Rib: Gold flat tinsel (narrow)
Shoulder: Peacock herl
Hackle: Red
Wings: Brown speckled hen or turkey, with sides of jungle cock
Head: Black ostrich herl

BENN'S BLACK PRINCE

John S. Benn, 1890s *page 31*

Tag: Gold oval tinsel
Tail: Yellow goose or duck primary section, or golden pheasant crest
Butt: Black ostrich
Body: Black floss
Rib: Silver flat tinsel
Hackle: Black
Wings: Black goose or swan quill segments (or convert to hair wing)
Cheeks: Jungle cock (optional)

BENN'S COACHMAN

John S. Benn, 1880s *pages 32–33*

Tail: Red hackle fibers
Body: Peacock herl
Hackle: Brown
Wings: White duck or goose primary strips with a few red primary fibers married on top

BENN'S MARTHA

John S. Benn, named after his daughter, circa 1900 *page 34*

Tail: Red hackle fibers
Body: Red floss (rear half) and yellow floss (front half)
Rib: Gold oval tinsel
Hackle: Brown
Wing: Mallard flank and jungle cock

BLACK BEAUTY

Karl Mausser, circa 1960 *page 35*
Tied by Ed Haas

Tail: Black hackle fibers
Body: Fluorescent red chenille
Hackle: Black

BLACK DEMON

C. Jim Pray, circa 1937 — *page 36*

Tag: Gold oval tinsel (fine or small)
Tail: Barred wood duck
Body: Silver or gold oval or flat tinsel
Hackle: Orange
Wing: Black bear or dark-brown bucktail
Cheeks: Jungle cock

BLACK DEMON (BLACK BODY)

Unknown (variation on Pray's pattern) — *page 36*

Tag: Silver flat tinsel
Tail: Golden pheasant crest
Body: Black silk floss
Rib: Silver flat tinsel
Hackle: Orange
Wing: Black bucktail

BLACK DIAMOND

Harry Lemire, circa 1969 — *page 37*

Tip: Silver flat tinsel
Body: Black silk floss
Rib: Silver flat tinsel
Underwing: Four peacock sword fibers under gray squirrel tail
Wing: Guinea flank fibers
Throat: Guinea
Cheeks: Jungle cock

BLACK GNAT BUCKTAIL

Unknown, circa 1930 — *page 38*
Tied by Cal Bird

Tag: Silver flat tinsel (optional)
Tail: Red hackle fibers
Body: Black chenille or wool yarn
Rib: Silver flat tinsel (optional)
Hackle: Black
Wing: Dark-brown bucktail

Note: This fly is more correctly tied without the optional rib.

BLACK GORDON

Clarence Gordon, 1930s — *page 39*
Tied by Bob Roberts

Butt: Red wool yarn
Body: Black wool yarn
Rib: Silver or gold oval tinsel
Hackle: Black
Wing: Black or dark brown hair

BLACK MAX

John Shewey, 1980s — *page 191*

Tag: Gold flat tinsel
Tail: Several orange-dyed golden pheasant crest feathers
Body: Bright orange wool yarn (rear 2/5) and black wool yarn (front 3/5)
Rib: Gold oval tinsel
Hackle: Black
Wing: Black bear or black bucktail
Cheeks: Jungle cock

Note: Many fly tiers have devised dark-wing versions of Doug Stewart's popular Max Canyon, which had been a staple on the Deschutes River (where it was born) since the 1970s.

BLACK PRINCE

Unknown, 1880s — *page 194*

Tail: Red hackle fibers
Body: Black yarn
Rib: Gold oval tinsel
Hackle: Black
Wing: Black duck, goose, or swan quill segments
Cheeks: Jungle cock (optional)

BLACK PRINCE (GORDON'S)

Clarence Gordon, late 1930s — *page 41*
Tied by Bob Roberts

Tail: Red hackle fibers
Butt: Yellow yarn or chenille (short)
Body: Black yarn or chenille
Rib: Silver oval tinsel
Hackle: Black
Wing: Black bucktail or calf tail
Cheeks: Jungle cock (optional)

BOBBIE DUNN

Peter Schwab, 1940s — *page 42*

Tail: Red bucktail
Body: Copper wire (extra-large)
Wing: Brown, red, and white bucktail, top to bottom
Throat: Red bucktail (optional)

BOSQUITO

Roy Donnelly — *page 43*

Tail: Red hackle fibers
Body: Yellow chenille
Hackle: Black
Wing: White bucktail

BOSS

Virgil Sullivan, circa 1950 — *pages 44–45*

Tag: Silver oval tinsel
Tail: Black bucktail (long)
Body: Black chenille
Rib: Silver oval tinsel
Hackle: Red
Eyes: Silver bead chain

BOXCAR

Wes Drain, 1950s — *page 46*

Tail: Red hackle fibers
Body: Peacock herl
Wing: White calf tail
Hackle: Brown, dry-fly style

BRAD'S BRAT

Enos Bradner, circa 1937 — *page 47*

Tag: Gold tinsel (long)
Tail: White over orange bucktail
Body: Orange wool yarn (rear half) and red wool yarn (front half)
Rib: Gold oval tinsel
Hackle: Brown
Wing: Orange over white bucktail, in equal amounts
Cheeks: Jungle cock

BRAD'S BRAT (AUTHOR'S VERSION)

Enos Bradner, circa 1937 — *page 195*

Tag: Gold flat tinsel
Tail: Several orange-dyed golden pheasant crest feathers
Body: Bright orange wool yarn (rear 2/5) and red dubbing spun into fine wool yarn (front 3/5)
Rib: Gold oval tinsel
Hackle: Brown schlappen
Wing: White hair topped with orange hair
Cheeks: Jungle cock

BRINDLE BUG

Lloyd D. Silvius, circa 1960 — *pages 48–49*
Tied by Al Brunell

Tail: Brown hackle tips or fibers
Body: Black/yellow variegated chenille
Hackle: Brown

CALIFORNIA COACHMAN

John W. Fricke, circa 1900 — *page 51*

Tag: Gold flat tinsel
Tail: Golden pheasant tippet
Body: Peacock herl, divided at midpoint with yellow floss
Hackle: Brown
Wing: White duck or goose primary sections
Cheeks: Jungle cock

CARSON COACHMAN

John S. Benn, circa 1890 — *page 53*

Tail: Golden pheasant tippet
Body: Peacock herl, divided by red floss
Hackle: Brown
Wing: White and red duck or goose primary segments

Note: Use white primary segments for the wing with a red segment married at the top. You can substitute white bucktail with red bucktail over.

CARTER FLY

C. Jim Pray, circa 1938 — *pages 54–55*

Tail: Bright yellow polar bear hair
Body: Bright red chenille
Rib: Gold oval tinsel (small)
Hackle: Bright red
Wing: Black bear or black bucktail

CARTER'S DIXIE

C. Jim Pray, circa 1934 — *pages 54–55*

Tag: Gold oval tinsel (fine)
Tail: Yellow polar bear
Body: Gold oval tinsel
Hackle: Bright red
Wing: White polar bear or bucktail

CHAPPIE

C. L. Franklin *page 56*

Tail: Two grizzly hackle tips
Body: Orange wool yarn
Rib: Orange silk or gold oval or flat tinsel
Hackle: Grizzly
Wing: Two grizzly hackles

CLIFF'S SPECIAL

Cliff Welch, 1930s *page 57*

Tail: Red swan secondary, or goose primary or shoulder
Body: Orange chenille
Rib: Gold flat tinsel
Hackle: Hot orange
Wing: White swan secondary, or goose primary or shoulder

Note: For small hooks, such as size 8, goose primary feathers are ideal; for larger hooks, goose shoulder or swan secondary feathers provide longer fibers.

COLVIN'S ROGUE RIVER SPECIAL

Frank Colvin, 1920s *pages 148–149*

Tail: White bucktail
Butt: Yellow wool yarn
Body: Red chenille or wool yarn
Rib: Gold tinsel
Hackle: Deep red
Wing: Salmon-pink and white bucktail

CONWAY SPECIAL

Dan Conway, circa 1934 *page 58–59*

Tag: Gold flat tinsel
Tail: Red and white hackle fibers
Body: Yellow wool yarn
Rib: Gold flat tinsel
Body hackle: Yellow
Hackle: Red and yellow
Wings: White goose shoulder segments with red strip married through the middle
Cheeks: Jungle cock (optional)
Head: Peacock herl

COQUIHALLA ORANGE

Tommy Brayshaw, circa 1946 *page 61*

Tip: Gold oval tinsel (fine)
Tail: Golden pheasant tippet
Butt: Black ostrich herl
Body: Orange silk (rear half) and orange polar bear underfur dubbing (front half)
Rib: Gold oval tinsel
Throat: Red hackle fibers
Wing: White over orange polar bear

Note: For a complete description of the other variations in the Coquihalla series, see *Fly Patterns of British Columbia* by Art Lingren.

COQUIHALLA RED

Tommy Brayshaw, circa 1950 *page 61*

Tip: Silver oval tinsel (fine)
Tag: Yellow silk floss
Tail: Red goose or hackle tip
Butt: Black ostrich herl
Body: Orange silk, orange mohair, and red mohair (in thirds)
Rib: Flat silver tinsel
Hackle: Red
Wing: Peacock sword fibers under gray mallard strips

COURTESAN

Syd Glasso, circa 1965 *page 62*

Tag: Silver flat tinsel
Body: Fluorescent orange silk floss (rear half) and bright orange seal dubbing (front half)
Rib: Silver flat tinsel
Hackle: Brown schlappen hackle with long, soft fibers
Collar: Hooded merganser flank (optional)
Wing: Four hot-orange hackle tips

CUENIN'S ADVICE (CUENIN'S FLY)

J. P. Cuenin, early 1930s *page 63*

Tag: Silver oval tinsel
Tail: Orange hackle fibers
Body: Silver oval tinsel
Hackle: Orange
Wing: Brown bucktail

CUMMINGS SPECIAL

Ward Cummings and Clarence Gordon, 1930s — *page 64*

Butt: Yellow floss or wool yarn
Body: Claret chenille or wool yarn
Rib: Silver oval tinsel
Hackle: Claret
Wing: Dark-brown bucktail
Cheeks: Jungle cock

CUMMINGS SPECIAL (AUTHOR'S VERSION)

Ward Cummings and Clarence Gordon, 1930s — *page 193*

Tag: Gold oval tinsel
Tail: Claret-dyed golden pheasant crest
Butt: Yellow wool yarn
Body: Claret dubbing
Rib: Gold oval tinsel
Hackle: Claret
Wing: Dark-brown black bear hair or bucktail
Cheeks: Jungle cock
Collar: Golden pheasant flank

DAVE'S MISTAKE

David McNeese, 1987 — *page 65*

Tag: Silver flat tinsel
Tail: Purple hackle fibers or purple-dyed golden pheasant crest, topped with fruit crow
Rib: Silver oval tinsel
Body: Red dubbing
Hackle: Purple
Wing: White polar bear hair or bucktail
Cheeks: Jungle cock

Note: Substitutes for the rare and expensive fruit crow (aka Indian fruit crow) include white feathers from the neck of a ringneck pheasant dyed a pale tan-yellow and then tip-dyed with bright red; these are troublesome to create and require expertise in dying feathers. Much simpler is to simply use a small red feather, including those taken from a dyed-red hen's neck.

DEEP PURPLE SPEY

Walt Johnson, early 1960s — *page 67*

Tag: Silver flat tinsel (short)
Body: Deep purple mohair
Rib: Silver flat tinsel
Hackle: Dark-brown ringneck pheasant rump from second turn of tinsel
Collar: Deep-purple-dyed long-fibered soft hen or rooster neck saddle
Wing: Two golden pheasant flank feathers

DEL COOPER

Mike Kennedy, 1970s — *page 68–69*

Tag: Silver oval tinsel
Tail: Red hackle fibers
Body: Purple wool yarn or chenille
Rib: Silver oval tinsel
Hackle: Red
Wing: White bucktail

DESCHUTES DEMON

Don McClain, 1960s — *page 70–71*

Tied by Marty Sherman

Tag: Gold-embossed tinsel
Tail: Hot-orange hackle fibers
Body: Antique-gold wool yarn
Rib: Gold-embossed tinsel
Hackle: Orange
Wing: Brown deer body hair or brown bucktail, topped with white bucktail

DONNELLY COACHMAN

Roy Donnelly, 1940s — *page 72*

Tag: Orange floss
Tail: Red hackle fibers
Body: Peacock herl, divided at the midpoint with a band of red floss
Hackle: Orange
Wing: White over yellow bucktail
Cheeks: Jungle cock (optional)

DRAIN'S 20

Wes Drain, 1946 — *page 73*

Tip: Silver flat tinsel
Tag: Fluorescent yellow floss
Tail: Golden pheasant tippet topped with yellow toucan or substitute
Body: Fluorescent red floss
Rib: Silver flat tinsel
Hackle: Purple
Underwing: Red cock-of-the-rock or substitute
Wing: Gray squirrel tail
Cheeks: Jungle cock

Note: Golden pheasant flank dyed fluorescent red makes a good substitute for cock-of-the-rock.

EVENING COACHMAN

Walt Johnson, early 1950s *page 74–75*

Tip: Silver flat tinsel
Tag: Fluorescent orange floss
Tail: Golden pheasant crest
Body: Peacock herl, divided at midpoint with a band of fluorescent red floss
Hackle: Grizzly

FALL FAVORITE

Butch Wilson or Lloyd Silvius, 1940s *page 76*

Tail: Red hackle fibers (optional)
Body: Silver flat tinsel
Hackle: Red
Wing: Orange or fluorescent orange bucktail

Note: Addition of an Optic-style head (black with red-on-white eyes) makes the Fall Favorite Optic.

FAULK

Emil Faulk, 1923 *page 77*

Tail: Red hackle fibers
Body: Orange wool yarn
Rib: Gold oval tinsel
Hackle: Red
Wing: White bucktail
Head: White bucktail

Note: Form the head with the clipped butt ends of the wing.

FOOL'S GOLD

Mike Kennedy, 1960s *pages 78–79*

Tag: Gold flat tinsel (optional)
Tail: Golden pheasant tippet fibers
Butt: Peacock herl
Body: Gold oval tinsel
Hackle: Brown
Wing: Fox squirrel tail

FREIGHT TRAIN

Randall Kaufmann, early 1980s *pages 80–81*

Tag: Silver flat tinsel (optional)
Tail: Purple hackle fibers
Butt: Flourescent flame wool yarn (rear half) and fluorescent red wool yarn (front half)
Body: Black chenille
Rib: Silver oval tinsel
Hackle: Purple
Wing: White calf tail

Note: The butt should form two-thirds of the total body length, while the body forms the remaining third.

GENERAL MONEY NO. 1

General Noel Money, 1930s *pages 82–83*

Tag: Silver oval tinsel
Tail: Golden pheasant flank feather fibers
Body: Silver oval tinsel (rear $2/5$) and black dubbing or black wool (front $3/5$)
Rib: Silver oval tinsel
Throat: Burgundy saddle or neck hackle
Wing: Orange swan or goose shoulder
Cheeks: Jungle cock

GENERAL MONEY NO. 2

General Noel Money, 1930s *pages 82–83*

Tag: Gold oval tinsel
Tail: Golden pheasant crest
Body: Black floss or wool yarn
Rib: Gold oval tinsel
Hackle: Yellow, from third turn of tinsel
Wings: Red goose, duck, or swan sections
Topping: Golden pheasant crest

GOLDEN DEMON

Unknown *page 85*

Tail: Golden pheasant crest
Tag: Gold oval tinsel (fine)
Body: Gold oval tinsel (large), lacquered
Hackle: Hot orange
Wing: Bronze mallard, with jungle cock on each side (optional)

GOLDEN DEMON (BUCKTAIL VERSION)

Unknown *page 85*

Tag:	Gold oval tinsel (fine)
Tail:	Golden pheasant crest
Body:	Gold oval tinsel (large), lacquered
Hackle:	Hot orange
Wing:	Brown bucktail
Cheeks:	Jungle cock

GOLDEN EDGE ORANGE

Harry Lemire, 1960s *page 86*

Tag:	Silver flat tinsel
Tail:	Golden pheasant crest
Body:	Orange floss
Rib:	Silver flat tinsel
Throat:	Guinea fibers
Underwing:	Gray squirrel tail (sparse)
Wing:	Bronze mallard with small jungle cock eyes on each side
Head:	Bright red tying thread

GOLDEN GIRL

Roderick Haig-Brown, 1940s *page 87*

Tip:	Gold oval tinsel (fine)
Tag:	Orange silk
Tail:	Golden pheasant crest
Body:	Gold flat tinsel
Hackle:	Yellow
Wing:	Orange polar bear hair, two golden pheasant tippet feathers
Topping:	Golden pheasant crest

GRAY HACKLE YELLOW (ROGUE RIVER VARIATION)

Unknown *page 88*
Tied by Al Brunell

Tag:	Gold flat tinsel
Tail:	Red hackle fibers
Body:	Yellow silk floss
Hackle:	Grizzly
Wing:	Brown bucktail

GREASE LINER

Harry Lemire, 1962 *page 89*

Tail:	Dark deer hair
Body:	Brown seal or angora dubbing
Hackle:	Grizzly (sparse)
Wing:	Dark deer hair
Head:	Clipped ends of deer hair used for wing

GREEN-BUTT BLACK

Art Lingren, circa 1983 *page 90*

Tip:	Silver oval tinsel (fine)
Tag:	Fluorescent green floss
Tail:	Guinea fowl fibers
Butt:	Black ostrich herl
Body:	Black silk floss (rear 1/3) and black seal dubbing (front 2/3)
Rib:	Silver oval tinsel
Hackle:	Black rooster neck hackle, one side stripped from second turn of tinsel
Collar:	Guinea fowl
Wing:	Black squirrel

GREEN-BUTT SKUNK

Dan Callaghan, circa 1975 *page 91*

Tag:	Silver flat tinsel
Tail:	Red hackle fibers
Butt:	Fluorescent green chenille
Body:	Black chenille
Rib:	Silver flat or oval tinsel
Hackle:	Black
Wing:	White calf tail

GRIZZLY KING (ROGUE RIVER VARIATION)

James Wilson, 1830s *pages 132–133*
Tied by Al Brunell

Tail:	Red hackle fibers
Body:	Green silk floss
Rib:	Silver flat tinsel
Hackle:	Grizzly
Wing:	Gray squirrel topped with natural mallard flank

HEADRICK'S KILLER (KILLER)

Frank Headrick, late 1940s *page 92–93*

Tag:	Silver flat tinsel
Tail:	Orange hackle fibers
Body:	Red wool yarn or chenille
Hackle:	Red
Wing:	Black bucktail
Cheeks:	Jungle cock

HELLCAT (HEADRICK'S HELLCAT)

Frank Headrick, early 1950s *page 95*

Tag:	Silver flat tinsel
Tail:	Golden pheasant crest
Body:	Pink chenille
Rib:	Silver oval tinsel
Hackle:	Purple
Wing:	White bucktail or white quill segments
Topping:	Golden pheasant crest

HORNER'S SILVER SHRIMP

Jack Horner, 1938 *pages 96–97*

Tail:	Light gray-brown bucktail
Body:	Silver oval tinsel (large), over a base of stout floss
Hackle:	Grizzly, palmered through body
Back:	Light gray-brown bucktail
Head:	Black tying thread, with painted white eye with black pupil

Note: The tail and wing can be made from a single bunch of long bucktail fibers by tying the bundle down at the rear, doubling the hair back over itself for a short distance and securing with thread wraps; the long butt sections are then ready to be pulled forward over the body.

HOYT'S KILLER

Clyde Hoyt, circa 1940 *pages 98–99*

Tail:	Bright red hackle fibers
Body:	Black chenille
Rib:	Silver-embossed tinsel
Hackle:	Grizzly
Wing:	Mule deer body hair or dark bucktail

ICTERUS

page 191

Tag:	Gold oval tinsel (fine)
Tail:	One bright-orange-dyed golden pheasant crest feather between two natural golden pheasant crest feathers
Butt:	Bright yellow (rear half) and bright orange wool yarn (front half)
Body:	Black wool yarn
Rib:	Gold oval tinsel
Hackle:	Black
Wing:	Black, white, and black hair, respectively

Note: This pattern began as a variation of the Black Prince but eventually morphed into a new pattern in a good example of how fly patterns evolve and change. Icterus is the Latin genus name for the orioles, bright black, white, yellow, and orange songbirds that are common along the Lower Deschutes River and other rivers feeding the Columbia and Snake Rivers.

IMPROVED GOVERNOR

Martha Benn, pre-1910 *pages 100–101*

Tag:	Gold flat or oval tinsel (fine)
Tail:	Red hackle fibers
Butt:	Red silk floss
Body:	Peacock herl
Rib:	Gold or silver oval tinsel
Hackle:	Brown saddle or neck hackle
Wing:	Brown mallard, fox squirrel tail, or brown bucktail
Cheeks:	Jungle cock

Note: The tail (red hackle fibers) is typically mounted in front of the butt section of red floss. The rib goes over the butt section.

JUICY BUG

Russ Tower and Ben Chandler, 1950s *page 103*
Tied by Al Brunell

Tag:	Silver oval tinsel (fine)
Tail:	Red hackle fibers
Butt:	Black chenille
Body:	Red chenille
Rib:	Silver oval tinsel
Wing:	White bucktail or calftail, tied at a high angle and divided

Note: Traditionally, this fly often tied on a double hook.

JUNGLE DRAGON (ENOS BRADNER VERSION)

Bill Hosie, circa 1948 *page 105*

Tag: Silver flat tinsel
Tail: Golden pheasant tippet
Body: Flat silver tinsel (rear half) and red silk (front half)
Rib: Silver oval tinsel
Hackle: Grizzly
Wing: Gray squirrel tail
Cheeks: Jungle cock

JUNGLE DRAGON (WASHINGTON FLY FISHING CLUB VERSION)

Bill Hosie, circa 1948 *page 105*

Tag: Silver-embossed tinsel
Tail: Golden pheasant tippet
Body: Silver-embossed tinsel (rear half) and scarlet seal fur (front half)
Rib: Silver oval tinsel
Hackle: Cream badger
Wing: Gray squirrel tail
Cheeks: Jungle cock

KALAMA SPECIAL

Maurice "Mooch" Abraham, circa 1930 *page 106*

Tail: Red hackle fibers
Body: Yellow yarn or chenille
Hackle: Badger or grizzly, palmered through body
Wing: White bucktail

KALAMA SPECIAL (AUTHOR'S VERSION)

page 195

Tag: Silver flat tinsel
Tail: Fluorescent flame-dyed golden pheasant crest feathers
Body: Bright yellow seal's fur or angora dubbing
Rib: Silver oval tinsel
Hackle: Grizzly, palmered through the body
Wing: White bucktail

KISPIOX SPECIAL

Karl Mausser and Roy Pitts, circa 1957 *page 107*

Tag: Silver oval tinsel (optional)
Tail: Red polar bear
Body: Hot-orange chenille
Rib: Silver oval tinsel (optional)
Hackle: Red
Wing: White bucktail

KNUDSON WHITE STREAMER AND KNUDSON WHITE MARABOU

Al Knudson, circa 1935 *page 108*

Hook: Salmon/steelhead iron, sizes 2/0 through 6/0
Tag: Silver oval tinsel
Tail: Red hackle fibers
Body: Silver oval tinsel
Hackle: Red or orange
Wing: White neck hackles (large)

Note: Lacquering the body prior to mounting the hackle and wings makes the fly especially durable. For the wing, use two to five pairs of large white neck hackles, depending on fly size, or substitute three to six white marabou plumes.

LADY CAROLINE (TRADITIONAL)

Unknown, circa 1870 *page 109*

Tail: Golden pheasant flank fibers
Body: Brownish-olive wool yarn or dubbing
Rib: Silver flat tinsel, silver and gold oval tinsel
Hackle: Gray heron or substitute
Collar: Golden pheasant flank
Wing: Bronze mallard

Note: Blue-eared pheasant rump makes a good gray heron substitute.

LADY CAROLINE (REDUCED)

Unknown *page 109*
Tied by Ed Haas

Tail: Golden pheasant flank fibers
Body: Olive-brown seal dubbing
Rib: Silver oval tinsel
Throat: Golden pheasant flank fibers
Wing: Bronze mallard

LADY COACHMAN

Walt Johnson, 1958 *page 110*
Tied by Walt Johnson

Tip: Silver flat tinsel
Tag: Fluorescent red floss
Tail: Cerise hackle fibers
Body: Peacock herl, divided at midpoint by fluorescent pink wool yarn
Hackle: Light fluorescent pink
Wing: White bucktail between two light-blue hen neck feathers

LADY GODIVA

Ralph Olson, mid-1940s *page 111*

Tag:	Silver-embossed tinsel
Tail:	Red and yellow swan or goose, married
Butt:	Red chenille
Body:	Yellow seal dubbing or yellow wool yarn
Rib:	Silver flat tinsel
Wing:	Red bucktail over sparse white polar bear

Note: Olson tied this fly on size 1/0 through 3/0 salmon irons.

LADY HAMILTON

Ralph Wahl, early 1940s *pages 112–113*

Tail:	Red goose quill section
Body:	Red floss
Rib:	Silver-embossed tinsel
Wing:	Orange over white bucktail
Head:	Black tying thread, with painted black-on-white eye

LORD HAMILTON

Ralph Wahl, early 1940s *pages 112–113*

Tail:	Red goose quill section
Body:	Yellow floss
Rib:	Silver-embossed tinsel
Wing:	Red over white bucktail
Head:	Black tying thread, with painted black-on-white eye

MAX CANYON

Doug Stewart, 1976 *pages 114–115*

Tag:	Gold flat tinsel
Tail:	Orange over white hackle fibers
Rib:	Gold flat tinsel
Butt:	Orange wool yarn
Body:	Black wool yarn
Hackle:	Black
Wing:	White calf tail topped with orange calf tail

MCGINTY BUCKTAIL

Unknown *pages 116–117*
Tied by Al Brunell

Tail:	Mallard flank and red hackle fibers
Body:	Black and yellow chenille in alternating bands
Hackle:	Brown saddle hackle
Wing:	Grayish-brown bucktail or gray squirrel tail
Cheeks:	Jungle cock

MCLEOD UGLY

George McLeod, late 1940s *page 118*

Tail:	Fluff from the base of a red hackle
Body:	Black chenille
Hackle:	Grizzly, palmered
Wing:	Black bucktail

MIGRANT ORANGE

Walt Johnson, late 1960s *page 119*
Tied by Walt Johnson

Tip:	Copper flat tinsel
Tag:	Fluorescent orange floss over upper half of tag
Tail:	Fluorescent orange hackle fibers or acrylic hair
Body:	Fluorescent orange-red yarn
Rib:	Flat copper tinsel
Hackle:	Soft-orange hen or saddle
Wing:	Fluorescent orange bucktail or acrylic hair
Topping:	Fluorescent red-orange yarn

Note: If you use acrylic hair for the wing, make sure to use it for the tail as well.

MYERS BUCK

Jack Myers, circa 1920 *pages 176–177*

Tag:	Silver flat tinsel (optional)
Tail:	Yellow goose quill section or yellow hair
Body:	Yellow floss or wool yarn
Rib:	Silver oval tinsel
Hackle:	Brown
Wing:	White bucktail

NIGHT DANCER

Frank Amato, late 1970s *page 120*

Tail:	Red hackle fibers
Body:	Black floss
Rib:	Silver flat tinsel
Hackle:	Deep purple
Wing:	Black calf tail or bucktail

NITE OWL

Lloyd Silvius, circa 1930 *page 121*

Tail:	Yellow hackle fibers
Butt:	Two turns of red chenille
Body:	Silver oval tinsel
Hackle:	Orange
Wing:	White bucktail

Note: Addition of brass bead at head, painted black, with fluorescent red-on-white eye, makes this the Nite Owl Optic.

ORANGE HERON

Syd Glasso, circa 1962 *page 123*

Tag:	Silver flat tinsel
Rib:	Silver oval or flat tinsel (medium)
Body:	Bright orange floss (rear 2/3) and bright orange seal fur (front 1/3)
Hackle:	Gray heron or substitute
Collar:	Teal or hooded merganser
Wings:	Bright orange hackles

Note: Blue-eared pheasant makes a good substitute for heron.

ORANGE SHRIMP

Unknown, late 1920s or early 1930s *pages 124–125*

Tail:	Red hackle fibers
Body:	Orange wool yarn
Rib:	Gold flat or oval tinsel (optional)
Hackle:	Orange
Wing:	White bucktail with long jungle cock

ORLEANS BARBER

John Borisa, 1930s *pages 126–127*

Tail:	Barred wood duck
Body:	Bright red chenille
Hackle:	Grizzly

PACIFIC KING

Roy Patrick, circa 1940 *page 128*

Tail:	Black hackle fibers
Body:	Insect green floss
Overbody:	Dark-brown floss
Rib:	Black silk
Hackle:	Black
Throat:	Black hackle
Wing:	Black squirrel tail

Note: Sweep the black hackle downward to form the throat.

PARMACHENE BELLE

Henry P. Wells, circa 1878 *page 129*

Tag:	Silver flat tinsel
Tail:	Scarlet and white duck or goose primary, married
Butt:	Peacock herl or black ostrich herl
Rib:	Silver flat tinsel
Body:	Yellow mohair, wool yarn, or floss
Hackle:	White, fronted by scarlet
Wing:	White with a strip of scarlet married through the middle
Head:	Black tying thread

PATRIOT

Frank Amato, late 1970s *page 120*

Tail:	Red hackle fibers
Body:	Yellow floss
Rib:	Silver flat tinsel
Hackle:	Deep purple
Wing:	White calf tail or bucktail

POLAR SHRIMP

Clarence Shoff, early to mid-1930s *pages 130–131*
Tied by Ed Haas

Tail:	Bright red hackle fibers
Body:	Fluorescent orange chenille
Hackle:	Fluorescent orange
Wing:	White polar bear
Cheeks:	Jungle cock (optional)

PROFESSOR (ROGUE RIVER VARIATION)

John Wilson, circa 1830 *pages 132–133*
Tied by Al Brunell

Tail:	Red hackle fibers
Body:	Yellow silk floss
Rib:	Gold-embossed tinsel
Hackle:	Grizzly or brown
Wing:	Gray squirrel tail

PROTEIN BUCK

Ed Haas, 1970s *page 135*
Tied by Ed Haas

Tail:	Red hackle fibers
Body:	Orange chenille
Wing:	Black squirrel tail
Head:	Bright red tying thread

PURPLE ANGEL

Bob Stroebel, late 1960s *page 136*

Tail:	Purple hackle fibers
Butt:	Two turns of fluorescent flame chenille
Body:	Purple chenille
Rib:	Silver oval tinsel
Hackle:	Purple
Wing:	White bucktail
Head:	Fluorescent flame thread

Note: Soft fibers from the base of a hackle work best for the tail. The Alec Jackson version of the Purple Angel omits the rib and instead uses silver-tinsel-core purple chenille for the body.

PURPLE PERIL

George McLeod, circa 1940 *page 137*

Tag:	Silver flat tinsel (wet version only)
Tail:	Purple hackle fibers
Body:	Purple chenille
Rib:	Silver-embossed or flat tinsel
Hackle:	Purple
Wing:	Dark-brown bucktail

QUEEN BESS

Peter Schwab, 1940s *page 42*

Tail:	Gray squirrel tail
Body:	Silver flat tinsel over .030- or .035-inch lead wire
Wing:	Gray squirrel tail over yellow bucktail

QUILLAYUTE

Dick Wentworth, mid-1960s *pages 138–139*

Tail:	Amherst pheasant crest (optional)
Body:	Orange silk (rear half) and orange seal fur dubbing (front half)
Rib:	Silver flat tinsel
Hackle:	Teal flank, palmered from second turn of tinsel
Collar:	Black heron or substitute
Wing:	Four matching golden pheasant flank feathers
Topping:	Amherst pheasant crest (optional)

Note: Substitute dyed-black blue-eared pheasant for black heron.

RAILBIRD (BENN'S RAILBIRD)

John S. Benn, circa 1880s *pages 140–141*

Tail:	Claret quill segment
Body:	Claret wool yarn
Body Hackle:	Claret
Hackle:	Yellow
Wing:	Mallard or barred Clapper or King Rail flank
Cheeks:	Jungle cock

RED SHRIMP SPEY

Walt Johnson, late 1960s *pages 142–143*

Tag:	Silver flat tinsel (short)
Body:	Red fur, loosely dubbed over hot-orange floss
Rib:	Silver flat tinsel
Hackle:	Dark ringneck pheasant rump, from second turn of rib
Collar:	Soft red hackle
Wing:	Red hen hackle tips
Topping:	Golden pheasant crest

RED ANT

Mike Kennedy *pages 144–145*
Tied by Bob Roberts

Tag:	Silver flat tinsel
Tail:	Red hackle fibers
Butt:	Peacock herl
Body:	Red wool yarn (fine)
Hackle:	Furnace or brown
Wing:	Natural fox squirrel

ROGUE RED ANT (RED ANT)

Unknown *pages 144–145*
Tied by Al Brunell

Tail:	Golden pheasant tippet
Butt:	Peacock herl or green-olive chenille
Body:	Red floss or wool yarn (fine)
Rib:	Gold oval tinsel (optional)
Hackle:	Brown
Wing:	Natural brown bucktail or fox squirrel
Cheeks:	Jungle cock (optional)

Note: Often tied on double hooks.

ROGUE RIVER

Unknown, 1920s *pages 146–147*

Tail:	Red hackle fibers
Butt:	Olive-green chenille
Body:	Red floss or wool yarn
Rib:	Silver oval or embossed tinsel
Wing:	Silver-gray squirrel or white bucktail, divided
Cheeks:	Jungle cock
Head:	Black tying thread, with white iris with black pupil

Note: Generally tied on double hooks but easily adapted to single hooks.

ROGUE RIVER SPECIAL

Frank Colvin, 1920s *pages 148–149*

Tail:	Yellow and white bucktail
Butt:	Yellow wool yarn
Body:	Red chenille
Rib:	Gold oval tinsel
Hackle:	Deep red
Wing:	Yellow over white bucktail

ROYAL COACHMAN BUCKTAIL

Unknown *page 150*
Tied by Al Brunell

Tail: Golden pheasant tippet
Body: Peacock herl divided by red floss
Hackle: Brown
Wing: White bucktail
Cheeks: Jungle cock (optional)

SAWTOOTH

Ray Bergman, 1930s *page 151*

Tail: Guinea
Body: Orange chenille or wool yarn
Rib: Gold oval tinsel
Hackle: Guinea
Wing: Fox squirrel tail
Cheeks: Jungle cock

SCARLET IBIS (RED IBIS, RED FLY)

Unknown, pre-1850 *page 152*

Tag: Gold flat tinsel
Tail: Red duck quill segment
Body: Red floss
Rib: Gold flat tinsel
Throat: Red hackle
Wing: Red duck quill segments

SHEWEY'S SPAWNING PURPLE

pages 196–198

Tag/under body: Silver flat tinsel or nickel-plated hook
Body: Fluorescent flame flat waxed nylon (used as tying thread until hackle is applied)
Wing: Five individual sparse wings of purple marabou from the top of the feather
Hackle: Purple rooster hackle
Collar: Hot-orange-dyed guinea flank
Head: Claret or red thread
Cheeks: Jungle cock (long)

Note: Apply the fifth and final wing on top of the hackle.

SILVER ADMIRAL

Ernest "Polly" Rosborough *page 153*

Hook: Eagle Claw 1197N
Tail: Fluorescent hot-pink hackle fibers
Body: Hot-pink wool yarn or chenille
Rib: Silver flat or oval tinsel
Hackle: Fluorescent hot pink
Wing: White bucktail or calf tail

SILVER ANT

Isaac "Russ" Tower, 1930s *pages 154–155*
Tied by Bob Roberts

Tail: Red hackle fibers
Butt: Black chenille
Body: Silver oval tinsel
Wing: White bucktail
Cheeks: Jungle cock
Hackle: Black

Note: Often tied on double hooks; wing is upright and divided.

SILVER DEMON

C. Jim Pray, 1935 *page 156*

Tag: Silver oval or flat tinsel (fine)
Tail: Barred wood duck
Rib: Silver oval tinsel
Body: Silver oval tinsel (large)
Hackle: Bright orange
Wing: Silver-gray or Eastern gray squirrel tail
Cheeks: Jungle cock (optional)

SILVER DEMON (AUTHOR'S VERSION)

C. Jim Pray, 1935 *page 193*

Tag: Silver flat tinsel
Tail: Golden pheasant crest, topped with wood duck flank
Body: Silver flat tinsel
Rib: Silver oval tinsel
Hackle: Hot orange
Wing: Gray squirrel tail
Cheeks: Jungle cock
Head: Red tying thread

SILVER HILTON

Henry Hilton, 1940s *page 157*

Tail:	Mallard flank or red hackle fibers
Body:	Black yarn or chenille
Rib:	Silver oval tinsel (optional)
Hackle:	Grizzly
Wings:	Grizzly hackle tips

SKUNK

Mildred Krogel, circa 1930 *pages 158–159*

Tag:	Silver flat tinsel (optional)
Tail:	Red hackle fibers
Body:	Black wool yarn or chenille
Rib:	Silver oval tinsel
Hackle:	Black
Wing:	Black skunk hair with a strip of white skunk hair or bucktail over top

SKYKOMISH SUNRISE

George McLeod, circa 1938 *pages 160–161*

Tag:	Silver flat tinsel
Tail:	Yellow over red hackle fibers
Body:	Red chenille
Rib:	Silver oval tinsel
Hackle:	Red and yellow, wrapped together
Wing:	White bucktail or polar bear hair

SKYKOMISH SUNRISE (AUTHOR'S VERSION)

George McLeod, circa 1938 *page 192*

Tip:	Silver oval tinsel (fine)
Tag:	Lemon-yellow silk floss
Tail:	Natural and red-dyed golden pheasant crest (two each)
Body:	Scarlet dubbing
Rib:	Silver oval tinsel
Hackle:	Red and yellow mixed, with red foremost
Wing:	White polar bear hair or bucktail
Cheeks:	Jungle cock

SOL DUC

Syd Glasso, late 1950s *pages 162–163*

Hook:	Low-water style, optionally painted bright orange
Tag:	Silver flat tinsel (optional)
Tail:	Golden pheasant crest (optional)
Rib:	Silver flat tinsel
Body:	Fluorescent orange floss (rear) and hot-orange seal dubbing (front)
Hackle:	Yellow neck hackle or schlappen, one side stripped, from second turn of tinsel
Wings:	Four hot-orange hackle tips
Topping:	Golden pheasant crest (optional)
Head:	Red tying thread

Note: The optional parts of this dressing indicate the variation the pattern was subjected to by Glasso and Wentworth. Though this fact has been all but forgotten, Glasso and Wentworth often used to paint their hooks using Testor's model paints; as the late Doug Rose explained to me, they at first used white and then yellow before finally settling on bright orange as the standard.

THE SOULE

John S. Benn, 1890s *pages 164–165*

Tail:	Red and white hackle fibers
Butt:	Peacock herl
Body:	Yellow floss
Rib:	Silver oval tinsel (fine)
Hackle:	Red
Wing:	White duck or goose slips with red strips inside the white or married on top of them
Shoulders:	Jungle cock

SPADE (ALEC JACKSON, FRONT)

Alec Jackson, circa 1980 *pages 166–167*
Tied by Alec Jackson

Hook:	Alec Jackson Spey hook
Tail:	Fine deer hair
Body:	Peacock herl (rear) and black ostrich (front), both twisted into fine wire
Hackle:	Soft hen grizzly hackle
Head:	Flame-orange thread

SPADE (REAR)

Bob Arnold, circa 1964 *pages 166–167*

Tail:	Fine deer hair
Body:	Black chenille (small)
Hackle:	Soft grizzly hackle

SPECTRAL SPIDER

Walt Johnson, circa 1972 *page 168*
Tied by Sean Dahlquist

Tail: Fluorescent yellow craft fur
Body: Silver flat tinsel or Pearlescent Mylar
Rib: Silver flat tinsel (optional with Mylar body)
Wing: Cerise, orange, green, and blue craft fur or Antron yarn, stacked in that order
Sides: Light badger hackle tips
Collar: Mallard flank, spider style
Cheeks: Asian kingfisher rump or bright-blue-dyed hen neck feathers

Note: At times, Walt Johnson would add a collar of stiff grizzly hackle under the mallard flank and fish the fly as a damp or dry fly.

STEELHEAD BEE

Roderick Haig-Brown, early 1950s *page 169*

Tail: Fox squirrel tail
Body: Brown, yellow, and then brown again dubbing in three equal parts
Wings: Fox squirrel tail
Hackle: Brown or iron dun

STEELHEAD CADDIS

Bill McMillan, circa 1975 *page 170*
Tied by Bill McMillan

Body: Pale-orange rabbit dubbing
Wing: Light turkey quill segments
Head/collar: Natural deer hair

STILLAGUAMISH SUNRISE

George McLeod, late 1940s *page 171*

Tail: Red and yellow hackle fibers
Body: Yellow chenille
Rib: Silver oval tinsel
Hackle: Orange
Wing: White bucktail

STILLAGUAMISH SUNSET

George McLeod, late 1940s *page 171*

Tail: Red hackle fibers
Body: Orange chenille
Rib: Silver oval tinsel
Hackle: Orange
Wing: White bucktail

SURGEON GENERAL

Robert P. Terrill, circa 1975 *page 172*

Tag: Silver oval tinsel (fine)
Tail: Fluorescent red hackle fibers
Body: Bright purple yarn
Rib: Silver oval tinsel
Throat: Guinea
Wing: Fluorescent white bucktail or polar bear
Hackle: Fluorescent red, tied over the wing
Cheeks: Jungle cock (optional)

THOR

C. Jim Pray, 1936 *page 173*

Tail: Orange hackle fibers
Body: Red chenille
Hackle: Brown saddle
Wing: White bucktail

UMPQUA/UMPQUA SPECIAL

Unknown, late 1930s *pages 174–175*
Umpqua, Joe Howell
Umpqua Special, Author

Tail: Red over white bucktail
Body: Yellow wool yarn (rear 1/3) and red wool yarn or chenille (front 2/3)
Rib: Silver oval or flat tinsel
Wing: White bucktail with a few fibers of red bucktail on each side
Cheeks: Jungle cock
Hackle: Brown

Note: Without the jungle cock, the Umpqua Special is simply called the Umpqua.

VAN LUVEN

Harry Van Luven and Jack Myers, circa 1920 *pages 176–177*

Tag: Silver flat tinsel (optional)
Tail: Red goose quill section or red hair
Body: Red floss or wool yarn
Rib: Silver flat or oval tinsel
Hackle: Brown
Wing: White bucktail

VAN SANT (VAN ZANDT)

Josh Van Sant Jr., pre-1900 *page 178*

Tail:	Red hackle fibers
Body:	Peacock herl
Hackle:	Red
Wing:	Red goose primary sections

Note: The addition of jungle cock cheeks makes this the Josh Van Sant.

WEITCHPEC WITCH

Unknown, circa 1949 *page 178*
Tied by Ed Haas

Tag:	Gold flat or oval tinsel (fine)
Tail:	Golden pheasant tippet
Body:	Black wool yarn or chenille
Hackle:	Black
Wing:	Orange polar bear or calf tail

WELLS SPECIAL

Sam Wells, circa 1920 *pages 180–181*

Tag:	Gold flat tinsel (short)
Tail:	Dark-claret hackle fibers
Body:	Peacock herl
Hackle:	Yellow
Wings:	Gray duck primary strip with section of black married through center or at top
Sides:	Blue, yellow, and red duck or goose quill
Cheeks:	Jungle cock

Note: The sides are married strips of duck quill in order from top to bottom: blue, yellow, red.

WHITESEL'S WINE

Mike Kennedy *pages 182–183*
Tied by Jerry James

Tail:	Black hackle fibers
Body:	Wine-colored wool yarn
Rib:	Silver oval tinsel (fine)
Hackle:	Black
Wing:	Black bucktail with a topping of red bucktail
Cheeks:	Jungle cock (optional)

WITHERWOX SPECIAL

Hal Witherwox, 1950s *pages 184–185*
Tied by Al Brunell

Tag:	Silver flat tinsel
Tail:	Mallard flank
Butt:	Bright-green chenille
Body:	Red floss or yarn
Rib:	Silver oval tinsel
Hackle:	Brown
Wing:	White bucktail

YELLOW HAMMER

Dan Conway, 1920s; bucktail version first tied by George McLeod *pages 186–187*

Tag:	Gold oval tinsel
Tail:	Red and white hackle fibers
Body:	Yellow wool yarn or chenille
Rib:	Gold oval tinsel
Hackle:	Red and yellow
Wing:	White bucktail with a wisp of red on each side
Cheeks:	Jungle cock

BIBLIOGRAPHY

Arnold, Bob. *Steelhead & the Floating Line: A Meditation.* Portland, OR: Frank Amato Publications, 1995.

———. *Steelhead Water.* Portland, OR: Frank Amato Publications, 1993.

Bates, Joseph D., Jr. *Streamer Fly Fishing in Fresh and Salt Water.* New York: D. Van Nostrand, 1950.

Baughman, Michael. *A River Seen Right: A Fly Fisher's North Umpqua.* New York: Lyons & Burford, 1995.

Bergman, Ray. *Trout.* New York: Alfred A. Knopf, 1938.

Berryman, Jack W. *Fly-Fishing Pioneers & Legends of the Northwest.* Seattle: Northwest Fly Fishing, 2006.

Bradner, Enos. *Northwest Angling.* Portland, OR: Binfords & Mort, 1950.

Campbell, A. J. *Classic and Antique Fly-Fishing Tackle: A Guide for Collectors and Anglers.* New York: Globe Pequot, 2002.

Combs, Trey. *The Steelhead Trout.* Portland, OR: Frank Amato Publications, 1971.

———. *Steelhead Fly Fishing and Flies.* Portland, OR: Frank Amato Publications, 1979.

———. *Steelhead Fly Fishing.* New York: The Lyons Press, 1991.

Gallagher, Sean M. *Wild Steelhead: The Lure and Lore of a Pacific Northwest Icon.* Seattle: Wild River Press, 2013.

Grey, Zane. *Tales of Freshwater Fishing.* New York: Harper & Brothers, 1928.

Harris, William C. "The Trouts of America." From the book *Salmon and Trout* by Dean Sage, C. H. Townsend, H. M. Smith, and William C. Harris. New York: Macmillan Company, 1904.

Haig-Brown, Roderick. *Fisherman's Fall.* Vancouver, BC: Douglas & McIntyre, 1964.

———. *Fisherman's Summer.* New York: William Morrow & Company, 1959.

———. *The Western Angler.* New York: William Morrow & Company, 1947.

Hellekson, Terry. *Fish Flies: The Encyclopedia of the Fly Tier's Art.* Portland, OR: Frank Amato Publications, 2005.

———. *Fish Flies, Volume II.* Portland, OR: Frank Amato Publications, 1995.

Hemingway, Jack. *A Life Worth Living: The Adventures of a Passionate Sportsman.* Guilford, CT: Globe Pequot Press, 2004.

Kreider, Claude M. *Steelhead.* New York: G. P. Putnam's Sons, 1948.

Langley, Henrey G. *San Francisco Directory for the Year 1882.* San Francisco: Francis Valentine & Co., 1882.

Lingren, Arthur James. *Fly Patterns of British Columbia.* Portland, OR: Frank Amato Publications, 1996, 2008.

MacDowell, Syl. *Western Trout.* New York: Alfred A. Knopf, 1948.

Marbury, Mary Orvis. *Favorite Flies and Their Histories*, 1896 (2013 reprint by Skyhorse Publishing, New York).

McMillan, Bill. *Dry Line Steelhead and Other Subjects.* Portland, OR: Frank Amato Publications, 1987.

McMillan, Bill and John. *May the Rivers Never Sleep.* Portland: Frank Amato Publications, 2012.

Moyle, Peter B., Joshua A. Israel, and Sabra E. Purdy, "Salmon, Steelhead, and Trout in California," Davis, CA: University of California Davis, 2008.

San Francisco City Directory. San Francisco: R. L. Polk, 1875.

Shewey, John. *Spey Flies & Dee Flies.* Portland, OR: Frank Amato Publications, 2002.

———. *Steelhead Flies.* Portland, OR: Frank Amato Publications, 2005.

Smedley, Harold Hinsdill. *Fly Patterns and Their Origins.* Muskegon, MI: Westshore Publications, 1950.

St. John, Larry. *Practical Fly Fishing.* New York: The McMillan Company, 1920.

Stewart, Dick and Farrow Allen. *Flies For Steelhead.* Intervale, NH: Northland Press, Inc., 1992.

Sturgis, William Bayard. *Fly-Tying.* New York: Charles Scribner's Sons, 1940.

Van Fleet, Clark C. *Steelhead to a Fly.* Boston: Little, Brown and Company, 1951.

Wahl, Ralph. *One Man's Steelhead Shangri-La.* Portland, OR: Frank Amato Publications, 1989.

Wahl, Ralph and Roderick Haig-Brown. *Come Wade The River.* Seattle, WA: Superior Publishing Company, 1971.

Wharton, Joe. *Rogue River and Its Game Fish.* Grants Pass Daily Courier, 1928.

Welch, Vince, Cort Conley, and Brad Dimock. *The Doing of the Thing: The Brief Brilliant Whitewater Career of Buzz Holmstrom.* Flagstaff, AZ: Fretwater Press, 2004.

Williams, A. Courtney. *Trout Flies: A Discussion and a Dictionary.* London: A. & C. Black, Ltd., 1932.

Wethren, Bob, editor. *The Creel, North Umpqua Edition.* Portland, OR: Frank Amato Publications, 2008.

NOTES

1. Jacob Juker, born in Switzerland in 1824, ran J. Juker's Old Variety Store on Main Street in The Dalles through the 1860s; contemporary sources say he ran a "cigar store," but old newspaper ads demonstrate that he sold a wide array of goods, including fishing tackle. Available evidence suggests he arrived in Oregon in the early 1850s with his wife, Catherine (1832–1913), who outlived him by more than 40 years. A veteran of the U.S. Infantry in the Mexican–American War, where he attained the rank of sergeant, Juker died in 1870 and was interred at the Masonic Burial Ground in The Dalles. Nearly 50 years later, on application by historian Lulu D. Crandall (1854–1931), the U.S. War Department approved and shipped a military headstone to place upon his unmarked grave.
2. Among the many references to the earliest popular steelhead flies was a story titled "Portlanders Get Fine Steelhead," from *Ashland Tidings*, August 14, 1916, in which the Professor, Gray Hackle, and Royal Coachman are cited as top Rogue River flies. These same standard British and East Coast trout flies and others like them had been the standard fare for steelheaders since the inception of the sport.
3. Emerson Hough's story about the Rogue first appeared in the March 18, 1916, issue of the *Saturday Evening Post*, and a week later was reprinted in the *Ashland Tidings* with the headline, "The greatest of all steelhead rivers is the Rogue river of Oregon." Because steelhead fishing on the Rogue commenced in autumn, I am assuming Hough had fished the river the previous fall (1915), but certainly he could have visited earlier, perhaps on more than one occasion.
4. Ken James McLeod told me that, according to his father, George McLeod, E. B. George introduced bucktail flies to Washington steelheaders. E. B. George taught George McLeod to tie flies in the early 1930s.
5. Additional source:
   Campbell, A. J. *Classic and Antique Fly-Fishing Tackle: A Guide for Collectors and Anglers*. New York: Globe Pequot, 2002.
6. Benn is listed "Among the fishermen who fished for steelhead trout in the streams of the Peninsula and along the coast within 100 miles of San Francisco from the sixties to the nineties" as recalled by Walter L. Welch in a 1929 story titled "Trout Fishing in California Today and Fifty Years Ago," published in *California Fish and Game* (volume 15).
7. Located at 7 Sutter Street, with a second entrance on the Market Street side of triangular block, Butler's English Ale House first opened sometime in the early 1870s. "His specialty," said the *San Francisco News Letter* of March 24, 1877, "perhaps is fine old sherry; but he keeps a full line of the purest wines, liquors, ales and porters to be found in the city." The building had previously been occupied by Henry Casebolt, an ingenious and enterprising maker of carriages, street cars, etc.; owner of Sutter Street Railway; and also inventor of the balloon horsecar, a fascinating, short-lived, and—in retrospect—odd conveyance. By 1916, the business was named "John Butler & Son, Liquor Importers, Wholesale and Retail" at "550 Market Street and 19 Sutter Street," according to an advertisement in the *California State Division of Labor, 1916 Yearbook*. Many of these details on Casebolt come from an article published in the *Sacramento Daily Union*, Jan. 31, 1867.
8. According to the *San Francisco Call* (May 22, 1907, and July 16, 1907), Butler willed his liquor business to his son, Louis, and his house at 2009 Steiner Street to his daughter, Mrs. A. H. Rising. Louis rebuilt and reopened the old business at the original location in 1907 and operated for at least another decade as "John Butler & Son, Liquor Importers, Wholesale and Retail," according to the *California State Division of Labor, 1916 Yearbook* and the *Crocker-Langley San Francisco Directory*. Sadly, John Butler's daughter, Mary Rising, committed suicide on September 14, 1913, by sealing the doorjambs of her house with clothing and then placing a tube from the gas jet in her house into her mouth. Her death was reported in the *San Francisco Call*, September 15, 1913. She had apparently never recovered from the death of her husband, Alfred Hunt Rising, general freight agent for Southern Pacific railway, at age 41, the previous year.
9. Additional sources:
   Railway Age Gazette, Volume 53, 1912.
   San Francisco Call, Oct. 15, 1912.
   San Francisco News Letter. March 24, 1877.
   Sacramento Daily Union. Jan. 31, 1867.
   San Francisco Call, numerous editions.
10. Original letters related to the conflict are posted (as of 2013) at www.usmilitariaforum.com/forums/index.php?/topic/153799-fall-from-grace-admiral-eustace-baron-rogers.
11. Additional sources:
    Daily Alta California. February 2, 1885; May 16, 1887.
    San Francisco Call. April 10, 1910; January 8, 1911; January 15, 1911; April 14, 1912.
    Western Field (1903), lists (in ads) Phil B. Bekeart, Co., as representing various Eastern gun makers, etc.
    Coy, Owen Cochran. *Gold Days of the Series California*. San Francisco: Powell Publishing Company, 1929.
    Flayderman, Norm, *Flayderman's Guide to Antique American Firearms and Their Values*. Iola, WI: Gun Digest Books, 2007.
    Gernes, Phyllis, *Frank Bekeart, Goldrush Gunsmith, 1822–1903: A Biography of a Coloma Pioneer.* Coloma, CA: Gold Discovery Park Association, 1984.

Hough, Cass S. *It's a Daisy*. Bolingbrook, IL: Daisy Division Victor Comptometer Corporation, 1976.

Sovenski, Cindy, *California Gunsmiths 1846–1900*. Fair Oaks, CA: Far Far West Publishers, 1977.

www.malakoff.com/mccolofb.htm

12. The 444-foot-long wood and iron *City of Chester*, struck by a ship twice its size in a dense fog, was split in two and sank on August 22, 1888, in San Francisco Bay with 106 passengers on board bound for Eureka and Portland. The tragedy killed 13 passengers, including 2 children, and 3 crew members, according to period reports in the *San Francisco Call*. More than a century later, in April 2014, the wreckage of the ship was located by a National Oceanic and Atmospheric Administration team in 217 feet of water just inside the Golden Gate Bridge while the scientists were charting shipping channels.
13. Additional sources:

    Eureka Times-Standard. August 28, 1970.

    Souvenir of Humboldt County. Eureka, CA: Times Publishing Company, 1906.

    Bareilles, Jack. "World War Comes to Humboldt County." Humboldt State University thesis project, 2005.
14. Additional sources:

    Mining in California. Vol. 24, 1928.

    Biennial Report of the Secretary of State of the State of Oregon. "Articles of Incorporation," 1895.

    Capital Journal (Salem, Oregon). January 20, 1894 ("Furniture Company—The C. F. Weber Co., of Portland, today filed articles of incorporation. Capital, $100,000, with J. Vogt, J. W. Fricke, and O. F. Paxton as incorporators.").

    San Francisco Call. July 25, 1912 ("Ho, Waltons, Now's the Time to Polish Up Reels!").

    San Francisco Call. August 4, 1912 ("Western Pacific Carries Fishermen to the Edge of Famous Trout Streams").

    The Architect and Engineer of California. March 1912 ("Death of C. F. Weber").
15. Additional sources:

    Bradner, Enos. "So You're Going After Cutthroats." The *Seattle Sunday Times*. August 22, 1943.

    ———"Brad's Fly of the Week: Conway Special." The *Seattle Sunday Times*. February 8, 1948.

    ———"Unexplored Sound Beaches Offer Uncrowded Fishing for Cutthroats." The *Seattle Sunday Times*. June 3, 1951.

    "Fishing Reports." The *Seattle Daily Times*. July 2, 1921
16. From Skip Hosfield's blog, "Fly Fishing Arts, Crafts and Memoirs," www.skiphosfield.com. Hosfield, along with Bill Nelson (founder of the longstanding McKenzie Fly Fishers club in Eugene, Oregon), Stan Walters, and a few others, conceived the idea for a national fly-fishing organization and a weekend-long gathering of fly anglers. Hence the first Federation of Fly Fishers conclave was held in June, 1965, in Eugene. Hosfield was tasked with finding demonstration fly tiers and organizing that part of the event, and his recollections are priceless, such as the following: "We had an upstairs board room with Polly Rosborough at one end of a long conference table and Roy Patrick at the other end. The only time I checked on them Polly was volubly expatiating in his inimitable way to a group packed around him. At the other end of the table Roy was quietly explaining his procedures to a couple of onlookers with an occasional comment on the sideshow at the other end of the table. Down in the lobby Lee Wulff drew a crowd with an impromptu demonstration of tying his famous Wulff flies without the use of a vise."
17. David McNeese sent Glasso an envelope of flank feathers from a hooded merganser around 1979 or 1980, as I recall, and thereafter, Glasso used the feathers as a collar on a few of his flies. He wrote back to Dave to express his thanks and to tell Dave how much he liked the merganser feathers (which are a rich chocolate brown in shade, with bold black bars); sadly, the letter from Glasso, which contained several of his flies, was lost in a basement flood that McNeese suffered one winter in his Salem, Oregon, home.
18. Geordie Shanks (1828–1915) served for nearly 50 years as head gillie at Gordon Castle and was the most celebrated Spey angler of the day; his father, Jamie Shanks (1803–1899), was equally adept at dressing flies and made much of his living, in Craigellachie, as a tackle maker. John Cruikshank (1827–1897) was the famous head gillie at Wester Elchies, near Aberlour; Charles Grant (1807–1892) was for many years the schoolmaster at the Aberlour school and ranked among the greatest of the Speyborn anglers.
19. Additional sources:

    "Examiner's Fish and Game Expert Will be Seen at Fortuna Sports Show."*Humboldt Standard*. April 6, 1953.

    Dollosso, Art. "First Cousins: The Origins of Fine Western Fly Rods." *Golden Gate Angling & Casting Club Bulletin*. July 2010.

    Schrenkeisen, Ray, ed. *Fishing Lake and Stream*. New York: Doubleday, 1946.

    Springer, Joe. "Early History of the Pacific Rod & Gun Club." *The Pacific Breeze* (newsletter of the club), 1949.

    World War I Draft Registration Card for Jules Patrick Cuenin.
20. Information about Wilson also sourced from United States World War II Draft Registration Card, 1942, Serial Number 3777, Claude Ellis Wilson, and *Eureka Humboldt Standard,* January 15, 1959.
21. Among the little-known Kennedy patterns are the following:

    Deschutes Special: Tail, red hackle fibers; body, fluorescent green floss; rib, silver oval tinsel; hackle, gray; wing, gray squirrel tail; cheeks, jungle cock.

    Dingbat: Tag, silver oval tinsel (fine); tail, golden pheasant tippet fibers; body, fluorescent flame chenille or wool; rib, silver oval tinsel (small); hackle, furnace; wing, fox squirrel.

    Maverick: Tail, Lady Amherst tippet fibers; body, black tinsel-core chenille; hackle, badger; wing, gray squirrel tail. This fly converts especially well to the Alec Jackson style, using black ostrich herl spun with silver wire.

    Park: Tag, silver flat tinsel; body, black chenille; rib, silver oval tinsel (small); hackle, yellow; wing, black or dark brown hair. This fly is variation of an Atlantic salmon fly designed by Dr. Edward Park, who worked at the Johns Hopkins Harriet Lane Home, Baltimore, Maryland.

    Red Fox: Tail, golden pheasant tippet fibers; body, red wool yarn; rib, small gold oval tinsel; hackle, brown; wing, fox squirrel.

    Salmo Le Sac: Tail, peacock sword fibers; body, salmon-colored wool yarn; rib, gold oval tinsel (small); hackle, furnace; wing, fox squirrel tail.

    Tranquilizer: Tag, gold oval tinsel (fine); tail, yellow hackle fibers; body, purple wool yarn; rib, gold oval tinsel (small); hackle, claret; wing, gray squirrel tail (originally digger squirrel, aka ground squirrel).

    Willow: Tail, Lady Amherst tippet fibers; body, white wool yarn; rib, silver oval tinsel (small); hackle, badger; wing, gray squirrel tail.
22. Dressings for these flies are as follows:

    Coal Car: Tail, black hackle fibers; body, one-quarter fluorescent red-orange yarn, one-quarter fluorescent red yarn, half black chenille; rib, silver oval tinsel; hackle, black; wing, a few strands of black Krystal Flash and black-dyed squirrel.

Flat Car: Tail, black hackle fibers; butt, fluorescent green yarn; body, black chenille; rib, silver oval tinsel; hackle, black; wing, black and pearl Krystal Flash and black marabou.

Signal Light: Tail, dark purple hackle fibers; body, one-quarter fluorescent red-orange yarn, one-quarter fluorescent green yarn, half black chenille; rib, silver oval tinsel; wing, blue, pearl, wine, and lime Krystal Flash under black marabou; collar, soft dark purple hackle.

23. In this context, the name silverside salmon probably refers to coho salmon, but even in the early 1900s there remained much confusion about the taxonomy of salmon and steelhead. For example, the *Morning Oregonian,* September 10, 1903, reported that Hickson fished the Deschutes ". . . on Sunday for some sport with the steelhead salmon, or trout, as some wiseacres choose to call these salmon." In that same issue the *Morning Oregonian* reported that the two anglers had been taking steelhead on flies on the Deschutes a year earlier, in 1902.
24. Hickson Donnell, Eileen (ed.), "Rowe Creek, 1890–91: Mary L. Fitzmaurice Diary," *Oregon Historical Quarterly,* Summer 1982. Eileen Hickson Donnell, Ned Hickson's granddaughter, also noted that Fitzmaurice was a "justice of the peace in Condon, a state legislator from that district, and at various times he sold insurance and promoted land sales." The two families were very close, with both homesteaded residences being on Rowe Creek, a remote area (to this day) south of Fossil, above the John Day River.
25. Additional sources:

    Hickson Donnell, Eileen, ed. "Rowe Creek, 1890–91: Mary L. Fitzmaurice Diary." *Oregon Historical Quarterly*. Summer 1982.

    Kilkenny, John F. *Shamrocks and Shepherds: The Irish of Morrow County*. Portland, OR: Oregon Historical Society Press, 1981.

    Grant County News. March 26, 1891.

    The *Dalles Times-Mountaineer*. February 8, 1890; August 2, 1890.

    Oregon Voter: Magazine of Citizenship. Volume 37, 1924.

    The *Sunday Oregonian*. June 6, 1915.

    Condon Chamber of Commerce, http://condonchamber.org/TheTimesJournal.htm.
26. Additional sources:

    The *London Gazette*. December 19, 1882.

    The *Teesdale Mercury*. October 10, 1900.

    Banks, Edward."Capt. A. W. Money." *Forest and Stream*. May 18, 1912.

    Berryman, Jack W. "Pioneers & Legends: Noel Money (1867–1941)." *Northwest Flyfishing*. Spring 2002.

    Van Valen, James M. *History of Bergen County, New Jersey*. New York: New Jersey Publishing and Engraving Company, 1900.
27. This comes from a story, titled "Guiding Light in the Keys," penned by Harrison for the December 3, 1973, issue of *Sports Illustrated*. Further describing Woody, Harrison wrote, "Sexton is to saltwater fly-fishing what an astronaut is to the space program—a superb technocrat. With his short gray hair and mesomorph physique, he reminds one of a retired NCO who has refused to go soft."
28. Additional sources:

    The *Herald Statesman*. Yonkers, NY. March 22, 1945.

    Personal conversations with Woody Sexton in the 1990s.
29. Additional sources:

    Arnold, Bob. "Not the Same—Not Quite." *The Salmon Flyer*. Summer 1997.

    Beatty, Danny and Tamara Belts. *George McLeod interview—December 18, 2006*. Western Washington University. http://content.wwu.edu/cdm/compoundobject/collection/ffoh/id/301/rec/18.
30. The *Breakwater* was one of a number of steamers that operated between Portland and San Francisco. She carried passengers and cargo; other steamers were dedicated for cargo, particularly timber and lumber. By the time the 1,065-ton iron-hulled *Breakwater* was built at Chester, Pennsylvania, in 1900, Coos Bay had already become an important West Coast port.
31. Additional sources:

    Contino, H. S. *Shipwrecks of Coos County*. Mount Pleasant, SC: Arcadia Publishing, 2011.

    Historical Notes from Oregon Health Sciences University. April 28, 2010, http://ohsu-hca.blogspot.com/2010_04_25_archive.html.

    Kirkpatrick, Jane. *A Gathering of Finches*. Colorado Springs, CO: Multnomah Books, 2011.

    Nelson, Shirley. "Bed and Breakfast Occupies Historic House in Coos Bay," Jefferson Public Radio, www.ijpr.org, March 25, 2011.

    Wagner, Dick and Judy. *North Bend*. Mount Pleasant, SC: Arcadia Publishing, 2010.

    The *Coos Bay Times* (numerous editions).

    The *Sigma Chi Quarterly: The Official Organ of the Sigma Chi Fraternity*. Volume 34 , 1915.

    Weekly Coast Mail Marshfield (various editions).
32. Additional sources:

    Ellensburg Daily Record. June 16, 1949.

    The *Seattle Times*. Various editions, including January 5, 1950; October 18, 1950; September 24, 1968.

    Spokane Daily Chronicle. July 20, 1956.

    Johnson, Walt. Personal correspondence with the author, circa 1995.
33. Berryman, Jack W. "Pioneers & Legends: Maurice 'Mooch' Abraham (1867–1936)," *Northwest Flyfishing Magazine*, Summer 2002. Owing to a misspelling in *Steelhead Fly Fishing & Flies* (Combs, 1976), Abraham's name is often misprinted as Abrams.
34. Abraham must have been a regular on the Kalama well before he decided to try his luck there in January, 1924. The *Morning Oregonian*, January 23, 1924 ("Big Catches Made by Oregon Anglers") reported, "'Mooch' Abrams and Jack Cullison are two anglers, however, who had never taken a fish on a fly in winter before last Sunday, although they knew that others had. But just to show that it could be done, they went down to the Columbia Sunday to the mouth of the Kalama river in Washington and started upstream with their fly rods."
35. Additional sources:

    The *Sunday Oregonian.* June 22, 1913.

    The *Sunday Oregonian.* April 26, 1914.
36. From Bradner's "Brad's Fly of the Week" column in the *Seattle Sunday Times*, which featured the Lady Godiva on December 12, 1948, less than two months before Olson caught his monster steelhead on the Skagit. This article contains the dressing for the Lady Godiva I give in this book.
37. Additional sources:

    Bradner, Enos. "Steelheading . . . Has Been Unusual Season." The *Seattle Times*. February 17, 1949.

    Personal communication and correspondence with Walt Johnson, 1992 through 1998.
38. In a 2006 interview conducted by Danny Beatty and Tamara Belts for the Western Washington University Fly Fishing Oral History Program, George McLeod recalled, ". . . when I was in high school in the mid-thirties [1935], a friend of mine, Bob Dahlquist, was jump shooting mallards along the sloughs and pot holes on the Skagit. He was at the mouth of Day Creek, where Day Creek

came into a small side channel that diverted from the Skagit. Both Day Creek and the side channel from the main Skagit were small shallow streams where they came together at a large log jam and big deep pool about 200 feet in diameter. Bob jumped some mallards and got two birds. He stood there looking around and saw trout swirling! The next week he said, 'We got to go up there, and take the shotguns and the fishing rods and see what's in there.' The next Saturday Bob Dahlquist, Park Johnston, and I drove to the Day Creek Bridge and waded down the creek to the mouth at the log jam pool. We started casting size 6 and size 4 Royal Coachman Bucktail flies, and low and behold this pool, it was almost like a small lake, it was full of sea-run cutthroat, Dolly Varden and Day Creek summer steelhead. We proceeded to catch limits of these fish—it was the only place that I ever fished where you could throw a long line, let it sink, and strip the fly and steelhead would take it. They were about four or five, six pounds. Well sir, we fished that for about four years and then Ralph Wahl found it, Shangri-La!"

39. Read LaFontaine's dissertation here: www.thebookmailer.com/Gary/FFLife.html.
40. In the May 29, 1909, issue of *Forest and Stream*, C. A. Cooper talks of grand adventure and of using the McGinty in Colorado in a story titled, "Trouting on the Rio Grande."
41. Additional source:
    The *Times-Standard*. October 8, 1973.
42. The actual spelling of the lake is "Parmachenee," but Wells himself used "Parmacheene" for his fly in the chapter titled "Fly-Fishing for Trout in the Rangely Region" that he contributed to *Fishing With the Fly*.
43. Additional sources:
    Cheney, Albert Nelson, and Charles Orvis. *Fishing With the Fly*. New York: J.J. Little & Company, 1883.
    Wells, Henry Parkhurst. *The American Salmon Fisherman*. New York: Harper & Brothers, 1886.
44. The *Art of Angling Journal*, a beautifully rendered periodical that lasted just a few years in the early 2000s, ran a two-part piece on Ed Haas in its first two editions. The first part (Winter, 2001) was written by Californian Scott Gingerich, and the second part (Spring, 2002) was penned by the esteemed New York-based writer and author Eric Leiser. This was the most complete record of Ed Haas ever published. The quoted material herein is from those articles (Leiser's story for the first quoted material, and Gingerich's story for the additional quoted material).
45. This quote and most of the details in this story of the Purple Peril are from: Beatty, Danny and Tamara Belts, *George McLeod interview—December 18, 2006*, Western Washington University, http://content.wwu.edu/cdm/compoundobject/collection/ffoh/id/301/rec/18. Additionally, Walt Johnson, on several occasions in the 1990s, explained to me how his own interest in purple flies began with McLeod's Purple Peril.
46. Enos Bradner conducted an interview with Walt in 1967 and then published the interview in the *Seattle Times* on December 12, 1967 ("The Only Way is Fly, Says This Steelheader"). Walt mentions the original Red Shrimp fly and also talks of his winter steelheading success, including the two 15-pounders from the Skagit.
47. From the *Rogue River Courier*, Grants Pass, August 23, 1907, which explains that Wharton opened his store in the building that had housed Paddock's Bicycle Den in Grants Pass.
48. Additional sources:
    The Plaindealer. Roseburg. September 19, 1898.
    Rogue River Courier (Grants Pass). September 20, 1907.
49. Robert Deniston Hume (1845–1908) was a remarkable figure in the early days of the West Coast salmon-canning and salmon hatchery industries; two informative books about this enigmatic and controversial character are: *The Salmon King of Oregon: R. D. Hume and the Pacific Fisheries* by Gordon B. Dodds (University of North Carolina Press, 1959); and Hume's own *A Pygmy Monopolist: The Life and Doings of R. D. Hume Written by Himself and Dedicated to His Neighbors* (University of Wisconsin Press, 1961).
50. Essentially forgotten today, the Bunnell sisters, Ardath and Irene, began tying flies in 1928 when their violin teacher, an angler, suggested the craft might be a way to earn summer money. Soon after, they had become proficient enough to tie flies professionally and they started Oregon Waters Fly Company, based on Sandy Boulevard in Portland. An interesting story about the two sisters appeared in the *Sunday Oregonian*, March 20, 1938, and they were featured in that paper on a number of other occasions. In addition to supplying Colvin with his Rogue River Specials, the sisters—at the behest of Wharton—were the first to commercially tie the irrepressibly popular Golden Demon.
51. Additional sources:
    Colvin, Edsel, "Frank DeLong Colvin," at http://home.comcast.net/~pvcolvin/frank.html.
    Colvin, Edsel and Paul. Personal correspondence with the author.
52. Additional sources:
    "California Offers a Paradise for Fishermen of the World." The *San Francisco Call*. May 16, 1909.
    "Angling at Salmon Creek Under Adverse Circumstances." The *Morning Call*. January 28, 1893.
53. The *Bonita*, owned and captained by O'Kelly, served as a water taxi in the bay and distinguished herself in winning local boat races; 48 feet long and 14 tons, she was built locally (and elegantly) by Max Timmerman. *Bonita* sported a 30-horsepower, 4-stroke Holliday gasoline engine, the first of its kind in the bay. Her sister boats, nearly as fast but not quite, were O'Kelly's *Monlita* and *North Bend*. According to ads in the *Coos Bay Times*, the boats ran every 30 minutes and served the entire bay area.

    O'Kelly garnered headlines in San Francisco in 1909 when a "Dr. Astro," playing con games as a clairvoyant, fleeced the gullible Coos Bay boatman out of $1,000. Three coconspirators were arrested on a complaint filed by O'Kelly, but Dr. Astro—aka C. A. Conlin—posted $1,500 bail and promptly escaped to Mexico, where he was eventually arrested.
54. Additional sources:
    "Thousands Enjoy 4th on Coos Bay." The *Coos Bay Times*, July 5, 1907.
    Whitty, John. "The Coos Bay Area From 1940 to 2012." *Leadership Coos*. September 11, 2012.
55. Andrew Genzoli (1914–1984) was a lifelong newspaper man whose specialty and passion was researching and reporting on the history of Humboldt County.
56. Roskelley, Fenton, "Writer Names Favorite Flies," *Spokane Daily Chronicle*, Sept. 23, 1969. From 1958 through 2003, Fenton Roskelley (1917–2013) was the outdoors writer for the *Spokane Daily Chronicle* and then the *Spokesman Review*; he was said to be the *Daily Chronicle's* only employee to have a company car equipped with a boat hitch.
57. Additional source:
    Beatty, Danny and Tamara Belts. *George McLeod interview—December 18, 2006*. Western Washington University. http://content.wwu.edu/cdm/compoundobject/collection/ffoh/id/301/rec/18.

58. Bradner notes that the Sol Duc is Glasso's pet pattern in "Inside on the Outdoors: Hoh Steelheading Calls for Accurate Casting," the *Seattle Times*, March 14, 1963; the pattern description comes from a story by Bradner titled, "Double the Fun of Fly Fishing," the *Seattle Sunday Times*, April 23, 1961.
59. Doug Rose was such a genial soul that he was never openly critical of other anglers and tiers, but in personal correspondence with me he often lamented how unfortunate it was that so much misinformation circulated about the flies created by Glasso and Wentworth. Rose and Wentworth were good friends, and Rose once told me that while ". . . most recipes call for the hackle to be tied in with the floss at the second tinsel turn, Dick tied his in directly above the hook point the day I watched him tie a Sol Duc. He stripped one side and tied the hackle in by the tip."
60. "Working the fly" can take numerous forms; the tactic described by Arnold is also known as "fishing the hang-down." Sometimes a steelhead will follow a swinging fly all the way to the terminus of the swing (the "hang-down"), and then, as the fly slows and stops directly downstream from the angler, the fish will either move off or make a grab for the fly. Such fish (regardless of whether you know they are there) can sometimes be tempted into taking by action on the fly, either with the rod manipulations described by Arnold, or by stripping and possibly controlled release of line. In fact, I've hooked several accidental "reel-up" steelhead: on the last cast over a particular run or pool, I've let the fly swing out to the hang-down and then started reeling up line and wading shoreward, when suddenly, "Wham!" Fish on in the most dramatic fashion.
61. Additional sources:

    Beatty, Danny and Tamara Belts. *George McLeod interview—December 18, 2006*. Western Washington University. http://content.wwu.edu/cdm/compoundobject/collection/ffoh/id/301/rec/18.

    McCleod, Ken James (son of George McLeod). Personal correspondence with the author.
62. Additional sources:

    "Acting President of Reed Leaves." The *Oregonian*. July 21, 1942.

    Bungert, Heike, Jan G. Heitmann, and Michael Wala, eds. *Secret Intelligence in the Twentieth Century*. London: Frank Cass, 2003.

    Classic Fly Rod Forum. www.classicflyrodforum.com/forum/viewtopic.php?f=64&t=55886.

    "Corps hears protest on Siletz dredging." The *Oregonian*. June 23, 1971.

    Edwards, C. D., ed. *A Cartel Policy for the United Nations*. New York: Columbia University Press, 1945.

    "Each retiree becomes his own man whether under age 40 or over 70." The *Sunday Oregonian*. July 26, 1970.

    "Lincoln City Moves Toward Adulthood After Stormy Start." *The Sunday Oregonian*. December 3, 1967.

    Robinson, Edgar Eugene. *Independent Study in the Lower Division at Stanford University, 1931–1937*. Stanford University, CA: Stanford University Press, 1937.

    "Reed Professor Leaves for East." The *Oregonian*. November 26, 1942.
63. Additional sources:

    "Big Fishes Caught By Anglers, 1916–1924," *The World Almanac & Book of Facts, 1926, New York World-Telegram* and The *Sun*.

    "Death Notice for Henry L. van Luven." The *Sunday Oregonian*. January 26, 1930.

    The *Oregonian*. July 9, 1911.

    The *Sunday Oregonian*. October 10, 1920.
64. In the early years of moving pictures, Eureka hosted many small theaters: "Nine storefront theaters appeared in Eureka between 1904 and 1914. . . . Veteran theater man, Joshua Vansant, recalled, 'It seemed as though every time there was an empty store building someone would move in and start a show house. Then the first thing we knew they'd be gone.'" From "Sweasey Theater/Loew's State Theater, Humboldt County, CA," *National Register of Historic Places Continuation Sheet*. United States Department of the Interior and National Park Service.
65. Additional sources:

    Appendix to the Journals of the Senate and Assembly of the Thirty-First Session of the Legislature of the State of California, Volume 2. 1895.

    Carr, John, *Pioneer Days in California*. Eureka, CA: Times Publishing Company, 1891.

    Dailey, W. R., ed. *Henry's Official Western Theatrical Guide, 1907–1908*.

    Eureka Business Directory 1893–4. Standard Publishing.

    Eureka City and Humboldt County Directory, 1914–1915. Polk-Husted Directory Company.

    Goldthwait, Nathan Edward. *History of Boone County, Iowa, Volume 2*. Chicago: Pioneer Publishing Company, 1914.

    Humboldt Times. September 1864.

    Odd Fellow's Talisman and Literary Journal, Volume 17. Independent Order of Odd Fellows, Grand Lodge of Indiana, 1884.

    Proceedings of the . . . Annual Communication of the R. W. Grand Lodge of the Independent Order of Odd Fellows, of the State of California. 1874, and Chicago: S.J. Clark Publishing, 1915.

    California. *San Francisco: Bancroft & Company, 1870.*

    Stevens, Walter Barlow. *Centennial History of Missouri, the Center State: 1821–1915, Volume 4*. St. Louis

    Sprague, C. P., and Atwell, H. W. *The Western Shore Gazetteer and Commercial Directory for the State of California, 1870.*
66. The *Grants Pass Daily Courier*, February 21, 2013, was an additional source for this fly.
67. In a story titled "West vs. Dry Again," the *Seattle Sunday Times*, July 2, 1933, Ken Binns writes, "Some of the best patterns for Western Oregon and Western Washington are the royal coachman, professor, yellow hammer, teal and red, Jock Scott, the above patterns being tied with bucktail instead of wings."

INDEX

Page numbers in italics indicate illustrations.

Abraham, Maurice "Mooch," 106, 263
Adams, James, 35, 45, 76
Alvord, Thomas Gold, 101
Amato, Frank, 43, 120, 139
American River system, 2–3
Anderson, Sheridan, 120
The Angler's Guide (Salter), 88
Angling & Hunting in British Columbia (Pochin), 57
Antoine, Charles, 6
Arnold, Bob, 167
Art of Angling Journal, 264

Backus, Jim, 147
Backus, Walter, 6, 101, 150, 177
Bair, Fred, 141
Barker, Fred C., 129
Bates, Joseph D., Jr., 29, 36, 55, 141, 149, 150, 156, 177
Baughman, Michael, 20
Bekeart, Jules François and Philip Baldwin, 30
Benn, John S., 4, *10*, 10–12, *13*, 27, 30, 31, 33, 53, 141, 145, 165, 178, 261
  Eel River fishing trips, 10–11, 33
  fly books, *12*
  fly patterns of, 11–12
  fly wallets, 11
  gravesite, *14*
  plans to move to banks of Eel River, 12–14
Benn, Martha, 11, 31, 34, 85, 101
  Calderwood marriage, 13
  Cloer marriage, 34
  gravesite, *14*
Bergman, Ray, 88, 151
Berman, Joan, 13
Berryman, Jack W., 42, 47, 106
Bétten, H. L., 63
Binns, Ken, 187
Bird, Cal, 36, 190
Black Bar Lodge, 185
Black Diamond community, 37
bodies, 216
  chenille and yarn, 216
  dubbed, 217–19
  tinsel and floss, 219–22
Bonita water taxi, 264
Borisa, John, 127
Bradner, Enos, 16, 38, 46, 47, 59, 73, 93, 105, 107, 111, 118, 163, 187
Brayshaw, Tommy, 61
The Breakwater steamer, 263
Brown, Robert B., 47
Brunell, Al, 24
Buckingham, Nash, 85
Buhr, Al, 65, 169
Bunnell, Ardath and Irene, 85, 264
Burden, Brad, 65
Burdick, George, 157, 179
Butler, Doug, 41
Butler, John, 12, 14, 178, 261
Butler's English Ale House, 261
Buzzacott, Francis Henry, 88

Calderwood, Peter, 13, 34
Callaghan, Dan, 91
Capps, Washington L., 27
Carlon, Madge, 106
Carson, Charles Sumner, 53
Carson, John Milton, 53, 181
Carson, William, 53, 181
Carter, Harley and Wayne, 55
Casebolt, Henry, 261
Cave, Edward, 178
Chandler, Ben, 103, 155
Cheney, Albert Nelson, 129
City of Chester ship, 262
Cloer, Lon C., 34
Closson, Mable H., 33
Colby, Frank, 18
Cole, Ralph, 45
Colvin, Frank, 147, 149
Combs, Trey, xi, xii, 7, 14, 42, 43, 45, 51, 56, 65, 69, 76, 77, 93, 108, 110, 119, 120, 121, 131, 139, 149, 161, 165, 172, 179, 181
  foreword by, vii
Come Wade the River (Wahl), 113
The Complete Camper's Manual (Buzzacott), 88
Conway, Dan, 28, 47, 59, 187
Cooper, Del, 69, 172
The Creel (O'Byrne), 175
Cruikshank, John, 62, 262
Cuenin, J. P., 63
Cullison, Jack, 263
Cumming, Al M., 101
Cummings, Ward, 64
Curtis Creek Manifesto (Anderson), 120

Dahlquist, Bob, 113, 263–64
Dan Callaghan's North Umpqua (Callaghan), 91
Day Creek, 263–64
Deschutes River, 71, 81
The Deschutes River Railroad War (Speroff), 71, 81
Dolbeer, John, 53
Donnelly, Roy, 43, 72
Drain, Wes, 7, 46, 73, 86, 110, 111
Dry Line Steelhead and Other Subjects (McMillan), 170
Dudder, Oral, 136
Dufresne, Frank, 29
Dunn, Allan, 101

Eel River, 4
  Benn's fishing trips to, 10–11
  Benn's plans to move to banks of, 12–14
  reaching the, 33
  towns of the lower, 33
Eel River and Eureka Railroad, map of, *13*
Eureka, town of, 265

Faulk, Emil Nathaniel, 6, 77
Favorite Flies and Their Histories (Marbury), 33, 40, 129
Federation of Fly Fishers, 153, 262
Fish Flies (Hellekson), 101
Fisherman's Spring (Haig-Brown), 8
Fishing With the Fly (Orvis and Cheney), 129

Fishing Lake and Streams (Bétten), 63
Fitzmaurice, Mary L., 263
Fitzmaurice, Maurice "Mossy," 71, 81
Flies of the Northwest, 172
fly books, *12*
fly fishing, xi, *190*
 on the Columbia River, *vii*
 on the John Day River, *xiii*, *15*
 on the Snake River, *5*
 working the fly, 265
fly lines, sinking, 171
fly patterns, *1*, *18*, *19*, 24–25
 Admiral, *26*, 27, 243
 Alaska Mary Ann, 29, *29*, 243
 Al's Special, 28, *28*, *192*, 243
 Bair's Railbird, 141
 Bekeart's Special, 30, *30*, 243
 Benn, 11–12
 Benn's Black Prince, 31, *31*, 243
 Benn's Coachman, *32*, 33, 243
 Benn's Martha, 34, *34*, 243
 Black Beauty, 35, *35*, 243
 Black Demon, 36, *36*, 85, 244
 Black Diamond, 37, *37*, 244
 Black Gnat, 99
 Black Gnat Bucktail, 38, *38*, 99, 244
 Black Gordon, 39, *39*, 244
 Black Max, *191*, 244
 Black Prince, 40, *40*, *194*, 244
 Black Prince (Gordon's), 41, *41*, 244
 Bobbie Dunn, 42, *42*, 244
 Bosquito, 43, *43*, 245
 Boss, *44*, 45, 245
 Boxcar, 46, *46*, 245
 Brad's Brat, 25, 47, *47*, 195, 236–39, *239*, 245
 Brindle Bug, *48*, 49, 245
 Bucktail, 4–7, 101, 150
 California Coachman (Yellow Royal Coachman), *50*, 51, 245
 Carson Coachman (Carson Royal Coachman; Carson), *52*, 53, 245
 Carter Fly, *54*, 55, 245
 Carter's Dixie, *54*, 55, 245
 Chappie, 56, *56*, 246
 Cliff's Special, 57, *57*, 246
 Coal Car, 81, 262
 Colvin's Rogue River Special, 246
 Comet, 45
 Conway Special, 28, *58*, 59, 246
 Copper Demon, 85
 Coquihalla Orange, *60*, 61, 246
 Coquihalla Red, *60*, 61, 246
 Courtesan, 62, *62*, 246
 Cuenin's Advice (Cuenin's Fly), 63, *63*, 246
 Cummings Special, 64, *64*, *193*, 247
 Dark Max, 115
 Dave's Mistake, 65, *65*, 247
 Deep Purple Spey, *66*, 67, 247
 Del Cooper, *68*, 69, 172, 247
 Deschutes Demon, *70*, 71, 247
 Deschutes Skunk, 71
 Deschutes Special, 262
 Dingbat, 262
 Donnelly Chappie, 56
 Donnelly Coachman, 43, 72, *72*, 247
 Drain's 20, 73, *73*, 247
 dressed by Ed Haas, *17*
 Duck Fly, *20*, 21–22
 Evening Coachman, *74*, 75, 248
 Fall Favorite, 76, *76*, 248
 Faulk, 77, *77*, 248
 Flame Chappie, 56
 Flat Car, 81, 263
 Fool's Gold, *78*, 79, 248
 Freight Train, *80*, 81, 115, 248
 General Money No. 1, *82*, 83, 248
 General Money No. 2, *82*, 83, 248
 General Practitioner, 90
 Golden Demon, *16*, 24, 83, *84*, 85, 156, 248, 249
 Golden Edge Orange, 86, *86*, 249
 Golden Edge Yellow, 86
 Golden Girl, 87, *87*, 249
 Governor Alvord, 101
 Gray Hackle Peacock, 88
 Gray Hackle Yellow, 88, *88*, 249
 Grease Liner, 37, 77, 89, *89*, 249
 Green Heron, 123
 Green-Butt Black, 90, *90*, 249
 Green-Butt Skunk, 91, *91*, 249
 Grizzly King, *132*, 133, 249
 Hackle, 88
 Headrick's Killer (Killer), *92*, 93, 250
 Hellcat (Headrick's Hellcat), *94*, 95, 250
 history of, 2–4
 Horner's Silver Shrimp, *96*, 97, 250
 Hoyt's Killer, *98*, 99, 118, 250
 Hoyt's Special, 38, 99
 Humboldt Railbird, 141
 Icterus, *194*, 250
 Improved Governor, *100*, 101, 250
 Juicy Bug, *102*, 103, 250
 Jungle Dragon, *104*, 105, 251
 Kalama Special, 106, *106*, *195*, 251
 Kennedy Special, 106
 Kispiox Special, 107, *107*, 251
 Knudson White Marabou, 108, 251
 Knudson White Streamer, 108, *108*, 251
 Lady Caroline, 109, *109*, 251
 Lady Coachman, 110, *110*, 251
 Lady Godiva, 111, *111*, 252, 263
 Lady Hamilton, *112*, 113, 252
 Lord Hamilton, *112*, 113, 252
 McGinty Bucktail, *116*, 117, 252
 McLeod Ugly, 38, 99, 118, *118*, 252
 Maverick, 262
 Max Canyon, *114*, 115, *191*, 252
 Migrant Orange, 119, *119*, 252
 Myers Buck, *176*, 177, 252
 Night Dancer, 120, *120*, 252
 Nite Owl, 121, *121*, 252
 Orange & Gray, 139
 Orange Heron, 62, *122*, 123, 253
 Orange Shrimp, 77, *124*, 125, 253
 Orleans Barber, *126*, 127, 253
 Pacific King, 128, *128*, 253
 Park, 262
 Parmachene Belle, *ix*, 129, *129*, 165, 253
 Patriot, 120, *120*, 253
 Polar Shrimp, 125, *130*, 131, 253
 Prawn Fly, 83
 Professor, *132*, 133, 253
 Protein Buck, *134*, 135, 253
 Purple Angel, 136, *136*, 253
 Purple Peril, 24, 46, 67, 75, 118, 137, *137*, 254
 Queen Bess, 42, *42*, 254
 Quillayute, *138*, 139, 254
 Railbird (Benn's Railbird), *140*, 141, 254
 Red Ant, 254
 Red Fox, 262
 Red Shrimp Spey, *142*, 143, 254
 Rogue Red Ant (Red Ant), *144*, 145, 254
 Rogue River, 145, *146*, 147, 254
 Rogue River Special, 147, *148*, 149, 254
 Royal Coachman, 51
 Royal Coachman Bucktail, 150, *150*, 255
 Salmo Le Sac, 262
 Sawtooth, 151, *151*, 255
 Scarlet Ibis (Red Ibis, Red Fly), 152, *152*, 255
 Shewey's Spawning Purple, 198, 255
 Signal Light, 81, 263
 Silver Admiral, 153, *153*, 255
 Silver Ant, *154*, 155, 255
 Silver Demon, 21–22, 36, *36*, 63, 85, 156, *156*, 193, 239–41, *241*, 255
 Silver Hilton, 157, *157*, 256
 Skunk, *158*, 159, 256
 Skykomish Sunrise, 24, 118, *160*, 161, *192*, 233–36, *236*, 256
 Sol Duc, *162*, 163, 256, 265
 Sol Duc Dark, 163
 Sol Duc Spey, 163
 The Soule, *164*, 165, 256
 Spade, *166*, 167, 256
 Spawning Purple, 21, *196*, 196–97, *197*
 Spawning Purple Spey, 197–98
 Spectral Spider, 168, *168*, 257
 Spey, 62, 67, 109, 123, 143, 163
 Steelhead Bee, 169, *169*, 257
 Steelhead Caddis, 170, *170*, 257
 Steelhead Special, 171
 Stewart, 115
 Stillaguamish Sunrise, 171, *171*, 257
 Stillaguamish Sunset, 171, *171*, 257
 style conversions of, 190, *191–98*
 Surgeon General, 172, *172*, 257
 Thompson River Caddis, 89
 Thor, 173, *173*, 257
 Tranquilizer, 262
 Umpqua Special, 24, *174*, 175, 257
 Van Luven, *176*, 177, 257
 Van Sant (Van Zandt), 178, *178*, 258

Weitchpec Witch, 179, *179*, 258
Wells Special, *180*, 181, 258
White Wulff, 75
Whitesel's Wine, *182*, 183, 258
Willow, 262
Witherwox Special, *184*, 185, 258
Yallarhammer, 187
Yellow Hammer, 59, *186*, 187, 258
see also fly tying
Fly Patterns of British Columbia (Lingren), 57, 61, 87, 90
Fly Patterns and Their Origins (Smedley), 4, 7, 27, 83, 165, 177
fly tying
bodies, 216–22
Brad's Brat, 236–39
hackles, 222–25
hair wings, 226–29
jungle cock eyes, 231–32
materials, 7, *23*, 24–25, *25*, *199*
recipes, 243–58
Silver Demon, 239–41
Skykomish Sunrise, 233–36
soft-loop technique, 205–6
tags, 206–10
tails, 210–15
terms, 200–4
Fly Tying (Sturgis), 173
fly wallets, 11
Fly-fishing Pioneers & Legends of the Northwest (Berryman), 42
Ford, Cory, 29
Franklin, C. L. "Outdoor," 56
Franzoni, Zelma, 127
Fricke, John, 51

Gallagher, Sean M., 45, 76
Gantner, John, 110
Gardner, Erle Stanley, 56
Genzoli, Andrew, 157, 264
George, E. B., 6, 118, 137, 261
Gephart, Joseph, 129
Gill, John, 81
Glasso, Syd, 7, 62, 67, 75, 123, 139, 143, 163, 262
Golcher, Will and Henry, 30
Gordon, Clarence, 31, 39, 41, 64, 151
Gordon, Theodore, 4
Gordon-Lennox, Caroline, Lady, 109
Grant, Charles "Schoolie," 62
Grant, James, xiii
Greenley, Dale, 159
Greenwood, Bessie, 45
Grey, Zane, 85, 147, 156, 183

Haas, Ed, 24, 135, 190
fly patterns tied by, xi, *17*
hackles, 222
hand-folded, 224–25
scissor-folded, 222–24
Haig-Brown, Roderick, 8, 57, 61, 83, 87, 109, 169
Hammond, Rocky, 89
Hance, John P., 4
Harkley & Haywood Sporting Goods, 57
Harris, William C., 40
Harrison, Carter H., 4
Harrison, Jim, 97
Hauser Bros. newspaper ad, *6*
Hawkins, John, 38
Headrick, Francis "Frank," 93, 95, 99
Hedge, Marvin, 106
Hellekson, Terry, 99, 101
Hemingway, Jack, 175
Henry, Bernie, 97
Hickson, Edward R. "Ned," 71, 81
Hilton, Henry, 157, 179
Hobson, Harry D., 69
Holbrook, Dawn, 105
Holbrook, Don, 73, 111
Holm, Don, 79
hooks, 24–25
Partridge Bartleet, 24
Spey, 24
Hornaday, William T., 63
Horner, Jack, 97
Hosfield, Skip, 61
Hosie, Bill, 105
Hough, Emerson, 4–6, 261
Hoyt, Clyde, 38, 99, 118
Hughes, Jene, 117
Hume, Robert Deniston, 149, 264
Husby, Joe, 161

The Inner Man (O'Connell), 12

Jackson, Alec, 136, 167
James, Jerry, 153
Jennings, Preston, 168
John Day River, *15*
Johnson, Les, 131
Johnson, Walt, 7, 24, 28, 36, 46, 47, 67, 73, 75, 86, 93, 95, 99, 105, 110, 119, 125, 128, 139, 143, 161, 163, 168, 187
Johnston, Park, 113
Johnstone, E. McDonald, 103
Juker, Jacob, 261

Kaufmann, Lance, 81
Kaufmann, Randall, 81, 115
Kelson, George M., 18
Kennedy, Mike, 69, 79, 106, 145, 172, 183
Kispiox River, 35, 99, 107, 161
Klamath River Angling Guide (Burdick), 157, 179
Knudson, Al, 6, 28, 47, 67, 73, 108
Korbel settlement, 157
Kraft, Virginia, 185
Kreider, Claude, 43, 128
Kroeber, A. L. and Theodora, 179
Krogel, Mildred, 159

LaFontaine, Gary, 117
Lake and Forest as I Have Known Them (Barker), 129
LaLanne, Jack, 97
Lambuth, Letcher, 105
Landis, Lauren, 37
Lemire, Harry, xi, 7, 37, 77, 86, 89, 159
A Life Worth Living (Hemingway), 175
Lingren, Arthur, 57, 61, 87, 90

McCarthy, Call J., 6
McClain, A. J., 181
McClain, Don and Lola, 71
McDonald, Stella, 149
MacDowell, Syl, 18, 149, 175
McLeod, George, 6–7, 38, 67, 75, 83, 99, 107, 111, 113, 118, 137, 161, 171, 187
McLeod, Ken, 7, 28, 73, 83, 93, 99, 105, 111, 113, 118, 137, 161, 171
McLeod, Ken James, 118, 187
McLeod, Mary, 118, 137, 161, 171
McManus, Phil, 149
McMillan, Bill, 171
McMillan, John, 170
McMonies, Jimmie, 149
McNeese, David, xii, 46, 65, 110, 123, 169, 172, 190, 196, 262
McNew, Hap and Lon, 45
Marbury, Mary Orvis, 31, 33, 40, 129
Martuck, Leon, 171
Mausser, Karl, 35, 107
Maxwell, Forrest, 64, 65
Maxwell, Herbert, Sir, 18
May the Rivers Never Sleep (McMillan and McMillan), 170
Money, A. W. and Noel, 83
Moore, Frank, 39, 41, 159
Moore, Roger, 77
Moyle, Peter B., 63
My Way was North (Dufresne), 29
Myers, Jack, 177

Nevins, Charles, 13
No Room for Bears (Dufresne), 29
North Fork of the Stillaguamish River, 46, 47, 93
North Umpqua River, 39, 91
Sawtooth and Surveyor pools on the, 151
Northwest Angling (Bradner), 38, 47, 59
Northwest Fly Fishing (Amato), 120
Northwest Outdoor Writers Association (NOWA), 47

O'Byrne, Victor, 175
O'Connell, Daniel, 12
Off the Beaten Track in Baja (Gardner), 56
O'Kelly, Jasper, 155
Olsen, Ray, 143
Olson, Ralph, 73, 111
One Man's Steelhead Shangri-La (Wahl), 113
Orvis, Charles F., 129

Pacific Northwest Fly Patterns (Patrick), 76, 128, 159
Patrick, Roy, 76, 105, 113, 128, 159
Pemberton, Harold, 161
Piatt, Larry, 115
Pitts, Roy, 107
Pochin, W. F., 57
Portsmouth Square, *9*
Practical Fly Fishing (St. John), 6
Pray, C. Jim, 6, 14, 36, 55, 63, 76, 85, 101, 127, 141, 156, 173
Putnam, E. Oliver, 165

Reminiscences From Fifty Years of Flyrodding (Rosborough), 153
Rising, Mary, 261
A River Seen Right (Baughman), 20
Roberts, Bob, 24
Roberts, Don, 86
The Rod and The Gun (Wilson), 133
Rogers, Eustace Baron, 27
Rogue River, 147, 183, 261
Rogue River Feud (Grey), 183
The Rogue River Indian War and Its Aftermath (Schwartz), 103
Rogue River and Its Game Fish (Wharton), 7, 8
Rosborough, Ernest Herbert "Polly," 127, 153
Rose, Doug, 123, 139, 171, 265
Roskelley, Fenton, 159, 264

St. John, Larry, 6
salmon, taxonomy of, 3, 263
Salmon Fishing (Taverner), 123
The Salmon Fly (Kelson), 18
Salmon and Trout (Harris), 40
Salter, Thomas Frederick, 88
San Francisco, 19th century, 2, 3
Schwab, Peter J., 6, 42, 177
Schwartz, E. A., 103
Scripture, William, 4
Sexton, Woody, 97, 263
Shanks, Geordie, 62, 109, 262
Shanks, Jamie, 262
Shasta (Johnstone), 103
Sherman, Marty, 115
Shewey, Al, 21
Shewey, John, vii, *25*
Shoff, Clarence, 131
Silvius, Lloyd D., 49, 76, 121
Skillman, B. F., 22
Smedley, Harold, 4, 7, 27, 83, 165, 177
Soule, Charles Parsons, 165
Spencer, Lee, 20–21
Speroff, Leon, 71, 81
Spey Flies & Dee Flies (Shewey), 229
steelhead, *ix*, 3, *11, 16*, 16–21, *213*
  recipe for, 64
  taxonomy of, 263
Steelhead & the Floating Line (Arnold), 167
Steelhead (Kreider), 43, 128
Steelhead Flies (Combs), xii
Steelhead to a Fly (Van Fleet), 53, 141
Steelhead Fly Fishing (Combs), 65, 93, 131, 149, 161
Steelhead Fly Fishing and Flies (Combs), xi, 7, 14, 42, 43, 45, 51, 56, 69, 76, 77, 119, 120, 131, 139, 159, 165, 172, 179, 181
The Steelhead Trout (Combs), 14, 110, 139
Steelhead Water (Arnold), 167
A Steelheader's Way (Waller), 8
Stewart, Doug, 115
Stovall, Jim, 36
Streamer Fly Fishing (Bates), 36, 55, 141
Streamer Fly Fishing in Fresh and Salt Water (Bates), 150, 156, 177
Streamer Fly Tying & Fishing (Bates), 29
Stroebel, Bob, 136
Sturgis, William Bayard, 173
Sullivan, Virgil, 45
Surette, Dick, 131

tags, 206–7
  on double hooks, oval-tinsel, 210
  oval-tinsel, 207–8
  speed method for tying oval-tinsel, 208–9
tails, 210
  golden pheasant crest, 212–13
  hackle fiber, 210–12
  wood duck flank, 214–15
Tales of Freshwater Fishing (Grey), 183
Taverner, Eric, 123
Taylor, Bob, 90, 167
Terrill, Robert P., 172
Thirty Years War For Wild Life (Hornaday), 63
Thoreson, Walter, 173
Tie Your Own Flies (Patrick), 113, 128
Tower, Charles W., 103
Tower, Isaac "Russ," 103, 155
Traherne, John Popkin, 31, 40
trout,
  Lahontan cutthroat, 3
  taxonomy of, 263
Trout (Bergman), 88, 151
Trout Flies (Williams), 30, 53
Trueblood, Ted, 156
Tucker, Phil, 187
Tying and Fishing the Fuzzy Nymphs (Rosborough), 153

Van Fleet, Clark C., 53, 141
Van Luven, Harry, 6, 177
Van Ness, Howie, 29
Van Sant, Joshua and Josh, Jr., 178
von Lengerke Meyer, George, 27

Wahl, Ralph, 7, 73, 86, 107, 110, 111, 113
Waller, Lani, 8
Washington Fly Fishing Club (WFFC), 93, 105
Weber, C. F., 51
Welch, Cliff, 57
Wells, Henry Parkhurst, 129
Wells, Sam, 14, 53, 181
Wentworth, Dick, 7, 123, 139, 163
The Western Angler (Haig-Brown), 57, 61, 83
Western Trout (MacDowell), 18, 149, 175
Wharton, Joe, 8, 22, 85, 145, 147
Whitesel, Jack, 183
Wild Steelhead (Gallagher), 45, 76
Williams, A. Courtney, 30, 53
Wilson, Butch, 76
Wilson, John and James, 133
wings
  hair, 226–29
  mallard, 229–30
Winter, Dick, 153
Wintle, Jerry, 167
Witherwox, Hally, 185
Wood, William, 4

Yurok Myths (Kroeber), 179